Pity the Swagman
The Australian Odyssey of a Victorian Diarist

'Joseph Jenkins… one of the most interesting Welshmen of the Victorian era.'
Bill Jones

'A truly fascinating book, bringing disparate corners of the 19th century world uniquely and startingly to life.'
Jan Morris

'As a window on both the Welsh immigrant experience in colonial Australia and the rural Wales the immigrants left, this account is unequalled.'
Carl Bridge

'This book casts an entirely new light on an Australian hero.'
Jack Murphy

'Save me from the curse of myself.'
Joseph Jenkins, 1878

Pity the Swagman

The Australian Odyssey of a Victorian Diarist

Bethan Phillips

First published in 2002 by Cymdeithas Lyfrau Ceredigion Gyf.
This new edition published by Y Lolfa in 2024

© Copyright the estate of Bethan Phillips and Y Lolfa

The contents of this book are subject to copyright, and may
not be reproduced by any means, mechanical or electronic,
without the prior, written consent of the publishers.

The publishers wish to acknowledge
the support of the Books Council of Wales.

ISBN: 978-1-80099-502-4

Published and printed in Wales
on paper from well-maintained forests by
Y Lolfa Cyf., Talybont, Ceredigion SY24 5HE
website www.ylolfa.com
e-mail ylolfa@ylolfa.com
tel 01970 832 304

This book is dedicated
to
Dr William Evans,
the grandson of the Diarist
and author of
Diary of a Welsh Swagman.
As an eminent cardiologist,
he played a crucial role in
the establishment of
the British Heart Foundation.

Contents

Preface by Dr Brinley Jones	ix
Acknowledgements	xi
Foreword	xv
1 Footfalls echo in the memory	1
2 May God help his creation	7
3 Her dowry I like	30
4 Master of Trecefel	47
5 A man for all causes	66
6 A wet canvass	83
7 Free of pain at last	97
8 Gathering storm clouds	112
9 A most troublesome year	123
10 At the end of his tether	141
11 Hell or Melbourne	162
12 I shoulder my swag	199
13 Gold Fever	209
14 My only husband	224
15 A slavish existence	244
16 The past lives most deeply in us all	261

17	Many storms	278
18	Trounced by fate	298
19	The Maldon Scavenger	311
20	I am rootless	343
21	I trust all of us will be reconciled	370
22	Grief Subsides – Love Abides	389
	Appendix	409
	Bibliography	427
	Index	431

Preface

This is a meticulously researched book telling a very moving human story, set against a backcloth of events in nineteenth century Wales and Australia. It is based on the life and times of Joseph Jenkins, a prolific, often ill-starred, Victorian diarist. Bethan Phillips has assiduously studied the original diaries, covering a period of 58 years, and has skilfully chosen extracts from them. The result is an expansive biography both readable and scholarly: two qualities which are not of necessity compatible.

It has been held that a diary is a 'personal way of imposing some kind of order on the chaos of the world around us.' In her analysis of Joseph Jenkins's complex world and of his accomplished but flawed personality, the author demonstrates the truth of this statement. She also gives us an evocative account of a Welsh rural society riven by poverty and ill-health, where the lives of the disenfranchised peasants contrasted starkly with the opulence and privileged existence of the gentry. We learn of the corruption endemic in parliamentary elections and of the economic changes which followed the coming of the railway. The impact of these developments upon Jenkins is analysed, as are the events which prompted him to make his ill-judged escape from family and friends to seek a new life in Australia.

Through the diaries we are afforded glimpses of the privations endured by the early migrants on the long and arduous voyage to Australia. We learn of the plight of the 'swagmen' and of the vain hopes of those who searched for gold. The travails of the Aborigines and the dreadful fate of the Kelly Gang also feature. Bethan Phillips has assembled and refined the entries to produce a work of real merit. I am confident that her efforts will be well rewarded and that her work will prove to be enduringly popular in both Wales and Australia.

Dr R. Brinley Jones C.B.E., F.S.A.
President National Library of Wales

Acknowledgements

I am extremely grateful to the descendants of Joseph Jenkins for their assistance and co-operation in writing this book. I am particularly indebted to Frances Evans, Tyndomen, Mair Owen, Penbryn and Beti Evans, Glasfryn, all Joseph's great grand-daughters, for giving me access to the diaries and for providing me with letters, photographs and miscellaneous documents. I was fortunate to have many valuable conversations with the late Dr William Evans, who first ensured that a selection from his grandfather's diaries was published. I also benefited greatly from the advice of the late Dr Eben Roderic Evans, a great grandson of the Diarist. My research led me to visit many of the farms associated with Joseph Jenkins, and I must thank Joyce Jenkins and Mair Davies, Blaenplwyf (his birthplace), for their assistance, and Beti and Gareth Davies, Sychbant, for allowing me to view the Blaenplwyf Account Book.

I must acknowledge the help given to me by Dr Bill Jones of Cardiff University, and Dafydd Ifans, Cyril Evans and Ceris Gruffudd, all of the National Library of Wales. Others who assisted me were Dr J. Geraint Jenkins, Emrys Williams, Robert Thomas, Guto Llewelyn, Dilwen Roderick, Dr Ann and Dr Glyn Rhys, Susan S. Roberts, Beti Davies (Castell), Roger Williams, Director of Education, Ceredigion, Roy Davies and

Robert Blayney. I wish to record my particular debt to Dr R. Brinley Jones C.B.E. for writing the Preface.

Many institutions provided me with valuable information, including the Guildhall Library, London, the National Maritime Museum, Greenwich, the San Diego Maritime Museum, the Merseyside Maritime Museum, the Public Record Office and the State Library of Victoria, Melbourne. I must refer specifically to the staff of the Manuscripts Department of the NLW, Aberystwyth, who saw to my many requests over the years.

During my time in Australia, following in the footsteps of the 'Swagman', I was accompanied by the film director Paul Turner, who opened many doors for me. I greatly valued the support given to me by so many who expressed an interest in the life and work of Joseph Jenkins. Much valuable information was provided by the late Frances Gray of Maldon as well as by John Grigg and Alan Russ. Jeff Jones of Bendigo was also very supportive during my visit. Many people in Australia have been more than willing to provide me with assistance and advice. I especially wish to thank Mary Ryllis Clark for her wise advice, and Jock Murphy for his response to my many requests. Sara Joynes of the Australian High Commission has been an invaluable source of encouragement at all times.

I have also relied heavily on the books of Professor Geoffrey Blainey for my background reading, and it is from a quote in his *The Tyranny of Distance* that the chapter heading 'Hell or Melbourne' is taken.

I wish to thank Cymdeithas Lyfrau Ceredigion for agreeing to publish this work and I owe a tremendous debt to Dylan Williams for guiding me through the various stages leading up to publication with such skill and meticulous care. I must also commend Eleri Roberts for her patience in typing the many drafts.

Finally, I must express my appreciation to my own family who have had to live with the 'Swagman' for so many years, and especially to my husband John and my son Geraint for reading the proofs and offering timely advice.

NOTE

In the interest of facilitating the flow of reading it was decided to include only the English translations of Joseph's poetry in the body of the book. These translations are marked with a †. The original Welsh can be found in the Appendix.

Foreword

It was almost by accident that I was first introduced to the diaries of Joseph Jenkins. In October 1985 I called at Tyndomen Farm, near Tregaron in west Wales, to research the World War I experiences of Dr William Evans, a distinguished London cardiologist, for an article. During the evening, his niece, Miss Frances Evans, showed me the 25 diaries written by her great grandfather, Joseph Jenkins, during his lengthy stay in Australia. Many of the diaries were in poor condition, as one might expect as some had been written well over a century ago. A few had been bound in leather, but others were backed by cardboard, their pages gnawed by mice and showing the effects of damp. One or two still contained bits of straw, relics no doubt of the days spent by the diarist labouring in the fields while attending to the threshing machine. Although some of the pages were made illegible by blots caused by a spilt ink bottle, most of the pages were written in a neat copperplate hand giving graphic and detailed accounts of life in Australia.

The discovery of the diaries is a remarkable story. After Joseph Jenkins's death in 1898, the volumes, which had been so assiduously protected by him during his lifetime, were stored in the attic of Tyndomen Farm, the home of his daughter Nel. There they remained more or less forgotten for 70 years until his great grand-daughter, Frances Evans, retrieved them. Their historical significance was recognised by Dr William Evans, the Diarist's grandson, and he undertook the arduous work of editing them. A selection of entries from the 25 Australian diaries was published by him in 1975 under the title *Diary of a Welsh Swagman*. This volume was widely acclaimed, particularly in Australia, and it received many favourable reviews. One reviewer even hailed the Diarist as 'the Welsh Pepys of the soil'.

This chance encounter with the diaries has taken me on a long journey, lasting over 15 years, in search of the man who had so meticulously chronicled the daily events of his own life and the lives of those around him. It has involved trawling through thousands of diary entries relating to his life in Wales and to his subsequent life in Australia. I was fortunate in being able to visit many of his direct descendants who still live in Cardiganshire (now Ceredigion). Through them I gained access to many of the Diarist's notebooks and to other fragments containing his writings and poems. I was also told the stories about him which have survived in the family's collective memory.

In 1993 I was able to visit Australia to follow in Joseph Jenkins's footsteps. It proved to be both a moving and a memorable experience, particularly when I visited the town of Maldon in Victoria, which is indelibly associated with his final years in Australia. Today, the town has been designated as one of national historic interest and many of its original buildings have been preserved. McArthur's Bakery where the 'Welsh Swagman' would eat his meagre lunch while browsing among the books kept there, still survives. The Welsh Chapel, where he would, on occasion, listen with undisguised impatience to the lengthy sermons on the Sabbath, also stands. Many of today's townspeople are descendants of the early Welsh immigrants who would have been known to Joseph Jenkins. Some of the streets still bear their surnames, such as Jenkins Street, Lewis Street, Beynon Street and Evans Street. The water channels that he laboured so hard to keep clean are evident even today, but only a forlorn heap of stones marks the spot where his cottage, North Railway Gate Lodge, stood. Here he spent his latter years in Maldon, veering between feelings of contentment and despair.

My guide and companion during my visit to Maldon was the late Frances Gray, whose house overlooked the site of the cottage. She was avidly interested in the 'Swagman' and had been corresponding with me about him since 1986. This is an extract from one of her letters:

> When I look through my window and over Joseph's place, I can almost see him turning his back on the town and heading towards the railway station a few yards away, knowing that there were some waiting to walk into his cottage and cast lots for the possessions he'd been forced to leave behind. He never accepted the Australian way of life and he suffered dreadfully at times, but he remained a loaner [sic] and went away. His cottage did not last long after his departure. It was occupied but not cared for, and before long it fell apart. He frequently mentions snakes inside the cottage, and the patch is snake territory. Whenever council fellows are clearing up there, the snakes are disturbed and enter my back patch. It has always been like that.

In spite of his differences with some of the townspeople and his occasional acerbic comments about them, Joseph Jenkins would have been flattered to learn that his significance as a diarist is still acknowledged today in Maldon and further afield. Frances Gray informed me that:

> In 1978 the *Diary of a Welsh Swagman* was added to the reading list for the Victorian High Schools Compulsory Examination. Students arrived by the coach load to do the 'Swagman's Tour'. The place has become a Mecca for teachers and students of sociology.

Of his 58 diaries, 33 were written in Wales. What remains of these are deposited at the National Library of Wales at Aberystwyth. The State Library of Victoria, Melbourne, has now acquired the 25 Australian diaries. These diaries encompass the full cycle of his life, starting among the hills of Cardiganshire, followed by the travails of his Australian experiences, and ending with the eventual return to his homeland.

The diaries reveal him as a man seeking to exorcise his own demons by attempting to escape from them, but they also reveal him as an astute observer of the people and occurrences impacting upon his own eventful life. His dogged determination in keeping a daily journal, often under the most difficult of circumstances and in the most unpropitious surroundings, has given us a uniquely valuable historical record of life in the nineteenth century.

BETHAN PHILLIPS
Llanbedr Pont Steffan, 2002

CHAPTER 1

FOOTFALLS ECHO IN THE MEMORY

It seemed an odd hour to set out on such a momentous journey, late of an evening in the cold of a Welsh winter. Most of his neighbours had already settled around their hearths with their families, basking in the glow of a peat fire. Yet this was typical of the man, ever impulsive, impetuous and driven. His name was Joseph Jenkins, a prominent and successful farmer in the county of Cardiganshire, west Wales, but he believed himself to have been cursed from birth. 'I was,' he grimly recorded, 'doomed from the start.' His favourite author was Charles Dickens, his favourite novel *David Copperfield*, and like Copperfield and Dickens himself, he was haunted by the idea that he had been 'born on an unlucky Friday.' On the evening of 7 December 1868, Joseph Jenkins must surely have felt justified in his belief that he was being stalked by some malevolent fate, for this was the night he chose to desert his family, his farm and all he held dear to him. He recorded his fateful departure in one bleak line in his little 'Black Book':

Monday, 7 December 1868
I left Trecefel after dark and caught the downtrain to Aberystwyth.

These prosaic words were to herald a sequence of events that would radically change his life. His action would open wounds that would fester for a lifetime.

Joseph Jenkins cut a solitary figure as he made his way along the lane leading from Trecefel, his farm near the town of Tregaron. Although he was by now over 50 years of age, he was still a man of striking appearance, erect, broad shouldered and well over six feet tall. In his hands he carried two heavy suitcases, but his troubled expression showed that this night he was more burdened by his thoughts than by the weight of his baggage. Small wonder, for he was leaving behind a lifetime of memories and achievements. The familiar lane, which had so often brought him home, was tonight leading him to an uncertain future.

Twenty years previously things had been so different. Then he and his young wife Betty, both brimming with optimism and confidence, had proudly bowled up this very lane in their new spring cart full of hope for the future. Behind them had trundled six wagons groaning under the weight of a Welsh dresser, a bog oak chest, a pine linen press and many other wedding presents generously given at their *neithior*, or wedding feast. The years that followed had been a time of building, of sowing and of reaping. He had thought then that the sun would never set on their happiness.

Now, however, his emotions were different. They were destructive and negative, for he was consumed with a burning hatred and seething with a sense of betrayal and humiliation. He could scarcely believe that it had all come to this, but there was nothing he could do to redeem the nightmare.

The sound of his hobnailed boots crunching the gravel of

the lane echoed in the cold stillness all around him. A soft, white mist rising from the river Teifi had settled on the blackthorn hedgerows, leafless now, which he had so carefully planted in double rows and succoured over the years. The land had always been an essential part of him; he had nurtured and cared for it, and the experience of leaving it was like being rent limb from limb. He had long agonised over his situation but had concluded that there was no way back. Old familiar sounds intruded from time to time and floated faintly across the chill evening. From his farmyard he heard the clanking of a bucket, the barking of a dog and the distant shout of one of his children. To continue on his way, he was forced to muster all his strength of will.

Within minutes he had reached the little grey stone, humpbacked bridge and scrambled down the steep bank leading to the new railway line. Here the rush of memories was overwhelming. The opening of this line had been a moment of triumph for him, for he had played a pivotal role in bringing the age of steam to this remote part of rural Wales. He knew every foot of it; he had assisted the engineers during its construction and had even 'held the chains as they'd measured the tracks.' By now, however, his sense of achievement had evaporated and, ironically, this very line would be the means of transporting him from the locality.

As he made his way along the embankment towards the station he glanced up at a velvet sky studded with stars. The sky had always fascinated him, and he often marvelled at the wonder of creation. But not on this occasion. Tonight, he attributed all his woes and misfortunes to one of those glittering lights shining down coldly from millions of miles above. In his diary he had written, 'I was cursed even in my mother's womb – born under an inauspicious star.'

Annoyed with himself for continually being at the mercy of such thoughts, he quickened his pace, for he would soon hear the laborious chug of the engine as it climbed the incline from Pont Llanio at precisely 8.42 p.m. on its way to Tregaron. He quickly crossed the bridge over the river Teifi and within five minutes had reached the still and dimly lit station.

It was deserted except for Edward the Porter. The sight of this man did nothing to improve Joseph's mood; only six months previously they had exchanged blows and he had been 'weltered with blood'. Tonight, they merely ignored one another, but Edward's curiosity must have been aroused when he heard Joseph purchase a 'single' ticket to Aberystwyth. Mercifully, the shrill blast of the approaching train deflected the porter's attention and within minutes the gleaming engine churned into the station, hissing to a stop in a great cloud of steam. It was driven by Joseph's old friend James Benbow. As was his custom, Benbow raised his hand in greeting, for Joseph had only recently composed a poem in his honour. Tonight, however, Joseph had no desire to exchange words with Benbow. For once, he preferred to slip away in silence and, if possible, in anonymity.

Promptly, at 8.52 p.m., the last train pulled away from Tregaron bound for Aberystwyth, taking Joseph on the first leg of his extraordinary odyssey. At least he was alone with his thoughts and felt thankful for that. But he also felt a sense of disquiet; it had been less than half an hour since he had left his home and as the train picked up speed he experienced a growing air of finality. A chapter in his life was closing, another was about to open, and he was of an age when most men sought the reassuring comforts of family and friends.

Outside he could see that the train was already skirting the large tract of brooding marshland known as Cors Caron. Old memories came flooding back as he recalled the times when he and his servants had dug peat from the bog. Slicing the long peat iron into the soggy earth and lifting the turf was heavy work, but he was glad of one thing, 'This year's harvest of peat had been a prodigious one.' Back at Trecefel he had left a huge stack of turf so that his family could fortify themselves against the ferocity of the Welsh winter which most surely lay in wait. Through the window of the train he saw the moonlight reflected in the pools of brackish water and he recognised the lights of Allt-ddu farm stabbing the darkness. Cors Caron had always fascinated Joseph; for him, this sullen stretch of landscape, with its heavy mosses and tough grass, seemed to convey an air of myth and mystery. It was enchanting for a brief while in late summer when it was covered with a great white eiderdown of feathery bog cotton, or *plu'r gweunydd*. 'At such times,' wrote Joseph, 'these dark acres become a place of haunting beauty.'

But some parts were treacherous; it was said that only the Cistercian monks of nearby Strata Florida Abbey, ghostly in their white cowls, had known the secret paths across its seeping surface. Many were the tales of hapless travellers being sucked into its 'bottomless pools' or engulfed by the peat, where their bodies lay hidden for centuries in a state of perfect preservation. Joseph had often heard how the old peat diggers had come across them.

As the train rattled on regardless, his pain began to bite deep. He felt guilty as he thought of Betty, his wife, and his eight surviving children, the youngest of whom had barely learned to walk. They would wake the following morning to discover that he had left them. Yet there was no turning back, for ultimately he was in flight, not from his family, but from himself. In his naivety he had convinced himself that only at the furthest point on the globe, which to him was Australia, could he find sanctuary and a release from his problems. With its steady hypnotic rhythm the train continued on its journey, stopping at Allt-ddu Halt, Strata Florida, Trawsgoed and Llanilar, names that would soon be distant memories as each one took him further from family, farm and friends.

Ahead lay a long and perilous voyage. Throughout his exile he continued to harbour the belief that he had been the victim of an ineluctable destiny, and was never able to accept that he had been solely responsible for his actions on that eventful night of 7 December 1868. He dolefully recorded in his notebook, 'I was given a stony path in a suffering universe.' This would be a constant theme in the Journal he kept so assiduously down the years. Even at the end of his life he still claimed that he had been 'born on a cursed Friday' and expressed the wish, 'If I happen to be reborn, I hope it will be on a more lucky day and under a brighter star.' What follows in this book is based, almost entirely, upon the written testimony of Joseph Jenkins himself as recorded in his diaries, his poetry, his notebooks, his fragments of miscellaneous thoughts, his letters and the recollections of his direct descendants.

CHAPTER 2
MAY GOD HELP HIS CREATION

Nowadays, red kites fly high in the sky over Blaenplwyf, their feathers flashing in the sunlight as they wheel and dive to snatch carrion from the crows below. Blaenplwyf is an old, white-washed Welsh long house; it was here, in the early hours of Friday 27 February 1818 that life began for Joseph Jenkins. The farmhouse still stands at the end of a narrow lane above the village of Tal-sarn in the county of Cardiganshire, mid Wales.

He was born in an area of great natural beauty which had a profound effect upon him. In later years he wrote, 'A man living so close to such a mystical landscape with its changing light and calling curlews understands life.' To the west of the farmhouse lay the sylvan slopes and fecund meadows of the Vale of Aeron stretching as far as Cardigan Bay. To the north, Joseph saw the three hills known as Trichrug often wreathed in morning mists, covered by a blaze of russet heather and yellow gorse. Turning to the north-east he beheld the rugged grandeur of the Pumlumon range of mountains above Tregaron; to the south of these rose the steep slopes of Craig y Foelallt guarding Llanddewibrefi with its ancient church of Dewi Sant, the patron saint. Such images became indelibly etched on Joseph's mind, and he was to draw on them for spiritual strength during the hardships that lay ahead. 'The wise man,' said Joseph, 'is content with nature and all the blessings it offers.' Sadly, however, he did not always follow his own good advice.

For much of his life he remained a troubled man. One factor which caused him much distress was that he was born with a harelip. He claimed that this was caused by 'being crushed in my mother's womb.' His brother John was similarly afflicted, but unlike Joseph, he never allowed it to dominate his life.

Joseph was the third child of Jenkin and Elinor Jenkins. This was a time of large families, and thirteen children were born at Blaenplwyf. His father was a tall man of imposing appearance, who played a prominent role in the community. He was a member of the Board of Guardians, dispensing assistance to the needy; he served as a juror at the Assize Courts and he was an agent to Lord Lisburne of Trawsgoed, one of the local gentry. Elinor, his wife, came from Coedparc, a prosperous farm. She was the niece of a fine poet and *litterateur*, Dafydd Dafis, Castell Hywel, who translated Gray's 'Elegy' into Welsh, and also established an academy to educate young people of the area.

There was a hunger for education in this remote farming community, and this was particularly so on the hearth at Blaenplwyf. Opportunities were few, however, and Jenkin Jenkins did his best by employing a private tutor by the name of Jac Llwyd, a colourful local character, to instruct his children in the rudiments of reading, writing and arithmetic. In arithmetic Jac did not achieve great heights, but he was remarkably successful in teaching young people to read the Bible and to write. He was already 67 years old when he taught Joseph and his siblings in what was known as *ystafell dan storws* – 'the room under the storehouse'. It proved an unforgettable experience.

Jac Llwyd was a strict disciplinarian and Joseph recorded sardonically that, 'He used the birch more than the Bible.' He frequently cuffed his pupils and, as a prelude to punishment, he would call a miscreant a 'blockhead fellow'. When his temper was really aroused he would shout with all his energy, 'Rascal! Booby! *Scampyn mawr!*' The unfortunate pupil would then be in no doubt about his ultimate fate as he felt the 'plaited birch cane' smartly catch his flesh. Jac was a cobbler by trade, but he could also trap moles 'mainly on Saturdays'. On one occasion he was appointed bell-ringer, and this aroused the anger of the parishioners, who felt it unfair that one person should serve as both schoolmaster and bell-ringer, enjoying the large salaries, especially with fees for tolling the bell for so many funerals. He was paid in kind by Jenkin Jenkins, 'with eggs, meat, milk and potatoes.'

Throughout his life Joseph rued the fact that he had never been given the advantages of a good formal education, and the memory of Jac Llwyd remained vivid, even half a century later. Forty-one years after Llwyd's death (aged 81), and separated from Blaenplwyf by a distance of sixteen thousand miles, Joseph still fulminated against him:

October 1881. Victoria, Australia
As yesterday I remember what I wrote down on a slate when under Jac Llwyd, Llangybi. The words were thus. 'I cannot learn the multiplication table in my lifetime!' . . . It was in the year 1828. Jac was an old mole catcher . . . he was a very hot tempered old man which made him unfit to teach mischievous children.

Realising, perhaps, that Jac Llwyd had his limitations, Jenkin Jenkins made alternative arrangements for the education of

Joseph and John. The two boys were enrolled as pupils at a school run by an Unitarian minister, the Reverend Rees Davies, in the small village of Cribyn some five miles from Blaenplwyf. They had to walk to school on a Monday morning carrying packs on their backs with a supply of *enllyn* – butter, cheese and meat. They lodged with their teacher during the week and returned home on a Friday night. Joseph proved to be an eager pupil and retained fond memories of his time with Rees Davies, whom he described as a 'teacher without parallel'. Even so, this was to be only a brief interlude in his formative years and he later testified that, 'I had only two quarters of English schooling when I was 13. I never had a single day in my native language.'

The shortcomings of his education notwithstanding, other civilising forces also prevailed at Blaenplwyf. An inherent respect for religion and culture was fostered by the chapels and nurtured in the homes of the scattered farmsteads. This, coupled with the ethos of hard work instilled in him by his father, was to sustain Joseph in his youth and to remain with him into old age. He also had an unquenchable thirst for knowledge and a curiosity about the world beyond the confines of Cardiganshire. 'My aim,' he wrote earnestly, 'is to learn all I can about all things which will stand me in good stead on my journey on this earth.' To achieve this objective Joseph made one of the most important decisions of his life, and one which ensured that his voice still speaks today: he decided to keep a diary.

The Victorians were ardent diarists; the Queen herself, who was much admired by Joseph, kept a detailed diary from the age of thirteen. He believed that keeping a journal would improve his English and with this object in mind he embarked upon a task that occupied him daily for the remainder of his life. He began at the age of 21, commencing on New Year's Day 1839 with the following simple entry:

> Tuesday 1st 1839
> John and I thrashing. After breakfast – hauling stones. My father was at Pentrefelin. John Jones and Thomas Jones were measuring walls. 189 children called for new year's gifts.

By the end of his life this 'simple entry' had grown into a vast compendium of recollection and comment, covering over twenty thousand consecutive days and spanning nearly 60 years. The diaries were to link two continents encompassing a life of high drama, tension and toil.

A contemporary who witnessed his early efforts portrays him as 'sitting in the room under the old storehouse, late into the night, writing by candlelight with the summer moths skirting the flame.' He cut his own goose quills and mixed his own ink from crushed berries and spring water. Even after a gruelling day in the fields, his first priority each evening was to retire to the room beneath the storehouse with its low-slung, oaken beams and stone floor covered in rushes. There, surrounded by scythes, billhooks, ropes and willow baskets – with a dictionary at his elbow at all times – he grasped his quill in his calloused hand and penned, not only the day's events, but also the dark areas of his soul. Neither his mother nor his father encouraged him in this project which they considered was 'a waste of precious time and good candles.' But having commenced upon this great undertaking, Joseph kept faith with it until the end of life.

In Australia many years later, as he began his forty-first diary, he recalled this early effort at educating himself:

PITY THE SWAGMAN

> 1 January 1880
> I commenced my 1st diary in 1839 in Wales. And when my MSS will be brought together, not a blank day can be found since . . . I had very little idea of either spelling or writing the English language. I had educated friends in London. I took advantage of Sir Rowland Hill's penny postage scheme as well as my own exertions . . . and through this I became able to . . . correspond and contribute to the most critical daily or weekly Journals in both Welsh and English.

His Journal ultimately came to dominate his very existence, and proved to be his one constant companion during his many trials and tribulations. He referred to it as 'my mind saving confessional . . . If I did not keep my Journal I could not escape the pain, cruelty and madness of this world.' Like Byron, he could also have said, 'this Journal is a relief . . . down goes everything!' Decades later, while sitting on a boulder in the Australian outback writing his Journal, he was asked by a sarcastic fellow worker why he bothered to spend time day after day on such a fruitless task. Joseph's reply was, 'This shall be my monument – for better or worse!' What had started as a means of learning English had now assumed a deeper purpose.

Regrettably, many of the early volumes have been destroyed or lost, and the earliest surviving complete diary is the one for 1845. It opens with a plea to God for protection, as was the convention among Victorian and earlier diarists:

> 1 January 1845
> I do beseech Thee to be my shield this year again, which I hope to outlive.

This was no mean hope in a period when life expectancy was notoriously short, and especially so among the poor, who suffered shocking privations. Nevertheless, the young still lived in hope, for the same diary entry informs us that no less than '300 children called [at Blaenplwyf] collecting New Year's gifts.' Each child was given one penny, known as *calennig,* after singing a greeting to wish the household *Blwyddyn Newydd Dda* – a Happy New Year.

This particular era was one of the most difficult in the annals of Welsh farming history, and for the Blaenplwyf family and their neighbours it was among the worst of times. The end of the Napoleonic War had brought in its wake a period of economic depression worse than anything the farmers had experienced before. The early years of the nineteenth century witnessed a sharp decline in the prosperity of rural Wales and this was particularly acute in Cardiganshire. Rents were high and, due to depressed prices, many farms were unable to pay their way and were even abandoned. Greedy landlords, eager to acquire more land, had enclosed vast acres of 'Common Ground' on which small farmers and cottage dwellers had formerly grazed their animals.

The frustrations felt by many in rural areas erupted into violence with the Rebecca Riots of the early 1840s. The numerous tollgates were a constant reminder of the exploitation of the farmers, who were required to pay for moving their animals along the turnpikes and for collecting lime. Bands of rioters with blackened faces, dressed in women's clothes, destroyed tollgates at night, and threatened those landlords deemed to be oppressive. They called themselves the 'daughters of Rebecca' – a name taken from a verse in the

Bible, 'they blessed Rebecca and said unto her, let thy seed possess the gates of them that hate thee.' There were serious outbreaks of violence on 1 August around Lampeter, when armed men destroyed six gates. Joseph and his brothers strongly objected to these tolls which were described as 'a great burden', especially when 'horses, cattle and pigs bred at Blaenplwyf' were taken to the fairs to be sold 'at unfair extra expense on account of the tolls.'

Blaenplwyf was a relatively large farm, which had five tied cottages to house its labourers. One of these was a small two-roomed damp hovel called Cefnbysbach, which stood a hundred yards from Blaenplwyf. In early January, Mary Davies, the mother of the household, lay dying on a straw mattress watched helplessly by her two small sons, David and Daniel. In times of crisis, neighbours and relatives supported one another in almost tribal fashion, and the following extract from his diary shows the strenuous effort made by Joseph to obtain medical assistance for Mary Davies:

> 9 January 1845
> Saddled the horse and went for the doctor. Mary Cefnbysbach is very ill. Went to Lampeter for the Union Doctor – thence to Gilgell for a certificate from Relieving Officer – came back accompanied by the doctor and thence to Lampeter for the drugs and then to Cefnbysbach.

Joseph rode over thirty miles that day; it was an age when people still made time for one another and helped bear each other's burdens.

The winter of 1845 was one of the longest and most severe in living memory. The whole of Britain seemed to have been gripped by savage weather. Even the river Thames was described as 'a floating mass of ice'. Life was a constant battle against the elements. For weeks on end blizzards howled around the farmhouse of Blaenplwyf. Sheep had to be dug out of deep snowdrifts; the ice had to be broken to provide water, and fodder had to be dragged on sledges to the starving animals. The servants draped themselves in hessian sacks in an attempt to ward off the biting cold. It was claimed that the warmest place was in *y dowlad* – the loft above the cattle byre in the cowshed adjoining the farmhouse. Here, the servants slept and were kept comfortable by the breath and bodily warmth of the animals below.

But far too many succumbed to the disastrous weather. Joseph's diary testifies to an average of three funerals a week, when 'the sad spectacle of a cortege winding its way along the narrow roads to the graveyard' was almost an everyday occurrence. 'Thursday 2 January, there are three funerals today. One of a child.' Attendance at funerals was an obligation; Joseph describes how, 'I and my brother John were cut by the icy wind to the marrow of our bones as we helped carry coffin after coffin. It is a terrible time, sometimes we are almost blinded by blizzards.'

Joseph's Journal at this time makes for grim reading and the catalogue of entries speaks for itself, '6 January, two deaths . . . Daniel Bryngolau and Mrs Evans, Bank; 22 January, John and I ploughing . . . My father at the funeral of the child of Jac Carn. I myself feel unwell.' Although the poor were an easy prey and usually the first to fall victims to disease, death was no respecter of rank or wealth. In late January members of the Blaenplwyf family paid their respects to their local squire, suddenly struck down by a fever at his mansion:

29 January 1845
Father and John at John Vaughan Esquire Brynog's funeral. The brethren of Ystrad Benefit Society were requested to meet the funeral at the Lodge. Heavy shower of snow.

The grief of a neighbour was the grief of the whole community and attendance at a funeral was regarded as a sacred duty. However poor the family, it was a mark of pride to ensure that an *angladd barchus* – a respectable funeral – was provided for the departed. These funeral rites eased the sorrow of the family, and the rituals, including the sermons and the hymns, bonded the community at a difficult time. In some areas an individual called *Y Rhybuddiwr* – the funeral announcer – would carry the news of the death and the funeral arrangements from house to house. He would be dressed in black with a black ribbon tied around his hat. If the family was poor, he would carry a bag to receive contributions from the neighbours to pay for the funeral. It was also customary for relatives or friends of the deceased to *gwyliad y corff* – to conduct a night vigil over the body – which was a relic of Catholicism when prayers were said for the soul of the dead; this entailed sitting up all night by candlelight in the room where the body was laid out. Joseph's mother undertook this task on many occasions and, from all accounts, Elinor was renowned for her compassion and charitable work within the community. On the day of the funeral the mourners would gather at the house and then follow the bier to the graveyard. Often, the bier was borne by four men, other times it was conveyed on a cart. After the funeral the male mourners usually retired to the nearest local tavern, where they were furnished with ale and food and reminisced on the life of the recently departed.

January and February were diabolical months; Joseph describes them as being so cold that 'the birds drop from the sky . . . and are tame almost to the point of extinction . . . We are drenched with rain and driving snow . . . and hailstones almost cut the flesh like flints.' In addition to the human tragedy, he worried about the animals. 'No doubt, many of the beasts will starve before the month of May next.' As the winter continued with its unrelenting severity, Joseph was also concerned about the cottagers who were 'obliged to huddle round their turf fires day and night.' They fell sick, 'one after another, for with their meagre diets they were ill equipped to endure the many diseases which ravaged the county.' His diary chronicles long, almost daily entries of deaths among his relatives and neighbours, whose lives were 'blighted by poverty and pestilence.'

The month of February 1845 was to prove particularly horrendous as one neighbour after another fell victim to the 'spotted fever'; others died inexplicably after very short illnesses. Joseph noted sadly that 'the fever now rules this vicinity... and we can but pray for deliverance.' The funerals amounted to as many as two a day, as they struggled to cope with the farmwork and attend to the needs of afflicted relatives and neighbours.

Infant mortality remained high and one of the saddest tasks which faced Joseph and John was when they were called upon to assist in bearing the coffin of a child. '21 February 1845. Clear and frosty. John and I went to meet the bier for carrying the child of William Smith.'

The Blaenplwyf family never neglected their servants when calamity struck. When a young servant, Thomas Evans, died aged 14 of the 'spotted fever', Elinor immediately set out to comfort the grieving mother. Together, they 'kept watch throughout the night over the young boy's body.' Joseph and his brother John assisted on the day of the funeral; they collected the bier and 'whipped by freezing sleet', helped to carry the coffin some five miles to Llangeitho cemetery.

The deaths continued unabated in the locality with the very young and elderly still the most vulnerable. March proved to be as cruel as February and Joseph's diary is a sad catalogue of death. On successive days members of the family attended the funerals of children at Trefynor and Spite. April brought no relief; 'Father at the funeral at Cwm Bettws of a young girl – died of consumption after a long illness.'

The word 'consumption' struck terror into the hearts of people. Joseph claimed that 'the county of Cardiganshire has no catastrophe equal to this disease where death, like bad weather, is ever present' and references to consumption appear with a fearful regularity in the diaries. The Blaenplwyf family was well acquainted with the grief caused by this affliction. When Joseph was 15 he witnessed his young sister Esther die at the age of eight from T.B.; in later years a second sister, Anne, aged 30, after a long and debilitating struggle, also succumbed to this dreaded illness. The sinister onset of the disease, 'which no poultice or remedy could alleviate,' was the nightmare of every family. Time and again Joseph described, 'hearing the hard cough echo in the cottages and farmhouses of the county with a terrible consequence.' He himself was to have personal experience of its malign progress later in life.

The 1864 Report of the Medical Officer to the Privy Council called T.B. 'the plague of Cardiganshire' and described 'the Infirmary at Aberystwyth as being always full of scrofula,' which was T.B. of the lymph glands. The causes of T.B. were attributed to poverty, poor diet, cramped conditions in damp habitations with inadequate ventilation, consanguineous marriages and possibly, an infected milk supply. Although Joseph's Journal tells us that hundreds of pounds of butter and cheeses were sold each quarter in the markets, and that 'eggs, fowl, lambs, pigs and cattle were regularly sold in the fairs,' it did not follow that the people themselves ate well. Indeed, the reverse was true, especially for the poor. The cash flow was so low and times so hard that they were forced to sell what they would have preferred to eat.

The findings of the Medical Officer show the appalling extremities of the farmer. 'Nothing,' he wrote, 'but the sternest frugality can ever hope to find gain . . . The farmer himself does not eat fresh meat once a month; his meal is the leanest cheese and lean beef or ham salted to the texture of mahogany, and hardly worth the difficult process of assimilation.' As for the servants in their tied cottages, they subsisted on a frugal diet of *sucan* – boiled oatmeal, and every day they ate *cawl* which was broth reheated. The Medical Officer reported that 'the victuals of a Cardiganshire worker consisted of a morsel of salt meat or bacon used to flavour a large quantity of gruel of meal and leek; day after day this is the labourer's dinner.'

During the first half of the nineteenth century the town of Tregaron was hardly a model of civic cleanliness. One visitor noted that 'dung heaps abound in lanes and streets' and that in the cottages 'there seemed seldom to be more than one room for living and sleeping in.' He also maintained that 'the pigs and poultry form a usual part of the family' and relates the following incident witnessed by him:

In walking down a lane which forms one of the principal

entrances to the town, I saw a large sow go up to a door, (the lower half of which was shut), and put her forepaws on the top of it and began shaking it; a woman with a child in her arms rushed across . . . and immediately opened the door . . . and the animal walked into the house grunting as if she was offended by the delay; the woman following and closing the door behind her.

All in all, the picture painted in the Privy Council Report depicts a people in desperate straits. 'A farmer in Cardiganshire must mean a person badly lodged and insufficiently clothed and fed. There were hungry people pining for want of food as soon as weaned . . . The physical condition of the people was declining; tuberculosis and scrofula were the scourges of rural society.' Professor Ieuan Gwynedd Jones has summed up the plight of the inhabitants thus, 'The condition of the people was so appalling that religion was their penultimate refuge, the ultimate refuge being emigration.'

Thousands of Cardiganshire people chose the 'ultimate refuge' by fleeing to America and the colonies to escape the inequality, poverty and pitiless toil with its ever-present backdrop of dung and death. Blaenplwyf consisted of 233 acres through which ran the rivers Denis and Dyfel, rendering much of it boggy marshland, which had to be drained laboriously. Joseph complained that as he and John dug trenches, 'the raw wind tightened my chest and cut my flesh.' Near to the farmyard lay a pond which, in summer, was covered in water lilies and bean bog; but in winter it became a solid sheet of ice. '14 March, freezing hard. It was with great difficulty that I cut the ice on the pond for having some water for the horses.' Most of the land was in the hands of a few rich landowners, and the powerful Lisburne family, housed at the grand mansion of Trawsgoed, owned Blaenplwyf. The five tied cottages which formed part of Blaenplwyf were Gwargors, Banc, Cefnbysbach, Blaencwm and Penrhiw.

Oxen were used to plough the soggy upland soil which was heavy, gruelling work. 'John and I did try to open a furrow in Froncaemawr against a bitter wind which burned the lungs, and even the yoke weary oxen, with their hides whipped stiff by the wind, looked fit to drop . . . Above us the dull skies sag with the weight of more threatening snow . . . and I fear for the harvest next year.'

The passing of the Enclosure Act made it necessary for hedges to be planted to define the boundaries, and Jenkin Jenkins made his sons stake out the land by planting thick double rows of blackthorn hedges as a protection against the driving winds. '8 March, John and I enclosing . . . Father bought hundreds of quick thorns which we were obliged to plant by digging trenches, and piling up the bank of earth on which we planted the thorns . . . My hands were scratched to ribbons and I had difficulty handling my quill.' As the inclement weather continued unabated he noticed how quiet the land became. 'The birds were hushed, and even the crows seemed too famished to caw.' But for Joseph and his brothers there was no respite; there were always dry stone walls to be repaired, horses to be brushed down, dung to be spread, and oxen, cattle, pigs, chicken and geese to be fed. On 9 March Joseph and John worked in the shelter of the barn where they 'threshed using a flail . . . until the arms ached.'

Their father was a hard but fair taskmaster who taught them all aspects of farming. Although the relationship was not always harmonious, Joseph was later to be thankful for this early training. It stood him in good stead later in life when he was sorely tested on many occasions. It was not only the men who slaved from dawn till sunset; the women also played a vital part in the economy of the farm. Joseph wrote that he never saw his mother 'be idle for one moment in her life.' Every day of the week for 52 weeks a year the women worked as hard as the men and shouldered the burden of milking the cows twice a day. Elinor never allowed the fire to go out, for it was regarded as an ill omen. Each evening the glowing peat was covered with ashes, and then brought to life the following morning with a bellows. According to Joseph, 'the aroma of the peat was sweet, but it caused the eyes to itch and burn.' The hearth was the focal point of the household; during the long winter evenings the family gathered around it; the men carved spoons, wove baskets and ropes and made brooms; stories were told, poetry recited and, prior to retiring for the night, verses were read from the Bible. Elinor and her daughters spun yarn from raw wool and knitted stockings for sale in the fairs; they also made cheeses and butter, which was stored in 'wooden tubs ready for collection by the carrier.'

A visit from the carrier was always welcomed at Blaenplwyf for he brought 'strange tales of the world beyond.' His name was John Jones, Llwynbrain, who drove his 'cardicart' from farm to farm to collect produce to sell in the industrial south. He could regale them with stories of his visits to Merthyr Tydfil which was, at this time, the iron capital of the world; he could tell them of the 'blazing furnaces which lit the skies at night,' of the deafening noise of the works, the teeming streets, and the less than respectable characters attracted to the town. Over the years he had regularly driven his 'cardicart', packed with eggs, cheese, butter and bacon, to be sold in south Wales. Hundreds had left rural Cardiganshire for a better life and bigger wages in the south, but they still yearned for the fresh farm produce and also for news of their relatives and friends at home. On 3 May, John Jones bought '9 casks of butter sold for eight pence and three farthings a pound from Blaenplwyf' to be taken to Merthyr.

The carriers provided an essential link between the isolated rural communities and the cosmopolitan industrial areas of south Wales. They are portrayed in Welsh poems as popular and happy-go-lucky characters; John Jones appears to have been in this mould. Like most carriers he called at the many taverns lining the route between Cardiganshire and Merthyr, ostensibly to feed his horse, but more often than not to slake his own substantial thirst. Sadly, in October, John Jones's merry and profitable excursions to the south came to a tragic and sudden end. After a heavy drinking session, he allowed his trusty horse to lead the way, for it knew every twist and turn on the road to Merthyr, but on this occasion something unforeseen happened. Joseph records the fatal mishap:

> 7 October 1845
>
> As John Jones Llwynbrain this evening was going towards Merthyr with a load of butter and a dead pig, he met his instant death. He drank rather freely at Troedyrhiw Lampeter – also at the Ram. He proceeded on his journey as far as Ty Gwilym when the horse suddenly turned right . . . the cart was upset and the deceased suffered his death.

The lives of these carriers were not without risk. In 1844, David Lewis, from the nearby village of Silian, was making his way to Merthyr Tydfil with a cartload of butter. Near Trecastle he was robbed and shot in the head. His murderer was subsequently apprehended and hanged before a crowd of 15,000 in Brecon.

On the whole, there were few opportunities for young men to break the monotony of life on the farm by visiting distant localities; as a result, the Blaenplwyf brothers eagerly anticipated the annual trek to the limekilns of the Black Mountain in Carmarthenshire. Lime was necessary to improve the land and counteract the acid in the wet upland soil; usually four tons an acre was scattered to make the fields more fertile. Joseph always welcomed the chance to venture beyond the confines of the parish and gain a brief respite from the grinding routine of work, but in 1845 his father decided that his brother John should be given the task. Rather enviously, Joseph records, 'On 26 May my brother John went for a load of lime to Carmarthenshire . . . he arrived back the following night at 7 o 'clock.'

When a boy was entrusted with a horse and wagon to collect lime, it meant that he had achieved the status of a man. It was customary to start out as early as 4 a.m. and many of the Cardiganshire farmers regarded it as a matter of pride to get to the kilns first. The journey frequently became a race between the various farms, but in so doing, they could risk a fine for going too fast. The load of lime cost two shillings and six pence and the driver was allowed three pennies for his expenses plus the cost of the tolls when having to go through the 'many hated gates'.

John had enjoyed his excursion but when, four days later, more lime was needed at Blaenplwyf, Jenkin ordered Joseph to fetch more, not from Carmarthenshire, as he had hoped, but from the nearby coastal kilns to which the lime had been transported by boat. A somewhat deflated Joseph wrote, '30 May, Jenkin, Timothy and little Benjamin came with me to Aberaeron for a load of lime,' – which was not nearly as exciting as racing toward Llandybïe and the Black Mountain.

However, other days lay ahead to compensate for his disappointment, not the least of which was shearing day. In the calendar of Blaenplwyf the annual shearing was a red-letter day, which almost assumed the importance of a rural festival in the locality. As dawn broke on 10 July 1845, a motley crowd of twenty riders made their way to Bronbyrfe, a mountain farm in the upland areas above Llanddewibrefi. On 8 April Joseph had recorded that the sheep had already been driven to these higher regions for their summer grazing after wintering at Blaenplwyf. The party which set forth consisted of Joseph and his brothers, several servants, 'two girls to pack the wool and help with the food,' and some half a dozen special shearers employed for the long day's work ahead; also included were special guests such as J.E. Rogers, Abermeurig, and the Reverend Evan Evans, the vicar, who looked upon the occasion as an exciting day's holiday. But not for them the arduous task of shearing! While the workers gathered, penned and clipped the wildly bleating flock, the guests 'spent their time pleasantly fishing for black trout in the clear fast running streams.' Frequently, the netted fish was cooked on the spot, and considered a great delicacy.

After the shearing had ended, the whole company rode

down the mountain to Llanddewibrefi where the young shearers played a ball game against the villagers. This was an age-old custom and the game resembled a form of squash played against the wall of *yr hen dŷ cwrdd* – the old chapel – or against the wall of the hostelry known as the Foelallt Arms. It was a tough contest where no quarter was asked or given. After the games were completed the party proceeded to the Deri Arms, Betws Bledrws, where copious quantities of 'home brewed ale' were consumed. In all, it had been an eight-mile trek from Bronbyrfe to Betws, and while the horses were being fed and rested the men took part in a game of quoits on the common. Finally, the company covered the remaining two miles uphill back to Blaenplwyf, arriving at 9 o'clock in the evening. It had been an exhausting but exhilarating day and they were greeted by Elinor with a fine repast of 'cawl, new potatoes, white cabbage, and gooseberry tart.' Thus ended one of the more enjoyable times experienced by the Blaenplwyf family, their servants and friends.

But such occasions were rare; the first six months of 1845 had proved harrowingly difficult for the farmers of Cardiganshire and Joseph wrote that, 'even nature herself seemed to conspire against the people.' His record paints a picture of 'deep drifts of snow . . . hard frosts . . . winds of hitherto unknown force . . . and rain falling like rods.' Fear and despair hung over the farmers like a dark cloud. On 1 March Joseph penned a moving invocation to God, which throbs with the anxiety of a man at the end of his tether:

> O Lord! What shall we do with the beasts, horses and horned cattle? . . . The fodder is entirely out in many

places and will out soon almost through the whole kingdom . . . The voice which enters my ears is my beasts will starve to death if the Spring is not at hand. Money is dear . . . but not half as dear as fodder this season.

Spring and summer came and went, bringing with them little relief; Autumn, far from proving Keats's 'season of mists and mellow fruitfulness', only turned into another winter of remorseless severity. Joseph voiced his concern for the crops, '6 November, we are behind with our work this year on account of the severe frost . . . so that stacks remain unthatched, potatoes remain in the drills and the wheat is unsown and in sacks.' It was a fearful situation. On 11 November, 'nineteen diggers lifted the potatoes from the field but there were only a few hundredweight because of the murrain or rot.'

In order to ensure that they would have a fuel supply 'against the winter cold', Joseph and the servants went to collect the turf from a stretch of moorland beyond the pond known as *y Waun*. The peat had already been dug in June and lay piled in small stacks – *crugiau* – so that it might dry in the wind. Even the younger children were made to work; childhood was short-lived as the six-year-old Benjamin was sent to gather rushes from the edge of the pond. These were then peeled and dipped in sheep fat to make rush candles. The nine-year-old Timothy was sent 'to cut willow rods for making baskets to hold the peat.' Joseph and John made extra fuel by 'mixing coal dust, bracken, dung and clay' and forming them into little balls – known as *pelau* – which radiated constant heat to keep the family warm.

They organised their lives around the seasons, the crops and their animals. The struggle to survive absorbed almost all their waking hours, but whenever the opportunity presented itself, Joseph would retreat to his 'cell' beneath the storehouse to record his feelings. His mood was often sombre and his Journal resonates with a deep spiritual side to his nature. Listening to the screech of the buzzard and the coot echoing from the marshland nearby, he prayed, 'May I leave every worldly lust aside, that I may have some comfort to look back on my writings.' Already, his diary had become like opium to an addict as, by the lamp-light at night, he struggled to make sense of 'difficult English words' and to use the language persuasively. But occasionally, he felt the weight of his task. In his notebook he wrote, 'I'm only an ordinary farmer – why do I endure it?' He went on to give the answer, 'Because I see life so full of curious turns, I do feel I must keep a record of each day for someone to see my life after I have gone, and be walking with history.'

As the year 1845 neared its end he described it 'as one of the most cruel and troublesome times I have known.' A frantic comment summed up his feelings of hopelessness in the face of the nigh impossible weather which had brought about such adverse conditions:

> What can be more miserable by any man than to see his dumb creatures starving to death in need of food? Everywhere, the frost has sealed our earth.

In July 1846, even worse was to follow when the storm which tore through Britain hit Cardiganshire with particular ferocity. Bridges and houses were swept away as was part of the cemetery at Llan-non where bodies were carried out to sea. Tal-sarn, Joseph's own village, witnessed its own tragedy when Dr J. Rogers, a respected local physician, and his manservant were swept away by floodwaters as the horrified villagers looked on. Joseph's reaction was, 'In the face of Nature's fury – man is insignificant and powerless. May God help his creation!'

CHAPTER 3

HER DOWRY I LIKE

The early diaries present an uncompromising picture of hardship and suffering. It was not all unmitigated toil, however, for there were lighter moments. Apart from his diary, Joseph had a deep interest in poetry. He confessed, 'My diary saves my mind, but poetry feeds my soul.' Both Joseph and his brother John were recognised as *beirdd gwlad* – country poets. Joseph turned to poetry throughout his life and his Journal is shot through with hundreds of verses written in both Welsh and English.

The Welsh have always held poetry in great esteem and the poet has acquired an elevated status within society. In medieval times the chief poet – *pencerdd* – had an essential role to play in the Courts of the Princes and was given a chair at their tables. Even today, the 'Chairing of the Bard' is still an important ceremony at the National Eisteddfod and the chair awarded to the victorious poet is greatly coveted.

In the rural society of Cardiganshire Joseph and John Jenkins were afforded a great deal of respect as local poets, and they played an important role in the community. They were called upon to record many significant events in verse, celebrating births and weddings and composing elegies. Their work lacks the excellence of the classical poets, but their verses would long be remembered within their localities.

From a very young age Joseph and his brother had sought to master *cynghanedd*, an intricate system of rhyme and alliteration. The rules of *cynghanedd* had been refined over the centuries and still feature prominently in contemporary Welsh poetry. Tradition has it that the two brothers constantly exercised their bardic skills by speaking to one another in *cynghanedd* as they carried out various tasks of ploughing, planting, shearing and scything. Aspiring poets were required to adopt bardic titles; Joseph called himself Amnon II as a tribute to another poet of the same name, and John assumed the name of Cerngoch, a reference to his reddish hair. Both brothers composed a great deal, but Joseph's work is, on the whole, inferior to that of his brother, who showed greater mastery of the Welsh strict metres.

Working life in the rural society was set by the seasons, and its social life was dictated by the fairs and festivals, the Saint Days, chapel functions, weddings and even funerals. An essential requirement for a 'country poet' was the ability to compose verses at short notice to commemorate notable events in the locality.

Joseph and John were able to compose such verses spontaneously, and much of their work reflects the natural gaiety and native wit of the Welsh. These verses are often full of humour laced with satirical references to happenings within the community. But it was at weddings that Joseph and John were most frequently called upon to display their bardic talents. A Welsh wedding was usually a dramatic affair and an occasion for great celebration and 'much merriment' when certain ancient customs were observed. In Cardiganshire the age-old practice of *pyncio* still existed. This involved a bardic contest between local poets, one representing the bridegroom and the other representing the bride. On the morning of the wedding, the groom, accompanied by his friends and a poet, would go to the bride's house. On arriving at the house, they would find the door barred, with the bride and her party inside, also accompanied by a poet. A bardic contest would then take place, with the poets composing alternate verses, one seeking to outdo the other in satire and humour.

Many of these *penillion pendrws*, or doorstep verses, have survived, including twenty-five stanzas composed by Joseph and his brother John at the wedding of 'David Hughes, Carpenter, Banc, and Elizabeth Evans, Blaencwm.' Both families worked for Blaenplwyf and a close relationship existed between master and servant. Some months previously Joseph and John had carried the coffin of the 14-year-old brother of the bride-to-be; but now the Blaenplwyf brothers were to play a happier role. The prospective groom and his friends had ridden on horseback to Betws Church and back in a mock abduction of the bride. The whole community joined in the merriment, indulging in the carousing and risqué banter, which inevitably followed. The arrival of the groom's party at the bride's door signalled the commencement of the duel in verse.

CERNGOCH (John)	Good day to you friends We have been sent By our faithful master On a message to you. †
AMNON II (Joseph)	What is all this wandering On your part from place to place? Has an old fox been caught And enticed to the Church? †

The groom's party soon became impatient:

CERNGOCH	Too long a conversation is a bad thing,
Time is nearly running out;
Lloyd of Bettws [vicar] is at the church
Expecting a portion of his money. †

After lauding the bridegroom's virtues, John asks on behalf of the groom:

CERNGOCH	Why do you frustrate our journey,
If you can get these possessions?
Deio has over three hundred [pounds]
To give her and the children. †

At last, after a long exchange of verses — much to the excitement of the wedding guests — Joseph capitulates on behalf of the bride:

AMNON II	Oh, come in friends
The door is fully open.
You will have food and drink
without let,
For the money is quite genuine. †

This final stanza by Joseph was the signal for the wedding to proceed and the union of David and Elizabeth was celebrated with the sound of gunshot and hunting horns, drums and great rejoicing throughout the locality.

Biddings were also an important feature of a Welsh wedding. A bidding provided gifts for the young couple given by relatives and neighbours to enable them to set up home. When a pair decided to marry, a *Gwahoddwr*, or bidder, would visit the cottages and farmsteads to inform all and sundry of the arrangements. The name of the bidder at Tal-sarn was 'Howel Howel of Ynys'. He was a colourful figure who wore a beribboned hat and carried a white willow stick decked with multi-coloured ribbons. His role was to invite all to the wedding and entreat them to be generous with their gifts for the married couple. He would enter the house and, after striking his staff on the floor, would deliver his message in verse.

The Welsh flocked to weddings as they flocked to funerals, and the Blaenplwyf Account Book, kept by Joseph, shows how the family attended dozens of bidding feasts held in the locality. The measure of their generosity can be seen, for Joseph kept a meticulous account of the sums given to the married couples. If the wedding were that of a close relative, a valuable piece of furniture such as a chest would be given; otherwise, smaller gifts or various sums of money, usually a few shillings, were contributed.

The *neithior* or wedding feast was often a riotous affair lasting until the small hours. The married couple, for future reference, would carefully record all the so-called 'bidding debts' given by the guests. Joseph himself attended countless biddings where he invariably describes himself as having had a 'hearty time with much good beer to drink the health of the happy couple.'

Weddings could be an expensive business, but there was always the expectation that neighbours would reciprocate when members of the Blaenplwyf family got married. Such an opportunity arose in April 1845 when Joseph's brother, John, was propelled to the altar with a degree of urgency by Margaret Evans of Tynygwndwn. Joseph, in a brief entry, records the event in his diary:

29 April 1845

My brother John is at the brink of getting married. The damsel is in a state of pregnancy.

On 3 May, while Joseph and his younger brother Jenkin took two loads of butter to the carrier, John rushed around frantically trying to procure a licence to marry. 'He found it at Llanarth.' The marriage took place two days later. '6 May, My brother John went down to Ystrad to be married today accompanied by my father and John Davies, Tynrhos.' Joseph described it as being 'a very wet day', but he was angry because his father refused him permission to attend the wedding. The reasons are not explained and Joseph referred to his father as being 'unfriendly'; indeed, it seems that the relationship between them was often tense.

Three weeks after John's wedding he records, '31 May, news came that the wife of my brother John is unwell.' But the following day contains the happy announcement that, 'My sister in law has been safely delivered of a son.' The son was named Jenkin Aeronian after his grandfather and was also to become a noted poet in later life. Meanwhile, the newly married couple were fortunate, for Jenkin Jenkins, Blaenplwyf, had secured a home for them. Joseph's diary entry confirmed that, 'my father . . . was the successful bidder for the tenancy of Penbrynmawr farm to which my brother John intends to go and live.' The circumstances surrounding the wedding had meant that the bidding feast was deferred. It took place six months later and Joseph's diary contains the following happy entry:

28 November 1845

I went to the Bidding at Penbryn [John's farm]. I went in

the morning for a load of Chamber utensils to Tynygwndwn. We were four men with carts. We spent a very merry day at Penbryn — about 50 chambermaids were present. 19 cheese moulds were presented to the young pair.

The extent of the generosity of the neighbours is evidenced by the fact that four cartloads of gifts were carried to John's new home. That evening there were refreshments consisting of bread and cheese and copious amounts of beer for the men. The presence of 'about 50 chambermaids', who were served with cakes and wine, ensured that it was a lively occasion with 'much banter, laughter, and sport.' Happiness is fragile, and tragedy was to strike John and his family many times in the years that followed. For that day, however, they and the wedding guests snatched what gaiety they could.

Fair days also proved a welcome respite from the rigid monotony of work. These occasional days were treated as holidays and members of the Blaenplwyf family and the servants were allowed sums of money to attend them. In the Blaenplwyf Account Book we get a glimpse of the amounts given specifically for attendance at these fairs. These ranged from 1 shilling to 5 shillings and the money was spent on 'gate expenses, beer, fancy biscuits' and other treats which broke the colourlessness of basic farm food of *sucan* and *cawl*.

Most villages had their own particular fairs. Tal-sarn Fair dated back to 1631, but the 'most ancient' fair in the county was *Ffair Garon* — St Caron's Fair — which had its origins in 1250. It was held over three days, 15, 16, 17 March. The third day of *Ffair Garon* was Joseph's favourite day and was known as the Tippling Fair, a name which speaks for itself. *Ffair Garon* heralded the end of winter with its long dark evenings and welcomed the advent of spring, offering new life and hope. To celebrate the fair, the inhabitants of Tregaron whitewashed their cottages and, at one time, placed herbs and witan, or sprigs of mountain ash, in the locks and above the doors in the belief that these kept witches and evil spirits at bay.

An extremely important fair, which combined business with pleasure, was that of the *Ffair Gyflogi* or the Hiring Fair, usually held in May or November. Servants seeking employment for the coming year would present themselves to potential employers. Once an agreement had been struck between the farmer and servant, he or she would be given an 'earn' of a shilling – *ernes swllt* – or half a crown – *hanner coron* – as a mark of good faith. The actual wage amounted to only a few pounds for the whole year. In 1845 Joseph hired a maidservant at Aberaeron Fair for £2 10s for the year.

In addition to the essential business of buying and selling stock, fairs were also of immense social importance, in particular for the young people. Flirtatious maidens dressed up in their best bonnets and wore their finest shawls to attract the attention of swaggering young men who came there with predatory instincts. The servants worked such long hours throughout the year that fairs presented the only opportunity for the young to meet in a free and easy atmosphere. Welsh fairs were notorious for amatory encounters: many a marriage was forged and the inhibitions of a moralistic society were cheerfully cast aside in order to snatch the pleasure of the moment.

There were various attractions. Ballad singers bawling out dramatic accounts of horrendous murders, shipwrecks and other sensational happenings entertained the crowds.

Hurriedly-printed news and ballad sheets were sold to the audiences at a penny a sheet. Smooth-talking peddlers from far afield set up their stalls or carts. They brought with them a glimpse of the outside world with its latest fashions, cheap fairings, and strange new-fangled devices, the like of which had never before been seen by the people of Cardiganshire.

The Blaenplwyf family rarely missed an opportunity to attend the local fairs. On 8 September Joseph and his brothers set out to enjoy themselves at the nearby village fair at Tal-sarn. Apart from the usual colour and clamour, this fair had the added attraction of a boxing booth. Drinking was rife; in addition to the two local taverns, the Blue Bell and Red Lion, a special beer tent had been erected to accommodate the thirst of the revellers. Joseph was a regular customer at the Blue Bell where he was known as a drinker and a clever talker who, tankard in hand, could hold forth on politics, religion, poetry and farming. He revelled in the atmosphere of a tavern where he could show off his natural ability with words, but at Tal-sarn Fair he drank so much that the brothers 'were obliged to help each other stagger up the steep hill leading from the village to the farm in the early hours of the morning.' That evening his diary lay untouched; but the following day, in the cold light of sobriety, smitten with guilt, he turned to it to unburden his soul:

8 September 1845
I and David were at Talsarn Fair . . . I did drink rather heavy there which caused me to promise and engage myself to abstain from drinking drunken spirits, Ale, beer, porter, cider and every other spirituous liquers to appease my thirst – also to hate and leave smoking and chewing tobacco.

There was another reason for such abject contrition. He had begun a relationship with a distant cousin, Betty Evans, Tynant, Ciliau Aeron, and Joseph was now anxious to present himself in as favourable a light as possible to his prospective father-in-law, Jenkin Evans. He was a prosperous farmer and also a committed Unitarian. The Unitarian credo differed from other denominations in that it stressed the free use of reason and rejected the doctrine of the Trinity. The prospects for Joseph looked good and the match seemed perfect; Joseph and Betty's father were already on close terms in that they shared the same religious belief, and Joseph now put his muse to good use in pursuit of this attractive young heiress:

> It's easier to live, I know, if
> Two hearts be together,
> To have you Betty in a happy home
> Is the wealth of my heart. †

As the relationship developed Joseph continued to demonstrate his affection for Betty in verse, and turned increasingly to spiritual matters. He prayed daily for guidance and gave 'thanks to God, the bestower of every goodness . . . for every power thou hast given to me up to this moment.' He even flirted with other denominations. 'I attended the Methodist Association at Tregaron when I heard four sermons.' Although he was prepared to endure the four sermons, which would have been lengthy and profound, he never really warmed to the Methodists. Instead, he remained loyal to the Unitarian credo of his family, regularly attending prayer meetings with Jenkin Evans, Tynant.

Even so, his mind was spinning with irreverent thoughts

about his daughter. The following verse suggests that he had his eye on both her money and her body:

> TO MY LOVE
> Betty is a pretty, pretty girl
> Her face and her dowry I like …
> Her kiss causes the heart
> To burn with passion,
> In love I will respect her.
> Oh! Leave your mother, come with me. †

By the spring of 1846 'as the primroses broke through the earth' they decided to marry. Strongly linked by religious and familial ties, the union of Joseph and Betty was welcomed by both the Blaenplwyf and Tynant families. Since Jenkin Evans, Tynant, also owned another farm, Caemawr, it would appear that Joseph had made a most propitious choice. On 31 July 1846, Joseph, aged 28, and Betty, aged 18, were married at Ciliau Aeron Church. The bride was four months pregnant. From his father, Joseph received a generous settlement. The Blaenplwyf Account Book recorded, '2 July, paid to Joseph as part of his marriage portion, the sum of £200.' A handsome dowry of £500 was also settled on Betty by her father. This was in addition to all the 'many stout pieces of furniture, stock, implements, household goods and cash' given at the *neithior*. The couple were, therefore, extremely well provided for. After the marriage, Betty remained for the time being with her parents at Tynant, while Joseph continued to help his father farm Blaenplwyf.

With the onset of autumn 1846 it was obvious that the health of Jenkin, Joseph's father, was beginning to fail. Up until September he had remained active in the community and could be recognised from afar riding Fly, his distinctive grey mare. He had farmed Blaenplwyf astutely, investing only in the best breeds of livestock, including the famous Welsh cobs, Castlemartin Black Cattle and well bred sheep dogs. But by October 1846 his familiar grey mare stood unsaddled in the stable and old Jenkin kept to his bed. According to Joseph, 'as the leaves fell from the trees, so did my father's strength begin to ebb . . . Mother is very worried.' Elinor, who had cared unstintingly for others in the locality, was now obliged to tend her ailing husband. At 53 years of age with eleven surviving children, eight of whom still lived at Blaenplwyf, she had to rely on Joseph for help with running the farm. He, in turn, was assisted by his younger brothers. There were ten mouths to feed at Blaenplwyf and Joseph himself now had new responsibilities. His pregnant young wife still lived at Tynant, and he could only visit her at weekends.

As Jenkin the old patriarch lay on his sick bed, he turned increasingly to his Bible for comfort. In his heyday he had been considered one of the most able, influential, and well read persons in the locality and he now faced his illness with stoicism and fortitude. The Blaenplwyf family did all they could to smooth Jenkin Jenkins's pathway to the grave. Elinor had remarked, *'Gwnawn yr hyn a allwn, oherwydd fe ddaw angau i ni gyd yn ein tro.'* ['We will do all we can, for death comes to us all in turn.'] No expense was spared by the family to see to Jenkin in his hour of need. Elinor called upon Dr Evans, of Lloydjack Farm, a respected physician and prominent Unitarian to attend to her husband. The doctor called almost daily and Joseph stood by to collect the prescribed medicines. He entered every detail in the Blaenplwyf Account Book. On 2 October

Joseph rode to Lampeter 'to procure drugs at Dr Evans' command at a cost of three shillings.'

As Jenkin's condition deteriorated a second opinion was sought from Dr S. Davies who, having examined him on 13 October, recommended 'pills at a cost of two shillings', which Joseph again collected from the Lampeter apothecary. Neither the symptoms nor the nature of the medicines are described by Joseph, but he carefully recorded all the costs involved. The prognosis for Jenkin Jenkins seemed bleak; on 2 November he requested that his favourite and most loyal servant, David Davies, Cefnbysbach, be allowed to tend to his personal needs. Joseph noted the extra expense incurred by this servant. 'Paid David Davies for the task of watching over father at a cost of one shilling . . . and paid three pence for grinding father's razor.' On 19 November he recorded his father's death in a single line, 'Father died today at 4 a.m. aged 70.' The cause of death was given as 'senile decay leading to pneumonia'. The 'old man's friend' had finally carried Jenkin away from the hearth he had occupied for 34 years.

Throughout the whole community there had been profound respect for his wisdom and authority, and his passing was deeply mourned. We learn from Joseph that, 'A great number of sympathisers' called at Blaenplwyf to express their sorrow. As befitted one of his stature in the community, he was given a respectable Welsh funeral. On 23 November 1846, after a service in the farmhouse, 'a huge concourse of many carts and hundreds of mourners' set out from Blaenplwyf for Capel y Groes, Llanwnnen. Joseph described it as 'a cold day with a keen frost.' The cortege followed an old route known as *y lôn gart*, the cart track, which led past the frozen farm pond and across marshy ground. Along the hedges the 'broken bracken was white with hoar frost, and the cart wheels crackled over the frozen puddles.' The coffin was strapped to a bier and carried by four bearers who were changed every half mile or so. The whole cortege was carefully supervised by Thomas Thomas the undertaker. The twisting narrow road led all the way downhill to the river Creuddyn; here, 'the bearers were paid the sum of one shilling each for carrying the bier over the river Croidyn.' When the funeral procession reached the crossroads at the main Lampeter to Aberaeron road, the mourners halted to sing a hymn in accordance with an old Welsh custom. They then crossed the road and proceeded the last few miles through the village of Cribyn until they reached the chapel on the outskirts of Llanwnnen.

At Capel y Groes, the Reverend Rees Davies preached a 'powerful' sermon recording the achievements of the deceased, and for this eulogy he was paid the princely sum of one pound. The chapel was overflowing and 'the whole area was black with mourners.' After the interment and a final hymn at the graveside, the male mourners adjourned to the nearby tavern of Abercerdin – now known as the Fish and Anchor – conveniently sited only some two hundred yards from the chapel. Here, the company partook of well-earned 'nourishment at a cost of one pound.' Joseph lists all the expenses incurred at his father's funeral, '5 December two shillings paid for ale, two pounds and two pence paid at the Benefit for dinner and beer to celebrate the life of father . . . To Thomas Howells, Carpenter paid 3 shillings for shaving Father and one pound for the coffin; Jenkin Mason paid six shillings for digging and walling the grave; Thomas Thomas, Pencader, the undertaker paid ten shillings for the funeral.' Joseph also ensured that he himself was remunerated, 'Due to Joseph from Father £1-7-6.'

Three weeks after the death of his father, Joseph's wife Betty gave birth to a son; he was born on 14 December at Tynant and named Jenkin after both his grandfathers. Significantly, Joseph recorded in his notebook that, 'the age of the moon was 26 days at the birth of Jenkin.' He feared that his child would be adversely affected by the position of the moon, as he believed himself to have been. The grief at the passing of one generation gave way to joy, for a son and heir was much prized. During the next eighteen months Joseph and Betty remained apart. He continued to help his mother and younger brothers to manage Blaenplwyf, while she enjoyed the comfort and support of the Tynant family in caring for her newborn son.

At Blaenplwyf each evening, even after a day of backbreaking work, Joseph would turn to the 'room under the old storehouse'. Here, he would light his lamp, take up his pen and record the day's events. He liked the isolation; his world consisted only of his Journal and himself, and 'the scratching sound of my quill which affords one great satisfaction.' He referred to his diary as, 'this long, lonely affair with myself.' Since 1839, when he had begun his first diary, rather shakily, he had come a long way towards mastering the English language. After seven years of commitment and dogged discipline, he had broadened his vocabulary, learned to fashion phrases and to express his thoughts, often in memorable and lyrical lines.

He read voraciously, seeking to immerse himself in English culture. He studied the works of Shakespeare which, he admitted, 'I found difficult'; he grappled with Milton's *Paradise Lost* and *Paradise Regained* which he found 'a challenge'; he enjoyed Keats and found himself truly in tune with Wordsworth because of his love of nature. But the one author he admired above all others was Dickens. He regularly ordered parcels of books to be sent to Blaenplwyf from London and remained eternally 'grateful to Rowland Hill for inventing the penny post in 1840.' The Blaenplwyf Account Book shows that the cost of postage for books was often as high as 'two shillings and nine pence', which was almost a servant's wage for three days work. By dint of sacrifice and sheer dedication he educated himself and, according to reports, 'he always had a book or paper in his hand.'

But even in these early years he was plagued by insecurities and self-doubt. He never ceased to worry about the date of his birth and often in his diary, observation turned to gloomy introspection. 'I was born on a Friday when the moon was in her twenty sixth day . . . it appears that no person born under such circumstances can ever be happy.' Ahead, however, lay greener pastures which would surely banish all such melancholic thoughts. The lavish marriage settlement made on Betty enabled him to acquire the tenancy of Trecefel near Tregaron, one of the most desirable farms in the county.

At Blaenplwyf, the old order had changed. Within a few years, two of Joseph's brothers, David and Timothy, decided to flee the harsh regime of work on the farm and joined the growing exodus from Cardiganshire in search of a better life in America. From the beginning of the century there had been widespread emigration from the county; many settled in Ohio, and the Jackson and Gallia counties became known as 'little Cardiganshire'. In the 1840s many from the county emigrated to Wisconsin and Joseph's two brothers eventually settled there, where their descendants still live today. Benjamin, the youngest brother, became a solicitor in Lampeter, and one by one the daughters left home to marry. Finally, it was left to Jenkin, the sixth son, to farm Blaenplwyf with his ageing mother and his tuberculous sister, Anne.

But Joseph's star now seemed to be truly in the ascendancy as 'all the oaken chests, linen presses, the dresser' and other valuables from his bidding were loaded onto wagons to be transported to his imposing new home. On 1 June, a month or so before he finally quit Blaenplwyf for Trecefel, he wrote in his diary, 'May God give me the strength to do right and guide me on a straight path.'

CHAPTER 4
MASTER OF TRECEFEL

On 28 July 1848 Joseph Jenkins, his young wife Betty and their first-born son Jenkin moved into Trecefel, a mile from the town of Tregaron. George Borrow, the 19th century travel writer who toured Wales in the summer and autumn of 1854, wrote of Tregaron, 'The place upon the whole put me very much in mind of an Andalusian village overhung by its sierra. The town, which is very small, stands in a valley, near some wild hills called the Berwyn.' Joseph's new home was a splendid three-storey building with ample room for maidservants in the attic and spacious, well-planned outbuildings. It stood on a commanding site overlooking the river Teifi as it meandered lazily through prime meadowland. But, as Joseph was to discover over the years, the river was an unreliable blessing, bringing in its wake both benefit and terror. His marriage to Betty had given him a prized farm, status and cash, providing him with a magnificent opportunity to prove his worth, and he was to grasp it with both hands.

However, their arrival at Trecefel was not all sweetness and light. When the family first moved in, their immediate neighbours and the people of Tregaron generally regarded them with some degree of suspicion. They were, apparently, the first Unitarians to settle in that area and were looked upon as apostates. It is difficult for us today to conceive of the hostility that once existed between the denominations, and in particular the ingrained hostility of the Calvinistic Methodists towards the Unitarians, who were regarded as the proponents of heretical beliefs. Joseph Jenkins, however, had no intention of becoming a martyr to his religion. Although at first he continued to adhere to the Unitarian tenets and travelled the fourteen miles to his old chapel, he soon saw the advantages of worshipping at the Anglican Church of St Caron and within a year both he and his family had become members. Almost certainly, he was influenced by the fact that his new landlord was the Reverend Latimer Jones, Vicar of St Peter's Church, Carmarthen. He was a prominent ecclesiastical figure who had contracted a profitable marriage and through his wife had acquired Trecefel and the neighbouring farms of Tyndomen and Penrallt.

For Joseph, marriage to Betty and the acquisition of the well-appointed farm Trecefel had changed his life dramatically, and even with his doleful disposition he must have felt well satisfied with his lot. His diary informs us that on 3 November 1848 he and Betty rode like minor gentry 'in the light trap' to Tregaron Hiring Fair, where scores of men and women offered themselves for employment in the coming year. They chose six servants in all: three men servants and three maids. The *gwas mawr* – the head manservant – was to be paid £11 per annum 'plus an allowance of dung and enough land to plant one bushel of potatoes.' A deposit, or 'earn' of half a crown was also given in advance to seal the agreement for one year. The second manservant was paid £6, and the *gwas bach* – young boy – received £3 per annum. The *forwyn fawr* – chief maid for the year – was paid £6, the second maid £4 and the young girl – the *forwyn fach* – earned £3 for the year.

His role as master of Trecefel suited Joseph. At 30 years of age he was still young, but with experience of all aspects of farming, having been well schooled by his father. He was capable and ambitious and determined to put these attributes to good use from the very beginning. The farm consisted of 183 acres, but included scrubland which needed to be cleared, and marshland which had to be drained. There were also many acres of fertile meadowland. The whole area was open land that had to be enclosed with fences and hedges. To drain the marshy ground near Cors Caron, Joseph undertook the task of diverting the river Teifi from its natural course. It was a bold step and a Herculean challenge. He set about excavating a dyke six feet wide and three feet deep to channel water from the wetlands, and the remains of this dyke can still be seen to this day.

Within some six months the Jenkins family had settled into their new home, and Joseph soon proved himself to be an astute farmer and an asset to the community. He firmly believed in the Victorian virtues of industry and piety, ending and beginning each of his diaries with a prayer. His tenth Journal begins thus:

1 January 1849
Should my heavenly Father think it proper to render me or my family life and health . . . may I follow my task with more fidelity and carefulness than before.

During the family's first Christmas at Trecefel snow fell silently blanketing the hills around Tregaron. Joseph described the weather as, 'freezing cold . . . The river Teifi is frozen all over . . . a man can cross it safely.' This picturesque scene soon turned into a nightmare when the roads became 'so slippery that it was impossible to take the horses out of the stables.' As the snow melted, the unpredictable Teifi river burst its banks and Joseph noted with dismay that 'the meadows were inundated with a great flood . . . only 40 acres remain uncovered by water . . . the sheep suffer very bad.' He and his servants were obliged to rescue the sheep from the floods at considerable danger to themselves. Joseph soon learned to have a healthy respect for the river in all its differing moods.

Joseph's interests were many and varied but he was particularly keen on politics. During the General Election of February 1849 he rode to Lampeter to witness the polling and to enquire about the result. He learned that Mr John Pugh Pryse of Gogerddan, one of the most powerful squires, was the new Liberal member for the Borough of Cardiganshire. There were, however, more pressing matters at home for Joseph.

At the beginning of March, Betty, who was pregnant with her second child, began to feel unwell. On 4 March she complained of severe pain. The following day Joseph found himself having to attend to his wife, a situation normally avoided by men in those days:

4 March 1849
Sunday – my wife began to complain about 11 o'clock. Monday – my wife began to complain loudly about 12 o'clock. I sent David the servant to Maesygalen and Lewis the servant to Tynant. She was delivered of a child about 2 o'clock. Only myself was in the room with her.

On that eventful night a second son was born to Joseph and Betty who was named Lewis, after Betty's favourite eldest brother. Just as he had recorded the age of the moon at Jenkin's birth, so he did for Lewis, stating, 'the Moon's age is 10 days.' Throughout his life he believed that the moon's position at birth had a huge effect on man's destiny. A Shakespearian quotation in his notebook reveals the depth of his lunar obsession, 'It is the very error of the moon; she comes more near Earth than she was wont and makes men mad.' So spoke Othello, the jealous husband who murdered his innocent wife Desdemona. It is also interesting to note that among Joseph's papers there were many books on astrology with natal charts predicting how the position of the planets at birth could influence one's life.

Each day, from dawn till dusk, Joseph occupied himself with farm work, but he also gave much time and energy to help the needy in the community. He was frequently called upon to assist with the drawing up of wills, the valuing of land and the settling of disputes. In recognition of these services he was eventually appointed to the office of Parish Constable with responsibility for maintaining law and order in the area. This pleased him greatly, for he had now climbed the first step on the social ladder he was to ascend steadily over the years. He proudly records, '28 April 1849, I was sworn in as a Constable Parish at Rhydfendigaid Bridge [today the village of Pontrhydfendigaid].'

The advent of the new year found Joseph fired up with the desire to succeed and he confidently wrote, '1 January 1850, I have plenty of room to improve myself in almost everything... Should I have permission to survive, may I prove useful as far as I can.' His opportunity to do so came sooner than anticipated in tragic and unexpected circumstances. January 19, 1850 had been a stormy, rain-lashed day. The river Brenig, a small stream that ran through Tregaron, swollen by the rushing mountain water, had suddenly grown into a raging torrent and burst its banks. Earlier that evening, a popular local character, Thomas Jenkins, the excise officer for Tregaron, had walked out of the Talbot Hotel. He failed to reach home and the alarm was raised. All attention was focused on the rivers, which had, over the years, swept countless victims to a watery grave.

Joseph, as Parish Constable, was responsible for organising the search which involved the whole town. He describes how 'hundreds of people walked the banks of the rivers Brenig and Teifi with poles without success.' He himself scoured the Teifi, walking for five miles as far as Llanfair but to no avail. A boat was rowed down the Teifi as far as Lampeter, but there was still no sign of the missing man. Finally, four coracles were brought up from Llandysul, and after a search of four days the body was discovered in a treacherous pool on a bend in the Teifi, only a mile from Joseph's farm. He attended the inquest, but no evidence was ever produced to explain how Thomas Jenkins had entered the river. It was the first of many tragedies that Joseph was to witness in the river Teifi over the years.

When Joseph and Betty arrived at Trecefel the farm consisted of open land. The poet Robert Frost wrote, 'good fences make good neighbours,' and he would surely have applauded Joseph's efforts to enclose the boundaries of Trecefel by planting double rows of black and white hawthorn bushes. Joseph did nothing by half measures. These thick hedges prevented the animals from straying and acted as windbreaks. It did, however, present Joseph with a great challenge, involving much expense and long hours of digging, planting and tending the saplings. But he laid the foundations of well-planned and tightly-secured fields which can be seen to this day.

Care of the soil was his primary concern, and he became obsessed with manuring the land, which he considered essential for good produce. 'Hauling dung' and 'composting' became regular entries in his diary. He even built a container for liquid manure, and near the entrance to the lane leading to his farm he set aside a parcel of land to store a vast stock of compost which he used to enrich the soil. Composting took place throughout the year; mud from the pond, muck from the ditches, all spare soil, rotting matter and dung were carried in carts to the mound where it was systematically turned and raked. Every foot of Trecefel soil was said to be richly manured so that the land became prodigiously productive, and the envy of many surrounding farmers.

Within a year or so the Trecefel family had become fully integrated into life at Tregaron. Betty became a familiar figure at the town market on a Tuesday where the Trecefel eggs, butter, cheese and poultry were sold. Joseph's standing as a figure of authority and influence in the town also grew rapidly. As a member of St Caron's Church, his qualities were soon recognised; in 1850 he was appointed Church Warden 'with care for the fabric of the building and the churchyard.' George Borrow, during his visit in 1854, had admired the 'massive tower of the church' and this was now the responsibility of Joseph. He became a firm friend of the vicar, the Reverend John Hughes, and was subsequently elected as a member of the Board of Guardians and appointed to serve on the Bench. He was also called upon to attend the Church Courts at St Peter's Carmarthen and to act as an arbitrator in Church affairs. Thus, a wide range of responsibilities was devolved upon him and his diary reflects the activities of a very busy man. 'February, 1851, at Aberaeron Quarter Sessions . . . Four prisoners transported for felony . . . April 1851, in town settling dispute between Tim Davies and Mr Hughes . . . June 1851, prepared an agreement between William and Mary Jones over a long disputed stable . . . September 1851, writing conveyance of sale between David Jenkins and David Jones of Tregaron.'

The demands upon his time were considerable, but he was a man of dynamic energy. On occasions, he could be fractious and cantankerous in his dealings with people. He admitted to this weakness in his opening remarks in the diary for 1851:

> 1 January 1851
> May I feel thankful . . . for the ceaseless care of me and my family . . . but may I be made less disagreeable... promising to repent in future and avoid many things which are dangerous to my moral and spiritual duty . . . Neither I nor my fellow creature know how soon the Father of all shall call us to another world.

Although Joseph had established a reputation as a mediator in disputes between his neighbours, it is ironic that all too frequently he found himself at the centre of altercations. On 9 September 1851 he was involved in a *fracas* with his neighbour, George Richards, Waunfawr. This resulted in a display of fisticuffs, for in his diary Joseph briefly noted, 'I received a black eye!' Whether or not he deserved this we do not know, for the cause of the dispute is not stated. Sadly, however, three months later, his adversary was to suffer a tragic end:

> 10 November 1851
> Richards of Waunfawr has committed suicide at the age of thirty-nine years by cutting his throat with a razor. He was buried at St Caron's Church burial ground on the

west side of the steeple. His tenants attended the funeral on horseback.

This was not the only black eye he received. On 10 July 1862, while giving evidence in a court case at Carmarthen he quarrelled with a witness and again came off second best. 'I received a black eye for trying to interfere at the White Horse, Carmarthen ... I got up early and did apply some leeches to my eyelid ... I did not attend the Hall today ... but moved from the White Horse to the Stag and Pheasant!' Evidently, Joseph could make an impact of sorts wherever he went. He courted controversy as easily as admiration. Even so, his grasp of farming and his knowledge of the land were widely recognised.

Within a few years, his astute crop management and careful animal husbandry had made Trecefel a model farm. This brought him many prizes at the various agricultural shows held in the county. In 1852, he won the first prize for the best bull and for the best ram at Lampeter show. He was so wedded to his farm that in summer he would set out at 5 a.m. to check that all was well before rousing the household an hour later. He cherished daybreak. 'I walk my fields early to the accompaniment of a dawn chorus of skylarks, thrushes and robins. It is a precious time for a man's soul to be at one with nature.' His servants were required in summer to work from 7 a.m. until dusk. During the shorter winter days there were other tasks to perform. Joseph records that on winter evenings the men 'made brushes, wove ropes, and made cattle ties before supper.' Even on Christmas Day he describes how 'our women were making candles before supper.' More than 500 candles were made each week by dipping wicks into molten tallow, which was a slow and laborious task.

The diaries provide sharp glimpses of 19th century life on a Welsh farm in all its facets. Many a modern fisherman and sportsman would envy the idyllic conditions of the river Teifi in the 1850s. Although it often boiled over into raging floods, it was at other times a silver thread of sheer paradise, glinting with salmon and darting speckled trout. Many of Joseph's happiest moments were spent on its banks. 'I went to net fish in the Teifi and landed forty pounds of trout.' Unfortunately, we also catch a glimpse of things to come, for in the tranquillity on the riverbank he informs us, 'I drank freely from a bottle of whisky during the exercise.' A frequent figure seen to be casting his rod in the Trecefel meadows was the vicar, often with great success. 'The Reverend John Hughes and Mr Francis caught 56 pounds of trout today in the Teifi.'

Some visitors to the Trecefel meadows pleased Joseph more than others. On 10 May 1856, two of the most prominent members of the local gentry, Captain Pryse of Gogerddan and Colonel Powell of Nanteos, participated in an otter hunt on Joseph's land. But they were not entirely successful. 'We found the otter at the river course . . . after 4 hours hunting, but the otter did beat them entirely. Colonel Powell did bring him once to the surface with his spear, but could not land him!'

An abundance of game made Trecefel a magnet for sportsmen. Joseph himself was an excellent shot and he proudly records his achievements in the company of a neighbour. 'I went with Richards of Llanfair to shoot for a few hours. We put up some 150 partridge and shot 12 brace.' Another frequent visitor was Tom Arch, Colonel Powell of Nanteos's gamekeeper, who, on one occasion, 'shot 27 partridges and 2 hares.' In February 1853 the hunters seem to have greatly outnumbered the quarry. 'We were over 60 sportsmen at it – had a good sport coursing, but caught only 4 hares!'

On market days the narrow roads were thronged with farmers, horsemen, travellers, carriers, carts and animals of every description being driven to town. Tregaron was an important droving centre. The sight and sound of cattle plodding along on their long journey to Barnet Fair near London was a common spectacle. Sometimes Joseph was inconvenienced by them. In April 1853 he wrote:

> I cannot shoe my horses with any blacksmith because they are all too busy with the Drovers in town.

Later in the year the fields were alive with farm workers:

> 26 workers, scythes on their shoulders, walked to the hay fields . . . 22 reapers are in the Trecefel field using hooks to cut the corn, which is short this year . . . and there are, in all, over 40 hands assisting.

During haymaking the whole family, the servants and many of the neighbours would help with the scything, the raking and the carting. It was also a common sight to see the women and children gathering stones from the fields in their aprons. These were then placed at the side of the roads for collection, to be broken up by paupers in the workhouses and used for repairing the highways. When Cardiganshire County Council assumed responsibility for the roads in 1888, the farmers were paid small sums for these stones. Another source of income was the collection of bark from the trees for use in the tanning process. Children did this and one schoolmaster complained that the number of pupils was down, 'because they were barking in the woods.'

Although the children were required to assist in the work of the farm from an early age, New Year's Day was an exciting and joyous occasion for them, even more so than Christmas Day. This was the day when they would collect *calennig* – New Year's Gift – from the scattered farmhouses. They sang their new year's greeting in exchange for 'one newly minted coin'. Joseph records that 'coppers were distributed, beside being given bread and cheese.' In 1850 he paints a lyrical picture of the young visitors. 'All the children carried little calico bags to hold their gifts of newly minted pennies.' The custom of collecting *calennig* still continues in Cardiganshire and some parts of Wales even to this day.

But life was precarious, and these descriptions of happy occasions are frequently outweighed by darker incidents. Each winter brought a crop of illnesses that assailed the population, and fatal accidents were all too frequent. In September 1849 Joseph's uncle 'died from injuries received when he fell under a cart while returning from Carmarthen.' In October 1850 a little girl of ten was killed at Abercarfan farm 'when a heavy load of peat fell on top of her.' In January 1850 Joseph's cousin John Evans of Gogoyan was 'gored to death by a bull'. And there was always the river Teifi. Deceptively tranquil in appearance, its dark pools on sharp bends with hidden currents regularly claimed young and old, and many members of Joseph's own family perished beneath its waters.

Although this was a remarkably harmonious society, occasional violent incidents shattered the peace with dire results. In 1857 Joseph was required to attend the inquest of a murder victim at the neighbouring farm of Llanio Fawr. A dispute took place between two menservants which turned into a vicious fight. A stone was thrown by one, hitting the other on the back of the head, killing him instantly. After a court hearing, a verdict of manslaughter was reached.

Life at Trecefel was, on the whole, sweet. The farm was flourishing, the family was growing and Joseph's status within the community seemed assured. His many talents had not escaped the notice of the local squirearchy. In 1852 the local squire, Colonel Powell of Nanteos, appointed him his agent and agricultural adviser. The diaries are soon replete with references to some of the most influential personages in Cardiganshire. We learn that 'young Mr Vaughan of Trawsgoed called at Trecefel' and that 'Captain John Inglis Jones of Derry Ormond Mansion sought advice on the diversion of water from the Lead Mines above Llanddewi.' We have already noted that the gentry availed themselves of the sporting facilities, and Joseph prided himself that 'Captain Pryse of Gogerddan came often to fish in the river near Trecefel.'

In spite of all this, Joseph could not escape the occasional mishap, a tendency that was to dog him all too frequently throughout his life. Colonel Powell had fancied a horse named Flower, owned by Joseph. 'It was an excellent pony for the trap.' A sale was agreed, but when Joseph went to fetch the horse in the stable, he found that it had been 'strangled by its own harness.' The diaries include other unfortunate episodes. In November 1851 he attended Tal-sarn Fair and bought two yearling steers for £4 14s, but managed to lose one on the way home. Whether he was drunk at the time is a matter of conjecture. On 27 January 1851 he killed a bull that 'weighed 172 pounds per quarter, but was obliged to sell the skin in Tregaron Market for only 1 penny a pound.' At Cilpill sale he bought hay for £17 15s, but on the way home the horse bolted and ran away upsetting the whole cart; the following day he had to buy a new wagon for £14 16s. In January 1852 he was badly injured. 'I was thrown from my pony on the icy roads and bled profusely.' Nevertheless, associating with the gentry gave him immense satisfaction and afforded him the kudos he craved.

His burgeoning friendship with Colonel Powell of Nanteos, the Member of Parliament and Lord Lieutenant for the county, brought him invitations to fox hunts, beagle hunts, otter hunts and hare coursing. Nothing pleased him as much as the thrill of the hunt with its blast and fade of the horn in the company of the gentry. All these occasions usually ended in sumptuous banquets at the Talbot Hotel, Tregaron. The Nanteos hospitality always ensured that there was an endless supply of good strong punch served in glistening silver bowls, which the chilled hunters eagerly drank without restraint to warm themselves at the end of a cold day's coursing. Joseph refers to one such occasion:

> I joined Colonel Powell of Nanteos to course hares. There were over 200 followers, 28 hares were started; 14 greyhounds were slipped 8 times, but only 2 hares were killed. After the coursing we adjourned to the Talbot Hotel at Tregaron. There we partook of a grand dinner with 24 of us in the party. There was plenty of champagne, wine and a punch bowl to keep us merry.

Although he found these occasions irresistible, his diary sometimes reveals a nagging conscience. At the end of each year he philosophically reviewed it and set out new resolutions for the year ahead:

1 January 1854
Let me leave aside what really proves injurious, not only to my own person, but to my family. Strong liquors often produce untimely deaths. Therefore, let me abstain! . . . I do rob my own family, my wife and my children.

It was a candid admission of a growing problem. In March 1854, the family was traumatised by tragic news from Tynant, Betty's home, which deeply upset Joseph and banished, briefly, all thoughts of 'carousing in the company of the gentry.' A messenger came to Trecefel to inform them that Lewis, Betty's beloved elder brother, had committed suicide on the day before he was due to be married. Whereas the family had been busy with preparations for a bidding and a wedding, they now found themselves having to make arrangements for a funeral.

Lewis was a talented, sensitive young man of 21. His father, Jenkin Evans, had held high hopes for his future. Sadly, at the last moment, Lewis, haunted by the fear that his health would fail, felt unable to face the responsibility of marriage. Joseph recorded the whole sorrowful affair in his diary:

27 March 1854
The servant at Tynant came up here about 4 o'clock with the mournful news that my brother in law Lewis has committed a daring suicide by drowning himself at Gors y Gelad . . . He wrote a letter to his parents . . . He was so determined, that he tied a stone about 32lbs weight to both hands and neck by means of a knot. There was not much above 2 feet of water, but in that condition, no man could rise from dry ground. He was found the next

morning by his lamented father. He was about to be married to Elinor, the daughter of Gilfach Frân.

In the depths of his despair, Lewis left a letter in Welsh in which he attempted to explain his reasons for taking his own life.

26 March 1854

My dear Parents.

My circumstances are such that I cannot withstand them as I am fairly certain that, should I marry, I would not live long because of my health. That and many other things tempt me to assist nature in removing me from this world, in the hope that the Omnipotent Father will forgive me for such a dreadful act.

My dear and beloved parents and relations, do not weep after me but rather live without blemish in this world so that no guilt, conscience or any other temptation will come to meet you in your journey through this wilderness.

Even though it is a shameful thing that I do, yet carry out this wish of mine which is to accompany me to the graveyard at Capel y Groes and the text that should be preached is this, – 'Prepare and pray . . . so that tribulation does not befall you. The spirit is willing, but the flesh is weak.'

Allow my sister Margaret and Jenkin to remain here after me because there are many drops of my sweat everywhere here – even though not much can be seen as yet.

Farewell, farewell to each one of you under the protection of the gentle Father.

This is the last time for me to write a word to you my dear Parents.

P.S. Give generously to the cause of the one who was crucified. I have a particular longing when I think of departing this life.

Even from a dead man to his friends and relations in this uncertain world. †

The Trecefel and Blaenplwyf families rallied to support the devastated Tynant family in their despair and Betty stayed at her 'old home' to comfort her aged parents. Joseph saw to the practical side of things and ensured that Lewis's wishes were carried out. He was buried at Capel y Groes cemetery, Llanwnnen, in a grave adjoining that of Joseph's father. 'The Reverend Thomas Thomas preached from the said verse . . . and the funeral was very thickly attended.' Joseph was so affected by the manner of Lewis's death that he composed a verse, which was etched on his gravestone and is still visible today:

> He was good and industrious in his life,
>   But low in spirit,
> He suffered under the weight of an affliction,
> And because of this burden, he departed this world. †

After a hard spring and summer of harvesting the hay and corn, Joseph decided that he deserved a break from the toil at Trecefel. In October 1854 he and his two cousins Daniel and David Lloyd ventured beyond the narrow confines of Cardiganshire 'to the great city of London.' A man of infinite curiosity with a thirst for knowledge, Joseph had long desired to visit the capital and to see for himself the many places he had read about. He particularly wanted to see Smithfield market where many of the Welsh Black Cattle ended up, and the Crystal Palace, designed by Joseph Paxton for the Great

Exhibition of 1851. Joseph proved to be an intrepid tourist as his itinerary reveals:

15 October 1854
Went to Carmarthen station to book ourselves to Gloucester . . . made for London. We were in the great city by 11 o clock . . . went from Paddington to Smithfield and took our lodging at the Coopers Arms . . . Many of the Cardiganshire Cattle dealers were there sleeping.

16 October 1854
Went to Smithfield Market where there were 7,000 head of fat cattle and 27,000 sheep . . . Prime beef selling at 7½d per lb. We went to the top of the monument by St Paul's and the Houses of Parliament . . .

17 October 1854
To the Crystal Palace, the great wonder of the world where we saw almost everything that is in existence – An exhibition of the Industry of All Nations . . . People throng the stands, farmers and gentry alike. It was built by the gardener Joseph Paxman.

18 October 1854
Went down a steam boat to Deptford Greenwich, Woolwich and Graves End . . . Splendid view of the river and Army and Navy at Woolwich and came back through the Thames Tunnel.

19 October 1854
Left Paddington at 7.30 a.m. Arrived Carmarthen 10 p.m. Slept at the Fountain.

20 October 1854

Left Carmarthen at 8 o clock by mail to Lampeter . . .
I was back here by dusk and found the family quite well.

Over the coming years Joseph continued to make improvements to the farm. Because of his vision and his practical ability to implement new ideas on agriculture, Trecefel soon became the showpiece of Cardiganshire. In 1857 judges from the County Agricultural Society, accompanied by the bailiff of Gogerddan, visited Trecefel to scrutinise his work. They were so impressed that they had no hesitation in declaring it the best-kept farm in the county. It was an honour richly deserved and Joseph's crowning achievement after a decade of dedication to his land. It seemed that the fates, for the time being at least, had truly dealt him a favourable hand. The Master of Trecefel could justifiably feel well satisfied with life.

CHAPTER 5
A MAN FOR ALL CAUSES

Joseph Jenkins was passionate about education; above all he wished to make available to others the privilege denied to him. It was a cause which he earnestly espoused in the interests of his own family and that of the community in general. Concerned about the inadequacy of provision in Tregaron, Joseph had made private arrangements for his own children by engaging a Miss Smith to visit Trecefel to teach them. The children of three neighbouring farms also joined them. '7 September 1857 Miss Smith here keeping school – Tyndomen, Waunfawr and Nantserni children came under her tuition today.'

Twenty-one years later in Australia he was to advocate that all young children be obliged to keep a journal to expand their knowledge and to improve their powers of expression. He also wrote a poem of 25 stanzas urging his young son Tom to follow in his footsteps:

> Learn to read as well as write,
> Learn to count and spell alright,
> Write down your thoughts in proper form,
> Explain them too, in clear light. †

Over the previous century many different schools had been established at Tregaron – most of them undistinguished and inadequate. One of Griffith Jones's Welsh Circulating Schools had been held in St Caron's Church 'between the pulpit and the door . . . with each child to bring turf fuel on Mondays.' Because the children had to work in the fields in the summer months, this school was only held during the winter. George Borrow caught a fleeting glimpse of such a school held in the town by the Reverend John Hughes:

> I did not fail to pay a visit to Tregaron church. It is an antique building with a stone tower . . . the name of the clergyman was Hughes . . . he was an excellent charitable man . . . who gave himself great trouble in educating the children of the poor. He certainly seemed to have succeeded in teaching them good manners: as I was leaving the church, I met a number of little boys belonging to the church school: no sooner did they see me than they drew themselves up in a rank on one side, and as I passed took off their caps and simultaneously shouted 'Good morning!'

George Borrow might have been impressed in the autumn of 1854; the inspectors responsible for the notorious 'Blue Books' report on Welsh education in 1847 had been less complimentary. The Tregaron Day School was characterised by 'a total absence of method and discipline . . . and the master was quite unable to maintain order.' The report came to be known as 'The Treason of the Blue Books', and was regarded as a prejudiced attack on Welsh religion, education and morals by persons who were devoid of any knowledge of Wales, its language or its culture. They claimed that the Welsh language prevented the Welsh from reaping the benefits of Victorian prosperity. As a result, only English was to be promoted in schools and children were punished for using their mother tongue. The infamous 'Welsh Not', a wooden board placed around the neck of a child caught speaking Welsh, was employed in many schools to enforce the policy of speaking English only. Joseph Jenkins campaigned vigorously for a better and fairer system of basic education. As early as 30 November 1854 Joseph and the Reverend John Hughes convened a meeting to consider providing a new school building.

Some three years later, on Tuesday 9 September 1857, a public meeting was finally held to discuss the establishment of a new school at Tregaron. Joseph chaired the meeting with his customary authority and the following unanimous resolution was agreed:

> A public and suitable schoolroom, with all conveniences should be erected, as . . . above 450 children between the ages of 5 and 16 years were entirely destitute of the privilege of being trained by a competent Master.

It was also decided that the schoolroom should be built and funded by means of a general subscription and that an appeal be made to the landed gentry and others for their support. Joseph was thanked for his guidance and pioneering spirit, and John Lewis, the 'sweet bard' of Tregaron, known by his bardic name Ioan Mynyw, signalled in verse a bright new era for the cause of education in the town:

> The time of inadequate schools
> And poor grey cottages has passed: †

Joseph was not only a thinker, he was also a doer who was prepared to lead from the front. He personally tramped the roads of his parish, Caron Isclawdd, calling at every farm and cottage urging the inhabitants to support the cause of the new school and to subscribe to it. The diary records that on 15 January 1858, 'in atrocious weather, up to my knees in snow,' he managed to collect the significant sum of £40. Just as importantly, he secured promises of labour from the farmers to build the schoolroom. A parcel of land on elevated ground to the rear of the present Bwlchgwynt chapel was chosen. Joseph managed to persuade Colonel Powell of Nanteos to give the land in trust for the purpose of the schoolroom. The work proceeded rapidly, 'on 26 April the foundation of the school was laid. On 1 May the farmers carted the corner stones for the school.' When the building was duly completed it was an example of superb co-operation among the inhabitants of a remote rural community, committed to providing education for their children. In 1859 Joseph's dream was realised when 80 pupils attended the school under the tutelage of Evan Jones, who was to be Headmaster from 1859 until 1872.

Not being content with the establishment of a new school, Joseph also turned his attention to the educational needs of adults. On 23 December 1857 he founded a Literary Society, which met in the Long Room above the stables at the Talbot Hotel. This proved to be a resounding success with scores of people packing the meetings. Every session was chaired by Joseph. There were debates on topics of general interest, and poetry competitions for the many up-and-coming bards in the locality. In February 1858 Joseph records that he 'gave another lecture to the Literary Society on Dedication to the Society.' No one was more qualified to deliver this, for few had served the Tregaron Society more assiduously than he had done.

The 1850s also saw Joseph turn his boundless energy to

another cause of far-reaching significance which would have a profound impact on the Tregaron area and upon west Wales in general. This was the era of railway expansion. As far back as 1844, the Railway Act had provided a legislative framework for massive railway construction which was to prove the major socio-economic development of the decade. Gladstone had stipulated that on each line there had to be a 'parliamentary train at least once a day', with a fare of no more than one penny a mile. In the 1850s many plans were discussed to provide a railway for west Wales. The age of steam would ultimately reach Cardiganshire, but it would take a decade before the dream was realised.

Among many others, one proposal put forward was to provide a railway line between Milford Haven and Manchester, which became commonly known as the M&M Line. It was intended to connect the deep-water harbour at Milford, which imported cotton from America, with the industrial manufacturing centre of Manchester.

The force behind the M&M was the intrepid entrepreneur David Davies, Llandinam. His great ambition was to drive a railway line through west Wales. Davies had already made a name for himself as a powerful industrialist, having built the Llanidloes – Newtown and the Vale of Clwyd railway lines. Along with his partner Frederick Beeston of Llanidloes, Davies became the contractor for the M&M line. In Tregaron itself one of the most indefatigable activists for the cause of the railway was Joseph Jenkins. He was enlightened and far-sighted enough to realise what benefits would accrue to agriculture and the economy in general from better communications.

The need for the railway was indeed a real one. The

prevailing mode of travel for most people was by horse and cart or on foot. The narrow, poorly maintained roads made the transportation of essential supplies such as lime and coal difficult and time-consuming. The drovers took two months to drive the cattle to England, but the advent of the railway would enable the animals to be transported in one day. This removed the expensive necessity of having to fatten the herds on the Surrey fields before taking them to the London markets.

Naturally, the inhabitants of Tregaron were keen that the railway should run through their town. Conscious of the importance of siting a station at Tregaron, Joseph became an ardent crusader for the venture. No stranger to the public platform, he deployed his natural eloquence in the cause of the railway by making his presence loudly felt at the meetings convened at the Talbot Hotel. The crucial role he played is highlighted by the fact that he was invited to address a committee meeting at the House of Commons on the railway and its benefits to agriculture. With his detailed knowledge of the area and its farming practices, he was deemed to be the ideal person to advise on such matters.

But the key figure behind the railway project was David Davies. In all, Davies and the M&M committee decided that a capital sum of £555,000 in £10 shares had to be raised to finance the whole venture. A committee was established in Tregaron and in other towns throughout the county in order to raise money. The £10 shares were offered to members of the public and Joseph embarked upon the task of selling these with a missionary zeal. He travelled to Aberaeron to address a public meeting, but there he found that the response was 'lamentable, only two shares were taken up.'

On 21 September 1857 he delivered a powerful appeal to a large crowd gathered at the Talbot Hotel. A self-congratulatory entry in his diary states, 'According to those present I made an excellent speech.' The local squirearchy fully supported the railway because they saw that it would bring economic benefits in its wake, thus increasing their own prosperity.

When the local squire, Captain John Inglis Jones of Derry Ormond, took up the cause and chaired a full house at the Talbot Hotel to drum up support for the railway, Joseph was present and gave him a ringing endorsement claiming that, 'several good speeches were made.' There followed three years of hard campaigning by all concerned until, on 27 January 1860, Joseph triumphantly wrote:

> I received a letter from London stating that £40,000 has been sanctioned by the Treasury in favour of the railway construction between Manchester and Milford Haven. Daniel Thomas of Hafod and myself have joined to canvass financial support for the venture and to arrange to sell shares at a meeting to be held at the Talbot Hotel. Forty shares were taken up at ten shillings each.

In principle, the battle for the railway had been won, but ahead lay years of careful planning and arduous work. Joseph's diaries for the subsequent years describe the impact of the project on the locality and in particular the upheaval on his farm resulting from it.

Although he had fought hard for the railway, when David Davies's gang of navvies finally descended on his land and began to 'move hundreds of tons of earth', Joseph became alarmed and his attitude somewhat ambivalent. His mood fluctuated between irritation and enthusiasm as he watched his fertile acres being inexorably ripped apart. Shocked by the ruinous impact on his land he grumbled, 'The major digging is done by an implement which they call the worm . . . This model farm is being destroyed.' Joseph felt that the toil of two decades was being imperilled, and he hated the intrusive presence of workers and onlookers:

> Large numbers of navvies are working on the Trecefel cutting and many curious visitors are coming to view the sight . . . My land is being overrun with people . . . This disruption greatly disturbs the farm which is already intersected by two roads . . . Now the fields will have to be replanned. In places the track is 36 yards wide!

It was one thing to want the railway, but another to have it literally on one's doorstep.

He lost his temper completely on 3 June when the surveyors spent two days on Trecefel land and ordered their men to cut 'twenty eight gaps in our hedges at different places.' For Joseph, this was little short of desecration. He had not anticipated the sacrifice of his precious hedgerows which had been so carefully nurtured over 18 years. But nothing was now going to stand in the way of the railway. On 4 October 1864 James Weekes Szlumper, the head engineer, arrived at Trecefel to supervise the pegging of the route. Joseph took an instinctive dislike to Szlumper and, with mounting agitation, wrote, 'The fields cannot be arranged. They are working out the exact route which spoils this model farm.' A couple of weeks later, Joseph relented and he once again became caught up in the excitement of the whole venture:

12 October 1864

The Railway Surveyor had driven his four-wheel carriage into our yard today. I and Lewis went along the fields to help him. The steam engine was drawn to Lampeter yesterday by 47 horses. The engine is to be employed from Pencader to Lampeter.

On 28 March 1865 his landlord, the Reverend Latimer Jones, came to Trecefel to inspect the railway from Tyndomen bridge to the end of Penrallt to assess how much he would receive in compensation for the loss of land. Amounts were agreed with Frederick Beeston the contractor: Trecefel land was valued at £14 per acre, and the neighbouring farms Tyndomen and Penrallt at £9 10s and £7 15s respectively. 'It was also agreed to fence through the three farms for 5 pence per set.' As the pace of work accelerated, the whole area echoed with 'clanging and banging . . . and Railway men began to swarm into the neighbourhood to begin work. No more than 3/- per day was paid to the most able labourers. Excavators began in Glanbrenig fields and 450 men pass to and from work every day.'

On 7 July Joseph received a special visit from David Davies, the contractor, ostensibly to discuss fencing-in the railway. Because of his involvement with the line and his early crusading zeal, Joseph had become well known to Davies as one who exercised considerable influence in the locality. This time Davies was not there to discuss the railway, rather, he had his eye on power and the future. The 1865 General Election was pending and Davies wished to become an M.P. He was by now extremely wealthy but remained enormously proud of the fact that he was a self-made man. In addition to being a railway contractor, he was a coal tycoon, owning collieries in the

Rhondda, and became known as 'Davies the Ocean' after one of his mines; he was also responsible for developing Barry Docks. Despite his vast wealth, Davies remained for the most part uneducated, and he was an indifferent speaker. He recognised that Joseph was a self-educated man with the ability to hold and influence his audience as an orator. He therefore sought Joseph's endorsement of him as the Liberal candidate in the forthcoming election. 'David Davies called,' wrote Joseph, 'to solicit my vote and influence, being a Parliamentary candidate for Cardiganshire against Lloyd of Bronwydd.'

Joseph and David Davies had much in common. They were born in the same year, 1818, and came from similar backgrounds. Davies had been brought up on Draintewion, a hill farm near Llandinam in Montgomeryshire. Both men were industrious, enterprising and ambitious: but they also differed. Whereas Davies was a thrifty, uncompromising, Calvinistic Methodist who never touched alcohol, Joseph disliked Methodists, spent his money liberally and 'drank freely' whenever the opportunity presented itself. Whereas Davies had spent every hour 'toiling and sawing', for which he gained the nickname 'Top Sawyer', Joseph had spent much of his time educating himself. Nevertheless, flattered by the attentions of the great contractor, Joseph immediately agreed to do all he could to support Davies in his bid for Parliament. Henceforth, Davies was to call frequently at Trecefel and Joseph records that they 'had a long chat at the Tyndomen cutting about sundry things.' Because of his association with Davies, Joseph was granted many favours, including the freedom to 'take private rides on the engines.' This afforded him a great deal of pleasure, and gave him a new feeling of importance.

Meanwhile, as the building of the railway accelerated, so did Joseph's irritation. In August he was particularly annoyed when he found that the workforce was not only tearing apart his land, but also compromising his maidservants. '22 August, The two Marys were not in bed. They spent the night in the barn lying with the navvies!' For Joseph, who often took a high moral stance, the situation was intolerable. Even worse, he now lost his 'faithful servant' David Lloyd, who decided to leave Trecefel for a more lucrative wage of 3/- a day on the railway instead of his annual wage of £8. Joseph then hired two men servants for £8 and £5 10s respectively, and a young lad for £3 15s per year. Each night Joseph plotted the progress. 'This huge upheaval and great enterprise continues apace, the men were very busy carrying timber for fencing and sleepers for the track – the stones are carted from Pantyblawd . . . Everywhere, there is a mess.' The curiosity of the local people showed no sign of abating. 'Hundreds of people are idling and walking along the contracting line – which lies only a hundred yards from the farmhouse.' But, always, the most hurtful sight of all was to note that 'our hedges are levelled!' The coming of the railway had its downside for Trecefel, but as one who had solicited applications for shares in the line, Joseph praised the promoters:

> It will pay each separate share holder
> More than four pounds in every tent.
> It will greatly profit the farmer,
> And pay all his taxes and rent.
>
> Come, praise the gallant Directors
> As well as the Manchester men.
> Hail to the skilful Contractors
> In earnest; Good cheers! Amen.

By 18 September 1865, the platelayers had reached the milestone at Bont-Ffrainc, the small bridge at the end of Trecefel entrance. On 20 September Joseph witnessed the first engine come puffing across Trecefel land carrying a heavy load of rail-sockets at full speed as far as the lane. He was so moved by the experience that he composed a verse to commemorate the occasion in which he described the engine as 'spitting fire and smoke, as it pulls and boils.' The lines captured the spirit of the event as 'the people clapped and cheered watching their dream of the railway at last being realised.'

But there were to be occasional setbacks. On 22 September 1865 the engine failed to go up the incline toward Trecefel and had to shed its load and return to the Teifi for water. Despite his periodic fury at the pillage of his land, Joseph still took a keen interest in the work of David Davies and Frederick Beeston. He regarded himself as no mean engineer and regularly inspected the mass of working materials which lay in sight of his farmhouse. These included hundreds of rails and sleepers and the scores of wagons and horses needed to move the earth. Six of these horses were kept by Joseph in the Trecefel stables. Neither could he resist becoming involved in the practical aspects of railway construction; when the chief engineer had pegged the track, Joseph insisted upon holding the chains and assisting in the work. Although he often cursed it, the whole extent of this Titanic undertaking secretly excited him and he never ceased to be amazed by the amount of timber, brick and stone needed for the track and the many bridges.

During this time Joseph struck up a useful friendship with James Benbow, nicknamed the 'Admiral', one of the most famous engine drivers on the M&M line. Originally from

Llandinam, he was employed by David Davies as his chief engine driver. Attired in the smart uniform of the M&M, he was noted for his obsession with punctuality. This friendship with Benbow enabled Joseph to indulge in one of the great thrills of his life, 'to drive a steam engine.' This went a long way to compensating for the 'loss of much of my fields.' For Joseph, 27 September was a special day as he 'rode on the Lady Elizabeth engine from Pont Llanio to Lampeter and back to Trecefel siding on the engine Montgomery.'

Christmas Day 1865 turned out to be more eventful than usual when David Davies invited him to ride on the light engine *Teifi*, known as 'the donkey', up to Cors Caron – Tregaron Bog. Joseph had taken a particular interest in the progress of the railway as it crossed Cors Caron. Because of the marshy nature of the ground, it had presented Davies with a difficult problem. Hundreds of tons of earth had been laid as a foundation, but the line kept sinking with the weight of the iron track. Eventually, the contractors discovered that a layer of wool placed under it would absorb the water and provide a firm foundation. David Davies then purchased all the wool he could procure and farmers took it 'by the ton in cartloads to Cors Caron.' Joseph congratulated Davies on his success and described the navvies as 'working wonderfully well along the turf.' He even wrote a rather limp verse to record their triumph over the tricky terrain:

> CORS CARON
> Success to David Davies
> F. Beeston, Master Duff
> All gangers and their navvies,
> They'll cut through smooth and rough.

By the end of 1865 the 12 miles of the Pencader to Lampeter line was completed. It was duly inspected by Colonel Yolland of the Board of Trade, and David Davies, Frederick Beeston and James Szlumper greeted him at Pencader. The line was tested by placing two M&M engines funnel to funnel so as 'to get the greatest possible weight per foot on the rails.' Davies Llandinam would have been well satisfied with the report in the *Aberystwyth Observer* 6 January 1866, which stated that, 'The cuttings are well finished, and the whole length is admirably ballasted . . . there has been no buttoning up of the pocket . . . Messers Davies & Beeston and their engineer have done their part in making a first-class railway with the least possible outlay.'

Joseph had referred to 'mountains of earth having been removed' from his farm. In fact, over one million cubic yards of earth was excavated between Aberystwyth and Pencader and he was fascinated to learn that '12,000 tons of iron had been used and no less than 60 bridges had been built' as the line criss-crossed the numerous rivers en route.

The grand opening of the entire line was held at Aberystwyth on 12 August 1867. To celebrate the event the dignitaries were driven in a special train around Pendinas before proceeding to Pencader. But the return journey proved to be an unexpected ordeal. As the train approached Trawsgoed, it careered wildly out of control down the steep gradient and flew past the station, leaving the assembled crowd of passengers standing agape on the platform. It was finally brought to a halt by the shocked driver some distance from Trawsgoed.

That evening the celebrations culminated in a banquet held at the Belle Vue Hotel, Aberystwyth. David Davies addressed the assembled dignitaries and reminded them that the M&M

Debentures were rapidly being sold. 'There are,' he said, 'only a few left, and if you want them, now is your time!' His words fell on fertile ground.

Davies emphasised the economic importance of his undertaking. 'Cardiganshire,' he said, 'is at this moment hundreds of thousands of pounds more valuable as a county. This line has put the county on a footing . . . with the commerce of the world.' When the Mayor heaped praise on Davies, he replied, rather immodestly, 'I feel we are entitled to it!'

The following day David Davies treated 50 of his faithful labourers to a farewell dinner at the Belle Vue Hotel. These men, who had toiled under his eagle eye for some 15 years, presented him with a clock. Davies, anxious to identify with his men, replied, 'I am a humble worker myself . . . I once worked as you are working now.'

In spite of his efforts on behalf of the railway and in spite of his acquaintance with David Davies, Joseph does not appear to have received an invitation to the celebrations. Nevertheless, his respect for Davies was undiminished. He maintained that, 'this Railway will change our lives for ever!' It most certainly did.

To the people of Cardiganshire, the railway meant far more than rapid conveyance of goods and the opening of communications. It was more than mere hissing steam on inanimate strips of iron and wood. It became an essential part of the landscape, with its picturesque stations, its liveried employees and the marvels of its cuttings and bridges. The sight of the puffing engine, the sound of the steam and the steady rhythm of the wheels over the tracks became one of the reassuring sounds of the countryside – as natural as birdsong. It became a feature of the people's lives; they set their clocks by it, they ate their food by it. The midday train was known as *y trên cawl* — the broth train. It signalled a break for lunch, and it is claimed that even the horses ploughing would automatically stop and retire for a rest when its chug reverberated across the fields. People would wave their handkerchiefs, and the passengers would respond in similar fashion.

Joseph's descendants also identified closely with this line. Later on, the railway would play a more tragic role as it conveyed the Cardiganshire Yeomanry to the bloody fields of the 1914-18 war. Many did not make the return journey, as the war memorials in the towns and villages testify. Joseph's youngest daughter Anne notes in her diary how she would stand on Trecefel bridge to 'see the train go by and wave to the soldiers going to war.' Later on she records that:

> On the 11th November 1918, as the goods train was proceeding through Trecefel fields, the engine gave many loud blasts and the engine driver shouted to me. From these signals I concluded that peace had come at last.

Today, only traces of the M&M Railway can be seen. The cutting below Trecefel is still clearly in evidence, but the rail is no longer in situ. Like so many other rural lines it fell victim to the depredations wrought by the Beeching Report of 1963. Joseph would, no doubt, have been appalled at the dismantling of the line, and his grandson, the late Joseph Evans, Tyndomen, campaigned forcefully to save it. But as Joseph Jenkins once wrote, 'Nothing on earth is static . . . time changes everything.'

Of those who were thrown together in the cause of the railway, David Davies and James Weekes Szlumper were destined for greater things. Davies became one of the most affluent and successful of industrialists and the first self-made millionaire in Wales. James Weekes Szlumper became High Sheriff of Cardiganshire and three times Mayor of Richmond. He was involved in the construction of the London Underground and ultimately received a knighthood. For Joseph, life would not be so kind. Ironically, the railway he had worked so hard to promote would be the means of carrying him from his homeland to a far-off continent to confront an unpredictable future.

CHAPTER 6

A WET CANVASS

The M&M Railway had absorbed much of Joseph Jenkins's time and energy; but politics, in particular general elections, were to drain his mental and physical powers to the limit.

Members of Parliament in rural areas were almost always drawn from the landed gentry because they alone had the wealth and power to bribe and bully their way to Westminster. Cardiganshire was represented by two Members of Parliament, one for the county, and one for the boroughs. The two dominant political families were the Vaughans of Trawsgoed, who represented the Tories, and the Pryses of Gogerddan, who supported the Liberals; Trawsgoed controlled the County seat, and Gogerddan the Boroughs. Political corruption was rampant and the elections of the time were bruising affairs. Threats, dirty tricks, coercion and oppression were the name of the game. There was no secret ballot and only tenants farming a certain acreage were allowed to vote in rural areas. Not until the 1884 Reform Act were farm labourers enfranchised. There was, therefore, plenty of scope for malpractice and trickery. M.P.s were not paid a salary, but the office conferred upon the holder a great deal of status and influence at both local and national level. So much so, that the gentry were prepared to spend inordinate sums of money to buy a seat at Westminster.

In 1859 Parliament was dissolved and on 16 April Colonel William Powell of Nanteos, the sitting Tory M.P., paid a visit to Trecefel to seek Joseph's support in the impending election. Colonel Powell had long noted the influential role played by Joseph in local affairs and felt that he could be of assistance in gaining the support of the tenant farmers. Already, there was rumbling discontent among the farmers directed against the gentry on account of the ever-increasing rents, the tithe paid to the church, and the enclosure of land. Joseph himself had suffered a rent increase at the hands of the Reverend Latimer Jones and when he was obliged to pay the half-yearly sum on 22 January 1859 he complained, 'Short of money this time.'

Nevertheless, Joseph acceded to Colonel Powell's request and agreed to back his candidature, although it might have been against his natural instinct to do so. By upbringing, Joseph was a radical, and most Unitarians would have been drawn to the Liberal cause rather than to the Tory camp. But Joseph had already switched his allegiance to the Anglicans and having been courted by the gentry, he now counted Colonel Powell among his friends. The many invitations he had received to the celebratory dinners at the Talbot Hotel had not been for nothing; it was now pay back time and the 'good Colonel' was collecting his dues.

Powell's Liberal opponent was A.H. Saunders-Davies of Pentre, Newcastle Emlyn. Within three days of throwing in his lot with Colonel Powell, Joseph virtually abandoned his stewardship of the farm; much to Betty's dismay he delegated everything to his wife and servants in order to devote his energies to the forthcoming election.

The weather for canvassing was atrocious, with the

surrounding mountains obliterated by snow and the roads 'glassy with frost'. Yet, each morning at sunrise, the intrepid Joseph doggedly set out in arctic conditions to drum up support for Powell. His diary reflects his punishing schedule:

> 19 April 1859
> I left here for canvassing in favour of Col. Powell. Went as far as Perthneuadd and did return along the Vale of Aeron as far as Llangeitho where I did stop for the night.

A stop-over at Llangeitho meant a night of drinking spent at the Stag's Head Inn where he could refresh himself with 'bread and ale'. Joseph had meticulously drawn up a list of every tenant farmer in the locality who had a vote, and he called at each farm exhorting them to support Powell. But not every farmer was compliant, and Joseph was obliged to attend frequent meetings held by Powell's agents at the Talbot Hotel in order to give a progress report.

Canvassing in such adverse conditions was arduous work requiring huge physical energy which, fortunately, Joseph possessed in full measure. Despite it being April, the snow piled high against the hedges and Joseph's horse 'slithered and slid on the icy lanes.' Battling against wickedly cold winds he visited every village and every sequestered farm occupied by an enfranchised tenant. On 20 April he recorded, 'out canvassing all day, then in the evening to Tregaron to attend the Committee, and after giving my report I returned home.' He barely spent six hours at Trecefel before he set out again the following morning, this time, 'to Llanddewi in order to canvass more voters.' The Llanddewi constituents seemed more amenable to his powers of persuasion, since 'many did promise support.'

The following day found him back again, trudging around 'the Tregaron area to see some electors.'

Joseph's dedication to the Tory cause was heroic. It was a grinding task to mobilise support among his neighbours, and Powell was taking nothing for granted. On 25 April a special meeting was convened, and Joseph 'went to town to meet Colonel Powell . . . It appears it will be a hard fight.' The next day he records, 'out again collecting votes for Colonel Powell – the weather is hostile but I had much success.' On 27 April, he felt optimistic enough to write that, 'the promises for Colonel Powell are favourable.'

His strenuous campaigning on behalf of the 'good Squire' brought its own rewards. Another meeting held at the Talbot Hotel was followed by a lavish dinner with the 'tables groaning under the weight of hams and venison . . . with plenty of claret and hot punch.' It was a welcome sight, for Joseph's appetite must have been whetted by tramping through the wilds of Blaencaron that day. On 28 April he truly felt that he was one of the 'gentlefolk' of the locality when he was conveyed in grand style. 'Went to the great meeting of the Tory landlords. Left for Aberaeron with the Rev. J. Hughes, Vicar, John Jones, Camer, Mr Williams, Sunnyhill. We were in the chaise and phaeton.'

Travelling in such comfort was the ultimate privilege, but a couple of days later Joseph was back on the rutted roads, canvassing on foot in his hobnailed boots because the lanes were too slippery for his horse. He walked four miles to Llanfair Clydogau and struggled up the steep hill of Rhiw Halen – Salt Hill – just to visit a few far-flung farms, such was his fanatical dedication to the Colonel.

On 2 May, Joseph was once again summoned to a special

meeting at the Talbot Hotel to review the campaign and, in particular to 'make arrangements to get the voters to the polling booth at Tregaron.' Colonel Powell and his advisers were leaving no stone unturned. It was one thing to extract a promise, but another to translate it into a certain vote. Joseph had conscientiously covered every mile of the scattered constituency, but on 3 May his canvassing was tragically interrupted. He received the sad news that his niece Elisabeth, the daughter of his brother John, had died of T.B. at the age of 13, and that 'she shall be interred to-morrow.' With the General Election imminent he could barely spare the time, but a family funeral had to take precedence, even over the interests of Colonel Powell. On 4 May Joseph and Betty set out for the burial at Rhydygwin Chapel; but immediately after the service, with what appeared to be unseemly haste, Joseph left Betty with the mourners and 'set out on foot to go about the country in search of voters.' His behaviour at that time scarcely endeared him to the rest of the family. But time was of the essence; 'the grand finale was nigh' and Joseph recounts the event in his diary:

> 5 May 1859
> Left early as it was polling day, which did open at 8 o'clock, where the friends of Col. Powell began to crowd at the Booth to tender their votes. The business was very active until 3 o'clock. The transactions were carried on very quiet and honourable during the day.

Elections could be rumbustious affairs, but the 1859 General Election appears to have been uneventful. When the count took place, Colonel Powell obtained 1,070 votes to his opponent's 928. The breakdown was as follows:

CENTRE	POWELL	DAVIES
Aberystwyth	607	169
Cardigan	105	528
Lampeter	160	176
Tregaron	198	55

Tregaron had polled heavily in favour of their local squire. This was partly due to the efforts of Joseph, but it also reflects the fear of their landlord experienced by tenant farmers. Because the secret ballot was not yet in existence, they were obliged to cast their votes under the menacing glare of Powell's agents, with the threat of eviction a powerful persuader. Nevertheless, 55 tenant farmers at Tregaron were courageous enough to follow their convictions and to vote for the Liberal A.H. Saunders-Davies.

Now that he was once again safely ensconced as an M.P., Colonel Powell had his dues to pay. The night of the Election saw Tregaron convulsed with celebrations. Three large casks of pitch were set alight in the town, and huge bonfires were lit in all the outlying districts. Ostensibly, the inhabitants were cock-ahoop, conditioned as they were by a mixture of longstanding tradition and oppression. Powell's agents had orchestrated a grand welcome for the Colonel. Joseph describes how, 'a procession, waving flags, met Colonel Powell M.P. at Camer Fawr, and escorted him to the Talbot Hotel where he made a speech from an upstairs window and showered monies on the scrambling children below.' Champagne was plentiful at the dinner that followed.

To reward his supporters, '300 gallons of beer were sent to Llanddewi, Llangeitho, and Derry Ormond.' What the

Methodists made of this, one can only guess. But this Election proved indeed, to be an extravagantly 'wet canvass'. Every effort had been made to bribe the voters with food and especially with drink. It had proved extremely costly, even for the deepest purse, and Joseph noted that, 'the bill presented to the committee was rather large.' But the expenditure had not been in vain. After the Election Colonel Powell called at Trecefel to thank Joseph personally for his support, which gave him a deep sense of pride.

Six years later, in 1865, Parliament was dissolved once more and Joseph found himself embroiled in yet another General Election. This time, Colonel Powell had decided not to stand as a candidate on the grounds of ill health, since he was now confined to a wheelchair. Instead, Sir Thomas Davies Lloyd of Bronwydd, regarded as a 'moderate Liberal', presented himself for the county seat. This, coupled with the fact that he was one of the gentry, made him an acceptable choice even for the staunchly Tory Trawsgoed family. As a result, they agreed to throw their weight behind him.

However, Colonel Powell suddenly changed his mind and decided that he would, after all, stand for Parliament, despite the chronic state of his health. This posed a dilemma for Lloyd of Bronwydd, but he decided to withdraw his challenge and yield the field to Powell.

In a letter to 'The Freeholders and Independent Election of the County of Cardigan', he wrote in *The Welshman*:

> As I had pledged myself not to offer any opposition to the gallant Colonel – so popular as a landlord and a neighbour, I am precluded from coming forward on this occasion.

However, many Liberals, incensed that their candidate had so meekly capitulated to the Tories, resolved to put forward their own candidate to oppose Colonel Powell. Two names were submitted to the Liberal committee. One was David Davies, Llandinam, who had already made a name for himself in the county as the industrialist behind the M&M Railway; the other was Henry Richard, an Independent Minister, born at Tregaron, who had already sown the seeds of what was to be an illustrious career. In 1848 he had been appointed secretary of the Peace Society, and would later earn the title of 'Apostle of Peace' for his efforts to promote international harmony.

The Liberals faced a difficult choice. A selection meeting was held at Aberaeron with both candidates invited to address the assembled delegates. David Davies made great play of his role in developing the railway and maintained that, 'few can have a greater or an equal interest in the general improvement and welfare of the county.' But one of Henry Richard's supporters caustically remarked that, 'Davies's task was to build a railway, not to make laws in Parliament.' Captain John Pugh Pryse of the powerful Gogerddan family, who normally supported the Liberals, also opposed Davies, whom he regarded as a carpetbagger, 'who had only come to Cardiganshire to serve his own interests.'

Denominational allegiances played a significant part. David Davies, an uncompromising Methodist, had already given thousands of pounds to various Methodist chapels and had promised much more. His vast wealth in a county where Methodists ruled the roost won him the day. Henry Richard, an Independent minister of more modest means, could not compete with Davies and was obliged to bow out of the contest. Later, Henry

Richard was to make his name as M.P. for Merthyr, but he was so hurt by his treatment in Cardiganshire that he never again spoke a word to David Davies, Llandinam.

While all this was going on in the Liberal camp, the vacillating Colonel Powell changed his mind again. He decided, after all, that his health was not good enough to enable him to contest the Election. This opened the door once again to Lloyd of Bronwydd, the 'avowed Liberal' with Tory support. Ever suspicious of David Davies, who was not viewed as 'one of us', the gentry threw their weight behind Lloyd, and Colonel Powell made it known that they would not bring out a Tory to oppose him. Thus, Cardiganshire found itself in the strange situation of having two Liberals contesting the same seat: one the choice of the gentry, and the other the choice of the Methodists.

A week after the selection meeting, held on 7 July at Aberaeron, David Davies called at Trecefel to request Joseph Jenkins's support in the coming election. Although Joseph had in the past pledged his loyalty to Colonel Powell, his departure from the scene now meant that Joseph was free to give Davies his full backing. He immediately proceeded to channel his prodigious energy into the cause of the 'railway man'. Without delay, his muse was employed. '10 July 1865 I did compose poetry in favour of David Davies which was printed at 3 o'clock.' Poetry and song could be powerful weapons in the maelstrom of Welsh elections. In order to whip up election fever these would be published and distributed far and wide. Joseph's verses, on this occasion, are not recorded in his diary or notebook, so we cannot judge their merit or their effectiveness in the campaign.

Because both Joseph and David Davies were driven men, a well-planned campaign was set in motion immediately. Meetings were arranged throughout the county, setting a relentless pace for the candidate. Joseph gives us a glimpse of Davies's commitments. '11 July David Davies spoke at Llanrhystud, 11.30 a.m.; Llanon, 1.00 p.m.; Tregaron, 4.30 p.m., and at Lampeter in the evening for a moonlight meeting.'

Joseph was given the task of covering the surrounding rural areas to persuade the tenant farmers to support Davies. He was, by now, vastly experienced in the art of canvassing and his appetite for the work was undiminished as he tramped the various parishes.

But he soon found out that this election differed greatly from the previous one fought on behalf of Colonel Powell. David Davies was hailed as 'a man of the people', but he was certainly not a 'man of the gentry'. Joseph complained in his diary that, 'Lloyd's supporters were screwdrivers,' – a term used for those who threatened the tenant farmers with eviction if they did not vote for their man. On 12 July Joseph wrote, 'if the screwdrivers do not interfere – very likely Davies will be our member . . . And he is the proper man of the people.'

Much to Joseph's dismay, a smear campaign in the press was conducted against Davies. A former mayor of Aberystwyth, T.O. Thomas, referred to Davies as 'an uneducated man . . . unable to speak properly.' John Pugh Pryse of Gogerddan dismissed Davies as 'a stranger . . . not suitable to represent the county.' With all the great landlords supporting Lloyd, David Davies faced an uphill task. He might have gleaned some comfort from the local paper, *The Montgomeryshire Guardian and Cardigan Advertiser*, which, on 26 July claimed that:

Never did a candidate receive from the people a warmer and more enthusiastic reception. But his opponent Sir Thomas Lloyd, moved about silently like death.

Joseph's diary confirms the warm reception given by the farmers to David Davies when 'scores of cheering people met him at Tregaron.' On 13 July, he returned to the Llangeitho district where he claimed 'to have received many promises for Davies.' On 14 July Joseph wrote that, 'Davies called at Trecefel at midnight.' The following day both men went to Cardigan for nomination day when Davies was met by engines and suitable carriages at Llangybi. At Cardigan, both Davies and Lloyd appeared on the stage, where they addressed huge crowds. After the speeches, according to Joseph, 'the county became inflamed' and both parties were locked in a bitter contest. Joseph was alarmed, for he knew only too well the power of the gentry. '15 July, It appears that we shall have a warm contest. Mr Lloyd and his friends are going to put the screw on tightly ... I work hard, but rough Tory tactics are in full swing.' Yet, Joseph retained a measure of optimism, 'should everybody have fair play – David Davies is the man of the people.'

Only three days remained until polling day and Joseph's efforts were such that he did not even have time to go to bed. However, it was an unequal struggle. David Davies had challenged the establishment, but the landed families of the county remained implacably opposed to him and united in their support of Sir Thomas Lloyd, whom they regarded as one of their own. David Davies used his wealth lavishly to promote his cause. He rode around the county in a wagonette drawn by four horses with two postilions. He was 'cheered everywhere by the ordinary people and his navvies, among whom he was not averse to taking off his coat to show how a job should be well done.' But unfortunately for Davies, most of these people did not have the vote. Yet Joseph remained hopeful to the end. '16 July, Davies has a good chance of success.'

The day of reckoning arrived on 18 July and Joseph's diary paints a scene of heavy-handed behaviour at the Tregaron polling booth. The opponents of Davies resorted to all manner of tricks in order to defeat him:

18 July 1865

I was at Tregaron by 6 o'clock a.m. Everything was active – well prepared for a hot contest. People waiting for 8 a.m when polling to commence. The sheriff's officers did prepare themselves and all against Davies. 32 local constables were sworn in, in addition to a swarm of police and constables. Davies' friends were not allowed to go near the Booth and damnable tricks were played there all day. False entry, throwing cards aside, false custody and so on . . . Thomas Davies Lloyd is a gentleman, but his supporters degraded him for ever.

Joseph was frustrated and distressed by the whole procedure, but he was impotent to act in the face of the open intimidation exercised by Lloyd's agents and by the special constables. His role of Parish Constable counted as nothing in this fraught situation. Yet, despite all the 'damnable tricks' perpetrated on behalf of Lloyd, when the votes came to be counted at Tregaron, 'David Davies, Top Sawyer' had a healthy majority. Disappointment was to follow.

When the votes for all the Boroughs were added up, Sir Thomas Davies Lloyd of Bronwydd emerged as the clear victor with a majority of 361.

	Lloyd	Davies
Aberystwyth	461	390
Cardigan	360	65
Llandysul	200	63
Aberaeron	299	215
Tregaron	96	290
Lampeter	94	126
	1,510	1,149

David Davies had fought a good fight and polled surprisingly well in spite of the opposition from old county families and the fact that he was a relative newcomer to Cardiganshire. He was in no way deflated by the result. When, four days later, David Davies and Joseph met at the Trecefel railway cutting, he found Davies in a resilient mood. '22 July, Had a long chat with David Davies about sundry things. He was in good spirit in spite of losing at the Polls.' On 29 July the *Aberystwyth Observer* published David Davies's letter of thanks to those who had supported his cause. He claimed that his achievement in 'putting down an iron road' would be more advantageous to the people of Cardiganshire than the freehold land held by his opponent, Lloyd of Bronwydd. The letter ended, 'I trust by the next time I ask for your suffrage I shall not be unknown to a single elector, while to many I hope to be known as having contributed to their prosperity and happiness.' To have challenged the might of the county families was in itself an achievement. To expect the majority of the tenants to disregard the commands of their landlords was a vain hope, although some were courageous enough to do so.

Joseph's forays into politics reveal much about his own character. He was a man governed by loyalty to individuals rather than to fixed political principles. In the 1859 election he had used his influence on behalf of Colonel Powell and the Tories because he had been flattered by the attention of the gentry. In 1865 he supported David Davies and the Liberals because he prided himself as being a 'friend of the great Railway man', whom he so admired for his achievements. In spite of the fluidity of his political allegiances, no one could accuse Joseph of a lack of enthusiasm for the cause he served at the time. Few could have worked harder than he during both elections. But there would be a heavy price to pay.

CHAPTER 7
FREE OF PAIN AT LAST

The first decade at Trecefel had brought Joseph success and recognition as one of the pillars of the community and his confidence soared. During those early years, his home life was comparatively happy with two young sons and four little daughters. Trecefel was now regarded as the most successful farm in the county and he had the support of a loyal and practical wife who helped to boost the income by selling cheese, butter, eggs and poultry at Tregaron market. The busy rhythm of life is reflected in Joseph's diary. 'June 1859, one horse sold at £21, two heiffers sold at £8 each, twelve lambs sold at 10 shillings each, 500 lbs of butter sold at 10 pence per lb, 300 lbs of cheese sold at 3 pence per lb . . . 250 candles made this week.'

Although the maids made hundreds of candles, they themselves were not allowed candlelight between February and October. It was the custom at Trecefel for the servants to hand over their tallow candles to Betty on 2 February in accordance with an ancient rite known as *Gŵyl Fair y Canhwyllau* or Candlemass, which was celebrated in the Church calendar. The custom probably had its origin in pagan times, to welcome the coming of light after winter darkness. The workers, however, were allowed to use rush candles, which were cheap and plentiful. Jane, the young maid, was often sent to gather rushes from the river bank in order to make candles for her fellow servants.

A farmer's life was to a great extent dominated by the vagaries of the weather. Joseph's diary illustrates the extremes that could disrupt life at Trecefel:

> December 1859
>
> Snow, the heaviest fall for 40 years fell during the last week in December. The road between Pont Llanio and Bont was blocked, also between Pont Einon and Tregaron. There were drifts 14 feet thick in places on the Lampeter road. The river Teify is frozen over hard. Large flocks of geese have alighted on the ice and on the Trecefel fields.

The freezing weather brought its own enjoyment for some. The diary describes local youths, 'skating on the solid Teifi below the bridge, with the ice supporting many tons in weight.' But conditions for man and beast were also hazardous, 'the horses slithered helplessly on the icy roads and had to have special sharp nails put on their hooves . . . It was impossible to stand and many people sustained broken arms or legs on the slippery surfaces.'

With a thaw in the weather, the melting snow caused disastrous floods, turning the Trecefel meadows into a vast lake. Joseph was obliged to wade thigh high into the water to rescue his animals. The situation became so serious that religious meetings, known as 'Humiliation Days', were held in the chapels to pray for a spell of fine weather because of the shortage of fodder for the animals. One writer described Cardiganshire as 'having suffered a most sickly time . . . with a prodigious quantity of vile weather . . . which wrought dreadful havoc among the people who were afflicted with many disorders.' The weather affected not only animals and crops, it predisposed people to crippling ailments such as bronchitis, pleurisy, fevers, distempers, and rheumatism.

As we have seen, the most prevalent scourge in Cardiganshire was consumption, known in Welsh as *y dicáu*, the decline, T.B. or the White Death because of the pallor of the victims. Joseph described the disease as 'a killer – no physic works against it!' It was most common among the youngest, the oldest, the poorest and the weak, but even those living in the opulent mansions of the gentry sometimes succumbed to its ravages. Edwyna, the 13-year-old daughter of Colonel Powell, Nanteos, died of the disease in 1858. Medicine as we now know it was still in its infancy; the people, in desperation, turned to local healers with their traditional remedies for relief. Many of these relied heavily on superstition but others had acquired a knowledge of the curative properties of herbs passed down from generation to generation.

The Trecefel family had their own local healer to attend to the ailments suffered by their children. She was a farmer's wife, Mrs Morgan of Lletem-ddu, renowned for making her own special ointments from herbs and other secret ingredients. In June 1860 Joseph recorded that, 'Betty took Jane, our youngest daughter, to Lletem-ddu for treatment of a painful leg.'

Many people, including Joseph, also believed in the healing powers of springs and wells. Such beliefs dated back to Celtic and pre-Christian times. There were many such wells in and around Tregaron. One of the most notable was Ffynnon Garon – Caron's Well – which was sited near Trecefel, where it was the custom for young people to meet on Good Friday to partake of the beneficial water. When Dyfed County Council replaced the Teifi Bridge in 1991, Ffynnon Garon was restored and preserved as a feature of historic interest. Farmers also believed that their sick animals could be cured by particular wells. A spring called Ffynnon Elwad – Elwad's Well – near Allt-ddu farm, a few miles from Tregaron, was reputed to cure 'sore beasts'. Tradition has it that the monks of the Cistercian Abbey at Strata Florida used this. Livestock was so valuable that sick animals caused almost as much concern as ailing humans.

In 1855 a well was discovered near Pont Einon – Einon's Bridge – on the outskirts of Tregaron. Its significance was such that an opening ceremony was arranged to consecrate it. As a local bard, Joseph was called upon to officiate and to compose special verses to mark the occasion. On 22 August 1855 a large crowd of people assembled at the well to sing hymns of thanksgiving and Joseph composed verses calling upon the sick to come and be healed. Feeling well satisfied with his contribution to this ceremony, held on the fringe of Cors Caron, Joseph informs us that, 'the company assembled at the well drank several halfpints of the clear water.'

The Trecefel family believed in the potency of healing springs and, being relatively prosperous, they sometimes chose to travel further afield, to 'take the waters at Llanwrtyd Wells,' one of the most popular spa towns in the Principality. At this time the popularity of towns such as Llandrindod Wells and Llanwrtyd Wells was growing. It was customary for those who could afford it to take a few days holiday to sample the water. A great deal of faith was placed in its healing properties, as was the case with the famous spas of England at Bath and Tunbridge Wells.

In 1856 there was a pressing reason for the Trecefel family to visit Llanwrtyd Wells. Ever since his birth, Jenkin, their eldest son, had been a sickly child. A favourite with both parents he is described by his father as a 'sensitive and religious soul, sorely enfeebled by frequent bouts of ill health.' In 1856 he was nine years old and had been plagued by a chronic cough and a persistent eye infection. In their never-ending search for a cure they decided to take him to Llanwrtyd Wells, a full day's journey from Tregaron. Joseph decided to accompany his son and hired a local driver, Wil Lamb, to drive the spring cart. Because Betty was still recovering from the birth of their daughter Mary, he also took along his second daughter, the three-year-old Elinor, known as Nel.

On 8 August they set out early in the morning taking the scenic but tortuous route over the Abergwesyn Pass. They climbed up Cwm Berwyn, passing Diffwys. The terrain was wild and remote; the road a rutted, twisting track cutting through hills clad with tough heather. There were steep winding ascents followed by precipitous downward slopes which caused the horse to slither dangerously, so that the children and Joseph had to walk behind the cart while the driver walked alongside the horse holding on to his bit to steady him. For the small children it was an arduous but thrilling journey. Joseph's diary states, 'I, Jenkin and Nel left in the light cart driven by Wil Lamb . . . driving over the mountains. Arrived at Llanwrtyd by 8 o'clock. Had a lodging with Eleanor Williams. I drank 6 pints of water.'

Llanwrtyd was at the height of the holiday season and was 'full of visitors'. He soon met many other farmers including Betty's brother, Thomas Evans, Tynant, who had come to Llanwrtyd for a short break. Although by this time it was late, Joseph left the children in the care of the landlady and visited a popular local tavern, the Belle Vue, where he met an old friend and 'partook of some gin and brandy.'

On the Saturday morning following their arrival, Joseph rose early to take Jenkin and Nel for some spa water. The sights and sounds and the holiday atmosphere was an exciting experience for the children, but this was soon tempered by having to drink copious amounts of the unpleasant-tasting healing waters. In the afternoon Joseph played quoits and then proceeded himself to drink the spring water to excess. Never a man for half measures, he claimed, 'I drank 37 pints to-day,' which seems an inordinate amount. In the evenings the water was chased by 'many glasses of gin and whisky' at one of the taverns. The vast quantities of water he consumed inspired him to write two verses in praise of the well at Llanwrtyd describing it as 'beloved of the lame and the sick and a blessing from God.'

On the Sunday Joseph attended the local church service where 'the Vicar preached in English to please the Gentlemen who were visitors.' It could scarcely have been a riveting sermon for Joseph confessed, 'I did sleep fast in Church.' It was highly unusual for Joseph to fall asleep in this fashion; he usually stayed awake, if only to criticise the preacher. Later that evening he met another old acquaintance Evan Williams, Abergwesyn. Deciding to give the spa water a miss for something stronger, they partook of a few glasses of brandy together at the local tavern.

On the Monday morning Joseph returned to the well and carried a gallon of water to Jenkin and Nel. He does not record their reaction to the 'medicine'. Joseph also decided to visit Llangamarch Spa, a short distance from Llanwrtyd, which was also full of visitors. Incredibly, he drank 36 pints of this 'spa water', but this time it had unpleasant consequences. 'My left side,' he complained, 'is rather bad after drinking the Llangammarch water.' He returned to Llanwrtyd where he spent the week 'imbibing enormous quantities of the water which,' he claimed, 'agreed with me.' He also forced his hapless children to drink substantial amounts.

On Monday 18 August after claiming to have drunk '45 pints of the health giving water' he left for home leaving Jenkin and Nel in the care of the landlady. He walked to Abergwesyn where he spent the night at the local alehouse, The Grouse. The following morning his friend Evan Williams 'came with 2 ponies and saddles to accompany me to Esgergelli.' He then walked the next six miles alone over the mountains arriving at Tregaron at 2 p.m. If his diary is to be credited, he claims to have consumed an average of 33 pints of spa water every day during the eleven days he spent at Llanwrtyd after which he wrote, 'I feel better!' Jenkin and Nel stayed on another week and returned from Llanwrtyd on 29 August, when 'Wil Lamb went with the horse and light cart to fetch the children.' Joseph added in his diary, 'I myself stayed at home all day.' Had he had more than enough of the spa water?

Despite the visit to Llanwrtyd Wells there appeared little improvement in Jenkin's health and he continued to suffer from various ailments over the years. On 28 July 1862, a third son, Tom Jo, was born, but by the end of that year Jenkin's condition had declined so seriously that it became a cause of concern for Joseph and Betty. Joseph closed his diary on 31 December 1862 by expressing a hope for 'better fortune and greater blessings in the coming year,' but within him there stirred a sense of foreboding. Hence his sombre entry for New Year's Day:

1 January 1863
The new year begins
With all its inherent perils.†

His words were to prove sorrowfully prophetic. In the early months of 1863, as winter gave way to spring, the diary contains disturbing references to Jenkin's diminishing health. He is described as 'afflicted by a dry cough . . . losing weight, being unable to eat and becoming weaker by the day.'

The outlook seemed bleak, and the shadow, which had so long hovered over the Trecefel household, gradually lengthened and darkened. Jenkin, as the first born, had been the source of so many high hopes; but now there would be nothing but tears. Betty, his mother, who had nursed him through many crises, was unable to accept the inevitable and frantically plied him with herbal remedies. These potions from local healers were accompanied by cold compresses applied to his fevered brow and hot poultices to his chest. As the tell-tale cough echoed persistently from Jenkin's room, Joseph recognised only too well the old familiar symptoms which had signalled the death of his own younger sisters at Blaenplwyf. He had heard that death rattle countless times in the dank overcrowded cottages of his servants, and so often in the early months of 1846 'had been obliged to help carry the bier to the grave.' Fearfully, he recorded, 'the tubercular curse has visited our home and his time is flying past like a cloud on a windy day.'

Terse entries in Joseph's diary reflect his anxiety. '26 April, Jenkin is very weak'. Even when Jenkin was a young child Joseph had been obliged to carry him on his shoulders, as he quickly became too tired to walk. By late April, Jenkin's cheeks were abnormally flushed by the rose red tint caused by the fever. Betty, who had tried everything to stave off this cruel illness, was now forced to accept the inevitable. When, in a fit of coughing, his *carthen* – quilt – became stained with bright red blood, his father wrote with resignation:

> The flower of the grave
> Now rests on his mien.†

During the coming weeks they were forced to look on helplessly as their consumptive son became sunken eyed, the phlegm rattling in his throat and his wasted frame racked by persistent painful coughing. On 5 May, Joseph, with a heavy heart, wrote, 'Jenkin is getting weaker daily . . . no appetite.' Life on the farm had to continue. Each morning he walked the fields at sunrise and saw all around him the glory of May; yet always in his mind was the pale image of his son fighting for breath. By the time May had given way to June, Jenkin was 'much troubled by the chronic cough . . . Outside, the cuckoo sings but Jenkin continues very weak.'

Although sorely burdened, Joseph found the space in his heart and diary to show compassion for others. He was very much opposed to war and suffering wherever it occurred. '27 June 1863. It is heartrending to read about the matchless cruelties performed by the Russian Officers and soldiers against the Poles. They do bury the men and women alive. The American War is carried on with great vigour and cruelty beyond description.' With two brothers domiciled in America, Joseph followed the progress of the Civil War with intense interest and was appalled by its ferocity. 'Let us come to our senses, we shall not live long – Quarrels and war are the most destructive evils under the sun. Each party is so bold as to pray to God for assistance to kill their fellow creatures.'

Unlike Betty, who had to confine herself solely to tending her sick son, Joseph's many interests gave him fleeting relief from the tragedy unfolding at Trecefel. On 28 June we find Joseph rejoicing in the triumph of the British explorers John Hanning Speke and James Grant. 'Speke and Grant have just returned from navigating the Nile. It appears that this mighty river has its source in Lake Victoria.'

He also continued to socialise and attended Ffair Iwan at Tregaron, noting that 'store pigs are selling for low prices . . . Wool is in brisk demand, selling for 1/6 per lb.' That evening, however, when he returned to Trecefel, he found 'Jenkin very weak and scarce able to clear up the bad matter from his lungs.' Betty was at his bedside vainly trying to ease his pain, but Joseph wrote, 'There is little we can do against the disease.' His breathing became more laboured and Jenkin could now scarcely speak. When the slowly progressive affliction finally claimed their son shortly after midnight on 4 July 1863 Joseph turned to his diary to record one of his saddest entries:

> Saturday 4th July
> Twenty minutes past 12 o'clock a.m. my eldest son Jenkin did breathe his last breathing in this uncertain world. He did bear about four months of illness and severe coughing.

Joseph describes how Jenkin had tolerated his illness strengthened by his faith in God, and quotes his dying words, murmured with difficulty, as he fought vainly for breath:

> With Christian fortitude the last words delivered from his mouth were these: 'O Dad, bydd drugarog wrthyf fi

bechadur a derbyn fy ysbryd.' ['Oh, Father, be merciful to me a sinner and receive my spirit.'] I never found him guilty of disobedience or falsehood. He was 17 years of age. He was born at Tynant on the 14th day of December 1846, and he never enjoyed a sound state of health.

The death certificate described the cause of death as, 'Phthisis, sick for nine months.' Phthisis, a Greek word that means wasting, is an appropriate term for the ravages wrought by T.B. For Betty, who had never left her son's side throughout his ordeal, with its terrible haemorrhages and coughing, the silence that now enveloped the house left her profoundly traumatised. Her optimism had been misplaced, and the reality of Jenkin's death overwhelmed her. Joseph described her as being 'low in the extreme.'

In the close-knit Welsh community, family and neighbours quickly rallied round to comfort Betty and to support Joseph in his loss. His brothers John and Griffith arrived on horseback soon after dawn. From Tynant, Betty's brother Thomas Evans also came at once. A special meeting to pray for Jenkin's soul was arranged at the farmhouse for 2 p.m. the following day. Large numbers of people visited Trecefel, among them 'a great many strangers', such was the communal grief felt by the whole locality. The funeral was arranged for Tuesday 7 July. As a mark of respect, the family acquired new clothes and Joseph records, '6 July, went to Tregaron to buy mourning clothes and returned to Trecefel by 2 p.m. to receive my son's coffin into the house.' His friend Evan Jenkins, the carpenter, had made the coffin. The servants helped carry it in and it was laid in the parlour.

The morning of the funeral, Joseph, unable to sleep, rose at 5 a.m. His diary describes the events of this sombre day:

Tuesday 7 July 1863

Strangers began to gather about 8 a.m. The sermon is at 9. The Rev David Evans and John Davies arrived with many of our relations . . . They began to sing, pray and proceed about 9.30. A large concourse of people was present. The body was taken out at 10.30. It was one of the largest funerals that I have ever seen. People from all quarters were present within a ten-mile radius. We did commence the journey towards Capel y Groes and were there before 3 o'clock.

Tradition has it that the coffin was borne for a short distance by some of the female mourners as a mark of respect for Betty because she had lost her first-born son. These women were her cousins from Cilgwyn, Llangybi. The coffin was then placed on a horse-drawn carriage to be carried to the graveyard of Capel y Groes, Llanwnnen, where the family had worshipped. Such was the number of mourners following the coffin that the road was clogged for over two miles.

Jenkin was finally laid to rest in a large family tomb next to the grave of his grandfather Jenkin Jenkins, Blaenplwyf, and Betty's tragic brother Lewis Evans, Tynant. The emotional intensity of the funeral had been a terrible ordeal for Betty. As they were being driven back to Trecefel she sobbed uncontrollably, but Joseph's reaction was more philosophical. He explored the depth of his own anguish by composing some verses in memory of his son, and committed them to paper even as he and his wife were taken home:

> Although unwell, he was obedient, he was truthful,
> He gave friendship;

> He was thoughtful, free of pain at last,
> He rises, in good health, to a better life. †

Joseph was fortunate in finding some release from his grief in poetry, and confessed that, 'the search for words dulls the pain.'

For Betty there was no such refuge, and she became gripped by a deep depression that only intensified as the year wore on. The previous July she had given birth to her third son Tom, and had scarcely had time to recover from childbirth before Jenkin was struck down. Joseph's constant involvement in community affairs meant that he had little time or energy to attend to the needs of his family. Betty had long been unhappy with the situation, and Jenkin's illness had drained her strength. Joseph's conscience was also disturbed and he wrote anxiously, 'Betty is feeling very mournful and very low in spirit.' But Betty no longer felt able to lean on her husband, and it was to her father that she turned for support in this, her darkest hour.

Within a month of Jenkin's funeral, she gathered all her family around her and ordered her son Lewis to get the cart ready for the journey to Tynant. A sad and chastened Joseph recorded, '7 August, Betty and the children left in the spring cart for Tynant. Not one of the children is at home with me.' Joseph felt their absence keenly, and it was with some regret that he had watched Lewis, now aged fifteen, drive his mother and the children away, holding in her arms the one-year-old baby Tom. From Tynant, the following day Betty and the children visited nearby Aberaeron, which Joseph described as 'a thriving seaside town . . . with a charming little seaport, ideal for bathing with salubrious air.' It was hoped that such surroundings would help to restore Betty's health and calm her state of mind.

Joseph, left to his thoughts at Trecefel, was far from pleased with Betty's departure and he sought solace in his diary by composing yet another poem to his dead son, describing him as, 'always obedient, and pleasant even in the throes of his illness.'

When Betty returned from Tynant some 10 days later she appears to have been in an aggressive mood. Joseph found her 'quite out of temper for many, if not all things that are carried on at Trecefel.' She indulged in bitter recrimination and compared his behaviour to that of her father and brother whom she saw as 'faultless . . . and like angels.' She was in no mood to tolerate the shortcomings of her husband any longer. She accused him of neglecting the farm; she held him responsible for a disastrous fire that had destroyed all the hay, and she criticised him for 'allowing the crops to rot.'

The losses had been serious and her accusations against Joseph were not altogether unfounded. Still distressed and confused by the loss of Jenkin, it was as if all her suppressed anger and frustration was now directed against her husband. Not surprisingly, by 20 August Joseph decided that he himself needed a holiday. A family outing was arranged in the Spring Coach, a horse drawn charabanc. Betty decided not to accompany him, so he took with him three of the children accompanied by some other relatives:

20 August 1863

Lewis, Margaret, Elinor, my sister Elizabeth of Tyndomen and myself did prepare to go with my brother Benjamin to Borth. We rode in the Spring Coach. We did arrive in Borth about 4 o'clock p.m. The place was crammed with visitors.

They stayed at the Fountain Inn, Trefechan, Aberystwyth, and the following day Joseph took the children to visit the 'ancient castle, and pointed out all the things of interest' to them.

When Joseph returned to Trecefel, freak weather conditions added to his difficulties. Heavy rain and flash floods caused more problems on the farm, and they even claimed the life of one of his friends. Joseph records the tragedy. 'John Davies of Lodge, Derry Ormond's agent, while returning from Llanddewi towards Llwyn fell into the river Brenig from the wooden bridge. He was carried down by the flood as far as the river Teifi and found at 7 this morning. Quite dead of course.'

1863 had been a wretched and tragic year for both Joseph and Betty, and the emotional ordeal of Jenkin's death was taking its toll on their marriage. Tragedy can sometimes weld a couple closer together; it can also drive a wedge into a relationship. This appears to have been the case at Trecefel. Husband and wife became increasingly alienated. As new problems surfaced, so the mutual recriminations mounted and Joseph himself began to show signs of melancholia. In despair, he wrote, 'I do feel that my life has become filled with sorrow and covered in darkness. It seems that we are governed by blind chance.'

CHAPTER 8
GATHERING STORM CLOUDS

Behind Joseph's confident and very public exterior, there lay an insecure and somewhat paranoid person. His diary frequently reflects his anguish. He complained that he was 'unfairly maligned', 'accused of things I had not done' and 'constantly duped by other people.' Acutely aware of his own shortcomings, especially of his neglect of his family, he regularly promised to remedy these in the future. The untimely death of Jenkin had left its mark upon him. 'I am,' he wrote, 'resolved to keep more at home enlarging my friendliness and to give more thought to the fact that I am a father, and refrain from alcohol.'

But his promise had a hollow ring. Within a comparatively short time he was again to be found at the Talbot Hotel in the company of Colonel Powell after a day coursing hares, 'drinking rather heavily again.' Betty was forced to turn increasingly to her father at Tynant, for he had remained her main source of support even after fifteen years of marriage to Joseph. She was not a submissive, obedient wife in the Victorian mould: she possessed an independence of spirit which led her to be highly critical of her husband's behaviour.

In public, Joseph was a man of many accomplishments, but his home life was increasingly blighted by tensions. He found it far easier to address large audiences on local problems than to face the wrath of a discontented wife; it was infinitely less demanding to fight an election campaign than to justify the smell of alcohol on his breath to Betty. Although he had built up Trecefel by dint of his own hard work, he was conscious that it was Betty's dowry and her father's influence that had enabled him to acquire the tenancy of the farm in the first place. Well aware that alcohol was at the root of much of the discord, Joseph tried, time and again, to face up to the problem, and he turned to his Bible for guidance. He repeatedly swore an oath to abstain from drink:

> October 1863
>
> I did sign the pledge not to drink in a public house for the remainder of my days, and let me have a fast resolution to keep it with the strictest fidelity. Should I drink a glass or two, people will say that I am guilty of being beastly drunk and disorderly. I was most guilty in my life of such.

His intentions were undoubtedly sincere and he could be disarmingly honest on occasions, but he admitted that 'I do find that I am often entrapped in some failing.' He never spoke a truer word, for sadly, his pledges came to nothing. Within weeks of signing this latest oath, his horse was found tethered in the stable of the Ivy Bush and he was to be found drunk at the Inn. This damaged, even further, the fragile relationship between himself and Betty. On another occasion he admitted to having stayed a whole night at the Ivy Bush, Lampeter, drinking and writing a lengthy treatise deriding the Pope, against whom he felt a pathological hatred. Wherever he went Joseph invariably carried a pen, ink and paper on his person and was often to be seen writing in taverns where there was heat and light.

Although he was beset by serious domestic difficulties, he managed to put these problems to one side while agonising over foreign unrest and distant wars. 'The world is in turmoil,' he wrote. 'The cruel Civil War in America continues . . . The French armies are fighting in India, Mexico and China . . . Italy is preparing for war . . . The Pope has been denounced.' He comforted himself by claiming that, 'nine out of ten families have quarrels. The big landlords are short of money, if not shorter than the tenants!'

His drinking was now leading to money problems for he had invested a great deal in the farm: he spent recklessly and borrowed heavily. As far back as 1855, using his father-in-law as a guarantor, he had borrowed £800 from the bank. He was usually the first to acquire modern machines, such as a potato picker, whatever the cost; he had also invested in massive and expensive drainage projects employing 25 men at 2/6 a day for 12 days to drain water from the bog. He purchased thousands of young fir trees and quick thorns to establish a plantation for protection, and 'to crown the hedges.' Eventually, he was forced to admit that, 'money is short.' However, a diary entry infers that the financial difficulties were not solely of his own making. Somewhat self-righteously he wrote:

January 1862
Our mode of living has been too luxurious and extravagant; money is scarce in the country. All our spare pennies have gone to the large firms in respect of things we were not in need of. Pecuniary distress stares us in the face.

Not one word about the cost of alcohol!

Matters came to a head when, for a second time, he was

unable to pay the half year's rent to the Reverend Latimer Jones and had to suffer the indignity of having to defer payment. He had also borrowed £60 from the owner of Foelallt, a grand country residence, to buy three cottages at Llanddewibrefi, but when the time came to settle the debt he was unable to do so.

Yet he continued to aspire to the life of a squire and to pursue interests beyond his means. When the *Great Eastern*, the biggest ship in the world at that time, docked at Milford Haven, Joseph found the time and money to go and see it. He was genuinely interested in the work and achievements of the Victorian entrepreneur Isambard Kingdom Brunel (1806-1859) who had designed the ship. On seeing the *Great Eastern* he marvelled at its gargantuan proportions. When a 'gentleman from London called at Trecefel with a photograph of Colonel Powell,' Joseph purchased it at a cost of 14/-. Such extravagance infuriated Betty who constantly tried to curb his improvident habits.

Each year, in late September, Joseph held a 'Harvest Home' at Trecefel. This consisted of a night of feasting and drinking to celebrate the end of the harvest. A great party was held in the barn, where gallons of 'porter and cider' were provided for the farm workers. Taking advantage of a captive, if somewhat intoxicated audience, Joseph would deliver a long address on the state of the world. We can only guess at what the workers made of this. Undeterred, Joseph thundered on in his authoritative didactic style. So convinced was he of the importance of his utterances that he sent a copy of one of his speeches to *The Welshman* for publication. Much to his delight, it was printed in its entirety on 3 October 1862. The following extract shows that it was a wide-ranging, but also a disjointed and somewhat sycophantic address:

> Let the corn be cut immediately after it becomes ripe and be secured in the haggard . . . Every industrious man can live comfortably within the Principality and need not think of Patagonia . . . loose the hero Garibaldi that he may echo the word liberty through Europe . . . I will conclude my remarks by proposing the health of our august Prince be drunk with cheers . . . The Welsh people are ready and willing to lose the last drop of blood in defending her Majesty's dominion.

The reference to Patagonia is interesting because in March 1862 a society had been formed in Tregaron to encourage Welsh people to emigrate to a new colony to be established in South America. Nationalists such as Michael D. Jones feared that the Welsh, who were emigrating in droves to America, were being too easily assimilated in that melting pot of nations. They feared that the Welsh identity and the Welsh language would soon be lost; already some five thousand or so emigrants from Cardiganshire had settled in America. Michael D. Jones dreamt of establishing a new Welsh colony in a remote part of the world, removed from alien influences. They chose Patagonia, and in 1865 a contingent of 155 Welsh emigrants boarded the *Mimosa* at Liverpool and sailed for Argentina.

A meeting was held in Tregaron to encourage emigration to the new colony. Joseph's eldest daughter, Margaret, attended and returned home full of enthusiasm for the venture. Her father, however, poured cold water on the idea, dismissing it as a fool-brained venture. He claimed it was far preferable for Welshmen to stay at home. This was richly ironic in view of his own actions within a few years. No one from Tregaron is listed among the original colonists who embarked upon the *Mimosa*.

One institution which provided a platform for Joseph's oratory was the Beehive Society. This had been originally founded in 1827 to raise money for persons in need. It was by now, however, as much a social club as a charitable association. Joseph soon became one of its most prominent members, serving as treasurer and also chairing many of its grand dinners held at the Talbot Hotel on New Year's Day. Much ceremonial was attached to the activities of the society. Prior to a grand banquet, the members processed through the town bearing banners and, accompanied by a brass band, went to St Caron's Church for a religious service. It was a lively occasion, full of sound and colour, with the streets thronged with people, when the New Year was greeted in a truly Bacchanalian manner.

Whenever the tensions at home got to him, Joseph would find comfort between the covers of a good book. His tastes were eclectic, ranging from Welsh poetry to Voltaire's *Philosophical Dictionary*, which he claimed 'is my favourite book these days.' He referred to Voltaire as 'a man possessing sense beyond the common.' His rational approach to religion and his attacks on the Catholic Church hierarchy appealed to him.

Joseph continued to be a prolific contributor to the correspondence columns of newspapers. On 3 October 1862 he sent a letter to *The Welshman* asking Princess Alexandra of Denmark to persuade the Prince of Wales, whom she was due to marry, 'to visit his own subjects for once before he ascends the throne of England.' His plea fell on deaf ears.

Because of his heavy drinking, his fitness to serve as Parish Constable was now being called into question. When St Caron's Vestry convened to elect a 'responsible person' to the office, he was not reappointed. His reaction, however, was a sense of relief, 'Thank God I got free this year!' His defiant response was to 'partake of a few glasses at the Red Lion in the company of friends.' His drinking continued apace throughout the following year and he unashamedly records, 'In Tregaron all day drinking all kinds of alcohol.' By April 1864 Betty had resorted to new tactics in an attempt to control her wayward spouse. Joseph was not amused!

26 April 1864

The tithes for Trecefel ought two be paid today. But I could not attend for the infernal pickpocketress. She took money on Monday last, being the 17th pound and fourteen shillings taken by her from both my pockets – hen pecked and robb'd – I'm kicked like a football in this world.

In the spring, a freakish spell of hot weather added to his problems when an uncharacteristic heatwave turned his normally lush meadows into a desiccated wasteland:

May 1864

The cattle are bellowing because there is no grass, while the meadows are scorched and there is no growth. We have been obliged to allocate nearly twice the usual acreage of land for cattle this year . . . A man cutting peat died of sunstroke. Never known it so hot in the month of May.

This unseasonal weather brought tragic consequences in its wake. 'We experienced a severe thunderstorm. A girl of 15 out in the fields gathering firewood was struck by lightning and killed . . . So were many sheep and lambs . . . and a house was demolished.' *The Welshman* recorded that, 'The oldest inhabitants of Tregaron did not remember such heat and such a rapid and dreadful thunderstorm.'

Sobered by the loss of stock and damage to his farm, Joseph once again tried to mend his ways. When Colonel Powell sent him an invitation to a ploughing match to be followed by a celebratory dinner at the Talbot Hotel, for once he had the courage to decline. He set out his good intentions for the future with this reply in verse:

> I wish from the turf to retire
> And tend to the horse and the cow,
> Wise rural transactions desire,
> And stick to the tail of my plough.
> Let those who have money to spend
> Go after the hare and the hound,
> I to the farm must attend
> To clear and manure the ground.

But Betty had seen it all before and no longer had any faith in her errant husband's 'good resolutions'. Their relationship continued to slide from the tense to the impossible as Joseph's mood shifted from one of defiance to one of depression. When a local figure of note threw himself off a cliff as a result of marital problems, Joseph actually envied his fate:

5 September 1864
> A lucky job for David Jones
> To kill himself, his neck and bones.
> He thus escaped from many strife
> The blows and tongue of scolding wife.

Having seemingly thrown all caution to the wind, he now spent most of his time in the local taverns. '8 September, up all night from one public house to another.' Unfortunately, the opportunities for drinking in both Tregaron and Lampeter were limitless. There were no less than 26 taverns in Tregaron apart from the many private houses that also sold alcohol. The problem was acute.

As far back as 1830, John Calcraft, a Tory M.P., had introduced the Sale of Beer Act, that enabled anyone to open a beer shop for a fee of two guineas. Such houses proliferated in both Lampeter and Tregaron. So prevalent were these alehouses that Sir John Harford, the Squire of Falcondale, became alarmed at the situation, claiming that, 'the proportion of public houses to the population affords a pretty fair index of the morality of a place. For every two private houses in Lampeter, one sells beer without any licence at all.' So concerned was he that he established a temperance society in the town. Writing in *The Welshman*, October 1862, he stated, 'I have let a small house at a moderate rent for the purpose of affording accommodation to travellers and others who may require refreshments, but do not desire drink which is sold in the town at an exorbitant price.'

Like Lampeter, Tregaron was an important droving centre, and public houses made a roaring trade, but denominations such as the Methodists vehemently opposed alcohol. Joseph despised the Methodists for their narrow views and ridiculed them in the following couplet:

Tregaron – Where Methodists live in abundance of grace
Which shortens their vision and lengthens their face.

In 1859 Wales experienced one of its periodic religious revivals. At Tregaron these revivalists attacked public houses and denounced drunkenness with missionary zeal. Joseph provides us with a graphic account of their activities:

> February 1859
>
> Scores of boys and girls are ballyhooing, clapping their hands, yelling like a pack of hounds and shouting 'God forgive me my sins'. At Bwlchgwynt chapel the preacher was unable to continue with his sermon. Sixty new members joined those 'jumping Methodists' today at Tregaron, and in the past fortnight there have been three hundred fresh recruits. This, which they call the 'Christian Reformation', goes on briskly in the Chapel here, and it is spreading to the north part of the county as well. At Tregaron, these jumping Methodists threw a barrel of beer in the river Brenig. Two preachers at the Chapel have denounced them as the 'fire of hell boys'.

Although Joseph was quick to mock the Methodists, he had never been able entirely to shed the Puritanism of his early Nonconformist upbringing. Try as he might, he could not resist the temptation of drink, but he was prepared to concede that alcohol was the cause of much evil:

> Drinking a glass sometimes
> Gives rise to the sins of the world,
> And if beer were to disappear,
> All men would become angels. †

One thing is certain, Joseph's hopes of reaching angelic status seemed slim in the light of the following entries, which peppered his diary in 1866. 'I did keep rather late in town last night ... Spent the night at the Black Lion, Lampeter ... Had a good few whiskeys at the Bush and caught the last train home.'

Such excesses caused Betty much heartache, but there was also a deep feeling of growing anger in the family. Lewis had lost all respect for his father and openly insulted him. Betty's father, alarmed at the spendthrift ways of his wayward son-in-law, asked him to reform his behaviour, but to no avail. As a result, Joseph's status as 'paterfamilias' at Trecefel was diminished.

Joseph was now a confirmed alcoholic. Drink provided him with a temporary escape, but it could never give him lasting relief from his problems. Ever prone to self-analysis he asked the question, 'Why am I a slave to drink?' He had no answer. Confession was good for his soul, and his diary was always there to receive the outpourings of his guilty conscience. Once again he swore, 'I will refrain from all intoxicants.' But such pledges had become repetitious and meaningless entries, and he admitted, 'I lack the resolve to follow my word.'

Mortified by his own inadequacy Joseph resorted to selfish lamentation to explain away his weaknesses, claiming that, 'the eternal human condition is one of failure and unhappiness. I was not destined to be happy. This is my lot in life from the day I was born. It is not my fault!' It seems a facile statement, and an easy way out.

CHAPTER 9
A MOST TROUBLESOME YEAR

At the beginning of 1866 Joseph embarked on a drinking spree. After visiting many taverns he turned up late in the evening at Tregaron Station in a drunken state. Ever fractious after alcohol, he quickly became embroiled in an argument and was set upon by an unnamed assailant who must have got the better of him, for he returned home 'bruised, dishevelled and weltered in blood.' The 'Master of Trecefel' was fast shedding all vestiges of his former respectability. But this incident had a sobering effect upon him and left him so full of self-loathing that he cried out, 'Lord, free me from myself. Why do I live like a slave to myself and others?' With renewed vigour he swore, 'I will never again sit in a public house to drink any sort of stimulants which have any sort of intoxicating effects.' On 21 January 1866 he confessed, 'It is high time for me to steer my life into a different course in respect of spending my money and time in public houses when I ought to be engaged at Trecefel . . . *The Weekly Dispatch* gives me a warning [regarding] those who are degraded through drunkenness.'

During the following months he made a determined effort to reform himself by focusing his mind on helping his family and assisting those in need around him. Tragedy had struck at the neighbouring farm of Nantserni, where two sons were dying of consumption, and both he and Betty called there daily to offer comfort and advice. Having suffered themselves, they were able to empathise with the stricken family. '6 February, both children there are very ill . . . very consumptive . . . in a hopeless way of recovery.' Three weeks later the inevitable happened. 'John did die this afternoon . . . he was 20 years of age and on the point of being married.' No one could accuse Joseph of lacking sympathy towards others and he did his utmost to ease the grief of the family. With true compassion he wrote, 'By helping those in need around us, we also help our own souls. This is how the world should be.' Regrettably, however, this philosophy was not consistently evident within his own family.

On 3 March the diary contains a further note of sadness as he refers to the loss of his friend Evan Davies. 'He was killed while loading timber . . . the cart did upset upon his mangled body . . . he died instantly.' Shaken by this tragic accident Joseph wrote, 'we don't know what may happen in one moment . . . Let us prepare for the worst and hope for the best . . . the deceased was 30 years of age.' On a cold morning, 'the land buried in snow,' he attended the funeral and wrote a stanza in memory of him. As though sobered by so many tragedies around him, for the first quarter of 1866 Joseph attended to his farm and faithfully adhered to his pledge 'not to drink'. He even wrote a poem entitled 'Home' which he described as:

> A place full of tranquillity . . .
> A temple, a castle, a tower
> Where one's burdens are lightened
> And the Father and Mother as one
> Make the hearth – the home.

The situation seemed truly to be taking a turn for the better, but *Ffair Garon* lay on the horizon with its usual temptations. The diary says it all, '17 March, I left for the Tippling Fair . . . which is the habit in Tregaron the day after the fair . . . which they also call the Pig's Fair.' This was the day on which the farmers celebrated the end of winter with its privations and its monotonous diet of salted meat, and welcomed the 'spring with full, foaming tankards'. This infamous Fair put paid to all Joseph's good intentions and rudely shattered the shaky domestic harmony that had briefly prevailed at Trecefel. Betty retaliated by once again running to her father at Tynant.

Although he had delegated a great deal of the farm work to the children and servants, Joseph would, even after a hard night's drinking, rise at dawn 'to walk the farm'. He scanned the fields checking for gaps in the hedges, counted the animals and noted the condition of the river. His entry for 22 March 1866 is typical, 'Up at 4 a.m. Went to see the sheep. Grass full of hoar frost . . . 12 lambs to be seen . . . began to snow heavily.' The month of March had come in 'like a lion' but it certainly did not go out as a lamb. It remained fiendishly cold, 'with such rain and wind that the labourers could scarce stand their ground and were obliged to seek shelter in the outhouses.'

Unfortunately, during the following months Joseph had even more opportunities for socialising. After two years of turmoil, the railway was, at last, nearing completion. With the excitement of seeing the 'new engines shunting back and forth, the people celebrated the dawn of a new era' and Joseph was not to be left out of such jollity. Alcohol remained the major source of discord between husband and wife, and a couplet written by Joseph reflects his resentment at Betty's anger towards him:

> The worst of all evils through life
> Are a lewd lass and scolding wife.

Joseph's behaviour continued to upset Lewis his son, now 17 years old, who had always been close to his mother. To add to Betty's distress, her mother died on 26 October. Joseph tried to make amends by writing a stanza describing his mother-in-law as 'an affectionate mother and a charitable worker who would be sadly missed by the whole community.' But this was scarcely enough to placate Betty. Joseph caused even more problems at Trecefel when, at the end of October, he refused to hire the two resident maidservants for the coming year. 'They left on rather bad terms.' He complained that, 'they were a very independent lot and too proud to learn their trade or to be taught anything.' But the sudden dismissal of these servants left Betty without help. On 17 November, therefore, Joseph 'was obliged to travel on the engine of the train to the Hiring Fair at Lampeter.' Here, he employed two new maids at £5 10s each 'with the granting of a bushel's planting of potatoes' as part of the bargain.

In late November Joseph took his usual dawn walk around the farm, and found that 'twenty sheep had been cruelly worried by wild dogs . . . six sheep were already dead and fourteen others were badly maimed.' He took these back to the barn and 'applied ointment to their wounds.' So disturbed was he by the sight of the mutilated sheep that he composed a verse cursing 'the cruelty of the bloodthirsty hounds.' The following night Lewis and a servant stood guard with guns, but the dogs did not reappear. When, early the following morning, Joseph himself went in search of the dogs, he was startled by a deafening crash from the direction of Tregaron. It turned out that

James Benbow, the engine driver, had driven through the railway gates and smashed them to pieces because 'the Porter had failed to open them in time.' This caused a huge stir in the town, and such was the commotion that Joseph 'could hear the men swearing loudly from Trecefel bridge half a mile away!'

For some time the Reverend Latimer Jones, his landlord, had been unhappy about Joseph's drinking and his neglect of the farm. With the approach of Christmas 1866, Joseph attempted to pacify him. He reached for his gun on the morning of 22 December and went in search of the 'abundance of game' to be found on the Trecefel fields. He quickly dispatched a bagful of birds which was made up as a Christmas hamper containing, '1 goose, 3 hares, 5 pairs of partridges, 2 snipes, 1 woodcock and 1 tail. Lewis took the basket to the station and it was sent by the 2 o'clock train to Carmarthen.' Whether or not it was sufficient to allay the concerns of the Reverend Latimer Jones is not known.

On Christmas Day the Trecefel family attended the *plygain*, a traditional Welsh carol service held in the church at 5 a.m. Although he had promised to join the family, Joseph refused to go in at the last moment because the Church was decorated with holly. This he regarded as 'an example of Popery', and he would have no truck with Catholicism. Instead, he went into Tregaron 'to see if there was any riot or disorder' he should attend to, although by this time he was not the Parish Constable. This was an excellent excuse for celebrating Christmas at the various taverns, but the only 'disorder' he encountered was at Trecefel later that night!

25 December 1866
I was in town before daylight. I did spend a Merry Xmas in town which is impossible for me to do here, because of

the bad feeling to-wards me by those who ought to love and harbour me. I was not home till supper time.

The last evening of 1866 found Joseph in a sombre frame of mind ruminating upon his failings over the past year. He had begun 1866 on an optimistic note, but he now confesses that:

> 31 December 1866
>
> The present year leaves us with many things that will tell during the next . . . we cannot complain against the year and the weather, but our own faults . . . I do know from my personal feelings that I am guilty of great negligence during the harvest time . . . Our hay ought to be cut down and the corn ought to be laid sooner, our own faults and folly remind us that we have soon to repent.

He had scarcely snatched a few hours sleep when he heard a loud banging on the door at 5.30 a.m. He opened it to see a group of hardy *calennig* singers who had braved the snow to wish the family a happy and prosperous new year. There had always been a welcome for them at Trecefel where they were rewarded with 'pennies, bread and cheese'. He had mellowed since his refusal to attend Church on Christmas Day and he accompanied his family to a special service on New Year's Day. '1 January 1867, we went to Church and had an excellent sermon from our worthy vicar.'

Nevertheless, any benefit derived from the sermon was tempered by his disgust on seeing that the Church had been elaborately decorated. It was an anathema to him. 'The Church,' he wrote, 'was artificially dressed by greens of all sorts. It was a great pity to destroy nature for the sake of ritual and popery and nothing else!'

The following day, however, he had no time for such theological wranglings. The snow had thawed on the surrounding hills, turning the river Teifi into a raging torrent which imperilled his stock, and he was soon to feel the shock of cold water rise up to his neck:

> 7 January 1867
> Large flood covers the meadows, 7 or 8 of our sheep carried away by the flood and cannot be found anywhere. I did save 24 and was obliged to enter the flood shoulder deep. The river continues to swell . . . went along in search of lost or drowned sheep. I could not find a single corpse.

For weeks he walked the riverbank and searched the water for his lost sheep. On 28 January he was informed that they had been swept some fifteen miles downstream with the bodies washed up at a farm near the village of Llanybydder.

It was the custom for some of the better-off tenant farmers to send their sons for six months finishing education to Kington School, near Hereford, and Joseph arranged for Lewis his son and the sons of Jane, his sister, to be sent to this school. Accompanied by one of the menservants, they set out on four ponies early on the morning of 19 January. The servant led the way through the Abergwesyn pass along the 'old drovers road'.

Within two days of Lewis's departure, Tregaron was again hit by severe weather involving 'a dreadful storm . . . ice, high winds . . . drifts yards high . . . the Lampeter road impassable.' Nevertheless, Joseph struggled 'to town to pay the tithes to Morgan Evans who receives it for the Vicar.' Unfortunately, the impact of Lewis's departure on Betty was considerable. She fretted and longed for his return. This situation annoyed Joseph, but there was little he could do about it. As the relationship between Betty and himself deteriorated, she had become increasingly reliant upon Lewis as well as her father for comfort. '14 February, Betty did not come home from Tynant . . . she took 5 cheeses.' However, she reappeared four days later on 18 February, 'arriving soon after supper.'

Embarrassed by this situation and fearing a scandal, his health began to suffer. On 22 February he complained, 'I am much vexed by a cough and the cold . . . I can but scarcely swallow my bread and meat.' The following day he managed to get into town to 'collect and pay money', but found himself and his dog 'much abused by the servant and landlord of the Red Lion.' For some reason they appear to have become implacable foes and, although they were both Church Wardens, little Christian charity existed between them. On 25 February he was still ailing. 'I do feel my ear and throat very bad to-day.' On the day of his birthday he lay ill in bed obsessed with all kinds of fears:

27 February
Should it turn out a sort of Lock Jaw, the number of my years are already reckoned, and it might be for me as well as for others, a good thing. I did reach my 49th year at 20 minutes past six this afternoon.

Haunted by the fear of death he renewed his pledge, 'I will never again drink beer and spirits.' Clutching his pen he fervently wrote:

O Lord, I earnestly wish
That you grant me the will
To avoid the place where drink is sold.
Give me the strength to flee it.

He continued in the same vein the following day, but he now had the consolation of knowing the nature of his illness:

28 February 1867

Feeling much worse to-day. Dr Rowlands came here from Llangeitho. He gave me some medicine. Tells me my complaint is quinsy. I can scarcely hold up my head when scribbling these lines . . . my jaw aches . . . can scarcely wield my pen . . . should the tender hand of providence think proper to allow me to rally this dreadful malady, let me be more cautious of my health.

Outside, the weather was foul. The snow had drifted so deeply that even the train could not get through and at one point it was derailed. Joseph spent a miserable month in bed, which was for him an unfamiliar and dispiriting experience. When he finally got up on 3 March he faced a further shock, 'Our mare Nans was stolen . . . I met her coming back from the direction of Lampeter with her blinkers on . . . She was greatly abused by somebody.' He never discovered the thief.

With the coming of spring, his health recovered. In April he was fit enough to attend an extraordinary stag hunt at Castell Flemish, a small hamlet a few miles from Tregaron. Stag hunting continues to be a controversial issue to this day, but this hunt was a particularly brutal affair. Although the hunt had been organised by his friend Colonel Powell, the cruelty of it greatly disturbed him. So moved was he by the events that he describes them in graphic detail:

10 April 1867

The stag was loosed on top of Castell Flemish in the presence of about 2,000 persons of all grades and size. I expected to see the stag and hounds running to-wards here against the wind, but the half starved and half murdered innocent creature took another direction. They were obliged to whip him off. He was too feeble to cover the lowest bank. It is said that he was bled the previous night and this morning. He crept on for 2 miles and was finished off by the dogs. It was a great pity to abuse the creature and keep him so long in a narrow cage.

He was so disgusted by the gratuitous cruelty of this stag hunt that he wrote three verses to express his concern, even at the risk of offending Colonel Powell.

By mid-April, Joseph was once again in rude health and all the good intentions when he believed himself to be at death's door quickly evaporated. He soon attended the fairs, selling his livestock at a profit. But, to Betty's chagrin, much of the money from the sale of animals ended up in the local taverns, increasing the acrimony between husband and wife. Yet Joseph remained defiant. On 14 April he stormed out of Trecefel claiming, 'I will follow my alleged trade . . . I took a jugful of warm ale, I went down to Llanio Bridge and had a quart of ale.'

The following day they patched up their quarrel in order to present a harmonious appearance at the funeral of a neighbour who had died of T.B. leaving a widow and many children. Following the funeral, Joseph was approached by the widow who was in despair because her landlord had recently increased the rent and now threatened to evict her from the farm. Tenant farmers were only allowed an annual lease, thus making their situation extremely precarious.

Joseph says that it was heartrending to see the crying of the poor widow Margaret Evan who pleaded with him, 'I do not know what to do . . . Our landlord is going to raise the rent . . . it was too dear before . . . we cannot afford to pay . . . it will be a fatal blow.' To his credit, he attempted to intercede on her behalf and 'met the Esquire at the station to plead her case.' He was, however, given short shrift by this particular landlord, who called Joseph a 'daily drunkard and further ordered the Porter to take me in his charge.' The whole incident was a personal blow to Joseph and highlighted his waning influence in the locality. He commented ruefully, 'When a man speaks the truth in favour of the oppressed he will be called either insane or a drunkard.'

After this humiliation, worse was to follow. Not only was Joseph unable to help others, he became quite unable to contain the situation at Trecefel, which had by now spiralled out of all control. After a bout of heavy drinking on May Day when he 'did stop in town all day', Betty reached the limit of her endurance. She packed her bags in the cart and left Trecefel stating that she intended to stay for good at her father's farm. It left Joseph shocked, furious and incredulous:

> 3 May
> I am not half pleased . . . She sent a man to say that she will not return again, but I do not believe her.

Her public departure was a crushing blow to his already dented image. Reputation was everything to Joseph, who believed a woman's place was in the home. Now, even the semblance of respectability was gone:

> 8 May
> No wife. Many stories.

To add to his embarrassment, Nel, his second daughter, also

decided to quit Trecefel and join her mother at Tynant. 'Nel is down since last Saturday. Her mother is down since that day's fortnight. She sent many messages up that she does not intend to return.'

Left in sole charge of the youngest children and with Lewis still at Kington, Joseph could scarcely contain his fury. He wrote many verses in Welsh vilifying Betty and cursing what he termed her 'treachery'. He now had to spend his days at home, but it had its compensations for he found a new comfort in his youngest children. 'Tom and Anne are fond of me, . . . they chatter in bed, in my lap without deceit . . . There is no thanks to Betty for this.'

But his anger against Betty continued unabated. '24 May The children are innocent. Their mother has absconded and left since April without the least provocation.' With an infinite capacity to overlook his own peccadilloes, he manages to attribute all the blame to his wife. 'She will have her own time to repent. Her conscience cannot be easy.' He felt betrayed by all except his two younger children.

The rift between Joseph and Betty became more bitter by the day. Acrimonious letters flew between Trecefel and Tynant in which Betty's father described Joseph as a drunkard and hopeless liability who neglected the farm. He even took steps to safeguard the inheritance he would pass on to Betty by setting up a trust for his grandchildren. Joseph retaliated by accusing his father-in-law of 'trickery, falsehood, lies and using the Tynant money to threaten me . . . all of which is enough to drive me out of the country!'

Meanwhile, because of the discord, the rest of the family and servants at Trecefel were also made to suffer. Unable to get at

Betty, Joseph became spiteful to those around him. The following entry reflects his vindictive mood:

> 6 June 1867
>
> Up at 4 a.m. I did arouse my children and the servants. They refused to get up before 5. They did prepare themselves for the bog. The turf cutters came home early. Showery and squally. I gave them 2 gallons of porter and cider instead of tea, but after they did send for tea! Bash! I did retire with my little children.

On 16 June Joseph decided that he himself needed a break from Trecefel and with his two young children, Tom and Anne, he returned to his old home of Blaenplwyf. There he met his brother John and they reminisced about old times. The children 'did enjoy themselves' and they all slept comfortably 'in the room under the storehouse' where Joseph had written the first of his many diaries. When he returned to Trecefel he was greeted with the surprising news that Betty was having a change of heart and was thinking of returning home.

But it was not for love of Joseph. She had missed her children, and had grown tired of life at Tynant. Most crucially, Lewis was due home from school in Kington on 21 June and Betty would once again have an ally at Trecefel. Joseph notes Betty's reappearance with this jaundiced comment:

> 20 June 1867
>
> Betty did return after being off since 20 April. I cannot tell what business she had in those quarters except causing abominable lies to be told against me . . . in spite of a kind and faithful husband and seven cheerful, sensible children.

The following day Betty made preparations to welcome Lewis

home, but Joseph was much less enthusiastic. '21 June, Lewis, came home from school ... he has been two quarters at Kington. I hope to obey and not to abuse as usual.' An uneasy truce now prevailed between husband and wife but the old suspicions remained. When, the day after his return, Lewis went to visit his grandfather at Tynant, the extent of Joseph's displeasure is obvious:

> 22 June
> Home all day. Lewis went down to Tynant. Where he expects his fortune. Nothing can be worse than a conceited and disobedient son. In fact, he is guilty of joining his mother to commit high treason against authority.

This far from happy situation persisted over the coming months as the hurt and anger congealed within Joseph. He carried on drinking excessively and was still subject to severe mood swings. The mutual hostility between himself and Lewis continued, but in mid August, his son's sudden illness brought about a truce and a moment of fatherly concern:

> 21 August
> Lewis ill . . . I left for Dr Rowlands of Garth to come over.
> He did operate on his throat; about half a pint of pus came out with other matters, which released him from his pain.

The sight of Lewis's suffering must have awoken memories of Jenkin's illness and its sad conclusion, but fortunately, for the time being, Lewis was restored to health.

Despite Joseph's disapproval, Betty continued to visit her father regularly, taking ample produce from Trecefel. Joseph sarcastically refers to one such visit on 12 October, 'Betty left for her favourite quarter in our spring cart. She took ten geese with her which Lewis did buy for Tynant.'

The approach of winter brought with it the usual round of local fairs which tempted Joseph to drink to excess. '18 November. Went to Llangeitho to the hiring fair. Did not hire anyone. I did stop a few hours at Stag's Head public house with some merry men.' The following day he went to Tregaron Fair, but this time he was accompanied by Betty and Lewis. They were warned to be on their guard for, 'there were several pick pockets there.' Many were robbed and Joseph's friend, John Davies, Allt-ddu, lost £55 after having sold much livestock. 'The empty purse was later found at Penlan.'

By late November the family had succumbed to various illnesses. 'Betty was unwell . . . while Tom and Anne laboured under the whooping cough.' Joseph himself complained of 'coughing and vomiting', which he interpreted as 'a bad sign for a long life.' Overwhelmed by a feeling that his end was nigh, he prepared himself for death, 'Let it be so and let me die in peace, with the following verse engraved on my tombstone:

2 December 1867
Here lies Jo, son of Jenkin
Body and soul in the earth,
And when the world condemns him
He'll find refuge in peace under his mother's cloak'.†

By Christmas Day, the whole family had recovered sufficiently to attend a church service. Even Joseph, thankful that he was still alive, took his usual place as Church Warden. But he may well have regretted his decision, for the text of the vicar's sermon was a harsh condemnation of beer drinkers and smokers. Joseph felt severely discomfited and, suspecting that the remarks were directed against him personally, he retaliated, 'The preacher might well find himself entangled in temptation soon!'

The sermon had little effect, however, for on 27 December he attended the bidding of John Jenkins and Miss Jones at Llangeitho, but here there was a slight hitch. Miss Jones had miscalculated her dates and 'was confined of a child early in the morning which naturally impeded the marriage.' Nevertheless, the bidding went ahead, 'and was warmly and thickly attended and a joyful time was had by all,' especially Joseph.

Nevertheless, 1867 had been a particularly difficult year. On 31 December he marked its passage by writing a lengthy commentary on events unrelated to Trecefel as if to get away from his own pressing problems.

The year had been dominated by the Irish Question and by the activities of the Fenians, who were prepared to use force to further their nationalist aspirations. The hanging of three Fenians in Manchester, following an abortive attempt to rescue a prisoner which resulted in the death of a police sergeant, added to the tensions. To most inhabitants of the mainland, this was a fate richly deserved, but to the Irish they became the 'Manchester Martyrs' celebrated in story and song. Although not condoning their actions, Joseph shows his opposition to the death penalty, a view repeatedly expressed within the diaries:

31 December 1867

Unrest is everywhere . . . Scores of thousands of Special Constables are sworn in popular towns . . . 3,000 are already sworn in the city of London. The Fenians are the principle notice of the day, not only in Europe, but in America and other parts of the world. Every country blames our Government for hanging the three Fenians at

Manchester . . . And they ought not to do that. They have no business to take another man's life which is quite contrary to the law of God and the law of Nature. Let every man have fair play for his life, but some ought to be kept in chains for life, as they are quite unfit to be chosen among society. Let the Government take care of every murderer and give him proper work to perform with safety . . .

Rather uncharacteristically, he criticises Queen Victoria, blaming her and her government for the situation in Ireland:

Queen Victoria and her underpriests are the very cause of Fenianism in both countries, – Ireland and America. I dispute whether Victoria can hold on under her advisers for 10 years more . . . Her government is craving for office instead of examining the welfare of the community at large. Time will bring them to their proper senses, but I fear it will be too late.

True to form, however, Joseph blames Catholicism and the Pope for most of the ills of the world:

People are backsliding to Catholicism and Barbarity . . . All sorts of iniquities are increasing faster than the population of every country. Let all the countries embark on the same golden rules which our saviour did properly teach to the world . . . Then no hatred will be kindled between nations. Down Popery! Down Fenianism! The Pope is the real root of discontentment of his religious subjects.

He also concludes that, in spite of the many grievances felt by the

Irish, the Welsh suffer more at the hands of the Government. Even so, he still wishes them to remain loyal to the Crown:

> I hope that the Welsh people will continue loyal to her Majesty's subjects, though they are treated worse than the Irish people. They are under a pretender prince who has visited various parts of the globe, but never visited his own subjects. We are tried by English Judges, Counsels & very often English Juries . . . We are ready to fight gallantly side by side with the Saxons against any invader of the British Flag . . . Our English neighbours have many advantages through us: nevertheless they scorn our language, they cannot either learn or pronounce it correctly . . . Should any important office happen to be vacant, they always choose the Irish rather than the Welsh . . . Let every honest Christian adore his Maker . . . the honest and industrious men can face death without ever being a member of any chapel or denomination. What has the Pope or any Priest or Preacher to do with salvation? . . . We must work out our own salvation for ourselves individually. No man can suffer my happiness or my torments.

He concludes his reflections on the year on a personal note, but without accepting sole responsibility for its many misfortunes:

> 31 December 1867
>
> I am going to give my adieus to the year 1867 with all its trouble – being the most troublesome that I have spent. The blame might have been partly on my fault, but not altogether. The deficient crops cannot be attributed to my faults . . . We bring all sorts of punishment on ourselves and we bring ourselves voluntarily to a state of poverty.

CHAPTER 10
AT THE END OF HIS TETHER

As he thankfully closed the door on 1867, Joseph hoped for an easier time in the new year. His diary opens with this sentiment, 'May the year 1868, leave things more pleasing than it is at present.' It was to prove one of his most supremely ironic entries. Nevertheless, it started well.

On New Year's Day, he enjoyed himself by attending one of his favourite events:

> 1 January 1868
> I prepared myself for the Club Feast of the Beehive Society. We paraded up to the vicarage and back to the church where we had a good sermon.

The 'good sermon' was, as usual, followed by the grand banquet with liberal amounts of alcohol provided. On 11 January he attended the Pigs Fair at Lampeter, where he met 'a few drinking friends' and staggered back on the last train, which reached Tregaron at 11 p.m. In the first week of February he attended a 'housewarming party' at the Royal Oak, Lampeter, and returned home at midnight. The following day he attended the St Silyn Fair at Tregaron where, after selling some cattle, he spent the money on drink. Temptation followed upon temptation. On 12 February he was invited to 'a coursing meeting at

Tregaron with numerous respectable gentlemen . . . We had a fine day and a good dinner.' The hunt was bracing, but for Joseph the potent punch, the claret, the port and the mulled wine provided a perfect end to the perfect day. But not every day ended on such a happy note. On 23 January he again became embroiled in a fight with one of his arch enemies. 'At the Fountain Inn I caught a blow from Edward the Porter, and was covered in blood.' It proved a humiliating encounter.

Unable to protect him from his self-destructive addiction, Betty watched in despair as Joseph continued to lose all respect and credibility among his neighbours, and even among his own servants. In a desperate attempt to remove all temptation, she ordered her maids to ensure that all alcohol in the house should be locked up and kept out of sight. This only made things worse for Joseph now suffered the indignity of confronting the *forwyn fach* – the youngest maid – who refused to inform him where the brandy bottle was hidden. With some justification he complained that he was no longer master in his own house. He had always held the Victorian view that the father should be the head of the household, but at Trecefel this was no longer the case. Betty continued to search his pockets for money from the sale of stock, which grossly offended his pride. To complicate matters further, she now found herself pregnant with her ninth child, which came as a tremendous shock to both husband and wife. To Joseph, it seemed incomprehensible.

Many times in his diary Joseph has written about the uncertainty of life. On 18 February a tragic accident occurred in one of the outbuildings that deeply upset the whole family. This unfortunate incident briefly deflected attention from the tensions within the house and put matters in perspective. Joseph graphically recorded the incident:

> 18 February 1868
> One does not know what will happen in one day, or rather in one hour . . . Lewis, Daniel Lloyd, Thomas, Nel and Jane the maid servant went to cut chaff before supper . . . At about 7 o'clock Daniel Lloyd brought news that the maid servant Jane had got entangled in the chaff cutter. Her left hand was off at the wrist. Only a narrow piece of skin was holding it together. Daniel went on horseback for Dr John of Garth and Lewis for his father Dr Rowlands of Strata Florida. I did stop the flow of blood. Dr John was here by 10.30 and his father by 12.30. Amputation was necessary . . . and skilfully performed . . . I never saw such a dreadful accident . . . The patient was wounded about the face . . . deep wounds were made on the left cheek. I told the patient that she was not wanted at the chaff cutter that night, but young persons are wiser than me! The patient's still unaware of the amputation. It was done without causing her much pain. The skilful doctors left about 2 o'clock.

Joseph was always fulsome in his praise of Dr Rowlands and his son Dr John of Garth, although the means of alleviating pain at their disposal still remained somewhat primitive. By the middle of the century Dr James Simpson had pioneered the use of chloroform in Edinburgh, and it is possible that Jane was given ether to alleviate her suffering. She survived the amputation and Joseph had her forearm respectfully buried in the old churchyard near Strata Florida Abbey. There was no compensation for accidents; disabled people were left to fend for themselves as best as they could. Fortunately for Jane, an aunt took her under her care. Joseph paid her 'due wages of £1 12s 6d calculated up to one day after the accident,' which does not seem particularly generous in the light of the circumstances.

Jane's misfortune particularly distressed Betty who, on account of her condition, was very vulnerable. Despite the pregnancy, the relationship between Joseph and Betty remained icy. Her main support now was Lewis, her son. Despite his youth he shouldered much of the farm work and had been well trained by his father, '2 February, Lewis went to plough with a team of four horses.' This allowed Joseph to follow his chosen path, '20 February I went to Lampeter . . . to the county court to be held to-morrow . . . I did sleep at the Bush Inn and had a good bed.'

On 27 February Joseph reached his fiftieth birthday. This, for him, was a significant milestone, as he had held an expectation of an early death since the age of 21. He contemplated his present way of life and confessed, 'I drink too much alcohol and I'm tempted to abstain!' But he did not seem to be impelled by any sense of urgency. It was, after all, only two weeks before *Ffair Garon* when carousing was the order of the day.

A week following the fair, Joseph's diary contains an entry which brought much misery in its wake, '25 March 1868, it appears that a great many of Colonel Powell's tenants were served with notices to quit yesterday.' On this occasion his friendship with Colonel Powell could not override his social conscience and he added in his diary, 'Let the landlords try to farm themselves.'

The morning of 9 April was frosty as Joseph 'went about the

farm at dawn to gather strayed sheep.' When he returned, he found that 'Betty had been taken ill . . . She became very ill at about 12 o'clock and had to bear a severe labour until half past two.' Lewis went for his aunt at Pwllswyddog and another midwife from Tregaron. Joseph also sent for 'Dr John of Garth, but the delivery took place about a quarter of an hour before he arrived at Trecefel. She was delivered of a male child.' Joseph seemed perplexed by the birth; he even composed a verse claiming that he was at a loss to understand how the baby had been conceived at all.

The birth of Betty's ninth and last child, John David, left her debilitated and depressed. Even Joseph expressed concern about her condition. '11 April, Betty is not as strong as usual in her confinement. She keeps to her bed. She is rather weak and thirsty.' The following day, Easter Sunday, Joseph decided to attend the church service but did not appear to have received a blessing. '12 April, 1868 I did prepare for Church. The Rev John Hughes was officiating . . . I did not like his sermon . . . being the worst I have ever heard from his mouth!'

The following day Betty's condition continued to give rise for concern. '13 April, Betty is rather bad again . . . Her appetite is rather weak.' She continued 'very unwell' for the next seven days. According to Joseph, '20 April, Betty is worse . . . She does not eat anything almost . . . she has kept her bed all day.' She received many visitors including members of her family, but Joseph did not greet them with good grace and complained, 'I was much bothered by them.' Neither did he express any joy at the birth of his new son. Largely ignored by his family, especially by Lewis, and frequently embroiled in confrontations with his neighbours,

Joseph was becoming increasingly isolated. On 27 April he found himself chastised by one whose respect he had always wanted to retain. '27 April, I met the Reverend Latimer Jones. He came over to Trecefel... We had a long chat... but he, like many, was blaming me for many things, especially drinking too much.'

Such crushing criticism from a man of his stature shook him. It preyed so much on his mind that he wrote in his diary, 'I will bid farewell to all quarrels and every kind of sin. After I have gone away, no-one will meet with any sadness.'

Joseph was not the only one to suffer at the hands of Latimer Jones. He was an intolerant man who had even offended the mild-mannered diarist and cleric Francis Kilvert, who had an unfortunate encounter with him. This led to the following entry in Kilvert's diary:

> Monday 6 May 1870
> Got into an argument with Mr Latimer Jones about people's legal and moral rights over their property and he spoke in such an insolent, overbearing, contemptuous way that my blood was up, and Mrs Bevan said afterwards she feared we should have fought.

Convinced that enemies surrounded him, Joseph became increasingly paranoid and exhibited wild swings of mood. May Day should have been a happy festive occasion, but he succeeded in ruining it for all. He arose at his usual early hour of 5 a.m. and went round the farm, but on returning he stormed upstairs and roughly roused the whole household calling them all 'sluggards'. When his daughters and servants later returned from a religious service he rudely greeted them with, 'The hypocrites are back!' He blamed everyone except himself for the problems confronting him, not least his 'star-crossed fate of being cursed before birth.'

In his disturbed state of mind he continued to neglect much of his farm, but it was imperative that the peat be harvested and set in stacks for the winter. '15 May, Took our cart and tools . . . and crossed the river Teifi to our turf pit. We were seven hands . . . the cutters, Daniel, myself, Nel, Margaret, Thomas and the skinners to remove the surface. We carted sixty six loads of peat from the bog; Trecefel was never better provided with fuel.'

Lewis was conspicuously absent from this party. Much to Joseph's fury, he had visited Tynant which reinforced his conviction that Lewis was in cahoots with his grandfather and plotting to destroy him. With father now pitted against son and husband against wife, the situation at Trecefel had become so fraught that it seemed inevitable that matters would come to a head. This occurred on the fateful night of 26 May 1868. The manner of the confrontation was to provide Joseph with a sense of grievance which was to obsess him for the rest of his life:

> 26 May 1868
>
> I was not home before a quarter to eleven and went to bed directly . . . But alas! I was disturbed very soon and brutally affected by those who ought to respect me in every sense. The bed clothes were dragged from me. I did change my bed and tried to shelter myself with my young children Tom and Anne. Lewis came from the garret and began to strangle me, but I was strong enough for him – but he was assisted by the big maid, my wife, Margaret and Elinor. They had me down and did abuse me in the

most brutal manner for nearly 2 hours. Three of my ribs and my breast-bone were fractured and I could not breathe for a long time.

We only have Joseph's version of events, but the animosity which had built up against him as a husband, a father and a master seems to have exploded with a vengeance at Trecefel on that unfortunate night. Despite the pummelling he had received, Joseph still tried to stir himself early the following morning but the extent of his injuries was considerable:

26 May
I was up about five but could not bear to keep on after the outrage last night. I found that my ribs and breastbone were fractured . . . I have an ugly black eye with about a dozen other different wounds . . . In fact I cannot handle my right hand . . . I am undone all over my body.

He felt so weak that he was obliged to return to bed where he remained fuming and unable to eat for two days. However, on 28 May he was ready for his revenge. 'I got up at half past 5 and compelled my two daughters Margaret and Elinor to leave their couches through means of a slender ground ash, being the first time to show myself master of the house . . . They did finish to gather stones at Cae James!' Ironically, those to whom he had been closest were punished the worst. Poor Margaret, who was generally loyal to her father, spent a back-breaking day picking up stones but there is no mention of any action taken against Lewis. He also feared Betty too much to confront her openly about that savage night's work. Instead, he wreaked his revenge with a venomous onslaught against her, not only in the pages of his daily diary, but also in a secret notebook he described as my 'Black Book'. 'This,' he claimed, 'will explain the cause and every particular concerning the foul attempt of murder.' He also described the violence of the night's work in verse:

28 May 1868

> I'm black from the crown of my head
> All down to the tips of my toes,
> So cruel my traitors did tread
> My life is despaired through the foes.
>
> Three devils were tearing my legs,
> My testicles, the serpent did squeeze,
> The demon was struggling with pegs
> While poking my ribs with his knees.
>
> The Devil did never commit
> Such cruelty during his time,
> No savage did ever permit
> To see such abominable crime.
>
> What answer, I'd like to be known
> Will they give to the world for the job,
> My wounds are too deep to disown
> The murderous attempt of the mob.

Joseph remained indisposed for a week or so following the attack, complaining that, 'I do feel my ribs very bad . . . and have been advised to go to hospital . . . feel very poor in spirit.' He attended Carmarthen Hospital where he was bandaged for cracked ribs and received treatment for severe bruising. Within a few weeks he regained his health and, surprisingly, affairs at Trecefel returned to as normal a state as was possible in the circumstances. But Joseph continued to seethe inwardly against

Betty, pouring his frustration onto the pages of his 'Black Book'. He returned to work, albeit uncomfortably, alongside his son and servants in order to harvest the crops. Defiantly, he still frequented the taverns and followed the hunts. '12 August, I met the hounds at Ystrad Dewi and had a good long hunt... They caught the fox . . . after loosing 24 dogs.' Later, the huntsmen convened at the Talbot Hotel to regain their strength and to fortify themselves for another day.

But for Joseph another new and unexpected challenge beckoned. Once again, he forsook all responsibilities for his own farm in order to serve the demands of other people. On 24 August Mr Philips, the agent of Colonel Powell, called at Trecefel 'enticing me to go to town to attend a committee on behalf of Mr Edmund Mallet Vaughan of Trawsgoed.' Parliament had been dissolved and a General Election called. Joseph dutifully turned up for the committee at the Talbot Hotel where he was met by 'Colonel Powell and many other gentlemen present.' He was formally asked by the gentry to support the Tory cause and to endorse the candidature of Edmund Mallet Vaughan. This placed Joseph in a dilemma. He had witnessed at first hand the wretchedness caused by the rise in rents and the evictions of tenants by the landlords. For once, he held back and did not immediately agree to support Mr Vaughan. '25 August, I did refuse my name in order to consider the candidate's politics. I wish for an explanation from them both [Liberal and Tory], who will support the Tenant's rights.'

Most of the tenant farmers believed that their best interests would be served by the Liberal candidate Evan Matthew Richards, a Baptist and shipbuilder who hailed from Swansea. Yet, after careful consideration and, no doubt, considerable pressure from Colonel Powell, Joseph decided to throw in his lot with the Tories and to support Edmund Mallet Vaughan.

It seemed like a bolt from the blue for neighbours and family alike. It put him even more at loggerheads with Lewis his son and even with his brother John, who was firmly wedded to the Liberal cause. There were already straws in the wind that seemed to indicate that the hegemony of the landlords was over, and that the Liberals would triumph. But perverse as usual, Joseph stood like a Canute on the reactionary shore, while all around him the tide of Liberalism was creeping in. He was always a complex man; if proof were ever needed, this was it. For the third time in under a decade Joseph was to find himself in the boiler house of Cardiganshire politics, and it did nothing to mend the fractured relationship between Betty and himself.

However, the die was now cast; the contest commenced and the county quickly became gripped by election fever. Joseph's first entry relating to the campaign indicated that it seemed to augur well for E.M. Richards. '28 August 1868, Mr Richards, the Liberal candidate came up by train. He was cheered at Llanio Station. He was going to Havod Uchdrud.'

From the outset it was obvious that Evan Richards had got off to a good start. It signalled a new mood of determination among the Liberals and the tenant farmers of Cardiganshire, who felt that they had suffered enough. Joseph began his campaign on behalf of Vaughan of Trawsgoed by writing a letter to *The Welshman* seeking to convince his fellow farmers that the Liberal Party was not the right one to address their problems:

A CARDIGANSHIRE FARMER

The farmers know who their real friends are, and are fully

aware of the fact that the Liberal Party will grant every privilege to the working class and none, if they can help it, to the farmer; he, poor fellow is screwed with rates and taxes.

Feelings were running high in the county. The day following Joseph's letter saw a serious attack on the house of one of the lesser gentry who had recently raised his rents. Joseph vividly describes the incident:

12 September 1868
The home of Stephen John Jones, Cilpill, was burnt down last night by a mob of 15 who had their faces blackened. The landlord was not at home. They dragged his wife and child out with a little lass and part of the furniture before setting the house on fire . . . all the hay burned.

This open demonstration of hostility against a landlord disturbed Joseph. Cilpill, the target of the assault, was situated at Llangeitho, only a few miles from Trecefel, and the victim John Jones was well known to him. It is likely that this minor landlord was an easier target for the wrath of the local malcontents that the better protected mansions of Trawsgoed and Nanteos with their extensive grounds, high walls and ornate wrought-iron gates. Cosseted as they were by vast wealth, these landlords were described in the *Chester Chronicle* as 'the most tyrannical and selfish on the face of God's earth.'

Three days later the Tories launched their campaign in the Tregaron area. Joseph, in defiance of his friends and family, greeted Vaughan publicly and threw his weight behind the Tory cause:

15 September 1868
I went to the Station to meet Mr Edmund Mallet

Vaughan, our candidate for the county. We gave him a good reception. We had several speeches from the platform by the Rev John Hughes, the candidate himself, and myself in a short address on behalf of the farmers. I did accompany Mr Vaughan to Penlôn. He was driving for Lampeter.

The landlords regarded Joseph as a positive asset for he could communicate with the farmers in their own language, and he himself was also a prominent tenant farmer.

On Saturday 19 September Joseph 'went up to the station to meet some of the gentlemen' to determine the best course of action for canvassing the electors. His commitment to Vaughan appeared firm, but John his brother was so uneasy about the situation that he had called at Trecefel in order to discuss 'different things, especially electioneering.' However, he failed to deflect Joseph from his promise to Vaughan, and the following day Joseph reaffirmed his loyalty to the Tories by setting out early. '19 October, I did canvass for Mr Vaughan to-day. I had some good voters.'

Two days later Joseph felt less confident. His attempts to cajole the farmers to support the Tory were proving more difficult than he had anticipated. The Liberals had by this time a well-structured organisation in the county and this was starting to achieve results:

Wednesday 21 October 1868
I went to canvass from here to Llangeitho, but not very successful. Richards' men had been before me. They had worked with caution. They have obtained the signature of the electors in many places. It shows me now that it will be a hard contest.

Nor did it get any easier. 'Thursday 22 October 1868, I have been canvassing to-day again; but was rather unsuccessful like yesterday. The signatures for Richards are firm and well kept.'

To counter the burgeoning support for the Liberals, Edmund Mallet Vaughan had published a notice in *The Welshman* on 25 September seeking to convince the tenant farmers that he was not an archetypal Tory:

> I am a 'Conservative' . . . not the old fashioned Tory . . . doggedly opposed to change or progress of every kind, but a Liberal Conservative and True Friend of Civil and Religious Liberty.

The following day, Joseph was requested by the Tory Managers to attend an emergency meeting at the Stag's Head. Obviously discomfited by the unfavourable signals, Vaughan was anxious to step up his campaign. Fifteen people attended this meeting and they arranged a list of those to be canvassed. After scrutinising the names of the voters in the seven parishes, they calculated that 'Mr Vaughan would be in a majority of 71 votes.'

On Tuesday 27 October Joseph rode into Tregaron to canvass and 'to meet Mr Vaughan and his entourage.' As usual, they met in the Long Room at the Talbot Hotel with Colonel Powell and other members of the gentry present. With only a month to go before the General Election, and witnessing the mounting support for the Liberal candidate, the alarm bells were ringing for the Tories. For the second time, Joseph and other campaigners were ordered to scrutinise the lists of voters. With an optimism born more out of desperation than reality, they again found that the situation was 'in favour of Mr Vaughan as far as our district goes.'

The following day Joseph rode on horseback to Pont Llanio to meet Vaughan and John Inglis Jones of Derry Ormond. He escorted them to Llanddewi where 'we made and delivered a few speeches at the schoolroom.' From Llanddewi, the party proceeded to Llangeitho, Penuwch, Capel Betws, Llwyngroes and Stag's Head where no stone was left unturned in the drive for votes.

Once again, on Thursday 29 October, Joseph was 'up early to canvass for Mr Vaughan.' After an exhausting day calling on all those farmers in the Llangeitho area eligible to vote, he returned to Stag's Head where he 'had some brew and cheese washed down by some stronger liquid' to help him on his way.

Joseph continued every day on his relentless crusade, traversing the districts, scrutinising lists at committee meetings in the Talbot and trying to keep up the momentum of the campaign. By Friday 6 November the weather had turned vicious and a fine dusting of snow had rendered the roads treacherous. Despite this, a huge committee was convened for Vaughan at Aberaeron. The wagonette of the Talbot Hotel conveyed the Tregaron Tory supporters to the meeting with Joseph in their midst. Every effort was made to create an upbeat atmosphere, as described by Joseph:

Friday 6 November 1868

I never saw so many landowners from the county together before. Several speeches were delivered there. They made out a calculation that Mr Vaughan is about 400 ahead of Richards should the electors stick to their promise. I left homeward with the others in the wagonette of the Talbot Hotel. It was snowing heavily.

Saturday brought a hard frost and a heavy fall of snow. Nevertheless, Joseph resolutely set out on behalf of Mr Vaughan. Utterly alone and despised by his neighbours, he trudged knee deep in snow 'to canvass our parish.' It was 9 p.m. by the time he returned to Trecefel 'numb with cold'. He added in his diary, 'Winter has set in early.'

On Tuesday 10 November he was obliged to attend another committee meeting at Tregaron, but by now it was increasingly evident that the Tories were trailing the Liberals. Exhausted and somewhat deflated, Joseph set out the following day 'to solicit votes for Mr Vaughan,' but by the end of the day he realised that the Tories faced defeat and he himself would have to pay the price for his unpopular stance. The following sombre entry was to prove the last in his 1868 diary:

Wednesday 11 November 1868
I went out to canvass for Mr Vaughan. I find that it will be against him very much. The dissenters are very determined in their promise for Richards.

From now until the end of the year, the pages of the diary are blank. This departure from his usual routine is unprecedented and one can only speculate about the reasons. His difficulties at home, coupled with his disappointment about the election and the hostility engendered towards him as a result of his support for the Tories, must have affected him deeply. In the past the diaries had been the means of sustaining him, but it may well be that not even their pages could assuage the anguish that now overcame him. Whatever the reasons, we are deprived of any record in his diary during those last few weeks at Trecefel. Instead, he penned his fragmented thoughts in a notebook.

The General Election was held on 28 November. It proved to be one of the most significant elections in Welsh history. The contest between Vaughan and Richards had been bitterly fought, and on occasions, it proved to be a brutal confrontation. The situation was so highly charged that it had been necessary to swear in one hundred special constables armed with staves, at a cost of five shillings each, to keep the peace in Aberystwyth. They do not appear to have been very successful, for Vaughan's personal valet was beaten up at the Railway Station and forced to flee for refuge in the nearby Cambrian Vaults. The windows of the house of Vaughan's election agent in Pier Street were smashed. Disorder prevailed everywhere as gangs of urchins roamed the streets and pelted Vaughan's supporters with mud. One Tory supporter, who had the temerity to shout out loudly, 'Vaughan for ever,' had his face kicked in and his 'left thumb almost bitten off.' To add insult to injury the undreamt of had happened. When the votes came to be counted, for the first time ever, a Liberal had beaten a Vaughan of Trawsgoed, the standard bearer of the land-owning class. Evan Matthew Richards received 2,074 votes and Edmund Mallet Vaughan polled 1,918 votes. The result was relatively close, but a new era had begun. The seeds of democratic progress had been sown, but it would be some years yet before they were to be in full bloom. Vaughan received a majority in both Tregaron and Lampeter:

	Richards	Vaughan
Lampeter	107	226
Tregaron	232	304

Joseph had slaved indefatigably in these areas, but it is more likely that the votes reflect the widespread fear of eviction. According to Professor Ieuan Gwynedd Jones, 'The landlords had learned their lesson . . . it was here that coercion was seen in its most naked form.'

Following the 1868 Election, Thomas Harries of Llechryd, on behalf of the Liberation Society, presented evidence to the Hartington Committee showing that the Tory landlords had victimised those tenants who had voted for the Liberals. At least 43 had been evicted, including a family who had farmed the land for four centuries.

Amongst the landlords harshly criticised was none other than Joseph's friend, Colonel Powell of Nanteos. Many of his tenants suffered abominably for supporting E.M. Richards. Among these were Thomas Morgan, Tynffordd, Llanfihangel-y-Creuddyn, aged 60 years, who had been born and bred on his farm; David Davies, Tymawr, and David Jones, Brynchwyth, who came from the same parish. It was claimed that Colonel Powell had summoned his tenants to a meeting at Devil's Bridge prior to the election and ordered them to vote for Mr Vaughan of Trawsgoed. Only one agreed to vote Tory, the others decided to abstain; but Thomas Morgan, David Davies, and David Jones adhered to their convictions and voted Liberal. They paid a high price for their principles. Also presented before the Hartingdon Committee was the sad case of David Jones, Llanbadarn Trefeglwys who, at the advanced age of 82 years was thrown out of his cottage for voting contrary to the wishes of his landlord.

A complaint was also made against Mr Vaughan of Trawsgoed that his agent had threatened the Reverend David Davies, Bethania, and forced him to leave his farm because he had supported the Liberals. A wave of sympathy for these political martyrs now swept across the whole of Wales. Collections were made on their behalf in every Nonconformist chapel in the land and thousands of pounds were raised.

Defeat at the polls was not the only blow suffered by the Trawsgoed family on that election night. Their gamekeeper, Joseph Butler, was shot by a poacher, William Richards, Cefncoch. In spite of sustained efforts by the police and the offer of a generous reward, not one of his neighbours betrayed him. He was hidden and protected by them for months before he eventually escaped to America. This is further evidence of the solidarity felt by the ordinary people and their dwindling respect for their landlords.

Although Joseph had temporarily abandoned his diary, he still felt the need to express his thoughts. The following line appears in his jotting notebook, '29 November, I went away for a while feeling extremely unwell.' Amidst the euphoria felt by the Liberals at their famous victory, a mixture of anger and gloom pervaded the mansions of the gentry. Joseph was now 'hoist by his own petard'; he could not bask in the glory of the Liberal victory and his erstwhile friends among the Tories would have little use for him henceforth. While those who had stuck firmly to their principles and had been evicted for their pains were treated as heroes and martyrs, Joseph would have been regarded as a traitor to the radical cause. With members of his own family arraigned against him and with a diminished reputation in the community, his whole world had collapsed around him. He was also beset by another problem.

Early in September of 1868 he had embarked upon a scheme to drain part of the marshland above Tregaron bridge. This involved deepening the bed of the river Teifi below the bridge and excavating a substantial quantity of gravel and stones. He deposited much of this on the bridge itself. Since it caused an obstruction it was brought to the attention of James Weekes Szlumper, the right hand man of David Davies, Llandinam, who also acted as a county surveyor. He decided to take Joseph to court. On 18 September, Joseph received a summons to appear before the magistrates. An account of the case was reported in *The Welshman* on 2 October 1868:

> J.E. Rogers Esq. and the Rev John Hughes. Mr Szlumper, Aberystwyth Bridge Surveyor for the county of Cardigan charged Joseph Jenkins, farmer, Trecefel, Caron Isclawdd, with having, on the 18th ult. on the highway at Trecefel Bridge . . . laid a certain quantity of gravel and rubbish to the interruption of persons travelling thereon.

Joseph decided to defend himself and gives his own account of the case in his diary:

> 29 September 1868
> I prepared to attend the Petty Sessions . . . I was soon called and went through my defence quite triumphantly. I acted as my own lawyer. Szlumper swore a downright lie before the magistrates both at Aberystwyth and Tregaron.

Because of the lack of evidence, the case was adjourned but it had been a humiliating experience. It only served to fuel further his feelings of paranoia, making him neurotically insecure. He refers to himself as 'a hare lipped persecuted fellow' while claiming that 'Szlumper needed a good punch on the nose.'

These many blows left Joseph severely depressed, and soulful entries in his notebook reflect his private agony. 'December 1868, I can see no sense or meaning in this life . . . I have lost my way . . . I was lacerated by family, friends and enemies . . . Life is nothing but a catalogue of misfortune . . . Fate, my family, my friends and events have all conspired against me. Would that I had never been born.' Escape seemed to offer the only hope of salvation. Yet, his Biblical knowledge still provided a grain of comfort for he admitted, 'Even in sorrow there is much wisdom to be learned.' Returning from a contemplative walk along the bank of the river Teifi he commented, 'He is the happiest who floats on the surface of life's river and does not think too deeply lest the currents drown him.' His lonely, ignominious exit after dark in December was a tragedy in more ways than one. Fearing that he might never again see his family and native land, his final comment was, 'If my diaries survive, I will not have lived in vain.' With that, he walked away from everything.

CHAPTER 11

HELL OR MELBOURNE

After slipping away from his farm on the evening of Monday 7 December, Joseph stayed overnight at Aberystwyth. Early on Tuesday morning he caught the first train on the Cambrian Line to Birkenhead and then boarded a boat for Liverpool. There he stayed at a lodging house for three nights to prepare for his escape to the colonies. After the serenity of Trecefel he found 'Liverpool a huge and frightening city, worse than London, where the streets rattled all night with traffic, where the noise of footsteps never ceased and where a man had to look sharp about himself to guard his belongings.' Well aware of the dangerous nature of the voyage ahead, he went to a solicitor to make his will. Despite all the ill feeling and family conflict that had built up over the previous years, he bequeathed everything he owned to his wife and children:

10 December 1868
I, Joseph Jenkins . . . in consideration of the love and affection which I have and do bear to-wards my loving wife and children . . . do freely give . . . all my property.

The schedule attached to his will reveals that he knew every detail of his beloved farm even down to the value of the stack of peat gathered from the bog for winter fuel.

Joseph described Liverpool as crammed with would-be emigrants all busily engaged in purchasing the necessities for the voyage. Among them were many Welshmen joining the mass exodus to America. By coincidence, he met two men from Llangeitho, a village not far from his home, who tried to persuade him to accompany them to America, but his mind was now firmly set on the furthest flung colony of all. 'Australia shall be my refuge.' On Thursday 10 December he went to the 'Australian Liverpool Co. Office' and bought a single ticket for Melbourne on the *Eurynome*, an iron schooner, built on the Clyde in 1862. The ship was due to sail on Saturday 12 December under the command of Captain W. Watson and the voyage was to take 140 days.

Considering the fact that his two brothers, David and Timothy, had already settled in Wisconsin, Joseph's choice of Australia showed a steely determination to get as far away as possible from his past, even from his own family. Australia was also becoming an increasingly popular venue for Welsh emigrants. The rush for gold to places like the Klondike and California in 1849 had largely subsided, and with the discovery of gold in Australia in 1851 the focus had shifted to the Antipodes. Advertisements now appeared regularly in Welsh newspapers encouraging emigration to this land of new opportunities. Gold mining towns such as Ballarat and Bendigo were becoming familiar place names in west Wales, and during the previous decade many of Joseph's own servants had left for Australia. He also knew many tenant farmers who had decided to seek refuge there from the tyranny of the landlords and the burden of the tithes, and he was later to meet up with several of them. But first, he faced a harrowing voyage in the claustrophobic confines of a cargo vessel following a long, circuitous route with its discomforts and many vexations.

Until the 1880's the voyage to Australia was still undertaken primarily by sailing ships which, unlike the steam ships, did not require regular supplies of coal. Prior to the opening of the Suez Canal in 1869, these ships normally followed the 'Great Circle' route. This took them into the South Atlantic Ocean passing Madeira and the Cape Verde Islands. They then sailed south of the Cape of Good Hope setting their course between the 40th and 50th parallels and sailing east, driven by the force of the constant trade winds, the 'Roaring Forties'. This took them close to the fringes of the Antarctic, exposing them to the dangers of massive icebergs, mountainous waves and strong winds that drove them on at speed for days on end. It could be a terrifying run, described by sailors and passengers alike as 'passing through Hell', before the clipper eventually reached Melbourne. Joseph was well acquainted with the driving rains of Tregaron and the icy blasts that blew across Cors Caron – but these would be as gentle Zephyrs compared to the fury of the 'Roaring Forties', sending the *Eurynome* scudding across the foaming ocean.

The *Eurynome* is described in Lloyd's Register of Shipping as an 'iron schooner of 1163 tonnage and 210 foot long.' It was not designed as a passenger ship, but as a cargo vessel. Ironically, in view of his problems with alcohol, Joseph noted with wry interest that the sailors were loading into the hold of the cargo vessel, '1,000 caskfulls of the best 3XXX's beer.' According to the ship's schedule 33 passengers had embarked at Liverpool; 12 travelled first class and the remainder had to endure less favourable conditions in the nether regions of the ship. On the ship's list of passengers Joseph is classified as a 'farmer'.

Although the schedule refers to Scotsmen, Irish and other nationalities, there was no provision for the 'Welsh' and Joseph Jenkins is entered as 'English'.

It was with mixed feelings that he went about the final preparations for the voyage. On the Friday before departure he bought clothes, utensils and medical supplies including laudanum and quinine. Saturday 12 December was a 'wet and gloomy morning'. Joseph was up at dawn and down at the docks where he was overwhelmed by the immense warehouses piled high with merchandise and hides, and enormous dray horses hauling huge loads. In the confusion he was unable to find the ship and had to be guided to the correct dock by a policeman. Finally, as he boarded the *Eurynome*, all insecurities, doubts and thoughts of his family were swept away by the hustle and bustle of settling in to what was to be his home for the next three months. It was a scene of intense activity, of 'swearing busy sailors . . . of passengers busily engaged in putting their berth and other things in order' and of weeping relatives at the quayside bidding their 'heartbreaking farewells which were like a death. – For when, if ever, would they see each other on this earth again?' No one from Trecefel stood at the dockside to shed a tear for him or to bid him a fair voyage, and we have no means of knowing what the reaction of his family was when they discovered that he had deserted them. At 9.30 a.m. the ship left the Queen's Docks, pulled by a powerful steam tug, to anchor in the river Mersey ready for the high seas.

Because he travelled second-class Joseph was obliged to share a berth with a C.N. Martin, aged 18, described as a 'Gentleman', who hailed from Cheshire. He proved to be an easygoing, amiable companion with whom Joseph struck up a good rapport. When he opened his eyes at dawn the following morning, he had a distinct feeling of *déjà vu*. 'When I awoke I thought I was at home, or rather Trecefel when hearing the cocks crow, dogs barking, pigs grunting, the sheep bleating, the geese gaggling, the ducks quacking and many things beside.' Joseph described the deck as resembling a farmyard with 'all manner of animals very much alive.' In the days before refrigeration these would provide luxury fare for the first-class passengers, but Joseph and his fellow voyagers were to taste very little of the fresh meat from this motley collection of livestock. Second-class passengers had to go to the storeroom where the steward provided them with 'messes', or supplies for the week. They were obliged to prepare their own food and were required to take turns with the cooking. Joseph lists the provisions he was given by the steward for the voyage:

> Biscuits, beef, pork, preserved meats, flour, treacle, rice, butter, tea, sugar, coffee, peas, potatoes, oatmeal, raisins, suet, mustard, pepper, vinegar and lime juice.

The lime juice provided Vitamin C to combat scurvy, a disease that had proved fatal to many sailors. On the second day on board, while she was still moored in the Mersey, a severe gale blew up rocking the ship so violently that it caused her anchor chain to snap. The departure had to be delayed until a new cable and anchor were provided. Finally, on 16 December, 'with flags flying', the crew once more weighed anchor and the ship pulled away 'amid much shouting and clamour.' The excitement was infectious. Passengers danced on deck and sang songs to the accompaniment of a concertina, fiddle and piano; everyone was fired with a sense of adventure and exhilaration.

Relieved that at last the ship was under sail, Joseph recorded, 'I feel healthy and in good spirits, but very anxious to commence my long intended voyage.'

The feeling was to be short-lived. Within hours of departure a 'fierce gale blew up in the Irish Sea opposite the Menai Straits' and Joseph was thrown out of his bed on no less than four occasions. Early elation gave way to a general feeling of trepidation among the passengers; many became alarmed about the safety of the vessel as 'seats, earthenware and other objects were knocked about in all directions.' Huge waves washed over the deck and the sailors were obliged to tack. Joseph had already found his berth too narrow for the comfort of his large frame, but during the storm it became so hazardous that he complained, 'I had to lash myself in my bunk to prevent being tossed out.' The gale lasted four days and the ship was 'still rolling badly' as it passed Milford Haven on 21 December. When Joseph tried to go on deck he 'had a good ducking and had to change clothes twice.' The seas were so rough that 'the cabin on the port staircase was washed away – swimming along the upper deck; nearly a foot of water poured into the first class saloon cabins and the Captain ordered the port holes to be opened. The ship was ungovernable for nearly 2 hours.' As the Captain sought to regain control Joseph heard the loud command, 'All hands on deck!' and he noted bleakly in his diary, 'The ship made little progress ahead for tacking against the wind . . . we will not reach Melbourne for years at the present rate of sailing.'

Nevertheless, by 23 December, despite the fact that the 'ship was rolling badly', it appears that the panic among the passengers had subsided and that the general mood had become more relaxed:

All go on merry, some are playing, some reading... We are 66 souls on board alto-gether. Thirty belonging to the ship and 36 passengers including two children, one under two years and another under seven.

One of Joseph's main concerns was the difficulty he experienced in writing his diary. He complained that 'the ship is rolling so violently I can scarcely write in any shape.' Unlike the saloon passengers, who paid three times as much for their private cabins, he slept in what was virtually a large communal dormitory with two tiers of wooden bunks along the sides of the ship separated only by a curtain and low wooden partitions offering little privacy. It was also dimly lit and the air was invariably foul and stuffy, 'like being in a dark, pitching prison.' Living in such close proximity to one another made it an inevitable breeding ground for quarrels and disputes, and Joseph was soon to clash with some of the other passengers. Nevertheless, in spite of everything, he never failed to keep his daily assignment with his diary. On a stormy Christmas Eve he wrote with characteristic fatalism:

> Every man must die just once
> And lose all vital sparks,
> Come, eat, drink, sing and dance
> Our graves may be the sharks.

Unfortunately for Joseph, his eccentricities marked him out, and he soon became an object of ridicule among certain of his fellow passengers. But at all times he comforted himself with the certainty that he was intellectually superior to most of them:

24 December 1868

As I am the only Welshman on board, that is to say, the

only one who professes to be a Welshman, I am rather bullied by some know nothings, ... there are mongrels on board who cannot either speak or write English, ... As long as The Captain and other Chief Officers will go on as they are, I must not fear anything unfair:

> To me, the Welshman, they do form
> All blame for nasty sauce,
> For wounds, for headwinds waves and storm
> You Welshman art the cause!
> If I am thus empowr'd,
> O let the bawling horde
> Be up on deck all gather'd,
> And fling me overboard.

It was, apparently, not uncommon for the Welsh to suffer racial harassment on such voyages, which is why they generally preferred to sail together in large groups.

On Christmas Day a rather queasy Joseph experienced the notorious weather of the Bay of Biscay. 'We approach the rollers of the Bay ... seas boisterous ... very squally all day ... the bow of the vessel dived underwater and everything except iron was swimming along the deck ... It took the cooking vessels out of the galley.' Such vile weather dampened the festive mood on board and the Christmas activities were severely curtailed. Joseph informs us that there was 'plum pudding' for dinner, but added ruefully, 'no geese'. His mind drifted back to Trecefel where the table would have been laden with fresh geese, his favourite dish. Those passengers who remained on their feet celebrated as best they could. Joseph's co-passenger, Mr Martin, weathered it well by 'partaking of too much alcohol . . . and is rather fresh to-night.' Joseph, rather self-righteously, emphasised that he drank 'only one festive glass of wine' after which, on a memorably sober Christmas Eve, he retired to his bunk to write a rather mundane verse:

> 25 December 1868
> She ploughs and splits the waves ahead
> South Western is her course,
> She has nothing now to dread
> But windward swells in force.

The rough weather of Christmas Day had left its mark in the second-class quarters, 'but the careful Captain visited our cabin and said that it should be soaped and cleaned after we have a dry deck.' Boxing Day proved kinder; those passengers who had previously felt indisposed were now able to go on deck to see 'scores of porpoises swimming and playing' alongside the ship in all directions. With some satisfaction Joseph recorded, 'We passed many ships that were sailing in the same direction.'

The next day being a Sunday, the Captain informed everyone that a Church Service would commence at a quarter to eleven but that there was no compulsion to attend. Joseph chose not to attend and sets out his reasons why:

> The inhabitants of this Cabin are all Roman Catholic except myself:
> No preacher, priest or parson
> Can answer for my sin,
> Let me judge and reason
> Not listening to their din.

The following days brought an improvement in the weather and the 'Royal Sail was hauled up' so that the ship was now almost under full sail and able to exploit the maximum potential of the wind. According to Joseph, 'she carried about 1,600 square yards of canvas which bore her swiftly across the surface of the seas.'

But down in the gloomy confines of the second-class passengers there were signs of growing discontent concerning matters of hygiene and of conditions generally. For a man used to wide spaces and the freedom of walking his farm at dawn, being closeted in a berth below sea level proved difficult for Joseph. 'My berth ... is rank with the odours of my fellow travellers, and the place reeks with the stench of urine.' There were only a limited number of toilet cubicles; but passengers were allowed one wooden bucket with a rope handle as a 'slop pot' alongside their bunks. These primitive conditions presented a health hazard and there was a constant fear of an outbreak of typhus. Such was the concern among the passengers that they wrote a letter of complaint to the Captain, 'about the dirty state of the water closet.' He replied curtly that it was their responsibility to keep their living quarters clean.

On the last night of the old year Joseph notes that, 'A great many of us agreed to stop up on deck until the New Year of 1869 be in . . . There was much music and singing; on the stroke of midnight the ship's bells were rung.' As he witnessed these New Year celebrations he could recall that soon the early *calennig* collectors would be venturing forth with their songs and greetings as they visited his farm Trecefel to wish his own family *Blwyddyn Newydd Dda* – A Happy New Year. 'Here,' he wrote, 'I look out across the Atlantic with the moon dazzling on the restless waves.' As the ship's bells clanged in the new year Joseph summed up the ill fortunes of the old year in four lines:

> Farewell the year of sixty eight
> With all thy pleasures and thy cares,
> Who can recall the wrongs and right
> Mixed with flowers, fears and snares!

He greeted the year 1869 cautiously. 'We cannot tell who will survive . . . Some are to lose, and a few to win.'

On New Year's Day he caught sight of the island of Madeira and noted that 'the temperature is gradually rising.' Joseph spent much of his time walking the deck and endlessly questioning the cost and purpose of everything. The Captain informed him that 'the ship and cargo are valued at £150,000.' Although he had endeared himself to the Captain and the crew, he suffered severe provocation at the hands of a few second-class passengers. With some distress he wrote, 'A certain person has stolen my slop pot!' Such a loss was the ultimate indignity and greatly inconvenienced him. Regrettably, he was to be the victim of many such malicious acts throughout his time on board.

His spirits were soon revived the following day when he became fascinated by the ship's water condenser. 'We have to drink artificial water . . . the Engineer told me that it can produce 280 gallons per diem . . . A good invention.' As a farmer, Joseph had been upset by the condition of the animals on board and when he saw one of the squealing store pigs being killed and dressed exclusively for the benefit of the saloon passengers, he commented, 'Poor half starved prisoner, his lucky fate came at last!' As the *Eurynome* continued on its southwestern course towards the Equator, Joseph was enchanted by the variety of the sea life around him. 'I did see a swarm of turtle fish swimming to-gether, and a whale was viewed about 100 yards from starboard . . . It gets warmer by the day.' With the rise in temperature the passengers emerged from their cabins in high spirits. 'There was music and much activity on deck; the concertina, fiddle and piano are played well and merry . . . The Captain is particular about keeping the ship clean; some sailors are washing, some painting and some of the crew busily engaged in washing the decks . . . which were dirtied by loose dogs, pigs, geese, ducks, sheep and so on.'

As the thermometer rose, Joseph became increasingly thirsty. Fresh water was at a premium and was carefully rationed. Only three quarts a day were given to each second-class passenger for washing, drinking and cooking. Whenever it rained, every possible effort was made to collect fresh water. On 11 January 1869 'it began to rain heavily . . . and all the empty buckets were set to receive the rain water.' Joseph rushed to collect as many bucketfuls as he could, but the weather was dramatically variable, and within a few hours the rain clouds disappeared, to be replaced by the heat of the blazing sun.

On 12 January he complained, 'I feel very warm in my berth. It is 78° in the shade. No sail or anything else to be seen. Cuba, Madeira and the Canary Islands are about the nearest lands to us. We are quite at a standstill . . . the timbers are so hot I can scarcely lay my hand on deck . . . We are 250 miles this side of the equator. Many big ships are hanging about us, all in want of a breeze . . . The Captain said we will not cross the line for seven years at this rate!'

Mercifully, on 15 January, it began to rain heavily and Joseph once again lost no time in taking advantage of the occasion. 'I was engaged in catching water . . . I carried thirty six buckets to the water tank on the condition that I was to have one bucketful for every dozen to wash when required.'

From the moment he had set foot on board Joseph had bombarded the Captain and crew with questions regarding the running of the ship. He struck up a better rapport with the sailors than with his fellow travellers. He was regarded as an inquisitive, colourful and erudite Welshman, affectionately called 'Taffy', who could write poetry and turn his hand to almost anything. Occasionally, Captain Watson gave Joseph pieces of cheese 'privately', but he was also severely rebuked by him because his heavy hobnailed boots caused damage by 'scraping the poop deck and the chapel floor . . . I had an order from the Captain not to take my heavy nailed shoes up the poop.' On account of this he was nicknamed 'Clodpole' by the other passengers, which caused him much distress. He was also ordered not to attend Sunday worship in his hobnailed boots, but this did not unduly worry him as he preferred to find his own salvation in solitude:

> The Church bell was striking . . . I was not allowed to go
> to Church for my heavy plated boots –
> God is love Almighty
> Unchangeable in his way,
> The Clodpole may have mercy
> In plated shoes some day!
> They go to church to pray and preach
> I will try to find my berth to lie,
> The laws of Nature always teach
> How to walk, live and die.

Although he did his best to be philosophical in the face of misfortune, he still suffered in silence:

> Poor Taffy . . . Nothing but Kicks for Jo –

> The Clodpoles are to sweat and strive
> To keep proud sluggards all alive,
> May I bear the cruelty of others equably.

As they neared the Equator the sweltering conditions only served to exacerbate the tension and discomfort among the passengers and Joseph seemed to suffer more than most. He complained that one man in particular, John Tait, a Scot, relentlessly victimised him. 'Tait spread lies . . . and unjustly accused me of transgressions caused by persons other than myself.' Joseph constantly attributed his rough treatment to the fact that he was a Welshman, 'I am unfairly bullied because of my race.' With a touch of dry humour he adds, 'Among 8 ducks on board there is one drake which does not go near the rest – I told the Captain that he is a Welshman!'

To combat the racist taunts Joseph records that, 'I was obliged to let loose my tongue sometimes in self defence against lies and petty thefts.' But he also had a secret weapon which infuriated his detractors. 'A few words in Welsh always bring them to a hot temper. Their reply was, "Don't talk Welsh, it's ungentlemanlike . . . you can speak English!" '

Joseph was not the only scapegoat on board. Frayed tempers often reached flashpoint between the English and the Irish. The Captain, however, rigorously enforced the ship's law of absolutely 'no blows' and threatened the offenders with handcuffs. The bitter disputes between the English and the Irish provided a respite for Joseph, and after witnessing one altercation he penned these lines:

> While the Hounds are chasing the Fox,
> The Hare has a chance to escape,

I am their principal hoax,
This quarrel will spare me a scrape.

Despite suffering much gratuitous abuse, Joseph proved his worth time and again on the ship. As a farmer, he was asked to shear the sheep on deck. Clipping sheep on board ship was an experience he had never envisaged even in his wildest dreams, and it was a far cry from the mountains of Llanddewibrefi where the Blaenplwyf family had always made shearing an enjoyable occasion. Despite having 'to make do with a small pair of clippers' instead of a proper shears, he and an Irish fellow-worker sheared for two days. He noted, however, that the sheep and pigs were not well fed and were getting leaner daily. 'The last sheep which was killed had weighed only forty nine pounds, whereas she would have made seventy pounds when she first came on board.'

As they neared the Equator it became so hot that even the sailors were obliged to retreat from the deck and to seek relief overboard. Joseph watched 'many of the crew dive into the sea from a great height . . . they seemed to fear nothing except sharks.' Each morning he found a great many bodies of flying fish on the deck which he described as 'having two wings and can fly a long distance. I did see one flying nearly half mast high. Their bodies look white . . . They are as delicious to eat as trout or fresh herring.'

Sometimes the ship remained motionless for days and Joseph found the stillness of the ocean eerie. He also noticed that this strange calm affected the general mood of the passengers, leading to a kind of lethargy and creating a surreal atmosphere. To combat this, Joseph would get up at dawn with some of the others to carry out his ablutions. 'I went to the forecastle before breakfast for a cold bathing. We took buckets which were plunged with a line into the sea so as to give each other a good cold bathing. I did wash my feet and cut the point of my nails off. I feel quite comfortable and do enjoy my voyage well so far.'

He described the sea 'as smooth as muslin'. Often sharks appeared alongside the ship and the passengers tried to bait one with a large piece of pork; others tried to stab it with a spear, 'but the wily shark took care to keep beyond reach.' The saloon passengers were allowed to shoot and amused themselves by aiming their guns at floating corked bottles which were tossed into the sea. Joseph, who was an excellent shot, remarked caustically that, 'they were very poor marksmen.'

On 16 January 1869 the watchman sighted a ship for which they had been on the lookout for some time. The vessel, which was bound for London with a cargo of coffee, was also to transport the many letters that had been written on board the *Eurynome* since embarkation. There was great excitement on board as a boat was lowered and four sailors rowed across with the mail. Among its contents were many letters which Joseph had written to relatives, including one to his eldest daughter, Margaret, at Trecefel. His folk back home would now have a taste of his new, strange and fascinating world and, no doubt, his experiences would soon be the talk of the locality.

Eventually, on 18 January, the ship crossed the Equator. Joseph had eagerly anticipated the event for weeks, but it proved something of an anticlimax. There was no celebration to mark the occasion and Joseph learned about it almost casually:

19 January 1869
Had a few words with the Captain about the Equator . . . He said that it was early yesterday that we did cross it. We

are between Africa and South America and many thousands of miles from land . . . The sea is turning and pitching like a whirlpool. Very close and foul air in the berth.

Unfortunately, most of the passengers were struck down with some form of enteric fever causing acute diarrhoea. This outbreak gave rise to another complaint against the conditions and the passengers drew the attention of the Doctor to the pollution caused by the 'slop pots on board'. Joseph described the sickness as 'a dangerous fever attended by looseness.' He himself felt so listless that he lay on his bunk 'sweating all over . . . with nothing on except my shirt.' Unable to endure the fetid conditions below, many of the passengers preferred to sleep under the stars on deck. To alleviate the situation, the Captain himself advised the second-class passengers to 'take their beds and bedding on to the deck for freshness.' Joseph found sleeping on deck a moving experience. 'I feel humble beneath such a sky of crystal stars more numerous than I ever saw in Cardiganshire.'

The task which Joseph disliked most on board ship was having to cook for the other passengers. It involved a lot of preparation. He had to carry water and prepare the food in a narrow galley, which proved to be an ordeal. 'I cooked for 19 people to-day, but not very successful with the plum pudding.' He complained, 'I cannot afford the time even to please my muse or *awen*! Each day is taken up with chores . . . washed four pairs of stockings, two towels, 2 handkerchiefs, 2 shirts and drawers.' The Captain's policy was to ensure that the passengers were kept so busy that they had little time to complain or to cause any riotous behaviour on board. Joseph, always a practical man, covered his precious dictionary 'with an old piece of sail' and, rather optimistically, he also 'made a new breast pocket of sail inside my waistcoat – strong enough to hold my Australian gold!'

Smoking on board was strictly forbidden. Nevertheless, Joseph's co-passenger, Mr Martin from Cheshire, clandestinely smoked his pipe, and much to Joseph's dismay, he even tore two leaves from a book of poems by Byron to light his pipe. He later gave the book to Joseph, who read it avidly. In spite of his frequent difficulties he managed to establish a good relationship with some of the first-class passengers who recognised his talents. He was asked on many occasions to write verses for their benefit and, as always, he was eager to extend his own cultural horizons. 'I had the loan of the poetical works of Robert Burns from one of the Saloon passengers. It is the best thing I've read . . . it contains the heart and soul of the learned ploughboy.' On the evening of Tuesday 19 January Captain Watson paid a sudden and unexpected visit to the second-class area. He caught four of the passengers smoking their pipes; fortunately, Joseph had given up his pipe five weeks previously. Those who contravened regulations were threatened with punishment and, as usual, 'handcuffs were full ready in case of misbehaviour.' Discipline on board was of paramount importance for the safety of both passengers and crew.

On the 37th day of sailing Joseph wrote in his diary, 'If I were to tell the people of Tregaron that the following were on board, I doubt whether they would believe me!' He went on to list the various items on the ship:

> 12 water pumps, 9 ventilators, 3 flower gardens, many ricks of hay, stores of turnips, carrots, swedes, mangols, onions, potatoes; 2 steam engines, 2 sailmakers, a Smith, tools and bellows, 1 engineer, 1 lampmender, 1 ship-

wright, many sorts of living birds, 3 dogs, 2 cats, sheep, pigs and many other creatures all alive . . .

Joseph had been brought up to abhor indolence and he was never happier than when called upon to do some work on the ship. 'I have been blowing the fire for the Smith. The bellows are similar to those they have to fasten the grid iron bridges of the Railways.'

On 22 January the temperature remained over 90°F in the shade and everything on deck was 'unbearable to both hands and feet . . . and the sea is as smooth as glass.' But the situation on board was not quite as 'smooth' as the sea. Tempers became frayed and a fracas broke out between the first and second-class passengers, 'accompanied by much swearing and foul language.' The cause of the quarrel is not detailed, but it was serious enough to warrant an intervention on the part of the Captain who 'sanctioned the use of handcuffs to restrain the offenders and ordered them to go to the other end of the ship to swear.'

The treatment afforded to the saloon passengers often stirred the envy of the second-class travellers. They were served with an ample supply of fresh pork and mutton and were allowed wine and brandy. When Joseph was later to beg for some cold beer to alleviate his thirst, he was refused. He recorded that his 'chief sustenance on the voyage was biscuits, treacle, raisins, salt beef and cold tea.'

As the temperature soared to 100°F in the shade, 'it seemed to be raining fire,' with the scorching rays of the sun making it intolerable on deck. Thus Joseph was obliged to lie on his bed all day despite the foul conditions down below. Water was rationed and he craved for a cool drink. 'I would give a shilling for a quart of pure spring water. There are nearly 1,000 caskfulls of the best 3XXX beer on board, but the second-class passengers are not allowed to have a drop of it.' Throughout the voyage his favourite drink was cold tea 'which best quenched my raging thirst.' In these near searing conditions, Joseph tried to get some relief, but without much success:

> 1 February 1869
>
> I began to feel thirsty and could not appease it. I went to the Stewards entreating them to sell me a bottle of either ale or porter. They refused. The Captain would not allow anything to second-class passengers except port or claret at 4 shillings a bottle, which I refused. I came down to my berth and prepared my epitaph.
>
> > A certain Clodpole died on board
> > From craving thirst among the horde,
> > Without a prayer, pomp or pride
> > His corpse was cast o'er seaward side.

Joseph's agony was further compounded by more provocation from John Tait, the Scot, who took such a sadistic delight in taunting him. This time, it took the form of a picture drawn by Tait which ridiculed him and was placed on public display on deck. Unable to express his disgust in English, he turned to Welsh:

> When things get difficult I have to recite some serious words in my mother tongue, which terrifies them all. They think I'm denouncing all their weaknesses, whereas I'm only reciting the psalms of poor Iolo. [A reference to Iolo Morganwg, a famous Welsh eighteenth century poet and antiquary.]

To many of his fellow passengers Joseph seemed a rather

peculiar figure, clad in his rustic clothes and wearing hobnailed boots. They found it difficult to understand why he should spend so much of his time reading and writing and this made them suspicious of him. Consequently, the crueller elements on board humiliated him relentlessly. The impression he gave of being self-righteous only fuelled their delight in ridiculing him. He was, however, extremely distressed by this treatment and he listed in his diary all the indignities heaped upon him by some of his fellow voyagers:

> The behaviour of my fellow passengers:
> Stealing my knife and fork, and my crockery
>   without shame
> Spitting on my trousers during the night
> Blaming me for every foul discomfort
> Preventing me from writing
> Stealing my sugar
> Stealing my knife a second time
> Wiping their shoes on my towel
> Breaking the lock of my box
> Stealing my belongings
> Placing slops in my food
> Defecating and urinating in my dishes
> Taking my box and defecating on it
> Preventing me from reaching the toilet
> Stealing my thermometer and placing it in a hot place
>   to deceive me
> Fabricating all sorts of lies about me to others on board
> Trying to persuade the sailors to throw me overboard
> Mocking the fact that I have a harelip.

Such an appalling catalogue of events would surely have tested to the full the resolve of the strongest personality, and it is to Joseph's credit that he was able to overcome such abominable treatment. Although the hurt went deep, his ability to record it all within the pages of his diary acted as a catharsis.

As the ship sailed southeast into the South Atlantic Ocean and towards the Cape of Good Hope Joseph 'saw swarms of birds called Cape Hens the size of common crows.' He also noted that 'many albatrosses flew round the ship with huge wing spans and soft brown down.' Sadly, these birds were regarded as fair game for the saloon passengers, but Joseph considered that their sport was little short of cruelty. 'Two albatrosses were shot and fell into the sea beyond reach; and the third hit the deck with a sickening thud.' These marksmen had either not read Coleridge's *The Rhyme of the Ancient Mariner* or did not believe in the Ancient Mariner's conclusion that shooting the albatross had brought disastrous consequences. Joseph himself was convinced that sinning against nature was the cause of man's problems, and he felt that the gratuitous slaughter of these birds was a violation of nature.

Many of the passengers occupied their time by fishing, but on one occasion, with an unfortunate result. A fish weighing 12 pounds was caught, cooked and eaten by some of the second-class passengers but 'it turned out to be poisonous and caused heads to be swollen very much with sore throats.' Joseph then included the following piece of useful information in the diary, 'The mode of testing the safety of a fish is to put a half a crown or piece of silver inside the fish for one night; if it is eatable, the silver will keep its proper colour, otherwise it will be black and mouldy.'

With the doldrums and the oppressive conditions of the

Equator now well behind them, and having crossed the Tropic of Capricorn, the *Eurynome* continued south of the Cape of Good Hope towards the fortieth parallel in order to catch the strong westerly winds of the 'Roaring Forties'. Joseph's diary reflects the rapid and dramatic changes as they approached the 'fury of the Southern Seas':

> 3 February 1869
> Heavy seas on deck . . . A gale blew up . . . all hands ordered to be ready . . . thermometer fell rapidly.

The passengers became alarmed as they passed 'a large ship with a broken main top mast.' Of all the things that the sailors feared most, a broken mast or rudder was their worst nightmare. It was an ominous sign of things to come. By 5 February Joseph described the ship as rolling heavily 'with a storm howling in the rigging.' The following day heavy seas washed over the decks, ducking the sailors and giving rise to plenty of 'cursing and swearing'. The weather became increasingly 'chilly and cold' as the *Eurynome* veered towards the Antarctic. Instead of being 'becalmed and stock still', the ship now made 280 miles a day whipped along by the relentless trade winds, 'wave piling upon wave with terrifying ferocity and with foul language from the sailors.'

On Sunday 7 February huge hailstones showered the deck and Joseph had a frightening experience:

> I was standing under the poop looking at the sails when a chain broke and the sail was rent like a piece of brown paper . . . All hands called on deck . . . A heavy chain fell on deck . . . I did retreat to my berth down below. Lookers are not wanted on deck when it blows hard!

Down below, an atmosphere of fear prevailed as the schooner, buffeted by the waves, rocked violently, turning everything upside down. This ferocious weather caused so much damage that 'the following day the sailors were engaged in repairing the broken things after the gale . . . The Smith for the chains and the sailmaker for the sails – He is a good and cheerful aged man.'

'Cheerful' was hardly an epithet which could be applied to Joseph. On 12 February he paced the deck in a gloomy mood reflecting on the fate of all living things on board should the ship sink, as many of the passengers feared it would:

> There are four and sixty souls,
> Three dogs, two cats and a German,
> Eight good sheep, six pigs and fowls
> And Taff the soul-less Welshman!
>
> This voyage is only a painful reminder of the fragile spark of our existence. We could all soon drown – cease to exist beneath the boisterous waves. And then what?

Joseph complained that the weather was so unpredictable that it could change in the space of one hour. 'The clipper bounced like a cork, and below deck the lanterns swung crazily and nothing remained secure. I had to lash my tea can to the table, as everything is on a slide . . . there is no place to roll about in the bunk . . . my shoulders are too broad.' The ocean became awesome. 'Mountainous seas crashed with 500 tons of water washing over the decks from the port side . . . everything rattling . . . sheets of spray engulfing everything . . . waves rose up like huge peaks . . . foam everywhere!' Sometimes the ship made little headway and the wind was so ferocious that 'the ropes snapped and the sail hung flapping about having been rent to pieces, leaving the ropes on the mizzen mast caught full spread in the wind.'

On 22 February, 'the sixty ninth day of the voyage the ship was sailing every day in the Latitude 48°, being steered East North East.' The temperature had again plummeted and in the distance Joseph could see mountains 'full of snow and ice.' He found it intolerably cold in bed but was fortunate enough to be able to purchase a 'velvet collared overcoat' from his cabin-mate Mr Martin, who had come better prepared than the Welshman. The sight of the ship engulfed in boiling foam and blanked out by the thick spray now unnerved even Joseph, who had previously found the tempestuous seas an exciting sight. Having already witnessed the destruction of passing ships, he now feared that the force of the wind would snap the vessel's three towering masts. It was with great relief, therefore, that he was informed by one of the crew that 'they would reach Melbourne in three weeks.' But it was to prove a long twenty-one days!

As the ship shuddered and shook, Joseph complained that the food was inadequate. 'I had a poor dinner of 2 ounces of pea soup and a sea biscuit with cold tea.' Even in the teeth of fierce gales he continued to keep his diary but confessed, 'I find it very difficult to write . . . Candles are getting short . . . and only one lamp between two berths. The incessant noise drives me mad . . . the wind screams in the rigging, the waves crash all round, there is creaking and groaning all night long . . . the poop's bells keep going and the one in the forecastle strikes every half hour . . . But thankfully we are being driven at the rate of 14 knots an hour covering 300 miles a day.'

On 25 February Joseph begged Captain Watson for some

cheese to relieve an upset stomach, and was given it 'in lieu of butter'. Nevertheless, he began to be critical of the course chosen by the Captain:

> 27 February 1869
>
> The ship rolls . . . heavy waves dashed against stern and sides. It appears they will sail thousands of miles from the nearest course for the sake of fair wind. They keep too much to the south for the trade winds. If we were on the right course, it would use moderate weather – All steamers take that course . . . We have not seen any other vessel for a long time.

But, of course, the *Eurynome* was not powered by steam, and was obliged to sail south to catch the trade winds – however much the discomfort and unease felt by the Welshman.

The masters of ships carrying emigrants to Australia competed with each other in their efforts to reduce sailing time. In 1854 the *James Baines* had completed the voyage from Liverpool in the record time of 63 days. The *Eurynome* was certainly not in this league and Joseph was uncomfortably aware of the fact that the route she was taking had proved to be disastrous for many ships. His experiences by this time had also convinced him that she was not entirely suitable for passengers:

> 27 February 1869
>
> She is a good sailing vessel but was never intended as a passenger ship and ought never to be engaged in that trade . . . She is too wet and heavy laden . . . she is beaten about furiously. The sails were taken in except eight – They have about twenty-seven set sails, sometimes above 2,000 yards of canvas.

It is somewhat ironic that in December 1868, the month of his departure, the following advertisement appeared in *The Cambrian*, a newspaper circulating in South Wales:

> PANAMA ROUTE: To New Zealand in 48 days and Australia in 56 days. Per Steamers leaving South-hampton the 2nd of every month. This cheap, direct and pleasant route has been in successful operation since June 1866 ... Passengers go direct from the Atlantic Steamer across the Isthmus on board the Pacific Steamer.

This route would surely have provided him with a much more pleasant passage, minimising much of the tedium and discomfort endured on the *Eurynome*. But the hurried nature of his own departure had not allowed him to give much thought to the most appropriate means of reaching Australia. There was nothing for it, therefore, but to suffer the rigours of the long voyage.

By 28 February many of the passengers became ill and Joseph himself felt extremely indisposed with 'looseness and spent much of my time in my berth, reading and lying in bed. No passenger can remain on deck which is seldom free of water ... We are sailing with the wind and waves. The Captain and the crew are looking cheerful and think we will be at Port Phillip in 14 days. The sailors see no danger:

> All hands are running to and fro
> Along the slippr'y deck,
> Called and ordered where to go
> To lose, to heave and check.

St David's Day, 1 March, was unforgettable, not because it commemorated the patron Saint, but because they experienced 'tremendous seas which visited the main decks several times right over the poop, over the forecastle and sides.' Severe damage was inflicted on the vessel. Joseph called it 'by far the worst gale and squall we had yet':

1 March 1869
Many things washed overboard . . . The Hen roost and shed . . . The second cabin Ladies Water Closet were completely carried away. The sheep pens were overturned, but saved with their inmates; some of the fowl went . . . Ship rolling heavily but going swiftly . . . and with the currents or else we could not bear so well. Dangerous shipping on deck . . . very few sails out . . . which are tightly filled and hard pressed by the wind. A wild and heavy sea all day.

Still plagued by his stomach ailment, Joseph once again successfully pleaded with the Captain for his usual relief. 'I had some fine cheese from the Captain this evening which must be kept private.' The following day brought no abatement of the storm, 'sprays dashing over from Port side . . . ship rolls badly . . . all chief officers are on their constant look out.' The loud command for 'all hands' was given and Joseph, braving the elements, went on deck to watch the sailors clinging to the towering masts set against the massive spread of canvas billowing in the wind.

Awestruck by the sight of the sailors pitting themselves against the elements, Joseph went below immediately to paint a dramatic scene in verse:

2 March 1869
As I was an eye witness I composed the following movements.

> The order came with out a check
> All hands directly upon deck
> From many quarters up came all
> Ready trim'd to meet the squall,
> All were ordered by their guide
> To climb the shrouds on every side.
> The gallant Boatswain never dreads,
> He took the lead, went over heads . . .
> Nine both sides the waving mast
> Were coiling on their bellies fast,
> All hands and feet were grappling hard,
> In equal row, half round the yard . . .
> Nineteen all, and a fearless lot,
> And each was busy at his knot . . .
> The ship will thus reach Melbourne soon
> And out again sail for Rangoon

It is not surprising that James Nicol Forbes, a notable clipper captain, coined the slogan 'Hell or Melbourne' as his ship hurtled through the gales of the 'Roaring Forties', and Joseph's account of the voyage vividly illustrates this experience:

> Heavy rolling of the ship . . . Great rattling and moving in about our berths; some were thrown clearly out of bed . . . Heavy seas came on main deck . . . This ship . . . is not nearly as big as a thimble in these frothing, foamy waters . . . which are as hell!'

But for Joseph, there remained many other kinds of hell. While he struggled to keep an exhaustive account of the journey in nigh impossible conditions, hell for him was also other people. The taunts of his fellow passengers continued, and one malign person even ripped out some of the pages of his diary. There was also the need to be secretive, since the shipping line officials generally frowned upon the keeping of diaries. Captains feared that incriminating incidents might be recorded in such journals to be used later in evidence against a ship's company. All diaries, therefore, were subject to scrutiny. This might account for all the obsequious references to the Captain and his crew that appear frequently in Joseph's diary. He called Captain Watson 'excellent, wise, good,' and referred to the crew as 'brave, disciplined, and expert'. He obviously believed that he was writing for posterity for he occasionally addresses his potential readership directly:

3 March 1869

The reader may see by the map and chart that we have sailed far south and that was to catch the Western Wind. They call it a Trade Wind . . . Should this wind continue we will be in Melbourne in another seven days.

The dreadful storms which raged on St David's Day proved to be the climax of this fraught period on board the ship. On 4 March it was being 'steered East North East' and Joseph, at last, was able to write, 'We are approaching the Colony.' For the first time in weeks the storms abated, the temperature rose and the passengers were able to walk the deck in safety. 'More sails set up to-day. They prepare for land . . . The Captain is walking to and fro . . . and makes out for something useful to do for all the crew.' The ship was still being driven along at great speed and Joseph was eager to provide precise data concerning its course:

5 March 1869

We are about Latitude 42° and Longitude 125° South.

This will show the reader the ship was steered as far South as the temperature allowed; two more days sailing would take her among the icebergs. We are within 1,000 miles of our destination. The ship sailed about eight hundred miles during the last three days — but had been above three weeks sailing the same distance at the commencement of the voyage.

Despite Joseph's previous misgivings concerning the route followed, he now accepted that Captain Watson had been justified in his eagerness to catch the trade winds. He reported, 'All well so far, and so is everyone on board as to their state of health.' Apart from some minor upsets such as diarrhoea, sickness and a mild attack of food poisoning, no serious illness had broken out on board ship. Unlike countless other voyages to Australia, there had been no death on board the *Eurynome*. Indeed, with a touch of black humour Joseph wrote that, 'Neither man nor beast has been very ill — but I do not know about the rats which are very numerous in the cargo.'

It is interesting to note that when Mary Jones of Llanfihangel-y-Pennant, north Wales, emigrated to Ballarat in 1856 on the clipper *White Star* she witnessed four burials at sea and also there were four births on board ship.

On arrival in Australia the port physician would inspect the *Eurynome* for cleanliness and the absence of disease. If any hazards to health were found, the ship would be quarantined. Joseph was well aware of this. When, on 1 March, he felt too indisposed to undertake his duty as the cook, he paid another passenger 1 shilling and 6 pence to act in his stead. He was too frightened to report sick lest it might affect his chances of disembarkation at Melbourne:

1 March 1869

I could have a certificate from the Doctor, but it might go against my landing in Melbourne, and my age is unfavourable. I might be better off for not telling the truth.

It was mandatory for each ship to have a doctor on board but Joseph had little faith in his abilities and disparagingly referred to him as a 'bloody quack'. 'They say the Doctor is paid a bonus for each of us who arrives alive . . . It will be no thanks to him if we do!'

Each day's sailing now took them closer to Australia and a sense of eager anticipation spread among the passengers:

5 March 1869

Some are ailing for land . . . There are those who think Australia is full of honey and gold, and the seamen will have an opportunity to spend money.

As the ship sailed north into calmer waters, Joseph reflected on the 'cursing and swearing' he had heard from the sailors during the hazardous days of the voyage:

Dam the bloody ship and dam the bloody spray
Dam the bloody fish we ate the other day,
Dam the bloody day, which yields to bloody night,
Dam the bloody moon which does not always light,
Dam the bloody sun, he is wanted when tis cold,
Dam the bloody time to Satan I am sold.

Although these sentiments were attributed to the sailors, one suspects that they also reflect Joseph's own subliminal feelings during the voyage. As the vessel entered the final leg of the voyage and the other passengers became increasingly excited, his own mood became morbidly subdued and contrasted sharply with the cheerful disposition of all around him. He pessimistically recalled the fate of the *Royal Charter*, which had foundered in 1859 near Moelfre off the coast of Anglesey with the loss of 400 lives, while on voyage from Australia. Jeremiah like, he wrote:

> 6 March 1869
>
> There is great talk on board of being in Melbourne early next week. Time will tell! The *Royal Charter* was within thirty miles of Liverpool, she was bound there from the Colonies, and a great talking was on board about a merry landing at Liverpool. We cannot foretell things with any certainty. Enjoy and take advantage of the present – we cannot either calculate or rely on the past or future.

Joseph describes the ship as 'bouncing ahead on the South Atlantic Ocean, she made a distance of 300 miles yesterday.' But the food had become almost inedible. 'I had a poor dinner of a small piece of nasty beef and dry biscuits.' Having survived the hammering of the 'Roaring Forties', Captain Watson now ordered his crew to make the vessel shipshape. The two cannons on board, kept in case of an emergency, were cleaned. Each could take 'six pounds of powder' and the sailors asked whether any of the passengers had beeswax to apply to the guns to stop them from rusting. The masts and bow sprit were cleaned and painted from top to bottom. On 8 March the 'land chain was hauled out by the seamen. It had six anchors and a heavy grapple with four hooks. The grappler was only used when the ship dragged her anchors . . . The crew had washed the deck and oiled the mahogany oars and handpicks etc.' Within a short space of time the whole ship had been transformed.

All around sea creatures once again appeared. An enormous whale broke the surface blowing water up as high as half-mast and Joseph had the opportunity of observing an albatross at close quarters. 'It was,' he wrote, 'very large with strong webbed feet much bigger than the common goose.' He watched it 'taking many fish and eat them just like our cranes do with eels.'

10 March was a memorable day. As usual, he had been looking around the vessel and had watched one of the sailors climbing precariously up the highest mast to scan the seas. At 1.30 p.m. the sailor descended quickly and told Joseph to climb the mast if he wanted to see land. Fortunately, the other sailors did not think it was a good idea for Joseph to attempt such a dangerous undertaking:

10 March 1869

I was not allowed to go up the mast, therefore I told the chief mate who came there directly. He ascended the mast, and before he was half way up he called Land Ahoy! All rushed up on deck with great glee on hearing the long expected news.

The passengers were euphoric; the thought of land gave rise to unbounded jubilation. But as the cheers resounded from all quarters, Joseph's heart sank. The 'Roaring Forties' had been terrifying, but they were as nothing compared to the fear that now gripped him. The ship had been a capsule that had cocooned him, temporarily, from his own troubled world. The end of the voyage meant that he would once again have to face reality. He was frightened; turning to his diary he confides his anxiety:

Everybody is cheerful, except myself. Some are going

home soon, others to meet their friends and relations at the harbour. Not a single acquaintance for Joseph. Only a strange place, strange people and no hope of meeting any acquaintance. Poor Jo!

As so often happens at the end of a period of intense excitement, a vacuum now set in, giving way to crippling doubts and uncertainties. All the old demons surged up causing him to cry out in despair:

O! What a dark fate I have been given! I'm sorry that I did not embark for North America to see my brothers... I could have seen plenty of nature there and be far enough away from my enemies in the old country. The effects of these enemies will very likely shorten my life. My heart is crushed. It may be my fate because I was crushed in my mother's womb which has caused many a disagreeable hour to me on this voyage through fouls and so on.

This morbid self-analysis was soon banished by an order from Captain Watson to the second-class passengers to clean out their berths. On completion of the chore, the Captain presented the men with a bottle of gin and the ladies with a bottle of claret. When the ship was within 12 miles of the 'Heads', which formed the entrance to Port Phillip Bay, the 'Union Jack was hoisted on the foremast and the red flag was placed half mast on the mizzen mast. This was the signal for the pilot to come on board.' Port Phillip Bay, named after Captain Arthur Phillip, the governor of New South Wales, was the safest and most extensive harbour on the shores of the Bass Strait.

As the *Eurynome* entered the bay Joseph caught his first fleeting glimpse of the new land:

11 March 1869

They prepare to enter the Heads of the Bay to-night. It is a narrow deep place with a current of tide. We have about 30 miles of Bay to sail over – How beautiful the clear sky looks – the southern lights are a grand sight . . . about a score of different lights to be seen ahead of us . . . The bush fires are throwing a good light to view the bordering brushwood which are half covered by drifts of sand, like the snow drifts in Wales, but more dreadful to man and beast.

With the end of the voyage in sight, Joseph reveals not a little anxiety about the fate of his diary, and adds a grovelling verse as an extra insurance should the Captain scrutinise his long and detailed record of the journey:

11 March 1869
I don't know whether the Captain will demand the diaries . . . Anyone found writing against him will be guilty of High Treason!
The voyage alto-gether
I have no fear to tell,
Could not be managed better,
All sail all right and well.

But he had no cause for concern; the Captain was far too busy to bother about Joseph's Journal.

During the voyage Joseph had, more or less, honoured a final pledge he had made before leaving Wales that he would resist the temptations of alcohol. Although he drank a Christmas and New Year toast, and occasionally attempted to purchase beer to quench his thirst, he mainly drank cold tea or water. Possibly, his removal from the various tensions that had beset him at home made it easier to resist the drink, plus the fact that he could not afford to pay the exorbitant prices charged on board the ship. Whatever the reason, during the voyage, he managed to control a habit that, in Wales, had almost brought him to the brink of destruction.

On 12 March 1869 the moment came which everyone had longed for. The anchor was finally dropped and the vessel secured alongside a wharf. At a quarter to seven, six government officers arrived; the Captain handed them the proper documents, and 'All well' was reported. Had Joseph known the future fate of the *Eurynome* he might have felt a greater sense of relief on landing safely, for in 1881 the ship disappeared without trace with the loss of all lives while on a voyage to Australia. Another clipper, *The Gossamer*, which left Liverpool at the same time as the *Eurynome* also sank with the loss of 13 lives, including the captain and his wife.

At last, after three months of storms, searing heat, intense cold and much angst, the long journey was over. But a longer one was about to begin.

CHAPTER 12
I SHOULDER MY SWAG

On 12 March 1869, after 87 consecutive days at sea, Joseph finally planted his infamous 'hobnail boots' on Australian soil. He stood a total stranger on a distant shore feeling desperately alone. He had reached the new land, but could he invent a new self? Already, he was assailed by doubts. 'My heart is crushed, and a man cannot do wonders without having the right heart in the right place!'

His ship had docked at Sandridge at 4 o'clock, and he had been enthralled by the beauty of Hobson's Bay:

> How wide and beauteous does the Bay
> Form'd by nature look to-day,
> Border'd white by chalky ground
> With growing brushwood all around.

At Sandridge there was intense activity. 'I can see ships from all quarters of the world . . . some from Bristol, and many from America . . . all discharging their different cargoes.' He found himself caught up in a seething mass of immigrants, all anxiously seeking a new start in the colony. 'There were exhausted women and pale faced children . . . tough looking diggers carrying heavy packs with pickaxes and shovels . . . with much shouting and confusion.' Joseph had disembarked carrying only his Welsh Bible and his diary. He had wisely left the remainder of his meagre possessions on board to be collected the following day. The ship was berthed a distance of four miles from Melbourne because navigation up the River Yarra was too difficult. Joseph was therefore obliged to pay nine shillings for a return ticket on the railway line which connected the town with the harbour. He considered it expensive, but previous immigrants had been forced to travel by boat or punts up the Yarra River and had had their possessions stolen and pillaged even before reaching Melbourne.

Stepping out onto the streets of Melbourne proved to be both a climatic and a cultural shock. Almost immediately, the scorching sun and the heat reflected from the hard stone sidewalks disorientated him. It made him feel 'dizzy and unwell'. Nevertheless, he was impressed by 'this grand new city' and claimed that, 'Melbourne had everything to compete with London – the streets were clean with streams of water running both sides between the roadway and the walks. It was a busy, lively and wonderful place.' Sweating in his heavy tweeds he trudged in search of the Melbourne Post Office, which he had given as his Australian address. During the voyage he had sent a stream of letters to Wales and, after three months away from his family, despite all the past bitterness, he was desperate for news. 'I did call at the Post Office ... but no letter for Joseph there ... I am very anxious to know whether my letters arrived.' Feeling low in spirit he wrote, 'Poor Jo!' Having taken the decision to leave Wales, he would now have to reap the consequences and they were to prove more hurtful than he had ever imagined.

'Troubled by clouds of flies under the merciless Antipodean sun,' he searched for lodgings, and finally found a bed at the

1. Blaenplwyf, Llanfihangel Ystrad, a traditional Welsh farmhouse. Joseph Jenkins was born here in 1818.

2. Joseph's mother, Elinor Jenkins, was a strong personality and highly respected in her locality. She was a great influence on her son.
(Picture: Miss Frances Evans)

3. Trecefel. Joseph and Betty's marital home. Through hard work Joseph made it one of the best farms in Cardiganshire.
(Picture: Bethan Phillips)

4. Tregaron Railway Station. Joseph played a key role in bringing the M&M Railway to Cardiganshire. *(Picture: NLW)*

5. The early locomotive *Aberystwyth*. *(Picture: NLW)*

6. James Benbow, the engine driver, otherwise known as 'the Admiral'. Joseph counted him among his friends. *(Picture: NLW)*

7. David Davies of Llandinam, the millionaire industrialist and entrepreneur. Joseph supported him during the construction of the railway and later assisted him in his efforts to be an M.P. *(Picture: NLW)*

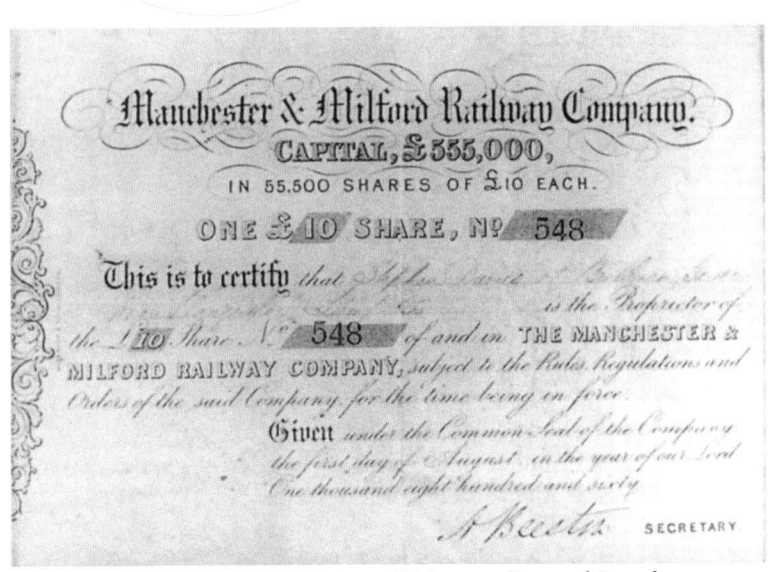

8. An M&M Railway share. With crusading zeal Joseph persuaded scores of the inhabitants of mid Cardiganshire to buy these shares. *(Picture: Mrs Mair Owen)*

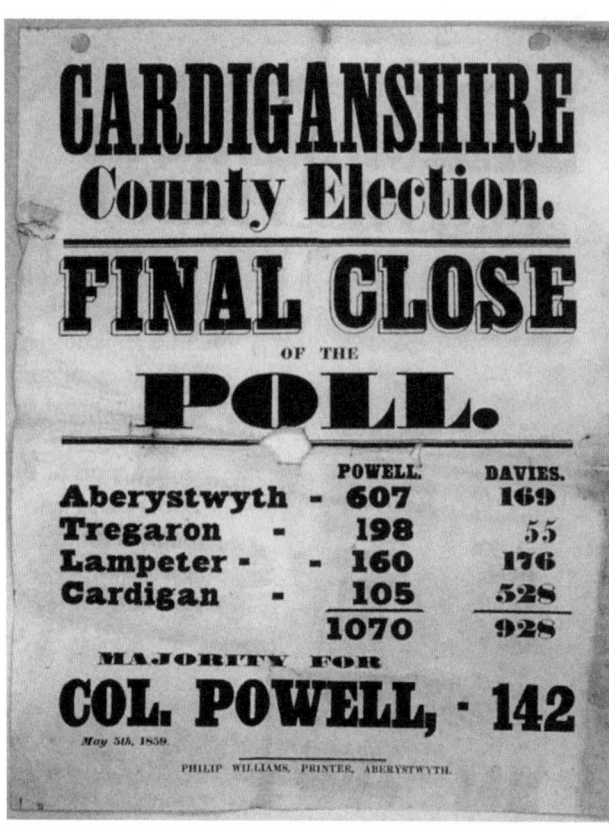

9. A poster giving the result of the 1859 election won by the Tory Colonel Powell of Nanteos. During this contest Joseph supported the Tories. Although a radical at heart he was prepared to switch his allegiance to gain favour with the gentry.
(Ceredigion Museum)

10. A leaflet showing the result of the 1868 election in Cardiganshire when the Liberals won and the Tory hegemony was finally broken. By supporting the Tory candidate in this landmark election, Joseph alienated both his friends and his family.
(Ceredigion Museum)

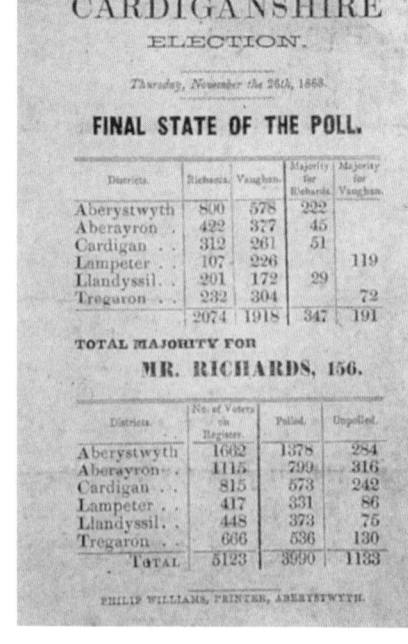

11. Joseph was an avid collector of the maps published by *The Weekly Dispatch*. His collection included a map of Victoria dated 1858. This may have influenced his ultimate choice of destination.
(Picture: Mrs Mair Owen)

12. A list of the second class passengers on the *SS Eurynome*. Joseph Jenkins was numbered 744. Since the Welsh were not recognised as a separate ethnic group, he is listed as an English farmer.
(Picture: Miss Frances Evans)

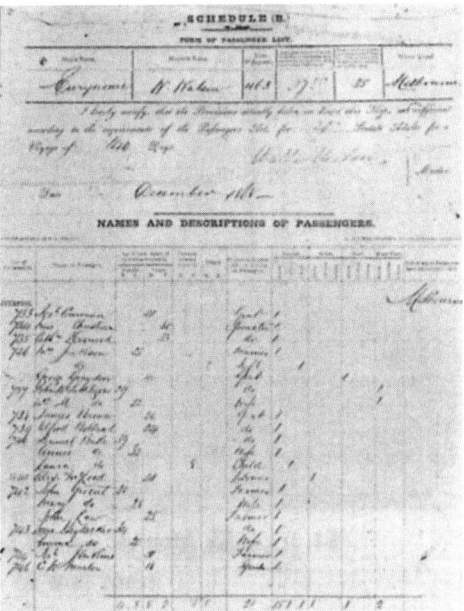

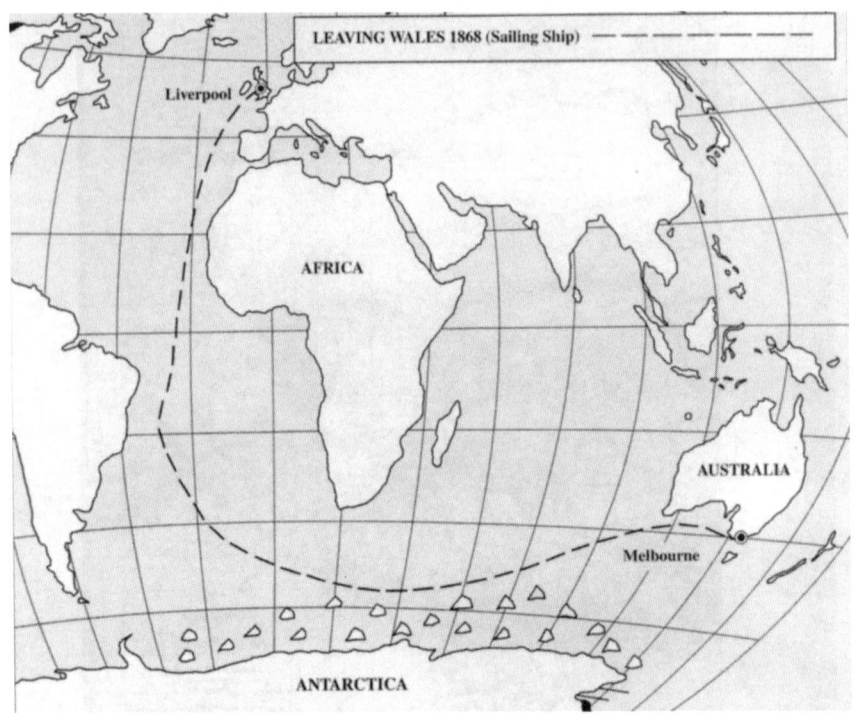

13. The Great Circle route to Australia followed by ships prior to the opening of the Suez Canal. Joseph chronicled in his diaries the hazards and discomforts experienced by passengers. His account is a valuable contribution to maritime history.
(Map: Ruth Evans/Siôn Ilar)

14. Joseph's port of arrival in Australia. He paid nine shillings train fare to reach Melbourne.

27th of March 1869
Queen's Head Melbourne

I was up early and before the sun appeared above the clear Eastern horizon. I went down to the Post office and posted three letters for Great Britain, one to my wife, one to my brother Jenkin, and one to the Editor of the Welshman. The Thermometer at the General Post Office was up at 70 so early in the morning. I had a good breakfast after returning. I intend to take up my "Swag" and leave my box clothes and many other things at Mr. Thomas until I will be able to pay the amount of 14/6. I hope that health honesty and integrity will be my guides, and let things turn out better than my expectation at this moment. It looks gloomy. Cheer up Joseph. Scores of Swag men pass to and fro every place on the road three or four times a day. Now for a life in the Bush. I have no trade, and was advised not to depend upon any lest I would be without the contents of my Swag. Thrashing is over, ploughing is not in as it is too dry. Farmers are disheartened in all quarters —

15. A page from Joseph's diary written soon after his arrival in Australia. It reflects his initial sense of disillusion concerning his new country.

16. Plantation and Sturt Street, Ballarat, as Joseph would have seen them in 1869. Ballarat was one of the most important centres of gold-mining and attracted many thousands of Welshmen. Joseph regularly attended the *Eisteddfod* held in the town.
(Picture: State Library of Victoria)

17. Maldon in 1872. Like Ballarat it was a gold-mining town with a strong Welsh presence. Joseph eventually settled here and became a well-known figure.

Waterman's Hotel. His first night on Australian soil was a waking nightmare. He slept very little. 'I was plagued by mosquitoes and feeling badly indisposed on account of the excessive heat.' The following day, Sunday, he set out to look for a Unitarian Chapel where he hoped to meet some compatriots, but his search was in vain. Once again the heat affected him badly. 'I feel unwell with a swollen head, body and legs.' He longed for the 'benign skies of Wales with their drifting, chalk white clouds and the soft rain.' He was in a state of physical and psychological distress. When he turned to write his diary on 16 March, the thoughts of times past overwhelmed him:

> Up at the appearance of the sun . . . But too far to reach Tregaron Fair after being there for the last 20 years . . . I do think of my friends who used to call by Trecefel to-wards the fair upon this day . . . I should think that it is not so hot there as it is here!

This emotional upheaval was more than he had bargained for. Having abandoned the close-knit community of Tregaron, he no longer had stability or status; instead of finding a refuge from his problems, he found himself steeped in impoverished obscurity. He had fled from all that was familiar to him only to be faced with different challenges and new burdens to bear. 'I enquired for work in the Town. No go. I did advertise myself, but no correspondence. Harvest over, land too hard and Labourers plenty. Nothing for Jo!'

On Wednesday 17 March Joseph again called at the Post Office, 'but no clue of any letters. I should like to know whether my letters arrived in Cardiganshire.' He found many shops and firms closed. 'It was a regular St Patrick holiday. The

Irishmen are very jealous about the day and they are very numerous here.' He found their celebrations an annoyance. 'I was kept awake nearly all night by the great zeal of the Irish with their fiddle playing.'

To Joseph, 'Everything in Australia seems to be back to front. Here, the sun passes on the left hand, contra to what it is in the old country.' But the sights of Melbourne were a pleasure to behold. 'I have seen all sorts of carriages drawn by the best horses that I ever saw . . . trotting and galloping with wonderful speed . . . At the dock a ship from Liverpool is loaded with horses to-day, not for England, but for Calcutta! The price of a good horse is £17. The Australians breed excellent animals.'

On the morning of 20 March Joseph found the presence of the mosquitoes intolerable. 'I was up at half past five for the mosquitoes . . . you must cover yourself in bed for these poisonous creatures.' For the third time he retraced his steps to the Post Office, and this time he was rewarded with a letter from Margaret, his eldest daughter. However, it only added to his agony. 'The letter made me cry a little when it said that Tom and Anne were calling for me.' He was so distressed that he walked to the port to see if he could procure a ticket on the ship *The Agamemnon* due to sail for Tilbury. However, he did not have sufficient money. Instead, he sent home his Log Book of the voyage in the care of Richard Jones, a compatriot, 'who hailed from Cricieth, Caernarfon.' Fortunately, this diary was safely delivered to his brother Jenkin at Blaenplwyf. In addition to the account of the voyage, it also contains some lines, hastily written, seeking to justify his decision to flee Trecefel for Australia, and possibly to assuage his feelings of guilt:

March 1869 Melbourne

This is my 40th Journal. I wish it to be kept. I was engaged in canvassing for a proper member to secure my native county . . . and looking out for a ship to embark in for the colonies. Both ideas may turn out a bitter sorrow to me. I was opposed in my politics even by my youngest children . . . I have done my best . . . and too much to bring forward the benefit of others. Neglecting my own business, which is a great fault – being my principal fault. My dear children, take care of yourselves first if you can. I dare any man to find any fault upon me personally except that I served others.

Joseph Jenkins

The following Sunday he again went in search of a Welsh Chapel. This time he was successful. 'I found a Methodist Chapel where I had a Welsh Sermon by the Reverend William Thomas of Llandysul . . . at 6 in the evening I went to-wards the Unitarian Chapel and had a sermon there.' However, in spite of the spiritual sustenance in his own language, his other problems were mounting.

By 22 March Joseph's money was fast running out. In Wales, Australia had been portrayed as the 'Lucky Country' where a man could quickly make his fortune; the reality was different. He had still been unable to find work and what faced him now was sheer survival. 'Up early . . . on an empty belly. Went in search of something to do and eat. I did walk 6 miles before breakfast . . . Melbourne is a place of extremes, where everything of the best quality can be obtained for money . . . It is new and the best men of the age were the planners. Unlike

London, the neat homes are all much lower built than our cities in general. On the streets I met native country men of different counties in Wales, and had the pleasure to talk the Welsh language at a distance of 16,000 miles from Trecefel!'

On 24 March Joseph was relieved to find new lodgings with a fellow Welshman, Mr Ellis Thomas, at the Caernarvonshire Temperance Boarding House, 132 Queen's Street, Melbourne. This was a less expensive hotel and he shared a room with two Welshmen on their way from Ballarat to dig coal in New South Wales. The following morning he set off early in search of work. Although Melbourne had previously captivated him, disenchantment quickly set in. On 25 March, he grumbled, 'this colony does not look very promising for immigrants!'

As he wandered the streets in search of work, he found himself accosted by dubious characters who were eager to get their hands on his money. 'I have to be on my guard,' he wrote, 'there is more liberty to sin here than I'd ever imagined back home. It appears that people are against emigration; as soon as they will get all the money from the immigrants, they scoff at them, and tell them to go home, as if they could enjoy the colony themselves without doing anything unless they can meet an emigrant man to rob and abuse.' He was now less than impressed by the motives of many of the inhabitants of Melbourne, and his earlier enchantment of the place soon turned to disillusion: 'This town is full of life and I have found out the gold diggers sooner that I wished to see them. They are up to many things here that London, Liverpool and Birmingham would be ashamed to do. Should the sharpers of such place be put together and coupled with those of Paris and New York, here are the tops!'

Joseph found that Australia was still a new country struggling to find an identity and 'a place of swirling uncertainties'. After 1830, many immigrants had been lured by the offer of a free passage. These were known as 'Bounty Immigrants'. At the time, there was a great shortage of skilled workers, particularly masons, carpenters, blacksmiths, wheelwrights, and shepherds, and such people were encouraged to settle in Australia.

With the discovery of gold in 1851, a flood of new immigrants had poured into Victoria in search of 'fast fortunes', and by 1852 vast numbers had landed in Melbourne. Until that time Australia had been the regular repository for convicted felons from Britain. But in 1852 the Mayor and dignitaries of Melbourne wrote to Queen Victoria protesting against the deportation of criminals to Tasmania, as they quickly crossed over to the colony of Victoria. The last convict ship, the *Hougoument*, arrived in Freemantle, Western Australia, as late as January 1868 with 279 prisoners, among whom were many Irish Fenians. When Joseph came in 1869 to exorcise his own demons, unfortunately for him he had arrived at a time of chronic unemployment following a severe seven-year drought.

On 26 March Joseph decided to explore the countryside around Melbourne, but was shocked by the scenes he encountered:

> The state of the country is deplorable to the utmost, looking more like a scorched hearth than grass fields . . . Cattle are bellowing for water and dying by the score. The stench of their carcasses is almost unbearable.

The smell of the putrefying bodies of thousands of sheep and cattle clogging the air deeply offended his sensitivity as a farmer.

It compounded his depression as he sought in vain for work. 'I walked hard with very little to eat for three miles . . . it looks gloomy, no work, no money, and no friend.'

As Joseph returned from his search for work along the muddy bank of the River Yarra, he witnessed a tragic incident which shocked him and made him realise that the ethos of this new colony differed greatly from the close-knit community he had left in Wales. On the river he saw hundreds of pleasure boats, with many ladies rowing and sculling. Suddenly, two boats collided and three young fellows were thrown into the water. Two swam ashore, the third, a young lad of about 16 years, disappeared. No assistance was offered to the crew of the capsized boat and Joseph was astonished by the callous indifference of people all around.

'What puzzled me above all things,' he wrote, 'is that a police constable was employed to keep the other boats away during the search. He [the constable] could neither persuade nor stop the people to sing and play about as if nothing had happened . . . They took not the least notice of the case more than if a common cat had been the victim of a watery grave. Even the relatives of the drowned young man were too drunk to assist in the search for him, and some of them commented that they would let nothing spoil their merry Good Friday.' Back in Tregaron Good Friday would have been as sacred as a Sunday. Here, it was a day for the unbridled pursuit of pleasure. Joseph sadly concluded that, 'Antichristianity prevails everywhere!'

His own position was becoming increasingly precarious and his lack of money was now a serious problem. He returned to his lodging but was 'obliged to sleep on a sofa in the dining room.' He already owed Mr Thomas, the landlord, 14 shillings and 6 pence for food and lodging. Despite searching hard, he had been unable to find work. Melbourne was still struggling to assimilate the vast numbers of miners who had flooded in to search for gold. Having failed in their quest, these men now sought any form of employment in order to survive. In the face of such competition, Joseph harboured no illusions about his chances. 'It looks bad. No work. No money. No friend or acquaintance.' Two lines of poetry reflect his feeling of destitution:

> I wander like a tramp
> On an empty stomach with an empty pocket. †

Joseph's only hope was to become an itinerant worker, or a swagman. Even then, his chances of employment were slim, for there were already 200,000 swagmen trudging the roads of Victoria in search of occasional work. In an attempt to lift his own spirits he wrote, 'Cheer up Joseph – Let things turn out better than my expectation at this moment.'

On 27 March, he rose early 'before the sun appeared above the clear Eastern horizon' and went down to the Post Office, where he posted letters to 'my wife, my brother Jenkin, and the Editor of the *Welshman* . . . The thermometer at the Post Office already registered 70°.' On returning to his hotel he was given a 'good breakfast' by Mr Ellis Thomas and he decided to leave in search of work. He left behind many of his books, his clothes and certain other possessions as a deposit for the money owing for his lodgings. Rolling his essentials in his blanket, he wrote, 'I shoulder my swag.'

His first fortnight in Australia had been a demeaning experience and he was now compelled to face up to the reality of his situation. He had no alternative other than to take to the road. He wrote, 'I will be torched by the sun and become an old crawler.' This was a derogatory term used to describe an aged ex-convict drifter. What would his family and friends in Tregaron make of him now?

CHAPTER 13

GOLD FEVER

'Now for a life in the Bush,' wrote Joseph on 27 March as he started his trek along the Castlemaine to Bendigo highway. The time was 10 a.m. The sun was already blazing down and the swag on his shoulders weighed in excess of 70 pounds. He carried his cooking utensils, his blanket, a few spare clothes, his medicine box containing laudanum, some books, a pen, ink, and his precious Journal. Before setting out he had expressed the hope that 'health, honesty and integrity will be my guides.' He travelled with the minimum of possessions because he had been warned of the dangers that lay ahead. 'I have no spade and was advised not to depend upon any lest the contents of my swag be stolen.' Joseph was only too aware that the prospects for work were limited. 'Threshing is over, ploughing is not in, as it is too dry. Farmers are disheartened in all quarters. It does not look good.' As he continued on his way he encountered 'scores of swagmen' and, like them, he had to contend with the elements.

In conditions of extreme aridity, trudging ankle deep in dust on unmade roads, he complained, 'I was obliged to lay down for the dust which was driven in clouds before variable gusts of wind . . . For the first time in my life I begin to appreciate the value of water.' His own dew-soaked meadows now seemed light years away as the sudden dust storms 'choked my throat, stung my eyes . . . and half suffocated me.'

Unfortunately for Joseph, he had set out on the day of the Melbourne Races, which was one of the most popular events in the district. He referred to the Australians as 'racing mad and betting mad', as he was being overtaken by 'hundreds of different vehicles thundering and clattering past – with the horses kicking up the dust like fine snow on their way to the Race Course.' Curiosity got the better of him and he admits, 'I did turn in order to see races once in my life time.' He was fascinated by what he saw. 'I was there just in time to witness the first hurdle race. The gallant horses came in very near to each other . . . Everything could be had for money . . . a glass of beer costs six pence. The Railway half encircles the course and four engines were in full motion all day . . . A great many wagers were laid from 1/- to £1,000!'

Unable to resist the temptation, he placed a shilling on a horse and, to his delight, it won; but when he went to collect his winnings the bookmaker had disappeared. Joseph was learning by painful experience the need for vigilance in his newly adopted country. It was money that he could ill afford to lose. Feeling peeved, he wrote, 'Here, there is no morality. Money is God! No more races for Joseph.'

Meanwhile he travelled 'along bare and dry fields calling at different farms for something to do.' But it was the same old story. 'No go! All disheartened!' In the rapidly approaching dusk he found a bed for sixpence 'under the shadow of the garden trees of the priest of St Paul's Catholic Church 9 miles from Melbourne.' He left the following morning without breakfast but was fortunate to have something to eat at a hospitable farmhouse. By 11 a.m. he was sweating profusely under the weight of his swag and saw from his thermometer that the temperature was 118°F. 'No wind and nearly unbearable for me . . . No water, but I had a drop with an old Irishman.' In the heat his need for water was desperate, but there were other dangers, undreamt of in Wales:

> March 1869
> As I was walking I saw something moving on my right hand side ahead in the dust. It was a black snake about 2 foot long. As I went forward I was challenged, its head was well up all the time. I had no stick and I threw my 'swag' between us. I picked up stones but I missed my aim. The snake crept outside the fence and I missed it the second time. It then slipped into a load of big stones. I was glad of that.

Having evaded the snake he came across another sickening scene in a large park. He estimated that, 'some 22,000 sheep were dying for want of water. The stench from the carcasses of dead sheep was so abominable that I was obliged to retire under a tree about 200 yards from the roadside.' After a few more hours on the road, darkness descended suddenly. 'It began to rain, attended by thunder and lightning . . . I came to the next Hotel and begged a bed for sixpence, being my last. I had a drop of water, but very small. I retired with an empty belly . . . slept badly and left without breakfast . . . Hotel keepers are the most inhuman beings.'

The following morning he 'went at a very slow pace about 2 miles an hour . . . no sign of work.' Suffering once again from severe thirst he was forced to give a traveller a pair of gloves which he had purchased in Liverpool, in return for a 'pint of small beer'. Longing for a drink of pure spring water he continued, 'walking west, north west, my face to-wards Trecefel, but I must have another two lives to reach it at this rate!'

During the afternoon he met a farmer who described to him the parlous state of agriculture in the colony. He complained to Joseph that the situation had become one of life or death, 'This is the seventh bad season . . . One more will settle the contest of living!' He then showed him his 'very bad crops of oats and barley . . . and thousands of long growing timber withered from the roots.' The farmer also told him that the following Friday had been designated as a day of general prayer for rain throughout the colony.

After only a week or so on the road Joseph had been so appalled at the state of the land that he commented, 'This country is very bad . . . there is downright mismanagement.' Compared with the small fields of Wales he found the terrain vast, alien and disorientating. 'I can see scores of thousands of acres with the naked eye resembling burnt couch grass, brown red earth and scrub bushes.' Often, the roads were little more than swathes cut through the bush and he found himself walking along wide bullock tracks full of ruts, scattered with boulders and tree stumps. These roads were '66 yards in breadth', offering no shelter and so unlike the narrow, shady lanes of Cardiganshire cushioned by banks of billowing cowslip and pink campions. Here the traffic was also different. Huge timber wagons and drays drawn by as many as 16 oxen lumbered and jerked along the highway. The human traffic was also considerable. 'I saw many immigrants, foreigners, who understood not a single word of each other, pass in silence as

they sought their different ways. And always, there were the scores of swagmen in search of work.'

By 30 March Joseph was feeling distraught. Exhausted and penniless, he was on the verge of starvation. Fortunately, he came across a fellow Welshman, Alexander Roberts of Carmarthen, who took pity on him by providing him with 'meat and drink and rest'. Joseph had survived another night, and had revived his flagging spirits. In his diary he wrote, 'I never before valued the gift of pure water, one of the principal comforts of life.' Nevertheless, he evidently felt frustrated and helpless and had to blame someone for his present predicament. In a fit of self-righteous pique he wrote, 'One of the principal causes of my departure was the unfaithfulness of my family!'

Disheartened and penniless he continued towards Kyneton, but the night was to prove more dramatic. With no money for a bed, a squatter, or small farmer, took him to a ramshackle shed. Here, at least he would have a safe haven for the night, or so he thought. No sooner had he settled down and 'made up my bed from my swag' when suddenly he saw the door being pushed in:

> 31 March 1869
> A traveller rushed to my newly made bed, a contest and scuffle for my bed clothes. I was the stronger . . . In the dark I lit a match and found that he had an axe; I had a pickaxe close by . . . I grappled the axe from his hand. He had a dog which I soon dispatched . . . Both on the road!

Joseph had been tough enough to withstand the attack, but the experience left him vulnerable and shaken, and he decided, 'No more rest there for Joseph.' Instead, 'since it was a fine and dry night,' he lay under the stars until dawn. It turned out to be a mystical experience. He was mesmerised by 'the brilliance of the Australian moon and the endless expanse of sky.' Everything seemed 'so much bigger and brighter in this country.' Throughout the night he was fascinated by the sounds of many different bells tinkling in the darkness. The following morning he discovered that, 'these were attached to the various farm animals such as goats, rams, bulls and cows . . . so that the owners might find them more easily in the wilderness. They also keep the kangaroos at bay!'

Travelling towards Castlemaine Joseph now entered the bush. Here, he was immediately captivated by the cool of the dense foliage and the peace to be found there. 'This place,' he exclaimed, 'has upon it the signature of the Almighty.' The birdsong was new to him. He was enraptured by the sound of the bellbird, and the chorus of the Australian magpies which echoed like evensong in an emerald cathedral, so different from the raucous call of Welsh magpies. He was so enthralled by his surroundings that he became hopelessly lost. But he was also starving and parched, and he wondered how much longer he could survive. Then, as so often happened in the life of Joseph, the unexpected occurred. By an extraordinary coincidence, a Welsh-speaking Welshman came upon him sitting disconsolately on a log. He was led immediately to safety and hospitality was provided. A quaint verse reflects his feeling of relief:

1 April 1869
> Through the Bush I tried my way
> And soon did find myself astray
> A Welshman came to my delight
> And said in Welsh I'd be alright,

Joseph did not name the man who had saved him, but hundreds of Welsh people had settled in the vicinity of Castlemaine, and the Welsh language was frequently heard on the streets.

Not all of Joseph's encounters were so fortunate. The following morning he rose early and entered Taradale. 'I went to a Baker, a Hotel keeper and a Butcher asking for a bit of bread to eat...But I was harshly admonished...I tried another Hotel, a big, tall, red faced landlady came to the door and very scornfully told me to go round the corner and don't bother me!...She was short of humanity!' Starving and thirsty, Joseph continued on his way until he reached Chewton.

Once again, he begged for a glass of water at a hotel, and lo and behold the landlord and his wife turned out to be Welsh-speaking. This time he was warmly welcomed and well fed. 'The grid iron was put over the fire and I had a good dinner with a glassful of good ale to wash it down.' It seemed that Joseph's luck had changed. Since taking to the road, he had sought the whereabouts of an old friend, John Lewis, formerly of Llan-non, in his 'old county'. The landlady knew exactly where he was and directed him to the diggings at Forest Creek near Castlemaine. He made his way there and eventually found his 'long searched and desired friend' hard at it prospecting. Joseph describes this meeting with John Lewis who was filling a cart while digging for gold:

> 1 April 1869
> I went to meet John Lewis and asked him in Welsh what he would take for his cart load? He looked at me and hollered out 'Tregaron! Trecefel boy! What brought you here?' Shaking hands was the next process . . . and to talk

about the old country and old times. I never was so glad to see a real acquaintance since I left Aberystwyth.

After wandering half-starved for days, he now found himself in a Welsh community. 'I saw many Cardiganshire and Carmarthenshire men. In fact, it was a regular Welsh neighbourhood, all speak Welsh in a homely manner and the children can talk both Welsh and English.'

John Lewis had been searching for gold for years. 'He owned three puddling machines . . . and was in partnership with his son Evan and brother-in-law Walter Davies, who also hailed from Tregaron.' Joseph was invited to join in the work and found the whole experience exciting. 'I will never forget the process of separating the precious metal from the earth . . . after 2 washings John Lewis had about £1 4s worth of pure gold in very small nuggets. If only I could come across a decent sized nugget!'

The enthusiasm for gold was infectious. He noticed that even 'the small children were busily engaged in searching for surface gold which appears in small lumps to the experienced and keen eye.' At the diggings Joseph met another party of diggers. 'I gave them good morning and was answered, *"Oes dim Cymraeg gennych chwi?"* ['Have you no Welsh?'] They were from Carmarthenshire, and had come out just over a month before me.' After the initial desolation of landing alone in Australia, Joseph felt that at last he had truly arrived.

Forest Creek appears to have been a Mecca for Welshmen seeking their fortunes. A contemporary writer vividly captured the scene at the diggings. The following extract is a translation from *Gwlad yr Aur* by ap Huw.

Enticed by the thought of getting rich, thousands of Welshmen went to Forest Creek where the Welsh language could be heard everywhere. Initially, the Welsh, bound by the language, tended to remain together. They squatted in thousands of hastily erected tents and humble abodes, indeed, many slept under the stars. The atmosphere was described as unbearably hot with dust everywhere like snow, making men parched. The grass was burned brown by the sun. Yet, this was, in one way, a land of freedom. It was a rich Colony, with plenty to offer hardworking Welshmen, and without the tyranny of ruthless landlords, without 'screws and agents' and no tithes. A few were to make their fortune, but thousands failed to find the hidden treasure of the yellow dust hidden beneath the earth.

The attractions of Australia were by now widely advertised even in the remotest parts of rural Wales. It is ironic that many emigrants had come from Joseph's own parish; among them were his former neighbours, David Jones, Rhiwonen, and the two brothers, David and Daniel Davies of Cefnbysbach; all three had worked for Joseph's family prior to emigrating. But the wheel of fortune had turned full circle. Instead of living in a dank cottage and working long hours for a meagre wage, the Cefnbysbach brothers had struck gold and were prospering. They did not have to tramp the roads like Joseph, but now lived in a comfortable bungalow in Ballarat.

During his time at Forest Creek Joseph met many other men from Cardiganshire. On 2 April, whilst walking round the 'busy scene' of the diggings, he came across an old acquaintance from the Vale of Aeron. 'I saw Walter Jones, late of Pen-y-wern Ystrad . . . had a two hour chat with him over a moderate glass of beer about the old county . . . he earns about £2 5s a week and looks stronger and healthier than when he left home.' Joseph also noted that 'the children appear healthy and taller.' It seemed that his fellow countrymen had found Australia to be a 'land of opportunity', which not only offered freedom, but also good health and a fair reward for hard work.

Later that day, Joseph climbed a high peak south of Castlemaine to view the land. The sight astounded him:

> I could see forty miles of countryside with scores of diggings . . . A man may think that millions of men could not perform so many holes and move so much earth . . . The area is full of thousands of holes as far as the eye can see; however, man has to work very hard to find the gold . . . Nature has made it scarce enough as not to endanger its high value . . . At the end, only a very few gold diggers and bankers are successful.

In the early days the gold had been easily accessible and Forest Creek was described 'as the richest shallow alluvial goldfield the world has ever known.' But what was previously pastoral landscape had been transformed by some 30,000 diggers into an eyesore of waste heaps, and abandoned potholes, the detritus of men delirious for riches.

Prospecting had gone on for some 18 years before Joseph landed in Australia, ever since Edward Hargreaves had struck gold on 12 February 1851 near Bathurst in New South Wales. He called it Ophir after the region in the Old Testament famous for its fine gold. By August 1851, rich gold fields were discovered in the colony of Victoria, and places such as Ballarat, Bendigo and Mount Alexander became world famous as the new El Dorado. Within weeks, gold fever had gripped the whole colony and people from all walks of life dropped everything in their frenzied quest for instant wealth. The impact on Victoria was enormous and posed overwhelming problems for the Governor, Lieutenant La Trobe. Affairs verged on the chaotic as civil servants, lawyers, shopkeepers, doctors, farmers, ex-convict shepherds, wardens and policemen joined the 'gold rush'. Law and order was threatened in Melbourne as 38 policemen resigned their posts to become diggers, leaving only two police officers to control a city of 20,000 people. 'Gold fever' even infected the ships at anchor in Port Phillip Bay. Out of 1,029 seamen, 521 abandoned their ships for the gold fields. The situation became so serious that captains refused to take their ships within two miles of shore, and the rate of pay for a seaman for the voyage home was increased from the usual £8 per man to a swingeing £120 per man in order to prevent mass desertion from the ships. The temptation was overwhelming, especially when it was said that, 'nuggets could be picked from the surface soil at Ballarat with a penknife.'

In 1862, of all British-born immigrants, 55% were English, 28% Irish, 15% Scottish but the Welsh made up only 2%. Many of the Welsh were concentrated in the Ballarat, Bendigo and Castlemaine areas.

During his time at Forest Creek Joseph stayed with John Lewis and his wife at their home, Bryncoch. He was well treated. 'Mrs Lewis has washed my things today . . . They are very kind to me . . . I was given tea and supper . . . good food.' Whilst at Forest Creek, Joseph himself tried his luck and dug for gold. But, as usual, he was obliged to record, 'No go for Joseph!' He described the diggings at night, 'Hundreds of camp fires glinted in the darkness which one old veteran claimed resembled the military encampments of the Peninsular War, fought in Spain at the turn of the century.'

On Saturday the men finished work at midday and he accompanied the Lewis family to Castlemaine market, where he felt entirely at home. 'The market was thickly attended . . . everything was there . . . potatoes 8 pence per cwt, butter 1/6 lb, beef 3 pence a lb, and mutton 2 pence a lb. I met many Welshmen in the Market. We were talking Welsh there all the time, in fact, it is a real Welsh neighbourhood here, and each Welshman claims his language with credit to his native place. Many farmers in the market gave me invitations to visit their homes. Castlemaine is well planned with broad streets and flourishing because of the alluvial gold which could once be picked up by every digger to the amount of an ounce a day.' There were two Welsh chapels at Castlemaine and he was overjoyed to learn that, 'they keep a National Eisteddfod here.' The town was also famous for its 'Castlemaine XXXX beer', first brewed there in 1859 and still a favourite drink. The following day, while Mrs Lewis and the 'smartly dressed' children went to the Welsh Methodist chapel, he and John Lewis went to watch the men shoot rabbits which 'looked big and more like hares.'

In addition to the Welsh and the other nationalities, Joseph described the place as being full of Chinese searching for gold. 'There are a great many of them here . . . They are at it now with their simple riddles which they can carry on their shoulders.' The Chinese were the largest group of non-European immigrants and made up one in every seven males in the colony of Victoria. They were hard-working, self-sufficient and law-abiding, working the tailings or abandoned diggings. All too often they were viewed as scavengers and were cruelly treated by many of the diggers. They were the target for racial abuse and violence. Many of them worked as market gardeners and Joseph mentions that at Castlemaine Market he saw 'much produce from the allotments of Chinamen.' He also describes their temples or Joss Houses, 'which were numerous.' Such was the concern about the Chinese entering the colony that the government, for a short while, imposed a levy of £10 on each one landing at ports in Victoria.

During his stay at Forest Creek, Joseph was disgusted at the action of a fellow Welshman, Griffith Joseph of Glamorgan, who callously persecuted a Chinaman. 'The Welshman jumped into the Chinaman's hole and took advantage of the gold therein.' Ever the champion of the underdog, Joseph complained that all sense of fairness had disappeared and that:

> The golden rules are now unknown
> To reap and take what we have sown.

But Joseph was growing restless at the diggings. Adopting a high moral tone, he now denounced the 'hunger for gold'. Gone was the initial euphoria on encountering John Lewis and trying his luck at prospecting. As so often happened in his life, his mood swung from one extreme to another, and his philosophy showed a double standard. He now claimed that, 'gold has become the God of the people . . . and the lust for wealth overtakes all else. This rush for gold is one of futility and a cruel illusion, for most men end up plunged into unhappiness and poverty . . . It is a sad sight to see men drawn to holes in the ground like moles on account of the tyranny of greed. They should know what the preacher says in Ecclesiastes – O Lord – how bitter art thou to a man at rest in his possessions.' Somewhat hypocritically, he then condemned 'gold, avarice and greed' in an 'epic' poem of 172 lines entitled 'Gold, Its Power and Influence' and sent it to a local newspaper he does not name. Joseph begins by addressing the Editor:

4 April 1869

> Dear Master Editor, will you
> Insert this subject, it is due
> To this Colony and the times,
> And here it is in awkward rhymes.

The 'awkward rhymes' ran to 168 lines of trenchant criticism and the following extracts illustrate the predominant theme:

> Gold has built the biggest town
> And gold, in time, will bring it down.
>
> The Hotel Keepers, through their tap
> For gold, all fools they will entrap.
>
> Town sharpers by their different tricks
> Take what the honest digger picks.
>
> There for gold the throng will seek
> Riddle the gullies, dry the creek.
>
> I wish you all to understand
> That gold won't stick to every hand.
>
> Gold is adored in every place
> Where we can find the Christian race.
>
> Too much gold has caused much strife,
> And want of gold bring peace of life.

'Peace of life' was a state to which Joseph constantly aspired, but it was to elude him for much of his time in Australia. He bade farewell to John Lewis and his fellow expatriates at Forest Creek and, heaving his heavy swag upon his back, he set out on the highway. He believed that the arduous track ahead offered the only means of escape from his troubled thoughts. 'I see struggle and strife ahead of me but only through action will I fill the void.'

CHAPTER 14

MY ONLY HUSBAND

On 5 April 1869 Joseph once again experienced all the discomforts and dangers besetting a traveller, as he humped his heavy swag and trudged along 'a gritty track strewn with large stones.' On his way he 'passed several suspicious looking characters, many of whom carried pistols and knives.' But as Joseph's appearance did not suggest that he carried gold or other valuables he was not a tempting target for their attentions. He set out for Smeaton in search of work, and described himself as 'Walking hard from farm to farm – With heavy bedding on my arm.'

The occupants of the first five farms 'all spoke Welsh... very kind... but no work.' Already, he was beginning to regret leaving the comparative security of Forest Creek:

> I am directed here and there
> No work for Joseph anywhere.

He passed huge stations where 'shepherds had to care for over 6,500 sheep.' This he found mind-boggling. What concerned him most was the condition of the pasture. 'It consisted of rough tufts of tough grass like the worst in Wales.' Sadly, the carcasses of newly born lambs lay rotting everywhere, and even the living sheep seemed too weak to bleat. Joseph himself soon felt the effect of the drought. 'I could not find spring water and was obliged to drink a very muddy mixture.'

He had no alternative but to keep going. 'I called on some squatters – but I could not have a bite to eat. Inhumanity!' He was close to despair when suddenly he heard the sound of water. 'I came across a creek with clear running water which was a treat . . . I took off my long stockings, shirt and so on . . . I had plenty of soap and two clean shirts . . . I washed myself all over.' At dusk, he discovered a shepherd's hut and was given shelter for the night. 'I made my bed on many sheep skins and the shepherd gave me a good bellyful of fresh mutton.' The following morning he journeyed towards Smeaton through fine agricultural land where the road was fenced with strong posts and ran 'as straight as a gun's barrel'.

On 13 April his luck changed when he was offered employment by an Irish farmer, Morgan Lane of Smeaton, at a wage of 15/- a week. For the first time since leaving Trecefel, Joseph was to work on the land again. But his conditions of work were dramatically different from those he had experienced at home. His new master set him the task of ploughing. 'It was,' wrote Joseph, 'like being in a furnace.'

> 14 April 1869
> Obliged to set out at dawn . . . because this is the climate to try a man's health . . . Felt it very hot . . . my neck was sunburnt. Thermometer in the sun 102°F. I never thought of such sudden variations . . . before ten o'clock the heat was nearly unbearable to my skin . . . I plough with the horses Tom and Prince, a good plough with a small land wheel – I greased the wheel to make my work easier.

Joseph described the land as 'stony and abounds in boulders'. But things were looking up. 'I am with nice people ... Good victuals ... I sleep in the stable with the horses. Better bed than I had since leaving Aberystwyth.' For the time being Joseph seemed satisfied with his lot. He was well fed and happy and doing what he liked best, which was working the land. There was, however, a certain irony in his situation. Back in Wales it was he who had allowed the tramps to sleep in his stables at Trecefel.

Although he was suspicious of Catholics, Joseph had to make an exception of Morgan Lane. On 4 May he records, 'I had a short chat with the master asking about his religion, but it was foolish on my side to interfere.' Joseph had been unable to conceal his contempt for the Pope, but his new master was having none of it. Morgan Lane replied frankly that, 'The praying of the Pope and the priests were the only things that keep out poisonous reptiles from Ireland.' Ever disputatious, Joseph responded, 'I then asked him why this same effect does not keep out the English Government, being their principal hatred? I received no reply to this question! Morgan Lane and his wife travelled 7 miles to Clunes to attend mass, but he kept neither a clock, a watch, a book nor an almanac in his house. Wise man! We are too much governed by time, and to keep a time piece only serves to remind us of the shortness of life.'

During his stay at Smeaton Joseph had to share the stable with a Chinaman, 'but very little we could understand of each other.'

He found the work on the farm increasingly demanding. Fencing was particularly arduous. 'The ground is like iron and it is tough work to make holes for the big posts ... It's a hard job to clean the horses, especially to clean the hooves inside the shoes ... The earth was fast there as dried putty!' Nevertheless, the prospect of the good food, which he described as 'the best I've had' and the certainty of a roof over his head, ensured that he stayed.

When, on 8 May, he was told that his services were no longer required, he became deeply disillusioned. 'No work for Joseph, he must take up his swag once again ... It is difficult to get work ... I hope I shall succeed soon.' On leaving Morgan Lane's farm, Joseph had to stay at the quaintly named Hit or Miss Hotel in Smeaton, which was owned by a Welshman, John Jones, from Gwent. Joseph generally disliked hotel owners, whom he regarded as 'greedy and unscrupulous'. Within hours of booking in at the hotel Joseph had quarrelled with John Jones. The reasons for the altercation are not mentioned, but Joseph had to leave abruptly. The landlord was so annoyed that he took his revenge by sending a friend disguised as a policeman to harass Joseph after he had left the hotel. The diary records the incident:

> 8 May 1869
> All the Welshmen were not very kind to me, especially Mr John Jones, Landlord of the Hit or Miss Hotel, Smeaton. He [the man disguised as a policeman] rode after me and did stop me on the road . . . stating that he had an authority to apprehend me for a bloody crime. I had no stick in my hand at the time or else I would apply it to the right quarters and in self-defence. He was obliged to ride back with speed . . . I was told that his name was Reuben Winterburn, the Landlord of the Karoo Chang Hotel, Smeaton . . . I will proceed against him as the road ought to be free for every honest traveller . . . I will leave a blank leaf for his report.

Joseph did indeed leave a blank page in his diary, but he never got round to writing his report. After spending the night at the

Sportsman Hotel, he took a walk the following morning along the highway, describing it as being '3 chains or 66 yards wide, not cleared of standing timber, with gum trees, box and stringy bark in abundance . . . One tree was 9 yards in circumference and three persons could sleep inside.' Within days, he found new employment with a German, Herr Minster, who was the landlord of the Cumberland Hotel. He was paid £1 a week for ploughing, cutting chaff and other duties. The work was hard, but he was delighted when he found a spring near the hotel, which provided him with clean and free drinking water:

> 13 May 1869
> Thanks be to God for a good drink
> Which quenches my thirst gratis.

The plentiful supply of water was not to Herr Minster's liking. He expected his labourers to quench their thirst by buying beer at his hotel. To his credit Joseph refused to do this. Herr Minster, who owed him two pounds in wages, refused to pay him in cash, insisting that he be paid in beer. Joseph kept to his resolution to abstain from alcohol, and decided to forfeit the money owing to him and quit his employment. This prompted the following diatribe against hotel keepers in general:

> Hotel keepers are the worst sort of swindlers that I have met in the colony . . . They will not forfeit a morsel of bread to save a man's life! I'm determined I will not take their drink for money. It looks dark on Joseph again!

Despite his dejection on leaving the Cumberland Hotel he quickly found new employment at Kangaroo Farm, Smeaton, which was owned by a Scot, Mr George Hepburn, a pioneer, prosperous farmer and businessman. He was an honourable man who paid a fair wage and fed his workers properly. Joseph was to work at Smeaton House, the Sportsman Hotel and Tea Tree Farm, all owned by Mr Hepburn. He sowed corn, cleared orchards, ploughed, cut chaff, helped with the horses and worked every day from 5 a.m. till dusk. He never shirked work, which gave him the dignity he craved. He confessed in his diary:

> I am ashamed of begging,
> But digging I can do,
> And any honest living
> I boldly can pursue.

He thrived on work and the conditions were the best he had experienced since arriving in the colony. He was so contented that he compared himself to 'Adam in Paradise', but feared that he might be turned out of his Garden of Eden. He slept in the saddle room of the groom's quarters with two blankets, a warm fire and good company. The food was excellent, 'each day we had tea, cream and sugar with plenty of beef and mutton.' Mr Hepburn and his family were teetotallers, which suited Joseph admirably. Nevertheless, he still seemed prone to accidents and misunderstandings. On 10 September he was paid £4 18s in wages by Mr Hepburn and decided to purchase a flannel jacket and a pair of trousers, but even this seemingly innocent transaction landed him in trouble. Instead of trying on the clothes in the store, he decided to go out into the privacy of the countryside to do so. 'I did put them on by the road in order to fit them, and who came but the police superintendent and his assistant. They took me in charge for stealing the clothes. I did go back a little with them, but they soon released their captive.'

On 13 September Joseph decided that he wanted a place of his own and he left his lodgings at Smeaton House to live in a small hut rented from a farmer named Bateman. He paints an idyllic picture of life in the hut, where he found the serenity of living close to nature deeply satisfying:

> 14 September 1869
>
> Joseph's Hut
>
> I slept comfortable. I have only a table and bed as furniture. It stands near a fine creek. Good water. Very convenient for washing... Two Chinamen are gardening near my hut. They put in peas, onions, carrots and so on. Some of their cabbage are nearly fit for use. Very few words of them I can understand... obliged to make signs ... Possums all around in the gum trees... Mr Bateman's children shoot them in the moonlight.

Here, Joseph seemed totally at peace, and in perfect harmony with his surroundings:

> 15 September 1869
>
> The croaking of young frogs are wonderful during the night – sometimes very much like young ducks at home ... There are millions of very small young frogs along the creek close to my hut... Black snakes begin to appear ... They swim in the creek – they are dangerous when trodden upon. I wash my clothes in the running creek and listen to the bird song in the overhanging gum trees. My soul is refreshed.

He found that the bark from the gum trees made excellent fuel. 'I am able to have a good fire in less than 20 seconds . . . This is a regular Bush life . . . I am far more comfortable than at Mr Hepburn's mansion . . . but the tucker is not as rich.'

Unfortunately for Joseph, his newfound state of bliss was to last for only a couple of days. On 17 September he began to feel unwell and past events came back to haunt him. He recalled the attack made upon him by his family and blamed them for 'the pain in my breastbone . . . The old complaint comes on again . . . it hinders my breath . . . I see that I cannot get rid of the kicks . . . It was a horrible affair – In fact, a downright murder, and ten times worse than a direct one. How much pain I have already felt! Lord! Free me from the memory of the torment I suffered!' After falling asleep he had a curious dream. 'I dreamt that I was with my friend Dr John at home, both of us were at the funeral of Dr Llewelyn, Dean of St David's College, Lampeter. I thought Dr John had a newly born child with grown teeth in his mouth!!' He was often prey to such bizarre dreams when he brooded on his past unhappiness.

Despite periods of recrimination, during his first six months in Australia Joseph had corresponded regularly with his family. He received letters from his daughters, from Lewis his son and from other members of his family. The writing and the receipt of letters was one of his greatest pleasures. Unfortunately, most of his letters have been lost, but among those that have survived is one letter – now deposited at the State Library of Victoria, Melbourne – which he received from his son Lewis in September 1869. Despite all the acrimony at Trecefel, and despite the problems caused by Joseph's abrupt departure, Lewis's letter is remarkably free of bitterness:

Trecefel
Nr Tregaron
Cardiganshire
South Wales

7 June 1869

Dear Father,
Many months have now passed since you have departed for a country, which has undoubtedly proved beneficial to thousands. Yet, many are the hardships in the best of countries, but very seldom we hear of that in either Australia, America or California and other colonies...

This Country, or rather Countrypeople you disliked to the utmost... deals miserably with us at present... Debts to the amount of above £600 have already appeared...

All of us expect and hope to hear from you often... and hope that peace and prosperity will prove your lot... A Correspondent from Sydney wrote to the *Dispatch* of Australia as one of the most favourable, Economical productive and healthy of the Colonies... The late droughts have been destructive to both Animals and Vegetables as I have read in the papers, but rain falls in abundance since then. The farm stock are looking about the same as usual, except the horses, which are exceedingly low; the cattle stock is light, only two could be sold this spring. Your landlord's mare fell over Trecefel Bridge to the river in April and was immediately killed...

We have not yet received the Diary. I send two papers off with this letter, viz *The Welshman* and *Dispatch*...

If we can manage to gather some money, and if there

be any necessity for the same, we shall try our best. It may be sooner than anticipated – But I don't see what need has a man for money in such a productive, fertile and lightly populated country where English gold is swiftly found.

I remain with our best wishes from all at Trecefel, and many others too numerous to be named have wished themselves to be remembered to you . . .

Lewis Jenkins

Clearly, Lewis believed that his father was in a land where wealth could be easily acquired, whereas the family was struggling at Trecefel. Nevertheless, Lewis offers to help his father if necessary. Joseph was obviously moved by this letter and composed unusually tender Welsh verses in reply.

At the end of September, much to his dismay, his employment with Mr Hepburn came to an end and he returned to the home of John Lewis, Bryncoch, Forest Creek, near Castlemaine. Here, he was given a warm welcome and he once again accompanied his friend to puddle for gold at a fresh claim in Sandy Creek, Newstead. His previous rantings against 'the ungodly pursuit of wealth' were now conveniently forgotten. John Lewis had invested in a new puddling machine which was powered by two horses. Joseph observed that 28 loads of earth were quickly reduced to 6 loads, mostly of clean gravel, and from these up to 12 grains of gold were procured. But in the midst of all this excitement on the gold field, suddenly, on 14 August 1869, he received unexpected and tragic news that left him shattered:

Forest Creek

The daughter of Jenkin Davies brought me a packet containing *The Welshman* newspaper and two letters from

Trecefel dated 26 July 1869 ... Alas I was astonished to read the following statement in the Deaths – 'Jenkins, on the 28th ult. after five days illness, aged 20 years, deeply regretted. Mr Lewis Jenkins, second son of Mr Joseph Jenkins of Trecefel, Tregaron, Cardiganshire,' O what an unexpected turn of news!!

Joseph then opened the two letters from home giving an account of his son's illness and his death. The cause of death was 'Encephalitis'. His grief was made more acute by the fact that he was half a world away from his family at such at time. He had been the last to know of his son's death and he could not even visit his grave. He found some release from his sorrow by recalling lines from Ecclesiastes, 'Then shall the dust return to the earth as it was, and the spirit shall return unto God who gave it.' Joseph added his own words:

> Peace to his soul when it awakes,
> From the dark grave without blemish.
>
> Death is an end to all storms
> To all sadness and joy†

But nothing could compensate for the fact that:

> Lewis has gone so far away
> That not one word will ever be heard from him again. †

His despair must have been compounded by the fact that Lewis had sent him a conciliatory letter just a few months earlier, and he must also have been tormented fact that the relationship between father and son had not always been a happy one. He was now a captive to these thoughts. With two sons having been cut down in their prime, he eased the pain with poetry.

Unable to contain his emotions, Joseph left the gold diggings. He sought to assuage his grief by plunging himself into hard work and taking up the cause of those less fortunate than himself. After reading a letter criticising swagmen in the newspaper *The Australian*, he took up his pen and wrote a robust defence of their life. They had been described as 'beggars, loafers and vagabonds'. This angered Joseph and he described it as 'a false representation open to create a bloody revolution through the colony.' He maintained that the swagmen were 'the backbone of the colonies'. His forceful response was published in *The Australian* on 18 November 1869:

> PITY THE SWAGMAN
>
> To travel 30 or 40 miles in search of work with 70 pounds of swag is not an easy task ... Going through the Bush on an empty belly ... to lie down on the bare ground on a severe frosty morning ... or during Summer where all sorts of colonial snakes abound is not a pleasant position. The time is at hand to provide work for the swagman ... to tax all the waste and neglected land to the amount of one shilling per acre per annum ... would amount to a round sum every year and let the same be laid out in public works.
>
> With due respects to honest labourers
>
> Yours Jos Jenkins, Swagman

The old fighting spirit that he had so often showed in Tregaron was now manifesting itself in Australia. He identified himself boldly and publicly with the cause of the swagmen, who were generally derided and mocked. His call for more public works to create employment was not to be realised for some years, and the plight of the swagmen never ceased to be of concern to him.

Anthony Trollope, the English novelist who visited Australia in 1871, described the swagmen as, 'One of the most remarkable institutions in any country on earth.' He later published a travel book on both Australia and New Zealand in 1873.

Despite all his efforts on behalf of others, Joseph himself was soon out of work again. He was forced to swallow his pride and to return yet again to the gold diggings:

12 November 1869
By digging and shovelling in every ditch
O would that I could have what I desire,
I sift and search for gold, but into debt I run.
But into debt I fly. †

After a mere two days he became disillusioned by the whole business of prospecting, and yet again he decided to quit Forest Creek and 'to try my old and honest calling again as a farm labourer.'

In his search for farm work Joseph passed through Ballarat where he stayed at the Temperate Hotel. As a prospecting town Ballarat had many taverns packed with rowdy, hard-drinking miners. Still painfully aware of the perils of drink, he decided to renew his pledge of abstinence. 'I took the pledge . . . I have an excuse now not to touch beer.' This seemed an unnecessary step as he had drunk very little alcohol since landing in Australia, but in a town so full of temptation it served to fortify his intent.

In Ballarat, he encountered the full impact of the gold rush:

14 November 1869
I entered the town through a broad street sided by ornamental trees – I have never heard so many dogs barking

in my lifetime – the streets rattled until midnight. I made for Sebastopol to the East of Ballarat – it is a well arranged place encircled by many claims of alluvial and quartz reef gold diggings . . . The Welshmen live well with plenty of all necessities . . . Great parts of Ballarat have been built on a flat . . . liable to flooding – ruined gardens and bridges are to be seen. The Prince of Wales claim is worked mostly by Welshmen . . . met crowds of men and women going to chapels and mostly talking in Welsh. I asked for David and Daniel Davies, being the sons of the late David of Cefnbysbach. Some Welshmen kindly led me to their neatly built residence. They were at home. I had an excellent dinner with many kindnesses.

Joseph received a regal reception at the home of the brothers and was loaned £1 by David's wife. He was conscious of his own penury and their prosperity and how 'fortunes were reversed'. He recalled how in Wales he had galloped to get medicine for their ailing mother, and he reflected on the uncertainties of life. 'A man cannot tell what shall be, or what shall be after him . . . I learned very early on in my life that nothing is for ever!'

Fortunately, he soon succeeded in getting new employment at Mount Blow Hard near Ballarat, the farm of Mr Wilson of Spring Gardens. He was to be paid 15/- a week. As usual, the work was back-breaking; it was made more intolerable by the savage heat of the Australian sun:

15 December 1869
Up at 4 a.m. – too close to sleep. Thermometer in the shade 135°F. At noon I had to carry the reapers' knives

home and was obliged to cut a handful of grass in order to save my hands from scorching. My two mates went to the adjoining Hotel. I took my Billy and had real 'tea total stuff' with ice water. The ice was very expensive.

On 24 December he received wages of three sovereigns from Mr Wilson, and on Christmas Day he went to the Ballarat *Eisteddfod*, founded by the Welsh miners in 1855. Since *eisteddfodau* had been such an integral part of his life in Wales, he looked forward to the event. He was excited at the prospect of meeting Welshmen and discussing with them the intricacies of Welsh poetry. He had mentally prepared himself and during the previous weeks he had composed verses ready for the *Eisteddfod*. He slept little the previous night and was up long before dawn:

25 December 1869

I was up at 3 o'clock and did prepare for Ballarat and began my journey at 4 o'clock. I reached town and had myself shaved and so on in order to attend the Welsh Eisteddfod I had to pay 2/- for my entrance ticket. A.R. Williams was in the Chair. I did ask his permission to address the meeting and he told me to be there early at 2 o' clock.

With some three hours in hand, Joseph decided once again to visit the brothers David and Daniel Davies. He paid three pence for a cab to their dwelling in the Sebastopol district of Ballarat. Here, he was given an excellent Christmas dinner of 'fat geese, mutton, and beef followed by various rich puddings.' The *Eisteddfod* was held at the Mechanics Institute of Ballarat, which, according to Joseph was 'a very fine place'. After his splendid repast, he caught another cab to reach the *Eisteddfod* in good time to address an audience. Wishing to make the most of this rare opportunity he stood on top of a staircase and loudly recited 22 verses of poetry, for which he was awarded the first prize. 'I was,' he boasted, 'warmly applauded by the very few that could understand it!' In essence, his speech was an appeal to the Welsh to stick together and to support and nourish their culture and language, something that they were reluctant to do. Whereas the Scots, and particularly the Irish, clung to their national identity, the Welsh were more willing to be assimilated in order to succeed in their newly adopted land. The following lines constitute the first verse of his long address:

25 December 1869 Ballarat
It's wonderful to see the sons of Gwalia [Wales]
Here today in Victoria
Gathering together to support their language
On the vast lands of Australia. †

He left Ballarat and the *Eisteddfod* that night well satisfied with his efforts, only to walk into one of the worst dust storms he had experienced since arriving in Australia. 'I never saw nature in such an angry mood. This land is so unpredictable!' He was forced to lie on the ground several times during the ten-mile journey back to Spring Farm and was 'almost suffocated'. Eventually, he managed to survive the storm and reached the shelter of the farm. With his one-day holiday over, an exhausted Joseph had only two hours rest before getting up at sunrise to thresh wheat. There was to be no respite from work, he was up at 4 a.m. and at the threshing machine by 5 a.m. He complained that it was so close and hot that 'all were covered by running sweat.' He himself was in the worst possible position. 'I was on top of the rick attending the tail of the straw elevator and nearly blind with sweat.'

His world had changed completely in the space of one long eventful year. Who could have foreseen that the former master of Trecefel would have to endure the rough tough life of a 'swaggie'? Yet, even in adversity, he had retained a measure of dignity and had shown great stoicism in the face of constant hardship.

At home, his wife Betty was also experiencing hardship. Without her husband, she was left to shoulder the responsibility for the children and the farm. In his diaries Joseph often blames her for his pain and troubles; Betty, however, does not appear to display a similar degree of antagonism towards Joseph.

The only known extant letter from Betty to Joseph, undated but probably written in October shortly after Lewis's death, reveals her struggle to survive at Trecefel. Despite her obvious heartache, she does not reproach him in any way:

My only husband,

I send this to you, perhaps to raise more hatred, but if it be so, there is nothing I can do. I read some of the letters to the children and to my cousin which show that Lewis and I were the cause of your departure. If so, and only you know, I am certain that no one desired more good to you than the children and myself. Neither they nor I can now help you, but we can send you some clothes and books. The watch is also to be had, but I would like to keep it, if you intend spending the rest of your life in Australia, perhaps the children will send it to you. Money is scarce and there is no prospect that things will improve as we have no one to do the work. I have only Daniel Lloyd and one small boy who cannot even hold the plough, but we did have a good harvest. I must try to get another boy, but I don't know where to find one. We are thinking of sowing wheat in Cnwcsarn field if it is not too late. We have not lifted the potatoes. I have no news to send you as your brothers, your brothers in law and the children send you an account of everything that goes on. You asked how much debt we have paid. I do not know how much Lewis paid, as he was doing his best to pay it all, as well as raising the little ones. Now, I have no one to care for them anymore, but I will do my best. Jane Llwyd, your sister, has not been well for five weeks – she complains of a headache.

Marged and Mary are far from well – Mary has an infection in her throat – it has broken three times – Mary has received a letter from you containing many topics of conversation. I am sorry to learn that you have not been well, but perhaps it is better that you are not here with me, as you imply that I am the mother of all your ills, it is better therefore for me to keep my distance – But remember there is bread and cheese for you and a place to sleep here.

Your brother David's wife and I went to an auction at Sunny Hill – it lasted four days. The children and I remember ourselves to you – hoping that you are better – and we will see you again if we are allowed to live.

Yours untidily from
Elizabeth Jenkins †

With only himself to care for, Joseph could indulge in frequent bouts of self-pity and introspection; but Betty's burdens were truly heavy. After the death of Lewis, the task of running the farm and looking after her seven remaining children was made even more difficult because she had to pay an increased rental of £150 per annum for the farm instead of the previous £120. Landlords, even the Reverend Latimer Jones, made no allowances for straitened circumstances. However, by virtue of her strength of character, Betty managed to survive. Her letter, written more in sorrow than in anger, reveals a generosity of spirit, compassion and a capacity to forgive, qualities that contrast starkly with the sentiments often expressed by her husband. Nevertheless, this letter must have had an impact upon him for he copied it and placed the original in his Bible where it remains to this day.

Despite everything, Joseph had survived his first year in Australia. It had been one of mixed fortunes, and the arrival of the New Year promised little hope of improvement. Nevertheless, he clung to his diary for consolation:

> 31 December 1869
> People, as yet unborn, will one day read my Journal and see how I did fare in the Antipodes and how we did live in Wales.

He ended what had been a turbulent year with the following somewhat bland entry:

> 31 December 1869
> Here I am on my last day of the year 1869. Very little had I thought of living one year so far from my native land. It

is strange; fate or not! Should life and health permit, I do really hope that I will be able to write and keep some sort of daily account of the remainder of my life whether here, at home, or on some other quarter of the globe.

CHAPTER 15

A SLAVISH EXISTENCE

When New Year's Day dawned at Spring Garden Farm, Mount Blow Hard, near Ballarat in 1870, no *calennig* singers called to wish the people a 'Happy New Year'; the only sound piercing the air was the shrill whistle of the threshing machine calling the workers to their duties at 5 a.m. For the first time since he had begun to keep his Journal, Joseph makes no reference to New Year's Day, which had always been such a significant date in his calendar, meriting a profound reflection on the events of the old year. Now, we only get one dismal entry recording the tedium of a working day of relentless toil lasting up to seventeen hours:

> 1 January 1870
> We were up at 4 o'clock and were called soon for breakfast. The whistle of the Threshing machine was opened soon after 5 o'clock. All hands attended.

In order to secure regular work Joseph had joined a team of eighteen threshers who trundled their cumbersome machines from one farm to another. They had an engine, a winnowing machine and an elevator drawn by a dozen or more horses. The workers usually stayed one or two weeks at each 'station', depending on the size of the farm, to thresh thousands of bushels of barley. It was noisy, dangerous and strenuous work, but at least it was well paid. His companions were a motley collection of itinerant workers who drank, swore and gambled. To them Joseph must have seemed like the quintessential 'wowser' – the Australian slang for a killjoy – who neither swore, drank, nor gambled.

On a Sunday Joseph spent his time reading his Bible, in particular the 'Sermon on the Mount'. He also washed his clothes, claiming that, 'Cleanliness is next to Godliness.' His fellow threshers, on the other hand, usually 'drank grog, and played cards'. Although Joseph described them as good company, their 'constant disputing, cursing and swearing' often interrupted his attempts at spiritual meditation.

As the threshing machine was hauled from one farm to another, Joseph was amazed at the 'vastness' of the stations, which so dwarfed the farms back in Wales. The pace of work was frenetic and hazardous. Accidents were common; one man fell from the platform and was temporarily disabled. Joseph himself had a 'strong blade of straw enter my eye as I was building the stack which caused great pain and discomfort.' At each new place, he called regularly at the Post Office to collect his mail. On 30 January 1870, he walked five miles to Creswick Post Office where he was rewarded with two newspapers, a letter from Nel his daughter, and a letter from his old friend Mr Charles Raw, landlord of the Talbot Hotel, Tregaron. This pleased him immensely and it evoked memories of happy times past.

The incessant grinding noise of the machines and the enervating heat, which could reach 102°F, was almost intolerable. On 5 February he wrote, 'Everybody tired . . . I was like

Wellington on the third eve of Waterloo.' But there were compensations. He confessed that, 'this land of Australia has a charm of its own':

> 17 February 1870
> What a glorious sight to enjoy the calm moonlight. Everything looks brighter than at home. The black spots on the moon are plainer and quite different . . . but we must watch we don't stare too hard or we'll get moon blindness.

During his period with the itinerant threshers, Joseph found difficulty in writing his diary. He often wrote during his lunch break, arousing the curiosity of his fellow workers, and many of his diaries still contain seeds and evidence of rain blotches. At dusk, it was too dark to write and no candles were allowed because the men were 'obliged to sleep among the straw stacks' and the use of a naked light posed a fire hazard. Joseph witnessed many fires caused by negligence. 'Nearly everyone smokes in this colony, the people are a hundred times more careless than at home. When a fire begins here, it is terrible. No water to master it.' Apart from the usual discomfort and inconvenience, the men also had to be on their guard against snakes. '22 February, 1870. There is no proper place for workmen for the night. I choose straw stacks, but the snakes are fond of approaching straw . . . they are out at night and fond of mice and rats. Everybody must be particular to hang his bedclothes during the daytime as snakes often crawl into them.'

Sometimes the men were accommodated in the stables, and despite the cramped conditions they often made their own entertainment after a hard day's work, even eschewing alcohol:

25 February 1870

At the Rose and Shamrock Hotel, 18 of us slept in a small stable of 6 stalls after enjoying merry songs . . . Not a glassful of intoxicating drink was called for! Too exhausted. O what a sober crowd!

Although a special camaraderie existed between Joseph and his fellow workers, sometimes his principles were in conflict with their actions. In early March, as the weather cooled dramatically, Joseph was affronted by the callous treatment of a Chinaman who had worked with them for some time. He was even prepared to court unpopularity in defending the rights of an abused fellow worker:

6 March 1870 Cavern Farm, Ascot

Piercingly cold. Obliged to pull straw over myself last night. We had a good supper. A Chinaman came in for his supper who had been working the previous days on the sheaf stack. No supper for John Chinaman. He was collared out of doors like a dog. It appears that he was not paid for his previous work done. O what a country of white Christians!

The following day, unable to tolerate the situation of 'no pay and no food', the Chinaman left the team, and Joseph was made to suffer at the hands of the supervisor for speaking up on his behalf. '8 March 1870. Mr Galaway made me prepare double duty . . . No Chinaman present, then the poor and helpless Welshman must be the Scoffing Pole, so goes the world. I took it without grudging. A powerful hand was in my favour. The wind! I did it very easy!'

March 1870 brought back vivid memories for Joseph. 'This

day,' he wrote, 'reminds me of my arrival in Melbourne. It was 12 March 1869 when I first set foot on Australian soil. Therefore, I have been one whole year knocking about in the colony. Sometimes sorry, sometimes merry. Sometimes full, sometimes hungry. But this colony looks better today than it was the same day last year! All is in my Journal . . . As a lowly worker I have seen life in a changing world which people back home would not believe – some things very wicked, how unjust life can be, but also much virtue.'

His diary was now 'getting too bulky to carry about', so he purchased a new book which he bound with leather. 'My diary,' he wrote, 'causes me much sweat and pain, but it is a sweet labour as vital to me as breath itself.'

He sums up his first year spent on the continent of Australia:

26 March 1870
This book contains my whereabouts in the Colony. It is badly written. I had neither time nor proper place to write. Should anybody like to read it, the reader will find my circumstances for one year. My state of health has been wonderfully well considering all the abusement I was obliged to go through both at home and here! I have more money in hand than the amount of debt I was obliged to run into after arriving.

Joseph's last two words are, 'All Paid!' Things were looking up.

At the beginning of April, Joseph and the team were at Mr Kinnersley's farm near Lake Learmonth. He took a walk into the surrounding area and was fascinated to see how the schools operated in the colony. Education had been an all-consuming passion at home, and he was full of admiration for the colony of Victoria's provision for its children in a land which was in a constant state of transition:

> 1 April 1869
>
> Education is carefully looked after by the government. Should the schoolroom be above a mile from the children's home, they ride their horses with a small leather bag strapped to their shoulders. The parents take chaff for the horses to eat at the stables that belong to the schoolrooms . . . The boys are well educated, but not accustomed to hard work.

Joseph feared that future generations would not learn how to cultivate the land. The government wisely invested in education to combat lawlessness and crime. Joseph constantly noted that the children in the colony appeared healthier than the children back in Wales. 'They grow tall and strong . . . The female children are women by the age of 14 years . . . they look as old and as big, if not more blooming than girls of 21 at home.' But seeing the happy, healthy children playing also revived painful memories of his youngest children, Tom and Anne, and he confessed, 'My thoughts fly back home – A heavy heart is too much of a burden.'

Spending almost every hour of every day nearly deafened by the pounding noise of the threshing machine failed to block out his anguish and he composed the following lines to express his feelings:

> YEARNING FOR HIS CHILDREN
> I look to-wards the yonder headland
> Expecting to see Tom and Anne
> Playing there hand in hand,

> Alas, I soon remember the distance.
> In the night whilst half asleep
> I am with my youngest children,
> I am conversing about country matters,
> But on awakening, there's the wound! †

He was prone to nightmares about his family, and a particularly stressful and vivid experience caused him to wake up suddenly one night sweating with fear:

> 3 April 1870
> Last night I dreamt that I was looking at my son Tom struggling in deep water. I could not render any assistance so he drowned in deep clear water.

Fortunately, this nightmare did not become a reality, but a tragedy similar to the dream did strike the family some years later. Two of Joseph's grandchildren, one aged 16 and the other 11, drowned in the river Teifi near his farm on a Sunday afternoon in August 1904. His dream in 1870 in Australia, somehow, was to be eerily prophetic.

But he was not to know this as he turned from his poetry to the threshing. In a perverse way he welcomed the endless toil. Being shook to atoms by the noise of the threshing machine helped to dull the pain of his guilt. His time in Australia had not only been a physical struggle, but had also been a profound psychological ordeal, and was not made any easier by the continued resentment against his wife and family:

> I remember my country
> And the time I left Wales,
> It is a bitter thing to remember the insults
> Which I endured from my family. †

On Good Friday, the threshing machine lay idle and he enjoyed his first holiday since Christmas Day. While the other workmen drank away their wages at the nearest hotel, Joseph preferred to spend the day alone writing a Welsh poem of 25 stanzas. With the ghastly image of his son Tom drowning still vivid in his mind, he felt it a duty to offer him some fatherly advice. Joseph composed no less than 26 Welsh verses of which the following two serve to illustrate the nature of his counselling:

Good Friday, 12 April 1870

> No idler be, hold sloth at bay;
> Record events each passing day.
> Some-one will profit from your work
> And praise your deeds always.

> Above all else remember
> To praise the World's Creator,
> For whatsoever path you take
> You're bound to Mother Nature. †

The advice was sound, but it seemed a poor substitute for his continued absence from Trecefel, particularly since both of Tom's elder brothers, Jenkin and Lewis, had died. At the end of April the threshing season came to an end. Once again he was out of work; but to add to his woes someone stole his personal possessions including his 'great crutch and lifeline', his diary. It was a shocking blow, and he made this impassioned plea to the thief to return his life's work:

> I've lost the labour of my brains
> Invaluable treasures, future gains ...
> You honest man I crave on thee
> Return'st my writing back to me.

Fortunately, Joseph retrieved the diary, which had been cast aside as useless by the thief, but he was once again reduced to wandering the countryside in search of work. Feeling depressed and adrift from his fellow countrymen, he decided to return to Forest Creek to seek work. But the labour situation there had also become difficult. '28 July 1870, thousands of men out of work and the gold fields deficient to pay wages . . . All complaining.' Joseph had recently sent John Lewis a postal order for five pounds; but when he arrived at Forest Creek Lewis asked for more money because 'he had puddled 24 loads of dirt which produced only three pennyweights of gold.' Although he felt uneasy, Joseph lent him the money, but he was later to discover to his cost that friendship could be a fragile thing, especially where money was involved.

Having suffered the privations and endured the indignities of life on the road, Joseph determined to use his pen once again to draw attention to the plight of itinerant workers in Australia. He was convinced of the need to adopt political means, and as a firm believer in the ballot box he decided to register his right to vote. '27 July, more than half the labouring classes are out of work or obliged to work for below fair wages. The Members of the Assembly should do something . . . Went to Castlemaine and did register myself as a voter . . . I was obliged to pay one shilling for the right to vote for a member of the Assembly House.'

Appreciating that this, in itself, was not enough, he used his writing skills to highlight the injustices suffered by his fellow workers. He composed tracts, poems and letters for publication in various newspapers 'defending the right of the swagmen to meaningful work and a living wage.' This was a cause close to his heart as evidenced in the following verses:

> Let all the Swagmen fairly state
> Their hapless life, their homeless state
> The squatters, miners, farmers too
> Having nothing now, for them to do.
>
> Without a home to lay his head
> He's scorn'd and starv'd till he's dead.
> The cruel tyrants can't enslave
> The tired workman in his grave.

On 26 September he found temporary employment on one of the huge sheep stations, and 'signed up an agreement to shear all the sheep on the station at one shilling and 3 pence a hundred.' It was a hard bargain and one that Joseph found he could not keep. After only a day's work he developed a sharp pain in his ribs which he attributed to the attack made on him by his family. 'Alas, I found I could not go on for my injured ribs and breast bone, the effects of the cruelties of my family tell so sadly.' Still desperate for work, Joseph sent the following earnest plea to Mr William Nash, who owned a large station at Lorrumberry:

> 8 September 1870.
> Sir,
> I am very sorry that my present circumstances compel me to implore your humanity. I am out of work . . . It was my intention to make myself useful to earn my bread and meat by means of honest labour . . . All my means are exhausted . . . I have a wife and 7 children to provide for. Am I going to be starved on this rich and plentiful land where men boast of their Christian like manner? . . . I am a stranger in these parts and do feel hungry . . . The produce of the land was ordained for the sustenance of the honest labourer . . .

As you are the governor of this fertile land about here, I considered it my humble duty to ask your immediate help during my present miserable position.

Your most humble servant

Joseph Jenkins

Travelling Swagman.

Receiving no reply to his communication, three days later Joseph wrote yet another letter:

11 September 1870

Sir,

Having applied for your sympathy, I had no reply. I went to the station keeper craving him for a bit of meat or anything eatable...I am hungry...Had only sugar and water for breakfast this morning...Pray let me have something to appease my hunger...I am not a loafer and never was

Obviously touched by the second letter, Mr Nash gave him work and supplied him with 'plenty of mutton and bread and tea to drink.'

In spite of his previous unfortunate experience, Joseph once again found himself shearing for a living. '12 October 1870, we were 7 shearers. The price was 12/6 per hundred . . . after it was signed, each had a glass of whisky . . . Each had to pay 10/6 for the shears, stones and oil. The Shears had to be sharpened by the stone after each sheep.' However, after Joseph had sheared the rams his old complaint returned, and he was unable to continue, 'because my breast bone is bad.' He also found the shears 'poor' and despised the supervisor for his inhuman behaviour and heartless treatment of the animals. 'The bounder was at me for not shearing close enough . . . The blood was frothing over the men's shoes . . . In fact, the poor sheep are nearly half skinned here . . . They care more for the fleece than the sheep . . . which can be bought after the clip for 9 pence each!'

The following day the situation grew even worse, and Joseph paints a pitiful scene. 'They were at me again for not cutting closer. I told them I could not be so cruel as to skin innocent creatures alive! After 6 sheep, I gave up and delivered the things back to the overseer . . . It was a pity to see the shorn sheep lying dead before going a few hundred yards from the hands of the shearer . . . Such an attitude would never have been found in Wales . . . The police ought to interfere and comply to the law of cruelty towards animals!'

Unable to endure such gratuitous brutality, Joseph left the shearing shed and returned to work for Mr Kinnersley of Spring Vale Farm, Lake Learmonth, where he remained until Christmas. The weather was untypically cold and his spirits were low on Christmas Day:

25 December 1870
>   Good times are passed. Who can be merry?
>   Christmas Day is cold and gloomy.
>   Gold is scarce and cant be found.
>   No wages and no work around.

On 31 December he again dwelt bleakly upon his fortunes during the past year, 'As this is the last day of 1870 . . . I consider that many strange things have happened during the year! . . . What benefit can be derived of all the wonders? Live and die! That is all!'

He opened his 1871 diary with, 'Here I do begin my 32nd diary but on different sides of the world . . . I wrote 17 pages to my daughter Margaret . . . I did write until my fingers got tired. Time is dull . . . No money to be merry.' With a touch of black humour he added the following verse:

> 1 January 1871
> TO A FRIEND IN THE OLD COUNTRY
> I'm far from the Land of my Fathers
> I'm feeble wherever I am,
> No-one except the grave diggers
> Ask me how I fare. †

Joseph felt the loneliness almost unbearable and missed his family in spite of his periodic bouts of anger towards them. Deeply depressed, he still maintained that his troubles were not of his 'own doing, but pre-ordained by destiny.'

> 1 January 1871
> After I was conceived in my mother's womb,
> Even before I could remember, I was wronged.

He continued in employment with Mr Kinnersley at Spring Vale Farm until 23 March when he left with a 'good reference'. His employer testified to the fact that he was a 'skilful man on the farm'. Joseph attributed his expertise on the land to his father, and many times in his diary he records his gratitude to him 'for compelling me to gain experience in every aspect of farming.'

Having received his wages from his master, Joseph set out for Ballarat where he stayed at the Railway Hotel and visited 'Mr Roberts the photographer to take my portraits in three guises.' One shows him posing at work, another spending wages, and one swagging in the bush with his billycan. He was anxious to obtain a pictorial record of his years as a swagman in

Australia and composed lengthy poems to accompany each one:

Joseph paid £1 5s for the photographs and promptly sent copies back to his family in Wales, which he hoped would suitably impress them. Fortunately, these photographs survived.

In mid-April he took to the road again and came to Clunes, which he described as 'a new golden sprung up town, the fifth biggest in Victoria with a population of 6,000.' According to Joseph, 'Melbourne was the first biggest town, second was Ballarat, third was Sandhurst or Bendigo and the fourth was Geelong.' He noticed that there was a large water plant on the outskirts of Clunes and in the hope of gaining employment there he wrote the following letter to the Manager, again claiming that he had a large family to keep:

19 April 1871

Sir,

Having a family of eight who are dependent on the returns from my daily labour, I am out of work. I do implore to be employed. I am able to perform the daily work of either a general or a heavy labourer.

Wishing my humble prayer to succeed

Yours obediently,

Joseph Jenkins

He failed to secure employment and once again decided to go into the bush, taking with him his medical chest containing cayenne pepper, quinine and a bottle of laudanum. He managed to survive the rest of the year precariously by working as a casual labourer in the Creswick, Smeaton and Maryborough districts. He still believed that his world was 'unfolding as it should' and he bade farewell to 1871 on a stoical note:

Man is a creature obliged to abide by circumstances as they happen . . . God never gave to mortal man authority to will and to work out his own plans. He, the harbinger of all thoughts, has ordained for man to be rewarded according to his knowledge and experience of things . . . Adieu 1871.

Meanwhile, back in Wales, the old order was slowly changing. He heard from his brother Benjamin that his mother had died at the age of 77 and he wrote a poem in her memory. In January 1872 his eldest daughter Margaret sent him a letter. Like the previous letters from Lewis and Betty, this letter shows the generous and forgiving nature of the family; they no longer harboured any bitterness against Joseph for his act of desertion. Margaret promises that the family will send Joseph the princely sum of £25 following his request to them for money. Betty, his wife, was the first to donate £5. The letter ends, 'I hope you will receive the five pound paper safe. We are all here giving our kind love to you and a Happy New Year.' The letter moved him deeply, for Margaret had always retained a special place in his affection and he had entrusted to her special care his many papers in Wales.

Yet he doggedly continued to live as a swagman in Australia, preferring to endure a nomadic existence which, despite its hazards, freed him from all other responsibilities. He continued to lurch from one crisis to another; he had many quarrels, he was often robbed, and even the snakes seemed out to get him:

Saturday 26 October, 1872, Mount Bolton
I did sweat much today and worst of all I was bitten by a snake which are very poisonous here. My thumb is very painful and swells. I must go to the Doctor if not to the

hospital. Could not sleep a wink for my hand and thumb. I did bathe them and applied my remedy.

In January 1873, he had another close encounter with a snake while he was working for John Hawkins at Coghill's Creek:

6 January 1873, Coghill's Creek
I went to reap and bind, o what a narrow escape I had from being bitten by a big black snake . . . The snake was under the swathe . . . as I had my hand under it, the big black reptile crept out from the swathe . . . Nothing was at hand to kill it, it was too big to tread upon. I called the binders but neither would go near it . . . I ran for a big stone and despatched it. It was 4 foot 7 inches long.

As a swagman he was exposed to all sorts of danger, from man and beast. Farmers, who did not generally welcome swagmen, usually set their dogs on them unless the swagman carried a revolver. Many swagmen also kept a dog on a leash for protection against attacks. As Joseph did not carry a revolver and did not own a dog, he was more vulnerable than most, and concluded, 'This is no land of milk and honey!'

On average he could earn about five shillings for a 17-hour day at the height of the harvest season. Always extremely careful with money and scrupulously honest, he was obsessive about keeping lists of his debts and expenses; on 6 August 1873 he set down his weekly requirements:

	s	d		s	d
Bread / 2 loaves		4	Onions		4
Candles		6	Salt		1
Oatmeal		6	Soap		7

Meat 12lbs	3	0	Pepper		1
Newspapers		6	Tobacco	1	4
Sugar 2lbs	1	0	Medicine		4
Tea 2ozs		4	Matches		1
Mustard		2	Tools and Clothes	2	0
Potatoes 14lbs		6	(Wear and tear)	2	0

Christmas 1873 found him at Mr McKay's Hut, Lake Learmonth. He writes that he is pleased with himself for joining the Good Templars, a temperance society, and 'after a rich dinner I went down to-wards the Lake and had a short swim.' On 26 December he notes that the 'All England Eleven Cricketers began to play against Melbourne Clubs.'

As usual, it had been a mixed year. Employers had cheated him and thieves had robbed him; yet most of the time he seemed reconciled to life's blows. He found solace in the bush by contemplating the natural order and his Celtic sensibility for nature had a religious dimension. He believed that man was responsible for the stewardship of the land, and he fulminated against those farmers who adopted a cavalier attitude toward the soil. 'They neglect to sow foreign grains like clover and lucerne, they crop the soil to death without bothering to manure the land... Although the land is rich, the land is Nature and Nature is honest... You may only take from it what you give to it. We violate nature at our peril and in so doing, invite disaster.'

CHAPTER 16
THE PAST LIVES MOST DEEPLY IN US ALL

Joseph's relationship with Australia was a complex one, almost a love-hate feeling. Sometimes he was fulsome in his praise for his adopted land claiming that, 'this is a vast, fine, glorious mysterious country.' On other occasions he could be scathing in his criticism. 'No honest man', he warned, 'should set foot in Australia.' A poem of eight stanzas composed while viewing the Australian landscape from a hill high above Smeaton reflects his ambivalent attitude. He called it 'The Ploughboy weeping over Smeaton' and began by singing the praises of this captivating continent:

> Behold what a beautiful country
> Formed through an imperative cause,
> For men to have comfort and plenty
> With peace, through good order and laws.

But he concludes by complaining that those who had 'invaded their country for gold' had sullied this idyllic state of affairs. Joseph could never reconcile himself to what he perceived to be slack and incompetent methods employed by the farmers:

> The land is ten times less value
> No shelter nor grass for the beast,
> Where's the civilised virtue?

> I cannot perceive it, at least.
> The heart of the land is exhausted
> The fences are withered and gone
> The dwellings are ruin'd and deserted
> And so are the homesteads thereon,
> Once was the garden of Victoria,
> Where plough boys and horses could feed,
> This beautiful spot of Victoria
> Is full of disorder and weeds.

He was firmly of the opinion that 'Australia could feed the whole of Europe if it were properly cultivated.' But the sight of thousands of animal carcasses littering the countryside prompted him to criticise the government for not making adequate preparations against the droughts by building dams to conserve water. 'This land,' he wrote, 'is neglected and exhausted owing to lack of forward planning and with no provision of manure to feed the soil.' He even went as far as to say, 'This country is wanting in high principles, humanity and morals. Melbourne is full of cheats . . . who rob a man if he does not look to his possessions.' This was in stark contrast to the description of Melbourne by the novelist Anthony Trollope who wrote, 'There is, perhaps, no town in the world in which an ordinary working man can do better for himself than he can in Melbourne . . . he has greater consideration paid to him than would have fallen to his lot at home.'

As a swagman Joseph had experienced life in the raw; unlike Trollope, he came face to face with the more brutal aspects of colonial life, being constantly 'overworked, cheated and abused'. Life was a constant challenge, and often what speaks most loudly in his diaries is his inward journey:

> This world is always full of strife
> Our age is only a race for life.
> Some are pleased to run uphill,
> And some run down against their will
>
> But few can here be found
> Who always run on level ground
> I cannot run, but slowly drag
> My ninety pounds of heavy swag.

By the beginning of 1874 Joseph had spent five years in Australia. He described the time as passing 'fast but also endless'. The posters in Wales for would-be emigrants had portrayed it as a land of limitless opportunities, but as far as he was concerned the dream had yet to be realised. He was nowhere near his goal of obtaining employment suited to his many skills and experience. In fact, he was still stuck on the bottom rung of the ladder, and this led to much frustration and bitterness. This was particularly the case when he saw a few of his fellow Welshmen thriving in the gold fields, but much of his envy was channelled towards the rich graziers, who owed their fortunes to thousands of acres of pastoral land. His ingrained sense of fair play led him to abhor the fact that, 'one man is allowed to hold a million acres of land with good surface soil . . . neither rated or taxed.'

By May 1874 Joseph was again without work. He immediately called at Learmonth Labour Exchange where he was directed to Mount Cameron Farm eight miles from Clunes and owned by a particularly ruthless farmer named William Clarke. His time there proved wretched and it ultimately affected his health. He described it as 'the most miserable place I have ever worked at . . . Both man and beast are worked to death and poorly fed.' He was paid two pence an hour and 'was obliged to sleep in a narrow passage leading from the barn to the stable.' On arrival at the farm he was ordered to plough a paddock of 140 acres made up of stony, rocky ground and was thrown to the ground twice because the horses drawing the plough were travelling at over four miles an hour. He started work at between 4 and 5 each morning and finished at 9, 10 or 11 in the evening. When his clothes became wet, there was no fire for drying them and all who passed trod upon his sleeping blankets. The horses fared even worse. William Clarke beat them mercilessly, forcing them to drag a plough for 14 hours a day uphill so that they developed 'the horrors', while he cursed and swore at them all day. Mrs Clarke was described as a 'nagging wife' who provided poor food and drove the workers as hard as her husband. After eight weeks of relentless toil and meagre rations, Joseph's health began to fail. He was now 56 years old. His constitution was so weakened that he was admitted to Maryborough Hospital suffering from quinsy and diphtheria. He became seriously ill and remained in hospital for 40 days.

Maryborough Hospital turned out to be almost as intolerable as Mount Cameron Farm, but it appears that Joseph must have proved a difficult patient. Despite feeling poorly and in constant pain, he struggled to write his diary each day. He was highly critical of the hospital regime which he described as 'harsh and inhuman'. During his stay he saw a 'very sick and lean Aborigine labouring under great shortness of breath' a few yards from his bed. When he finally died, Joseph claimed that, 'no more heed or notice was taken of his passing than if he were a fly or a moth.' The indifference to this man's death prompted the following lines:

12 July. Maryborough Hospital. 1874
> All class of people, race and tie
> Were born to life, to live to die.
> This world is nothing more
> Than tragic shipwreck near the shore.

Joseph was far from satisfied with his own treatment and, on occasions, felt that he was either ignored or victimised. He complained that the porters had deliberately placed his bed in a draught in front of an open window, causing him severe muscular pain. All night long the coughing and groans of fellow patients disturbed his sleep. He even went as far as to say that, 'A bed in the bush would have been more comfortable.' At last, 'after forty days in the wilderness I gained my freedom.' He was heartily glad to leave Maryborough Hospital. His stay there had seriously depleted his funds and he ruefully recorded that he was 'getting stronger ... but also getting further into debt.'

Still unfit for work and starved of companionship, Joseph now sought the home of a former friend and neighbour, David Evans, who had hailed from Bryn Madog, a mile or so from his family home of Blaenplwyf. He knew that David Evans and his wife Margaret had emigrated to Australia a few years previously and he found them living in Rheola, Johnstown, also known as 'Old Berlin', in the Castlemaine district. They had a small-holding and a vineyard and David Evans also supplemented his income by panning for gold in the nearby creeks. Joseph was warmly greeted at their home, for they had known him back home when he was a prosperous farmer; nor did they hesitate to offer assistance to this now 'down and out swagman', but they were shocked by his lowly condition in life. He had once spent many evenings at their old home of Bryn Madog where he invariably participated in the *eisteddfodau* which were often held there. The reunion with the Evans family was a truly joyful and emotional experience for Joseph. He described how, 'with full hearts we relived the old days with rivers of talk until the small hours.' With good food and rest he regained much of his former strength and was able to help David Evans clear the orchard, dig the garden and put up wooden posts as fences. At last, Joseph had found someone he could trust, and with whom he could safely leave his precious diaries and his few valuable possessions. But, by mid September, it was obvious that Joseph's health was yet again beginning to fail.

His symptoms were alarming. He complained, 'I cannot hold a scythe or button up my coat . . . It is a paralysis of a kind.' A doctor rather insensitively informed him that his condition was 'a grim, chronic and hopeless case!' On 10 October Joseph was again admitted to a hospital; this time at Inglewood. He found the experience as distressing as that at Maryborough. Although the doctor was 'very good and civil', he took great exception to the 'proud nasty cook who goes round scoffing at everybody.' He also objected to the 'wardsmen' whom he described as being 'lazy and indifferent, much to the discomfort of the patients.' Joseph's second visit to a hospital mirrored his previous experiences, and he proved to be an awkward, argumentative patient.

Once again Joseph had occasion to sympathise with the plight of the Aborigines. While he was convalescing with other patients in the grounds of the hospital, the conversation turned to the topic of the 'Australian natives'. Joseph was shocked to hear the majority of them express the opinion that, 'it was a right, and even a Christian obligation, to be rid of them all!' Appalled by this sentiment, Joseph's riposte was, 'In the name of everything, whence came such authority?' He also concluded that of all the immigrants to Australia, 'the Welsh prove the best colonists because they do not heed a man's colour or nationality.'

Joseph remained under duress at the hospital for one month, grumbling about cross draughts, disagreeable patients and the insensitive staff. He again declared unashamedly that, 'I would have been better off making my bed beneath the stars in the open bush . . . How I pine to leave this miserable place . . . kindness and even civility are in evidence only when the doctor is around.' Fortunately, his condition improved. He had, apparently, suffered an acute attack of rheumatism which cleared up of its own accord. When, finally, he was able to leave the hospital, so great was his relief that he remarked in his diary, 'thank God I escaped from their clutches.'

It was to David and Margaret Evans, Rheola, that he turned, yet again, in order to recuperate, for it was here that he felt closest 'to home'. His frequent bouts of illness had made him even more philosophical. In the company of the Evans family he was able to recall the colourful characters and events from his past in Cardiganshire, but there were still ghosts to exorcise. In a reflective state of mind, he wrote, 'times past are precious . . . nor can they be forgotten . . . If only I could remember the best and forget the worst . . . Separation has taught me that the past is where I belong.' It was a brave admission. He remained in the company of David Evans for six weeks, but on 20 December 1874, not wishing to impose further on his friend's hospitality, he left his diaries and other possessions with him for safekeeping and again took to the road. Within two days he had found work, picking peas for an

Irishman, John Whelan, at Warrenheip. He had arrived just in time for the holiday and wrote, 'on Christmas Day I had a splendid dinner of two geese among five people.' It was a reminder of happier times at Trecefel where geese were always plentiful at Christmas, but his contentment was short-lived. A fortnight later, Joseph's fragile composure was upset. '12 January 1875 . . . I had a dispute with the boss about a water cart . . . He called me a liar when I was right! So I left . . . He refused to pay me for Christmas and New Year's Day . . . I was very tired after being under the nigger driver . . . I told him I was not born in the right country to abide among Irishmen!'

Although he had stormed away from John Whelan's farm under a cloud, for once the sun broke through quickly and fortune smiled upon him. '14 January . . . I had a letter of introduction and obtained a position with Mr C. Ibbotson, a millionaire.' His new master owned a grand mansion called Spray Farm situated on the coast near Geelong. Joseph was enthralled by his new surroundings and wrote with delight, '15 January, O what a beautiful bay . . . I can see the Heads at a distance where all the ships of the world are obliged to enter for Melbourne . . . This spot of Australia is a tongue of land extending out to the Hobson Bay.' Not only was there a glorious outlook, but 'the conditions are the best I have ever encountered . . . The working hours are 3 or 4 hours shorter every day . . . and the living is 10 times better! Good tucker. No hurry . . . In fact, this place is too good to last for an unfortunate man like myself!' He could not believe his luck. He even approved of the farming methods. 'There are half a dozen fine water dams . . . the sheep and cattle are in excellent condition with pine fences . . . and the crops are the best I've seen in the colony.' At last, he seemed at peace with his surroundings and content with his world.

Compared to the other places, the work on this farm was not only pleasurable but relatively easy. He tended vegetables, such as carrots, peas, potatoes, and hundreds of acres of onions, as well as being responsible for the thatching. The land extended down to the beach, but there were certain dangers, 'sharks are in the bay and they have just killed a man.' Nevertheless, Joseph took full advantage of his new situation and even braved the dangerous waters. '24 January, I went down to the beach after breakfast and had a fine bathing in seawater. I don't remember that I had the pleasure of doing so in this country before . . . Feeling active in both body and mind.' The last time he had swum in the sea had been at Aberaeron, but this was a far cry from the safe bathing in Cardigan Bay. '26 February, I went down to the Bay in order to bathe . . . The tide was full . . . The sharks are numerous and ferocious. Either a living man or dog are desired bits. They devour fish, and a shark club is talked of.'

On 27 February he celebrated his sixtieth birthday with the words, 'When I look back on my past, it is only as yesterday, of tomorrow I know nothing!' His world seemed carefree, but his optimism was, as usual, tempered with a degree of pessimism. 'This is too good for an unlucky wanderer like me! Here there is no growling . . . All look cheerful and greet me with the glad words, "Good morning to you, old man."' On page after page of the diary he waxes lyrical about his perfect existence.

A happy Joseph sowed, weeded and harvested crops and 'threshed the peas with a flail.' The weather, however, was scorching, registering 113°F in the shade. In addition to the ferocious sharks in the bay, there was the constant peril of venomous snakes, but Joseph had long since learned to cope with this danger, claiming, 'I killed a snake four feet long on the verandah.'

Sundays were very relaxing. '7 March I went down to the beach and had a swim and did drink two pints of sea water. It soon took effect!' The precise effect is not noted! Rarely had there been a time of such happiness since he had landed in Australia, and time flew by too quickly for him to count the hours let alone the days.

Seldom had his diary been so free of acerbic comments as he praised the quality of life at Spray Farm. 'Oh, I was never better pleased that I am at this farm! My life is idyllic.'

In April, Joseph received a letter from David Evans informing him that Betty had sent him £5 from Wales, after learning that he had been unwell. Unfortunately, Joseph jumped to the wrong conclusion and believed that the sum had been sent to cover the cost of his funeral. Rather ungraciously, he recorded in his diary that, 'She [Betty] ought to be told that a man cannot be buried decently in the colony under £14. A grave in the cemetery costs £2; hire of a carriage or hearse £5; undertaker's fee £7.' This money had, in fact, been sent by his family as a gift. Although Joseph lent money to innumerable 'friends' in Australia, there is no evidence that he sent one penny to alleviate his family's plight in Wales. In his own mind he was always the injured party, believing that he had a monopoly on suffering.

His thoughts were constantly with his family, although they are sometimes tinged with malice. 'Sunday 18 April, I owe my daughter Margaret two letters, but to pay her in her own coin, she did not answer my letter to her for two years.' Relenting somewhat he added, 'parents do not generally take revenge on their children, I must try and write by the next mail.'

Despite his agreeable situation, he did experience the occasional mishap. In mid-April he became blind in one eye when a chip of wood caught him as he chopped a tree. He 'bathed it in hot water but suffered dreadfully.' On 9 May he was afflicted with an agonising attack of toothache when 'all my head and gums were painful . . . I cannot even bear my spectacles on to read and I pace back and fore like a madman.' Luckily, he recovered from these ailments and was carried on a wave of euphoria for the remainder of the year:

> 10 October 1875
>
> O what a glorious country this is, and the present climate ideal . . . My heart sings as I look out on the blue lustre of the Bay. How I wish I could acquire twenty acres of land to farm it on my own . . . Here the land is watered and the sheep and cattle graze as they should. Land was sold earlier for only one pound an acre.

The year ends on a note of unusual cheer and contentment. 'I have nothing to complain of. I was endowed with all necessities of life in every respect.' His good luck was to last three more months. Then, much to his dismay, his employment at Spray Farm was suddenly terminated on 31 March 1876 when his master, Mr Ibbotson, ran into financial difficulties:

> 31 March 1876
>
> I went to mend bags and overhaul potatoes in the barn. Very squally. As my master Mr Ibbotson is giving up cultivating the farm, my quarter is at an end today. No

more work for Jo here. I had over 14 months work and thanks for that. I saved £30.

Reluctantly, he took his leave of Spray Farm with a cheque for £20 5s in his pocket. Resigned to his fate he wrote, '1 April, I prepared myself again for the road.' He set out along Wallowby's track towards Castlemaine and 'his own people'. On 3 April 1876 he arrived at Tarnagulla and found accommodation with Mr and Mrs Edward Lewis at the Golden Age Hotel. Considering the vastness of Australia, it still seemed to be a small world, for Mrs Lewis hailed from the Vale of Aeron and had actually been at school with his wife Betty. She also had been well acquainted with Jenkin Evans, his father-in-law, and with the whole of the Tynant family. Needless to say, she knew all about the widely publicised quarrel between Joseph and Betty and, according to Joseph, 'She recounted to me my personal history, most of which was grossly distorted, even before I revealed to her my own identity. She heard my version and invited me to stay as their guest for a week longer, but I left the next morning to visit my friend David Evans, Rheola.' Joseph does not detail his 'version', but his abrupt departure from the Golden Age Hotel suggests that he was not keen to stay for another free week with the insatiably curious Mrs Lewis.

On his way Joseph, hoping to meet more Welshmen, called at the site of a 'new goldrush', four miles from Tarnagulla. Always keenly observant, his diary provides a fascinating glimpse of a town mushrooming following the discovery of gold:

10 April 1876

[The site] consists of a rugged hillock surrounded by trees

and scrub land ... some 1,500 tents and all sorts of temporary buildings had been erected there ... It already has the appearance of a small town with stores, banks, hotels, butcher shops and bakeries, a printing office, saw mills, carpenter shops, blacksmiths, and police headquarters ... some were engaged in blasting rock, others were using steel chisels and hammers. Picks are useless. Each claimed-plot measures 20 square yards, on which they sink pits varying from 15 to 30 feet in depth ... The area is taken up by prospectors, and hundreds of would be diggers leave without the chance of trying their luck, for the exercise is luck rather than skill.

This time Joseph chose not to try his luck at prospecting but continued to look for casual labour at various farms. Although work was still difficult to come by, he kept his spirits high by exploring the surrounding countryside. Unexpectedly, he found an ideal niche for writing his diary:

12 May 1876
This being Sunday ... I visited the creek. There I found a big stone, which served me as a chair; another one I adopted as my writing desk, which suits me admirably because it does not shake. There is nothing here to disturb me. The water murmurs as it runs over the pebbles in the creek, the magpie sings melodiously overhead ... I am deliriously happy.

Yet again, Joseph's joy was shortlived. He found himself in straitened circumstances, but the only work he could find was with a former employer, William Clarke of Mount Cameron Farm, a man whom he truly detested. It was a case of Hobson's choice. He turned up at the farm only to find conditions as bad as ever and a far cry from the blissful time he had enjoyed at Spray Farm. He described William Clarke as 'as mean as he ever was'. Although he had 'thousands in the bank he did not provide candles for dressing or undressing, nor did he provide soap.' Mrs Clarke was even more vicious; she proved a demanding, ungracious woman who immediately ordered Joseph to undertake a particularly demeaning and exhausting job:

14 May 1876
Mrs Clarke ordered me to clean out the two pigsties. They were last cleaned nine years ago. The litter was over six feet deep. I had to take off the roof before I could enter. It is written of Hercules that he did much heavy work, but it could hardly be heavier than cleaning out those pigsties. When I completed the work, Mrs Clarke's only remark was, 'Wash your boots before you come in to supper!'

Joseph was able to endure such treatment for only two weeks. With an enormous feeling of relief he left the Clarke farm at the end of May. After various other odd jobs he found a permanent position with Mr William Westcott of Moorabool Creek, near Bungaree. He was paid 17/6 a week and was well treated. His employer was a religious person and every morning prayers and services were held in the house where 'the gardener played the organ and some thirty workers attended.' His work consisted of hoeing and ploughing, but he still had to rise at 4 a.m. and work 17 hours a day. On freezing mornings he could scarcely grasp the handles of the plough and found it almost impossible to cut through the frost-bound earth. He found the work strenuous, especially when compared to the pace at home in Wales. 'Back in Cardiganshire, they talk of working hard... I do more work in a day than two men did working for me at home.' He also had to be ever vigilant. 'Snakes are abroad and numerous . . . They are of many kinds, black, carpet, tiger and whip varieties.' By now he was adept at confronting such hazards and managed to 'dispatch a venomous snake six feet long . . . They often drop from withered timber . . . My life is exposed to constant danger.'

One of Joseph's tasks on Mr Westcott's farm was to train young boys in the art of ploughing. This troubled his conscience, for he could not help thinking of his own two young boys growing up in Trecefel without their father. Joseph had been taught expertly by his father how to handle horses and follow the plough. He ruefully admits in his diary, 'Sometimes I think I should be at home training my two boys in the way of living.' However, he then justifies himself with the usual refrain, 'It was not my fault that I absented myself from their home!' In his notebook he admitted, 'The past is never past,' but he was never able to confront his own hypocrisy.

In June 1876 he received a letter from home with the news that Jenkin Evans, Tynant, his father-in-law, had died at the age of 94 years. Betty would have felt his loss keenly, but Joseph was not exactly grief stricken, having long fallen out of favour with him during his last year in Wales. He was more upset to receive news in October from his daughter Nel that Judge John Johnes of Dolaucothi had been murdered by Henry Tremble, his butler. He had great respect for Judge Johnes. He had heard his eloquent address at the 1867 National Eisteddfod at Aberystwyth and he described him as a 'cultured and honourable landlord':

22 October, 1876

Mr John Johnes was shot dead by his own Butler and afterwards his daughter was shot, but not mortally. The assassin shot himself after the cruel and dastardly deed. Mr Johnes was a man of unequal usefulness . . . an important Judge and Justice, a Liberal landlord and a great antiquarian. He was a gentleman in every sense of the word.

At Mr Westcott's farm Joseph continued to be well treated with 'good food and plenty of it.' He spent long hours hoeing beneath the fruit trees in the immense orchard, where the 'blossoming trees blazed in the bright sun.' Each morning, after breakfast, he attended a religious service when all the employees knelt to pray. His master was a devout Wesleyan Methodist. Joseph claimed that these were no different from the Calvinistic Methodists whom he had always hated. 'I found the tenets of the Wesleyans more Calvinistic than I'd thought possible.' Although Joseph faithfully attended the religious service held on a Sunday, much to his chagrin he was never invited to the supper that followed the sermon. He never understood why.

Joseph was reasonably content in the employment of Mr Westcott, but the conditions could be a 'mixture of religion and violence'. During the fruit-picking season he often found himself among 'a rowdy lot' and remarked, 'There have been two stand up fights already.' Despite the prayer meetings, 'swearing, fighting and thieving continued among the pickers.' Joseph complained, 'I had no peace to write my diary.' On 3 June 1877 a fellow workman scoffed at him whilst he was attempting to write his diary, and mockingly enquired of him what he was trying to do. Joseph retorted, 'I am building and carving my own monument, whether it will be for good or for bad.' It is unlikely that this reply held any significance for the picker, who clearly considered him to be odd. The farm was productive and the workers were kept busy as many varieties of fruits, such as cherries, plums, raspberries, gooseberries and rhubarb, were transported daily to Ballarat to be sold in the markets.

In December 1877 Joseph heard that his erstwhile landlord, the Reverend Latimer Jones, had died. Although the relationship between himself and the vicar had soured before he left Wales, he was nevertheless distressed by the news, which made him reflect on happier times at Trecefel. 'We may think that what has been has gone, but everything is stored in the memory. Two of the Trustees over my children until my return to Wales are now both dead.' (The other one being Jenkin Evans, Tynant.)

In his notebook he added, 'I'm 16,000 miles away from Trecefel but the past is not out there somewhere; it lives most deeply in us all.'

CHAPTER 17

MANY STORMS

So often in his diaries Joseph is immersed in morbid thoughts stemming from what he terms an 'unquiet heart'. He believed that some of his problems originated from childhood. Rather poignantly, he opened his diary for 1878 with these lines:

> 1 January 1878
> When I was a baby on my Mother's lap, no person would dare to upbraid her of her depressed hare-lipped child, as she considered her baby both innocent and faultless. But since then I have been forced to ride many storms.

Dogged by insecurity and plagued by elated highs and catastrophic lows, he starts the new year with this epitaph:

> Born for troubles, pain and distress
> To think, to toil for meals and dress,
> Abiding hunger, cold and dearth
> Retriev'd at last by Mother Earth.

With the passing of the years he felt increasingly isolated in Australia, becoming ever more conscious of his own mortality. Fear of a lonely death preyed on his mind and he penned this note as a precaution:

18. These photographs of Joseph in his working clothes were taken in Ballarat in 1871 and sent home to Wales. He maintained a regular correspondence with his family throughout his time in Australia.
(Pictures: Mrs Mair Owen)

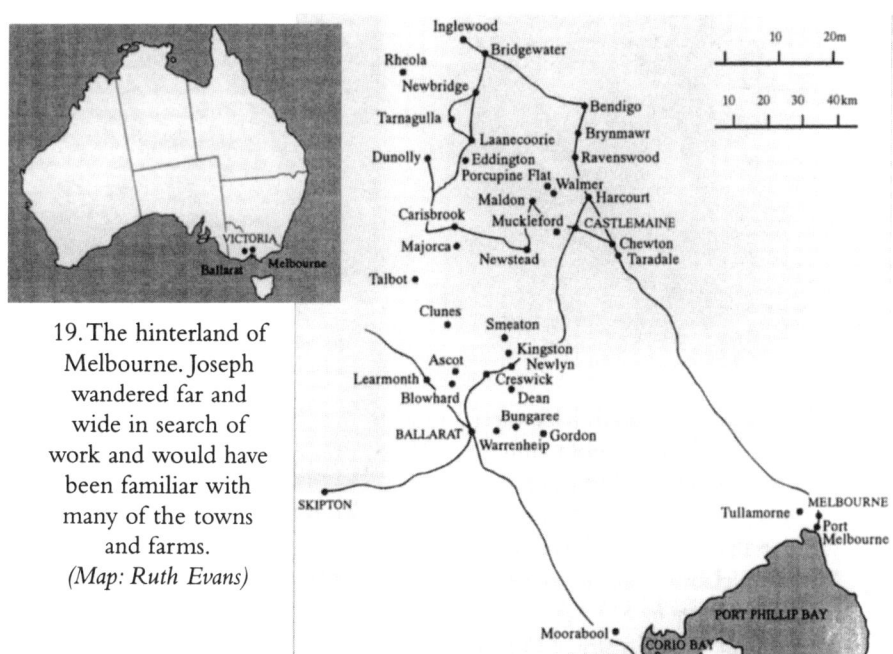

19. The hinterland of Melbourne. Joseph wandered far and wide in search of work and would have been familiar with many of the towns and farms.
(Map: Ruth Evans)

20. The Australian bush where Joseph found solace
in times of difficulty and stress. *(Picture: State Library of Victoria)*

21. Digging for gold in Victoria. Joseph's attitude to gold-mining was ambivalent. Although he referred to it as the 'bane of Australia', he himself staked out many claims – unsuccessfully. *(Picture by S. T. Gill. Copyright: State Library of Victoria)*

22. Joseph records his devastation on learning of the death of his son Lewis in Wales.

23. The barns at Spray Farm where Joseph spent his happiest hours. At a time when there were more than 200,000 swagmen looking for work in Victoria, Joseph counted himself fortunate.
(Picture: State Library of Victoria)

24. A group of Aborigines. Joseph felt a genuine compassion for their condition.
(Picture: State Library of Victoria)

25. Inglewood Hospital, circa 1870.
Joseph complained of cruelty at this establishment.

26. The Welsh Baptist Chapel, Maldon.
Joseph felt that the services were long!

27. Joseph, dressed in his
Sunday best.
(Picture: Mrs Mair Owen)

28. The Welsh Congregational
Chapel, Maldon. Although he
occasionally attended, he
preferred to stay at home and
read the Sermon on the Mount.

29. Ned Kelly prior to his execution. His escapades were followed with intense interest by Joseph.

NOTE: Every effort has been made to contact the copyright owners of each picture. In the cases where no source is given, relevant information would be appreciated so that any accreditation may be incorporated into future editions.

30. The armour forged by the Kelly Gang. Joseph sent vivid accounts to his family in Wales of the events leading up to the pursuit and capture of Ned Kelly by the forces of law and order.
(Picture: State Library of Victoria)

31. McArthur's Bakery in Maldon. Joseph regularly spent his lunch hour browsing through the excellent collection of books owned by his friend McArthur.

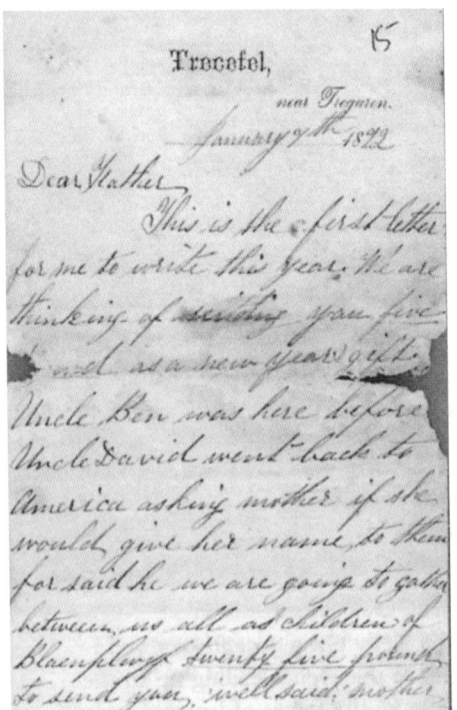

32. Over the years many letters must have reached Joseph from his family and friends in Wales but few have survived. This letter, sent by his daughter Margaret in January 1872, informs him that the family intend to send him some money.
(Picture: Miss Frances Evans)

33. Betty's letter to Joseph copied in his own hand. We can only speculate as to why he transcribed this letter into his notebook.
(Picture: Miss Frances Evans)

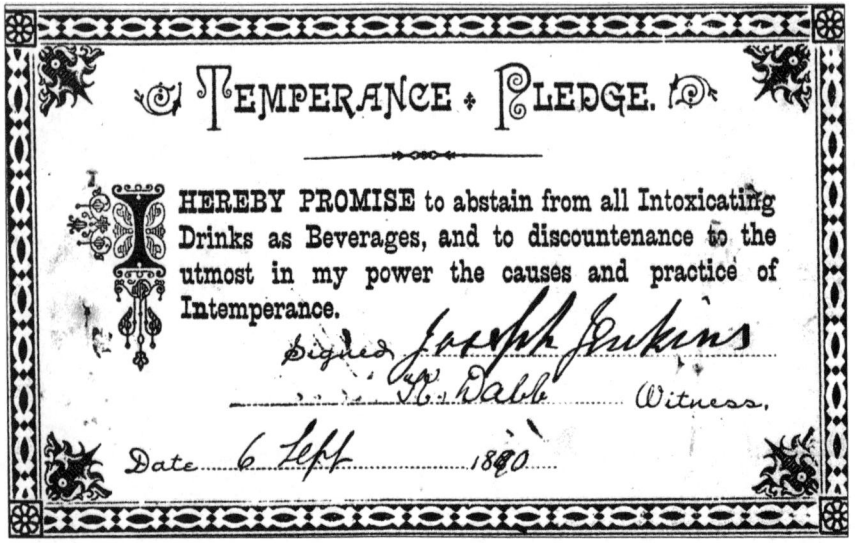

34. A Temperance Pledge signed by Joseph. During his years in Australia he managed to overcome the weakness that had so blighted his life in Wales. Sadly, he failed to keep to this pledge on his return home.
(Picture: Eryl Evans, Tangraig)

35. A final demand for rates owed by Joseph to the Council in respect of his cottage in Maldon.
(Picture: Miss Frances Evans)

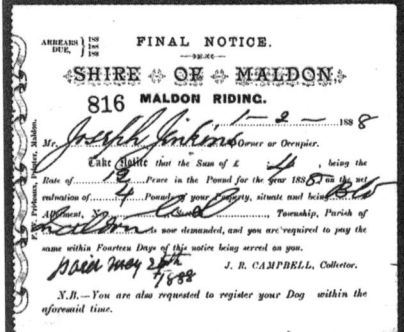

36. Joseph's brother John, an accomplished local poet who assumed the bardic title 'Cerngoch'.

37. *SS Ophir*, known as the 'Queen of the Indian Ocean'. There was a world of difference between Joseph's journey out to Australia and his return to Wales. He would have been delighted to learn that in 1901 the *Ophir* was chosen as the Royal Yacht for the Duke (later King George V) and Duchess of Kent, when they toured Australia.
(Picture: The Board of Trustees of the National Museums & Galleries on Merseyside)

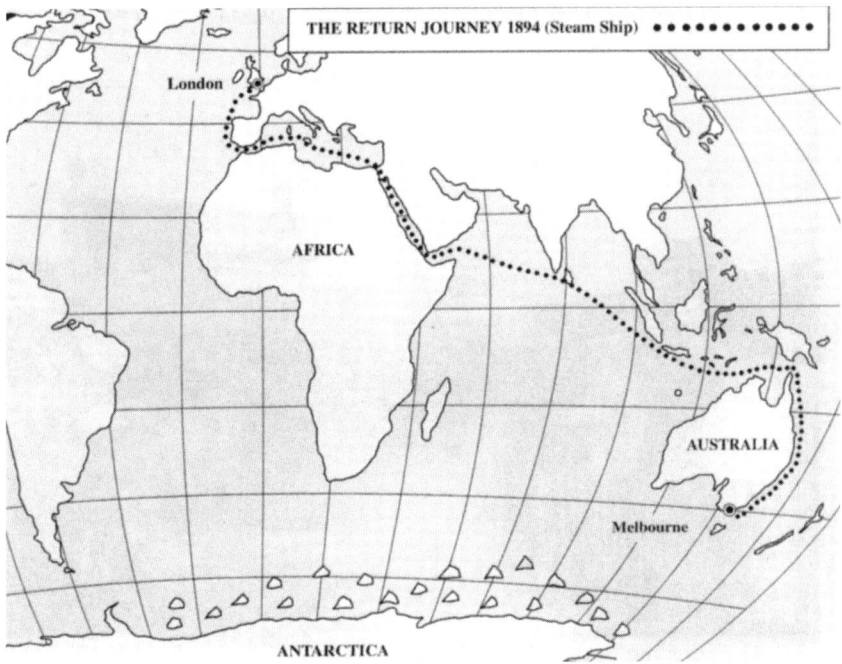

38. The return voyage via the Suez Canal proved to be much more pleasurable – and six weeks shorter – than the outward journey to Australia 25 years previously. *(Map: Ruth Evans/Siôn Ilar)*

39. Joseph's daughter, Anne. Like her father she was a prolific diarist. She was also an inveterate campaigner for the Temperance Movement.
(Picture: Mrs Mair Owen)

40. Although a radical by nature, Joseph was intensely loyal to Queen Victoria. He frequently lauded her achievements in verse and invariably celebrated her birthday.
(Picture: NLW)

41. Unveiling of the statue of Henry Richard M.P., the 'Apostle of Peace', in Tregaron square in 1893. In the background stands the Talbot Hotel where Joseph spent many convivial evenings in the company of the local gentry. *(Picture: NLW)*

42. A family group at Trecefel circa 1900. The photograph is believed to have been taken by Dr Evan Evans, Betty's nephew.

43. Tyndomen Farm, the home of Joseph's daughter, Nel. He spent many hours here following his return from Australia. The diaries were given to her for safekeeping and remained in the attic until they were rediscovered 70 years after Joseph's death.
(Picture: Robert Blainey)

44. Betty, Joseph's wife, in old age. She survived her husband by 21 years, dying at the age of 91 in 1919. It was she who looked after the children and kept the farm going during her husband's long absence in Australia. *(Picture: Mrs Mair Owen)*

45. The imposing memorial of the Trecefel family at Capel y Groes, Llanwnnen. Here Betty was laid to rest beside her errant husband. *(Picture: Mrs Evans, Glasfryn)*

46. This is all that remains of North Railway Gate Lodge, Joseph's home near Maldon station. However, in 1994 a water drinking fountain and a plaque were erected in Maldon to commemorate Joseph's achievement, citing his own words, 'Through this [diary] I am building ... my own monument.' *(Picture: Bethan Phillips)*

1 January

Should I happen to die or being disabled and could not speak for myself, I would be thankful for some of my survivors to let the following countrymen of mine know of my position. Mr David Evans . . . Mr John Lewis . . . Walmer Post Office.

N.B. Paper and postage stamps are generally plentiful in my books, which I always carry in my 'Swag.'

Joseph Jenkins.

The new year began on a less than happy note. Shortly after midnight he was rudely awakened at the crack of dawn. '1 January, I was annoyed in bed early this morning . . . I was awoken by a gun's report close to my bedroom . . . I would not welcome the foolish group.' The group consisted of a boisterous crowd of Scottish and Irish revellers celebrating the new year by discharging guns and cannons. They had assembled at the Lal Lal Falls where, later in the day, over 3,000 would attend the horseracing. Joseph strongly disapproved of such activities. 'There is too much gambling in this country, but the people will have it.' Joseph's idea of welcoming the new year was to listen to the dulcet tones of the *calennig* singers who would visit Trecefel on New Year's Day. He concluded that it would be far better if these rowdy revellers provided water for their dying cattle and sheep, as the temperature during the day soared to 103°F in the shade.

In such scorching conditions, Joseph greatly feared the outbreak of bush fires. The destruction caused by these was terrifying and widespread. His fears were soon to be realised for on 9 January he noted that 'scores of bush fires burned all around.' He was convinced that many of these were started by disgruntled swagmen taking revenge on farmers who put their 'savage dogs on men'. The punishment for starting a bush fire was £50 or six months in prison, but he claimed that it was 'impossible to detect a man setting fire to some corner, and lighting a single match would burn perhaps 90 square miles of grass, corn and homesteads.' Joseph described the pollution caused by these fires. 'The air was foul with smoke and visibility down to 2 yards from the rising dust and ash which drifts up to 6 feet in parts.' He repeated his belief that many fires were the work of 'hungry swagmen in retaliation for no work . . . and numerous farm workers are obliged to sleep and starve on the dusty roads because the farmers refuse to employ them over the weekend to save on Sunday meals.'

Joseph was constantly mystified by the unpredictable Australian weather. He claimed, 'it can change dramatically in the space of a day and even in the space of one hour . . . Ten days ago I could not hold the stone to hone my scythe because it was so hot; today I could not hold the rake and fork because of the cold. I sweat one day and shiver the next.' By the end of February the drought was so severe that sheep were dying by the hundreds and selling for four pence each.

On 27 February Joseph reached the age of 61, but he saw no reason to celebrate the occasion. 'I have not had much glorification . . . because I have had more kicks than either half pence or kindness in this world . . . after all the troubles and disappointments through traitors, fictitious friends and indifferent relatives.'

On 1 March, St David's Day, he felt somewhat more cheerful, possibly because he saw an opportunity to cover himself with glory. It was the day of the Ballarat *Eisteddfod*. It began disastrously. When he went to catch the coach, he found that, 'It was full of my countrymen, and no room for poor Jo.' He then rushed to Warrenheip Railway Station, but missed the train by half a minute. As a result, he was forced to walk nearly five miles in the intense heat to reach Ballarat in time for the afternoon session. Although exhausted, he was still eager to compete and found the *Eisteddfod* 'numerously attended'. The title set for the *englyn* competition was 'H.M. Stanley, the Explorer'. Joseph had composed his *englynion* on the road to Ballarat. The subject appealed to him, for he was immensely proud of the fact that Stanley, who had found Dr Livingstone in darkest Africa, was a Welshman whose real name was John Rowlands. There were six competitors for the *englyn*, but for the ninth successive year he was declared the winner. He was by now a well-known, popular and respected figure at the annual *Eisteddfod*, and in 1878 he was given a special prize:

1 March 1878

A certain young Lady presented me with a silk purse full of silver to hang it round my neck. Several knots of flowers were thrown up on the stage to me.

A euphoric Joseph, always a brilliant public performer, then proceeded to regale the audience with a seventeen-verse poem, reminding those present of the purpose of the *Eisteddfod*. The following verse will serve to illustrate the general theme:

Meeting to acknowledge the language of our forefathers
And to use it with respect,
Meeting to improve our lives
Making true brotherhood our aim. †

He confessed that, 'scarcely one third of the meeting could

understand my address, yet I had long and warm cheers and continual clapping of hands.' With the plaudits still ringing in his ears, he rushed to catch the coach home. 'But alas, I was too late again as all the seats were taken.' He was obliged to stay the night at Ballarat, having secured accommodation at the Bridge Hotel, a favourite place for Welshmen to celebrate St David's Day. Leaving his compatriots singing loudly at the bar, a fatigued but triumphant Joseph crept wearily to his bed. 'Having retired at 9 o'clock sharply and left scores of my countrymen singing the compositions of 'Dai'r Cantwr', David the Singer, I have an excellent bed, but dear for a shilling. It is a respectable house kept by Mrs Ann Thomas – in fact, it is a Ballarat Hospital for Welshmen whether they have money or not. My room was No. 19. Very warm.'

The following day Joseph was back 'at the tail of the plough', his only company being 'the odd snake about'. While ploughing on the farm he noticed a number of surveyors who had come to plot the track of the new Gordon-Warrenheip railway line. Victoria had now embarked on a massive scheme of public works in order to stem the rising tide of unemployment, and hundreds of miles of railway tracks were soon to be laid. The sight of these men brought back memories of those long distant days when he himself had been involved in the planning of the M&M Railway in Wales. Now he stood as a lonely bystander, whose only vocation was that of a lowly ploughman struggling to open a straight furrow through the rock-hard earth.

But when he was not labouring in the fields, Joseph continued to campaign on behalf of the unemployed and alleviate the 'abysmal conditions of the swagmen'. The arrival of wave after wave of new immigrants into Victoria had increased the population of the colony to over one million and unemployment had soared. Joseph bombarded the *Geelong Times* with letters drawing attention to the 'scores of half starved men craving for work without success.' In July 1878 he had 'the satisfaction of seeing a few sentences I wrote in the Geelong Times quoted by the Governor.' The Government had borrowed £50,000,000 from public and private creditors and there followed a boom-style extravagance, with spending on buildings, railways, communications and irrigation schemes. But Joseph saw this as a 'Fool's Paradise'. The public debt rose from £20 to £50 per head of the population, and he predicted that such reckless borrowing would end in economic disaster. 'They will surely saddle their children with debts.'

Letters from his family and friends arrived periodically, many of them containing sad news. 'On 18 July I read of the death of my generous friend Colonel Powell, Nanteos.' He proceeded forthwith to write a poem in memory of the Colonel, whom he described as 'humanitarian, warm hearted and excellent, who opened his hand and gave to the poor.' By any measure, this was an effusive assessment of his landlord friend.

Unfortunately, in September 1878, Joseph was again struck down by illness. He had worked for over two years at the Westcott Farm, but was now obliged to give up his employment because of severe stomach pains and bladder trouble. He records his last day at the farm, which was still hectic, in spite of his weakened state:

28 September 1878
Westcott Farm, Morabool Creek
After an early breakfast I went to mend fences . . . I did cut and earmark the Lambs. After dinner, went to plough at

the orchard . . . Very likely the last job of ploughing to be done by me on this farm or any other farm during the remainder of my advanced life. Having settled for my wages after supper, twenty pounds and four shillings and ten pence were due to me.

On 2 October 1878 he was admitted to Ballarat District Hospital which accommodated 30 patients under the care of Dr Owen, a Welshman from Denbigh. He was naturally apprehensive. 'I cannot be easy in my mind thinking of the painful operation which awaits me.' He was taken immediately by a wardsman to a room, where he underwent an excruciating examination of his bladder. 'I was laid down on a frame and the wardsman was holding me. I cannot express in words the pain I had when the doctor was injecting some stuff up to the neck of my bladder . . . Painful in the extreme.'

When he was returned to Ward 8, in a somewhat macabre turn of events, he found that he was placed next to the mortuary. He observed bleakly, 'the Dead House was right before my eyes!' Convinced that he would not survive any of the treatment, he seemed to accept his condition with an air of gracious resignation:

> In peaceful rest the humble abide,
> No more ambition strife or pride,
> Whatever troubles here might bring
> I thank God for everything.

Once again, death passed him by, but the agony endured. 'I could not sleep a wink all night . . . the pain was so constant, not a moment of intermission.' Nevertheless, he was buoyed up by the many unexpected visitors who came to see him, and his flagging faith in mankind seems to have been revived. 'It shows me that people are very kind and brotherly to each other . . . to add to my comfort.' He was touched by their compassion and realised that, possibly, he was not so unloved after all.

His feelings toward the hospital itself were less charitable. 'Up according to order between 6 and 7 a.m. I had to make my own bed . . . I'm scarcely able to stand . . . I could not make my bed to please the wardsman.' Although Joseph admired Dr Owen, he loathed 'one particularly cruel wardsman' whom he called a 'growler', and claimed that he was 'inhumanly treated'.

On 13 October he was delighted when some of the ladies visited him 'loaded with presents for old Jo. Jellies, cheese, cakes, tobacco and Flannels ready made.' Dr Owen visited him daily and on 18 October he was told that he was sufficiently recovered to leave the hospital. Thankful that the ordeal was over, Joseph spent the night at the Bridge Hotel, where his old friend Mrs Ann Thomas provided him with a bed and a meal for two shillings. He was so relieved at his recovery that, once again, he had his photograph taken and arranged for twelve copies to be sent to Wales.

He returned to John Lewis's farm to recuperate, but within a fortnight he was again laid low by illness. On 3 November he remained in bed 'too unwell to move'. The next day he passed 'urine as red as blood' and, as usual, blamed Betty for his condition. '5 November – I'm getting worse – what my tormentors at home will gain of this business I cannot see. The mother of my children is the sole cause of it all.'

In addition to the poor state of his health, the isolated location of John Lewis's farm on rough, high ground, many miles from the nearest neighbour, also caused him great anxiety. 'I am in a very inconvenient place to die, 15 miles from the cemetery and among those that cannot go to much expense on my behalf. I wish I was with my friend and countryman David Evans.' He dreaded the thought that he would be deprived of a respectable funeral and that he would leave this life without having paid all his debts. These concerns had their origins in his Welsh background, where the measure of a person's worth in the community would be reflected by the size and nature of the funeral. He worried that if he were to die at John Lewis's farm, he would be buried like a dog, 'as cheaply as possible'.

By Saturday 9 November his condition had deteriorated so much that Evan, John Lewis's son, had to take him to Castlemaine Hospital. It was an agonising journey. 'The rough road on a cart without springs gave me a good shaking . . . We left at 8 o'clock, very warm . . . I was obliged to cut some thick bush to screen the rays of the sun. We reached the Hospital at 11 a.m. and Dr McCrea saw that I was very bad. On admittance I was given a good bathing with leaves from the gum tree . . . and through the shaking of the Dray over the rough road in the Bush . . . the sore place broke out into puss and bad matter. I was eased of my great pain and fell dead asleep for three hours.'

Over the next few days he slept badly and felt he was 'getting weaker in both mind and body.' The greater his pain, the more he fumed against Betty:

15 November 1878

Very painful; All is the work of my female tormentor at Trecefel. I am very ready to forgive always, but I am very doubtful of her – as she continues still in her frolics. No person is entitled to forgiveness while going on in the most infernal transactions.

In the above entry we get an oblique reference to Joseph's belief that Betty had been unfaithful to him in Wales. There is no firm evidence for this conviction on his part, but his obsession was such that he often wrote sexually charged stanzas openely accusing her of adultery. In one such verse he indulged in a violent sexual fantasy about Betty. Afterwards, trapped by the conflict of his own morality and what he considered to be sinful desires, he cried out in self-loathing, 'Who will save me from the curse of myself?'

Meanwhile, another more pressing and immediate problem beset him, that of chronic constipation. He complained that the Doctor and staff refused to give him medicine to remedy the condition, but the wily Joseph had come prepared. 'I take my own opening pills on the sly!' Joseph had always been his own physician and carried on his person concoctions to remedy most ailments. His motto was 'Heal thyself wherever possible.'

The nights proved the most troublesome. He complained, 'I cannot find a comfortable position, sometimes I lie on my back, sometimes on my belly . . . but always I am tortured by pain.'

He did not endear himself to the staff or his 'fellow sufferers' as he readily confesses:

> While groaning, moaning all in train
> I cannot shake off the twinging pain,
> When all I do is mourn and weep
> Disturb my comrades of their sleep.

If Betty had any psychic tendencies she, also, must have been disturbed, for his sustained rage continued unabated:

> My pain is so severe
> I'm tired of my life,

> More I cannot bear
> I wish for final strife;
> The very cause of this
> Is half the globe away,
> She can't enjoy the bliss
> Of my tormenting day.

A little charity might have worked wonders to redeem his warring state of mind, but he became so low that he desired to end it all. 'I cannot choose, or wish anything other than for death to release me.'

Added to all this distress was another worry – the predatory designs of the Lewis family. Over the years John Lewis had been an incompetent farmer. He had neglected the land and wasted his time and energy in a fruitless search for gold. In consequence, he could scarcely make ends meet. Many times in the past he had begged Joseph for loans and the total debt now stood at £37. Seeing Joseph in his vulnerable state, the Lewis family stepped up their visits to the hospital. Evidently they were motivated by interest in his money rather than concern for his welfare. '24 November, John Lewis called on me today and brought me some cheese. They are very kind and attentive these days. They wish to borrow £8 or £10. So the world goes!'

On 26 November 'poor Jo' was in no condition to withstand the pressure of the Lewis family. 'Evan Lewis came to see me with a piece of sweet cake . . . according to his wishes I went out with him and drew £10 out of the Bank in order to lend his father.' Joseph added rather plaintively in his diary, 'When shall I see the money again?' The answer would be never. In intense pain he nurtured one deep wish, 'My body begins to swell and I would like to see my children before I die.' His situation was not improved by the scant sympathy shown by the doctor towards one of his more troublesome complaints. 'How long the day is when under desperate pain! The piles are my principal tormentors, at which the Doctor only laughs!' There seems to have been little sympathy for Joseph in Castlemaine Hospital, and his tendency to question everything proved to be a constant irritation to the staff.

During his illness he wrote, 'Rest is my healer, but books are my salvation.' He studied his Bible daily and pored over the works of Calvin, Voltaire, Milton, Shakespeare and anything else he could find in the hospital library. Despite believing himself to be *in extremis* he managed to write his diary every single day, noting every itch, twitch and irregular pulse beat in his body.

At last, on 2 December, the doctor declared Joseph fit to leave Castlemaine Hospital. He stayed once more at the home of John Lewis where, as usual, he was made to pay dearly for his accommodation. His health remained fragile and he complained, 'I feel so weak and tired that I am scarcely able to walk.' Since it was never in his nature to be idle, Joseph struggled to help on the farm, but it was only with great difficulty that he was able to get about. He had become increasingly irritated by the slovenly and inefficient manner in which Lewis managed his 200 acres; he also felt offended by the Lewis family's treatment of him generally. Above all, he hated the isolated situation of the farm, which he deemed unsuitable for a man in his debilitated condition:

18 December 1878, Ravenswood
This is a very curious spot in the Colony. No travellers passing by. No newspaper can reach it. No Post Office

near the place and the inhabitants are so indifferent to the transactions of the rest of the world. The Bush Rangers [the Kelly Gang] might have ransacked all the Banks throughout the Colony as far as we know!

During the past fortnight he had been informed by 'Bush Telegraph' – his friends – that there was a registered letter for him at Walmer Post Office, but he still did not feel sufficiently fit to walk any distance to collect it. His recent suffering had made him more solicitous of his health, 'It is my personal duty to look after my own health . . . and I am not doing it when working 16 hours out of 24.' As the tension grew between himself and John Lewis, Joseph decided that this was not the ideal place for recuperation and made arrangements to leave. He was taken to Walmer Post Office to collect the registered envelope, which contained four £5 notes, sent by his family at Trecefel. He does not record a note of gratitude or thanks in his diary for this generous sum, which was obviously sent at some sacrifice. He deposited the money at the New South Wales Bank and went on to visit his friend David Evans, Rheola, whom he knew he could trust. Feeling groggy and dispirited, he decided that it was time to put his affairs in order:

> 23 December 1878
> I left my will with David Evans with all the security I have for my little money, in order to defray my funeral expenses should I happen to die in this country.

In the meantime he was disturbed to hear that John Lewis had sunk even more deeply into debt. As one of his principal creditors, it caused him considerable anxiety. He was much concerned about his own future and how much longer he could survive. He had tried scything, but had found it too difficult. 'I fear I shall be unable to get work, for my poor health will not stand the strain of hard work ... the present rate of pay is two shillings for a day's work of sixteen hours.' His disenchantment with farming conditions continued, 'The crops here are destroyed by hares, kangaroos and parrots ... Bush fires are frequent ... the farmers have not prepared fodder for their cattle. No work for labourers ... Rain is wanted badly ... It is 103°F in the shade and 117°F in the sun.' He ended the year by passing judgment on the farmers around him – accusing them of enjoying themselves at the cost of the land:

> 31 December 1878
> I should like to see the Colonials taking as much interest and using their skill in farming as they do in cricetting. Lord Harris and his Team of All Eleven from England are here now.

He referred to 1878 as having been 'been full of pain, physical and psychological.' Although he never admitted to it, possibly the worst pain was caused by the unresolved conflict between himself and Betty.

His attention was soon diverted in a totally different direction. In the coming years Joseph became obsessed by the activities of four young men whose escapades gripped not only Australia, but the whole of the Western World.

They were known as the Kelly Gang, consisting of Ned Kelly, aged 23, his brother Dan, 17, and two accomplices, Joe Byrne, 21, and Steve Hart, 18. Ned was the son of 'Red Kelly' who had been transported from Ireland for stealing two pigs. The Kelly family felt a deep-rooted sense of injustice, claiming that the police were unfairly harrying them. The abject poverty caused by unemployment and unfair land laws led to a great deal of social unrest. This fuelled the young Ned Kelly with such a hatred of the establishment, especially the forces of law and order, that he and his young friends became bushrangers. They indulged in many criminal activities, such as 'duffing' horses, robbing banks, and even murder.

Joseph Jenkins, always an avid reader of newspapers, took an intense interest in their exploits and recorded events as he saw them unfold:

> 15 December 1878
>
> I had the Leader and The Age. Full accounts of the Bush Rangers were in the papers. They are 4 in a gang and did rob a Bank, a Station etc., all in broad daylight and in a populated place. The Bank was in a township. Scores of Troopers and others are after them since the last three weeks. The Bank was only 93 miles from Melbourne and close to a Railway station.

Because he snatched his accounts from newspapers as they appeared, Joseph's diary entries are often sketchy and incomplete. The above is a reference to a raid on a Police Station at Faithfull's Creek, near Euroa. The gang cut the telegraph wires and took over an entire township, managing to steal £1,942 from the National Bank. It was executed with incredible panache. Over the next eighteen months, other flamboyant raids followed, including the shooting of three policemen. Despite the offer of substantial rewards for their capture the Gang continued to evade the law.

A climax was reached on 28 June 1880 when the Gang took at gunpoint the local inn in the small town of Glenrowan.

Ned's intention was to lure the police into a trap by derailing a train carrying troops to Glenrowan, but the plan was foiled with tragic consequences. Joseph's diary takes up the story:

> Tuesday, 28 June 1880
>
> Latest news – 50 policemen got the outlaws inside a certain Hotel so that they have not the least chance of escape. A terrible report is spread about the Bushrangers today asserting that three of them were burnt intentionally inside an Hotel at Glenrowan over a hundred miles from Melbourne. Today it was a regular battle, shooting volley after volley on both sides. Two children and the Landlord were shot inside the Hotel with another man. The outlaws had about 30 prisoners inside. Quarter Cannon was sent from Melbourne, but the house burnt down before the cannon arrived. It is said that the Bushrangers inside were shot before the house was set on fire. Two bodies were left inside to roast. The Bushrangers had steel armour and helmets. The contest took place on Sunday night and yesterday. Ned Kelly is alive to be hanged.

Ned Kelly and his gang had forged for themselves suits of homemade armour from iron ploughs, hoping that this would make them invulnerable to bullets. Encased in this medieval-like armour, Ned Kelly advanced toward the police as a hail of bullets ricocheted from his huge bucket-shaped helmet and breastplate. He returned fire until, shot in his unprotected legs, he crashed to the ground riddled with 28 bullets.

By 1 July 1880, the horrific circumstances surrounding the death of Ned's friends raised questions concerning the actions of the authorities. A general wave of sympathy arose for the

Kelly Gang, and Joseph, who had previously condemned them unreservedly, now became more ambivalent in his stance:

> I went to the reading room and found columns of additional news about the captured Bushrangers. It is evident that two of them, Dan Kelly and Steve Hart actually joined to shoot each other inside in order to avoid the pain of being roasted alive . . . they stripped the armour plates for the purpose. The Authorities are now ashamed of their unusual cruelty and torment used after getting the gang hemmed in without any chance of escaping alive ... The Bushrangers were a terror among the country Bankers, but they came to a bad end at last like every other wickedness.

Eager to share this excitement with his family back in Wales, he tried to purchase newspapers, to no avail:

> 7 July 1880
>
> I cannot obtain a copy of the Leader this time to send home with portraits and the history of their capture – Having paid for 4 copies!! But I am afraid that they will be scarce and dear if can be had at all. Should the picture be in shape and character of a renowned preacher or Bishop, the demand for them would be different. Bush Ranging is the taste of the people.

On 28 October 1880, Ned Kelly was tried for the murder of Constables Lonigan and Scanlon in the Central Criminal Court at Melbourne. He was found guilty and condemned to death. The presiding judge was Sir Redmond Barry, a distinguished Ulsterman, Attorney General and Chancellor of the University of Melbourne, but Ned remained unimpressed by the high status of his fellow Irishman. When the judge donned his black cap to pronounce the sentence, Ned, disputatious to the last, continued to interrupt him and finally remarked, pointing his thumb downwards, 'I will see you where I'm going!' Ironically, within ten days Judge Barry himself had died of diabetes.

Often the prospect of a young man about to die evokes a groundswell of sympathy while his misdeeds tend to be forgotten. This was the case for Ned. Petitions of clemency were signed by 30,000 people and presented to the Crown. But the authorities were not to be persuaded; they had already suffered numerous humiliations and sustained too many losses because of Ned Kelly.

Confined in Melbourne Gaol, Ned faced the prospect of imminent death with equanimity. His mother, to whom he was extremely close and who was also imprisoned in the same gaol, exhorted him, 'Be sure to die like a Kelly.' Defiant to the end, Ned sent out his own message to his followers, 'Tell them I died game.' A 'battler' to the last, on 11 November 1880 he faced the hangman with courage and dignity. Joseph described his end:

> Friday 12 November 1880
> It appears that Edward Kelly the notorious Bushranger was hanged yesterday morning at 8 o'clock a.m. All his confession on the scaffold were three words – 'Such is Life!'

Another aspect of this story affected Joseph. The executioner was a white-haired septuagenarian, and the spectacle of an old man taking the life of a young man appalled him:

> 12 November 1880
> The hangman was an ex-convict over 70 years of age known by the name of Up-John. It is reported that his

hair was as white as snow. I do not think that any nation will thrive by authorising the old to hang and murder the young.

Joseph even made a play on the hangman's name:

> Up-John and drop the Kelly
> Give him a mortal swing,
> You'll have his clothes with money
> And be called the Hangman's King.

The life and death of Ned Kelly posed a problem for Joseph Jenkins. He could not condone the crimes, particularly the murders, but he was nevertheless troubled by the actions of the authorities. He was also concerned about the social injustices which might prompt others to follow in these young men's footsteps. In an age when the Old Testament exhortation of 'an eye for an eye and a tooth for a tooth' was widely accepted, his abhorrence of the death penalty shows an independence of thought in one who was, in most other ways, a conventional Victorian. The spectacle of public executions, which were in vogue in England and Wales until the 1860s, he had always viewed with distaste and he harboured serious doubts about their effectiveness as a deterrent. Writing in July 1866 he said that:

> The English lawmakers believe that public hanging will reduce crime and put fear into the hearts of the beholders. Yet, it is nothing but a public spectacle.

The 'uncommon calmness' of Ned Kelly as he met his death at the hands of the geriatric Up-John impressed Joseph. The last words uttered by Ned as he stood on the scaffold moved him deeply. This fatalism was in tune with Joseph's own philosophy of life, and such stoicism from the lips of a young man about to die left its mark upon him.

As the memory of the Kelly Gang's excesses faded, their exploits began to be invested with a mythical quality and to assume heroic proportions. Ned Kelly's death took on an aspect of martyrdom as his story became enshrined in legend and as he himself became lionised in song:

> So sing of Ned Kelly the lad of renown
> The pride of Australia, the scourge of the crown,
> Sing of his bravery and God bless his head,
> And bury the truth as you bury the dead.

Men die easily, but myths die hard, and this is true in the case of Ned Kelly, whose legend seems to grow with each passing year. For Joseph, the sequence of events he had followed so closely had been an exciting interlude, providing a welcome diversion from his own seemingly endless troubles.

CHAPTER 18
TROUNCED BY FATE

The exploits of the Kelly Gang had brought a touch of drama to Joseph's diary, but he confesses that the greater part of his Journal is made up of mundane happenings. 'I wish the reader to understand that my diary is principally an account of my movement and whereabouts. I know that the reader of it would find it very dreary and distasteful . . . but that is the reality of life. Yet, it has given me more pleasure than labour.'

It is true that much of what is written in the diaries can be 'dreary', but it is remarkable that he managed to sustain the mammoth task of keeping a daily diary in the midst of all his travails. Frequently, he had no suitable place to write and often could scarcely hold his quill from illness or fatigue. He conceded, however, that much of what he wrote would be of no interest to anyone but himself:

> No user of my diaries can profit from reading about . . . what time I rise in the mornings . . . what I do during the day . . . but he may appreciate the care and labour taken under great disadvantages . . . it is no common thing for a hard toiling man to do.

Amidst all his crises, obsessions and often purgatorial existence, writing his diary was a catharsis which, he claimed, 'saved my sanity.' Joseph's hero David Copperfield commented that, 'trifles make the sum of life,' and this dictum could well be a description of the diaries. He also genuinely believed in the discipline of keeping a daily Journal and strenuously advocated its educational worth. 'The present state of compulsive education would be more complete . . . if the Government were to provide a blank diary for every boy and girl to be filled up regularly . . . it would lessen crime in the Colony . . . Writing a diary would nurse their learning throughout life.'

In the early months of 1880 he wrote 'life is no joke' and not without some justification. He earned a mere two shillings a day and was paid only six shillings for digging a whole ton of potatoes. Ever concerned about unemployment and low wages, on 20 January he wrote a letter to *The Leader* under the heading 'The State of the Working Man', in which he again urged the government to provide a basic minimum wage for labourers. On 27 February he reached the age of 62 feeling low in spirit. 'I have nothing to glory in except the general rain that falls to cheer up both man and beast; I was born on Friday 27, an unlucky day!'

He was invariably unhappy with the political situation in Victoria. In June 1880 the newly elected Parliament was dissolved after only 45 days in power. Much to Joseph's vexation, the Liberal party had been defeated over a new Reform Bill for improving working conditions in the colony. Joseph's answer was, 'We ought to petition the Governor to manage this colony alone . . . the national debt has risen from £4 14s 6 per head since I arrived here to £22 10s at the present time.' In July the Liberal party was returned to power with a majority of 15 over the Conservatives.

However, the colony remained in a state of economic

depression; in September Joseph was paid only half the wages due to him. His personal affairs became so desperate that in October 1880 he yet again cast to the wind his former objections to 'the evil of avarice and the corrupting influence of gold' and turned once more to prospecting.

> 23 October 1880
>
> I tried my hand at digging, having measured and registered my claim ... Had a pick sharpened by a blacksmith for one penny. I dug a hole 5 feet by 3 feet but found nothing ... Like David Copperfield I was born on a Friday evening, during a waning moon, so I am not destined to be happy and rich.

Two of his former Cardiganshire neighbours, David Evans, Rheola, and David Jones, Rhiwonen, also joined him. In all, eighteen holes were dug, but without success. To commemorate this abortive joint enterprise, he wrote the following lines:

> Three Cardis dig for gold
> Among the grit and stone,
> Their prize and pay all told
> Is just a speck alone. †

Joseph gave the 'small specks' to David Jones who posted them home to Rhiwonen. 'One thing is certain,' wrote Joseph, 'it will not be too heavy!'

Towards the end of October he received a letter from his daughter Nel informing him that he was a grandfather. She had given birth to a daughter, Elizabeth, on Friday, 13 August. Joseph's gloomy reaction was, 'So like her grandfather and David Copperfield she is unlikely to be lucky.'

He spent the last week of 1880 at the farm of David Evans,

where he again dug unsuccessfully for gold. 'I am,' he wrote, 'very downhearted in that I have neither constant work nor money . . . More immigrants have arrived, and this will harm the labour market.' In the new year Joseph was forced to tramp the roads again.

He found occasional work with Mr Glendenning of Summerset Farm, Kingston, but more often than not he earned nothing. For a few weeks he was given accommodation at a labourer's cottage. '5 March, I work without a wage and in lieu of board and lodgings . . . Work is life's principal comfort . . . I owe a great debt to my parents for compelling me to work when I was young . . . I have no reading material except the Bible, but I can have none better than this, and that other compassionate book, Nature.' He philosophically concluded that things could be worse. 'I read that the Tzar of Russia has died. He and I were the same age. I am the better off now!'

In 1881 he decided to visit the Great Exhibition at Melbourne; 27 years previously he had visited the Great Exhibition in London. He praised the layout and buildings of the Exhibition but complained that 'pickpockets were at work everywhere.' He was fascinated by the displays and stands from all over the world but was disappointed not to see a model of 'an improved dung cart and dung spreader'. What struck him most forcibly was 'the pride and vanity of the people there clad in their costly and ornate dresses as they paraded along the beautiful walks.'

He returned from the Great Exhibition to work in a sodden field picking potatoes at Seven Hills Farm, Kingston. The field was so wet that his employer 'had to use six pairs of bullocks to draw out half a load.' He left the potato picking after filling 360 bags, but the prospect of finding other employment seemed hopeless. Potatoes were selling at a mere 2 shillings a ton. With no income whatsoever, he decided to visit John Lewis to ask for the £47 which was still owing to him. To Joseph's dismay, Lewis informed him that he could not repay a farthing. After all his generosity, he felt badly let down and gave vent to his feelings by calling the Lewis family, 'ignorant, self centred, self-righteous, proud, penniless, dishonest grudgers.' To gain some relief he visited his 'faithful and honest friend' David Evans, Rheola, where he received hospitality and helped to tend the vines. He admired his friend for his winemaking venture which 'paid better than most occupations, especially prospecting for gold.' He even helped David Evans to dig an underground cellar to house the wine, and planted trees and bushes to protect the vineyards.

In August 1881 Joseph took to splitting timber in the bush. It was back-breaking work and poorly paid at the rate of only two shillings per ton, and he was obliged to pay five shillings for a three-month licence to cut the trees. The wood was sold for fencing posts, as firewood for the engines in the gold claims, and the burnt wood was also sold as charcoal. On 20 August, Evan Lewis, the son of John Lewis the debtor, joined him. Despite having quarrelled with his father, Joseph was still on friendly terms with Evan who 'turned up with his gun and two dogs.' But Joseph was to have a narrow escape. He relates the incident, 'The dogs disturbed a big bear which came my way and I only had an axe to defend myself . . . fortunately the ferocious creature charged after the dogs . . . Evan shot the bear and took him home where he skinned the animal.' It is likely that this was a circus bear which had escaped to the woods, or possibly a large

Koala which the early settlers called 'monkey bears'.

Although Joseph often waxed lyrical about the tranquillity of the bush, it could also prove a barbarous place where men fought over land, possessions and work. He soon experienced at first hand the dangers of working there. 'I do not feel pleased, because I am living among thieves.' Unfortunately for Joseph, he clashed with a gang of Irishmen who had 'claimed the land and its produce in the name of the Pope!' Such a declaration only fuelled his anger. A quarrel between himself and the Irishmen quickly developed. He ended up having his 'axe, cross-cutter and wheelbarrow stolen, and had to endure many insults beside.' When an Irishman set fire to his temporary hut, Joseph's volcanic temper erupted. 'I told him my revolver was loaded and at the ready.' The Irishman quickly retreated. 'On 26 September a policeman paid us a visit looking if any of us were without a licence.' Joseph, as honest as the day, was able to produce his licence, 'but there were many Irish wood splitters who were obliged to flee the policeman!'

Joseph continued to split wood, but made scarcely any money. After slaving for many months he built up a supply of '47 tons of split timber, but it was stolen, and carried away by some carters in the night.' Wearied by the dishonesty all around him, he complained, 'It is not fair to rob an old man in this way.' But in the bush it was every man for himself, and there was no respect for age or person. 'Grey hair and rectitude,' he complained, 'are dishonoured here.' Alone at the age of 63, Joseph was an easy prey for the many rogues and criminals who hid in the bush as a cover for criminal activities. Victoria was still a young colony with many problems, not the least of which was a rootless, shifting unemployed population which had no respect for the law and scavenged for what they could get to survive.

In August 1882 Joseph attempted to establish some stability in his life by building a hut for himself, complete with a chimney, and clad with stringy bark as thatch. His new home gave him a sense of security and independence. Under the Miners Rights Act he could claim ownership of one acre of land, a roadway, and a permanent spring that he had dug for himself. He called it Ants Mole Cottage. It was located near Ravenswood, North Walmer. Living in his hut in the bush he was now at ease with himself, and felt safe from 'the swindlers and cheats' who so riled him. 'I feel happy to be alone with my Creator and feel the presence of the Author of Nature. What more could one wish for?' At Ants Mole Cottage he records an odd and amusing dream, in which his great heroine, Queen Victoria, visited him:

> 18 December, 1882
>
> I dreamt last night that the Queen of England came to visit me at Ants Mole Cottage and the Queen herself presented me with half a dozen ripe and delicious apples. My brothers Griffith and John in their smart buttoned overcoats passed by, but of course they did not stop, nor interrupt my conversation with the Queen.

At the *Eisteddfod* on St David's Day in 1882, Joseph had won the first prize for verses commemorating the visit of the two Royal Princes, the Duke of Clarence and the Duke of Kent, Victoria's sons, to Ballarat. He went so far as to send her a letter of condolence on the death of John Brown, 'her faithful servant and intimate friend.' He even kept 10 February 1883 as a private holiday because it was the anniversary of the marriage of the Queen to the Prince Consort. He recalled with pride, 'I once stayed at the Royal Hotel in Birmingham at a time when the Prince was resident there.' However, he had scant regard for the many peccadilloes of her son, 'the Prince of Wales is in the news again, as having an affair with Mrs Campbell. The Naughty boy!'

Dreams feature frequently in Joseph's diaries and notebooks, but more often than not they are nightmares, particularly when they relate to Wales. It is obvious that the old demons never slackened their grip on him. Even in sleep there was no sanctuary and Joseph, like Lady Macbeth, found that 'infected minds to their deaf pillows will discharge their secrets.'

20 December 1882
I had very undesirable dreams about dead and living people in Wales. There were crowds about me and I had not the least chance to defend myself as they were all talking at the same time.'

He also dreamt that he was being sucked into the bog at Cors Caron and swept downstream in the river Teifi, but no person would throw him a rope.

Despite the provocations from his fellow workers, Joseph achieved a rare measure of contentment in his homemade cabin. Living in the bush seemed to revive his spirits as it put him in touch with the healing forces of nature, but he still suffered severe mood changes. The beginning of another year filled him with fear, and New Year's Day 1883 saw him, yet again, consumed by the dread of dying like an animal in the bush, alone, unburied and unlamented:

PITY THE SWAGMAN

1 January 1883

As I am very lonely in this homeless colony and somebody might come across me dead in the Bush . . . Whoever they may be, let them write to Mr David Evans, Rheola, Berlin, who knew me at home, and my books, boxes etc are in his custody.

For the next six months he survived by selling timber and doing odd jobs such as fencing and grubbing trees, earning 'just enough to buy my tucker.' His mood had swung back to one of reasonable contentment and on 8 July 1883 his life seemed again to be comfortable and relaxed. Cheerfully, he confessed, 'I have a warm cottage with plenty of ready cut firewood close to the door and I have thirty seven papers to look over.' This, to him, was bliss. Newspapers from Wales were sent to the nearest Post Office at Walmer where he would collect them in bundles. Reading of life back home was something he anticipated with great pleasure. On this occasion, however, the pleasure suddenly turned to a deep anguish, which was to remain with him for the rest of his life. On scanning the papers he unexpectedly came across an account of the death of his favourite and eldest daughter, Margaret. She had died on 29 April at 32 years of age and was buried on 3 May in the new cemetery at Tregaron, 'being the first person to be interred there. So alone!'

The news left him reeling and he confessed, 'there are no words to describe the death of one's child.' For the second time since leaving Wales he had suffered the trauma of reading about the death of one of his children in a newspaper. It was almost too much for him. Margaret had always been closest to him in Wales and now his grief was mingled with lacerating guilt for not having been present at her final hours. While he was left to suffer the keenest torment alone, he knew that back home at Trecefel, Betty and the whole family could derive some comfort from a shared grief in the outpouring of sorrow at the funeral. How he longed to have been at Trecefel at this point in time. But there was no one for him to turn to for comfort, and no one with whom he could reminisce about the qualities of his beloved daughter. No one, that is, except his one 'faithful, compliant companion', his diary. In his notebook he wrote, 'I lost my first-born son in July 1863 and now I've lost my first-born daughter in July 1883. Twenty years is like yesterday, and to-day is like twenty years long . . . What a cruel time to have to stay alive':

> 8 July, 1883
> Margaret is on my mind all day. When I left Wales I placed my accounts and my books in her custody. She was very social and open hearted always . . . when my deceased daughter was only a child or as a baby, she would leave her mother's breast for my arms especially when she was ailing. I thought to see her again and never thought of her dissolution.

He turns to verse to express his longing:

> 8 August 1883
>   I would have wished to see her again
>   Before she went to her grave;
>   But such was fate,
>   I've nothing now but to remember her appearance
>   This one who was dear to me . . . †

The following day he wrote again that, 'my daughter Margaret is on my mind all the time. I had a warm hope to see her and speak to her before my dissolution.' His shock at her early death had a profound effect on him. 'I never thought that she would be the first to leave this not only uncertain world, but one that is mixed with many disappointments and many unbearable afflictions. I cannot find any good reason why I should continue to live to endure such sadness, but perhaps my grief is also sorrow for myself.' Without the consoling presence of family and friends Joseph expressed the wish to join his daughter. 'I'd rather lie with her and wish I'd never been born. Life is too cruel for me to understand. But at least Margaret has died young. She won't fade or age like me and will be impervious to time.'

His only escape from this living nightmare was to throw himself once more into grinding work. He went at it for 17 hours a day, splitting timber and hacking at the tree trunks as though he were hacking at his grief. At this point he seemed dogged by misfortune. In September he lost his penknife, which convinced him, 'I was born for destruction by the fates . . . 15 September 1883, Something undesirable often happens to me on a Friday. I was born after sunset on Friday evening which has frequently caused my life to be nothing but a black hole, where all is madness and folly.'

Worn out by grief and hard work, Joseph decided to seek a more settled existence and applied for a job with Maldon Town Council clearing land and grubbing trees for new roads. He procured temporary employment and moved into the stable of Mr Rowe, a local butcher and affluent farmer at Maldon. Although the work itself was strenuous, he still found the strength and time to agitate for improved conditions of work for his fellow farm labourers. On 23 September he wrote a letter to *The Leader* complaining that employers did not even provide a meal for workers, let alone a living wage. Meanwhile, during the day, he 'cleared boulders and stumps with a pick and shovel from land compacted rock hard by bullocks and drays.'

On Christmas Day he was 'given a good forequarter of lamb by Mr. Rowe', which he then carried on his shoulders back to his cabin in the bush. On his way he encountered 'scores of people picknicking in the bush, enjoying themselves.' He observed them for a while and described the scene. 'The young man is allowed to tickle the young lady a little above the hip joint, well to the front on the left side . . . Picnicking may be precious when young ladies wish to pick their men . . . Let the old customs have their sway.'

For Joseph 1883 had been a tragic year. He also foresaw that Australia itself was set on a course of self-destruction:

> 13 December 1883
>
> I consider 1883 . . . to be the most unfortunate year for me since my arrival in Australia . . . I have been half the year without work at all. Most of the people are shouting 'Advance Australia', but in my opinion I never saw anything going faster to a complete destruction than this colony . . . The advance of its inhabitants towards all sorts of iniquities surpasses the history of the destruction of Jerusalem!

Despite the hyperbole, his opinions held a modicum of truth. Although the 1880s were a boom time in Australia, the colony was to a great extent living on borrowed wealth. The end of the decade was to see it plunged into a serious economic depression. But, ultimately, it was the death of his daughter Margaret which had defined the year: it was a blow from which Joseph never really recovered. He recorded his anguish in his Black Book:

> I'm only flesh and blood. There is so much suffering in this world that the pain of it will surely destroy me; and if I think too deeply I will be crushed . . . Everyone has troubles, but I was truly trounced by fate.

CHAPTER 19

THE MALDON SCAVENGER

Joseph's nomadic existence ended in 1884. He obtained another contract to work for Maldon Council as a road cleaner at a wage of one pound a week and the remainder of his life in Australia was to be linked with this historic town. It is now regarded as Australia's 'First Notable Town' and the Welsh Swagman's association with it is still recognised. Maldon's history began with the discovery of gold at Mount Tarrangower in 1853 by John G. Mechosk, a Polish captain. The town, which stands 90 miles north-west of Melbourne, was named Maldon after a town in Essex, England, and it soon became world-famous for its rich alluvial gold fields, second only to Bendigo.

Welshmen played a significant part in the development of Maldon. Welshman's Reef or Cymru Claim was discovered in 1857 and yielded 3,000 ounces, making a fortune for its managers Jones & Co. Many Welsh miners emigrated from Cardiganshire where they had originally worked in the lead mines; others came from the South Wales coalfields and North Wales slate quarries. The Welsh tended to settle among the rugged gullies of Parkins Reef, which was to yield over 200,000 ounces of gold. They brought with them their language and religion and were regarded as thrifty, industrious and competent. Some became extremely rich, including John Lewis from Llandeilo. He emigrated to Maldon as a farmer, but was one of the lucky few, for on his land a substantial quantity of gold was discovered. His wife, Mary, hailed from Glyn Uchaf, Llangeitho, in Cardiganshire. Overnight they became millionaires and built a grand imposing residence roofed with Caernarfon slates in Adair Street. He also owned three other 'fine, well built houses'. Joseph noted that, 'He had two or three countrymen as mates, and they made their piles too!'

Unlike his affluent countrymen, Joseph's status was the lowest of the low as he set about the task of cleaning the streets of Maldon. Although the town had more money per head than any other gold town in Victoria, the streets, gutters and waterways were in a deplorable condition. At first, Joseph rented a cottage in Maldon for one shilling a week, which he described as 'a smoky room, with no fuel or water, and not fit to harbour an otter when it rains.' Not only was his new work arduous and unpleasant, but he now came under constant public scrutiny and was to suffer perpetual humiliation. 'I came under the notice of all passers by . . . Rain turns the dust to mud . . . wind turns the dust to thick clouds. Whichever state presides, the ladies complain of soiled dresses, the children provoke me, and the shopkeepers and hoteliers grumble about the state of things.' As usual, he was in a no win situation.

Armed with a wheelbarrow, a spade, a pick, a rake, a hoe, a brush and a crowbar, he cleared 'tons of muck every week and tipped it into the deep holes left by the diggers.' He was now 66 years old and soon became a familiar part of the scenery of Maldon as he conscientiously followed his gruelling schedule day after day. The town Surveyor commended his work but he was badly abused by others. 'Dogs and small children are fond of me, but the mothers call them away immediately – and the older children abuse me on their way home from school but I ignore them.' If he had been able to peer into the future, he would have been gratified to see hosts of students, now familiar with extracts of his diaries, visiting Maldon and walking its streets. But in 1885 and in subsequent years he was, all too often, an object of ridicule and cruel mockery.

Despite his menial status, his spirit was good and his heart still retained its sense of poetry. 'All the almond trees,' he wrote, 'are beautifully covered in white sheets of blossom as I work.' On 3 October 1885 a Salvation Army Officer approached him as he was shovelling muck and rather sanctimoniously enquired of him, 'You are cleaning the gutter, but is your heart clean, that is the thing?' The Officer must have regretted asking the question, for he received a reply which was little short of a sermon, revealing in no uncertain manner that Joseph knew his Bible better than his interrogator. The Officer was left stultified, but Joseph had evidently enjoyed the encounter. 'To my sorrow, he left without asking any more questions!'

So many Welsh immigrants had settled in Maldon that during the 1880s the Welsh language could be heard on every street and corner. Even in Australia Joseph lived much of his life through the medium of Welsh and he complained in May 1885, 'I will never become proficient in speaking English here because half the time I converse in Welsh.'

In the 1870s Welsh religious life flourished in Maldon. A Welsh church and two Welsh chapels – one Baptist and one Congregational – were built. The wealthy John Lewis, Llandeilo, generously supported the latter. Joseph's friends seem to have consisted mainly of Welsh farmers, struggling diggers, artisans and shopkeepers. As the town cleaner, he was known to every shopkeeper in Maldon and when Edwin John, his grocer, who hailed from Glamorganshire, died in April 1885, he described his funeral as 'being thickly attended with between 900 and 1,000 marching the streets to the cemetery.' Joseph also wrote a poem in memory of him, 'O death why fellest thou a tree . . . And leave a rotten stump like me?'

He did not express the same degree of grief when he heard the news that his erstwhile friend John Lewis had died in November 1885. Despite their warm reunion at the Forest Creek diggings in April 1869, a month after Joseph's arrival in Australia, the friendship had soured when Lewis failed to repay his debt of £47 to Joseph. He never forgave his 'old friend' for his dishonesty. Instead of the conventional panegyric composed for his funeral, we get the following attack on John Lewis's character:

> November 1885
> Looking over my accounts I see now I was wronged and betrayed by my countryman John Lewis, Llannon. I never thought that any man of the worst principles would attempt to treat his fellow creature as he treated me. I am not willing to allow people like John Lewis . . . to do me out of my hard and honest savings. Lewis was dishonest, mean, a liar, and cruel to man and beast – ill-treating his horses and his friend. He abused his cattle, his dogs and his cats, and above all, me!

The extremes of the Australian weather feature prominently in Joseph's diaries and played havoc with his work in Maldon.

During hot weather he complains of 'being unable to hold the crowbar which was like a red rod of hot iron.' He had to wear 'a soaking muslin cravat over my cabbage hat to prevent sunstroke . . . the gutters stink abominably of filth swept from the butchers fronts and every other type of objectionable rubbish which has to be cleared. In winter, heavy floods fill the drains with mud and gravel and wash away the footbridges.' Deluged with torrential showers, he often found himself having to work in uncomfortable oilskins for as long as eleven hours a day repairing the storm damage to pathways and bridges, and all for only one pound a week, while the national wage was five shillings a day. Despite this, he cheerfully recorded in December 1885, 'I have spent a most pleasant year – and I'm 67 years old . . . I enjoy my labour.'

Within a few years of settling in Maldon Joseph quickly built up a reputation as one able and willing to express an opinion on any current topic. His letters, articles and poetry were printed frequently in local papers. In December 1885 a poem entitled 'From the Scavenger's Diary' appeared in the *Tarrangower Times*, reflecting the unequal struggle of this existence, where few prospered but most were cast down. He ended the year by admitting, 'When young I was for ever longing for something in the future. Man is never contented with the present. My health has been reasonably good, and I have been in constant work, although at low wages.'

His contract was renewed for 1886, and in February he bought a small cottage for himself on a piece of wasteland near the railway line at a cost of £15. Ironically, his old farm Trecefel was about the same distance from the M&M Line as was his new home, called North Railway Gate Lodge, from the Maldon Line. However, his newfound independence in an exposed cottage on open ground brought with it its own perils. It quickly became a target for the larrikins who robbed and violated his humble dwelling so often that they made his life a misery, almost driving him to distraction. 'In March 1886, children broke into my cottage and destroyed many of my papers, parts of my diary and stole much of my property.' To the younger generation of Maldon he was a figure of fun, and an easy target. To those who did not really know him, he presented something of an oddity as he wheeled barrow-loads of filth along the streets and cleared the offensive cesspits. The fact that he was a learned man, a bibliophile, and a poet seems to have made him even more vulnerable to their taunts and ridicule. He, in turn, retaliated by accusing the larrikins of a 'lack of morality'. Even so, he still claimed, 'I am very happy in my work and grateful to the Author of every good cause for this gift.'

Joseph took his work as a road cleaner extremely seriously. From his youth he had clung to the belief that, 'If a job is worth doing, it is worth doing well.' Keeping the water channels clean was responsible work, especially as 'typhoids and fevers are mowing down young colonials by the dozen each week.' He was approached by the Medical Officer of Health to 'ensure that sewers and drains were kept as clean as possible from pollution.' Joseph had to check that contaminated water did not seep through the soil into cracks in the water pipes, thereby transmitting infection. In March he was given an assistant, but this only irritated him because of local corruption and the gross inequality in their pay. He complained that, 'The man who joined me today gets a wage of seven shilling a day whereas I get three shillings and four pence . . . Influence and partiality are the world's curses, especially here in the state of Victoria!' Working in the public eye had its drawbacks, but it also provided him with a superb vantage point for observing, at close range, everyday life around him. During the day he used his brush, pick and shovel; but each night, closeted in the quiet of his cottage, he took up his pen and meticulously recorded everything that he had seen and heard during the day, depicting Maldon in all its facets.

The contrasting scenes and differing life styles he witnessed in this burgeoning gold town fascinated him. In the background there was the ever-present noise of the machinery creating wealth for the few. As he cleaned the streets he could see the opulent mansions of those who had struck gold, but he could glean some comfort from the fact that even they had to relinquish their wealth eventually. He described their lavish funerals with the black-garbed mourners processing to the sombre notes of the Dead March played by a brass band, while the 'indifferent goats foraged for food on the waste ground nearby.' He paints a noisy, vibrant town where fortunes were made and lost overnight through gambling, where the crowds thronged the streets for the Easter Parade and where a variety of sports were held.

By July 1886, the sheer physical demand of clearing one square mile of streets, which 'amounted to 27 miles of channels and sewers,' soon began to tell upon his health. He complained of a loss of appetite and suffered from severe dysentery. He rarely touched alcohol in Australia and when he did so, it was usually for medicinal purposes. In November he resorted to 'taking medicine at the Albion Hotel to relieve my dysentery.

I had three glasses . . . but to no avail.' To add to his discomfort he complained that, 'there is a great heat everywhere . . . 100°F in the shade . . . 150°F in the sun . . . Ash from forest fires fills the air and drifts like snow . . . the smoke clogs my throat.' He compared the conditions to those experienced on 5 February 1851, known as 'Black Friday', when the whole colony was ablaze, and when it was claimed that the glow of the flames reflected in the sky could be seen as far as New Zealand.

But even in the midst of sickness, toil and heat, there was still one day that provided him with a modicum of rest and spiritual solace, so essential to his nature. 'I enjoy Sundays when I can rest my withering limbs, wash my clothing, read my Bible, and trim my beard which is the only part of my body which grows!' Sometimes, however, there attached to him a sense of deep loneliness as he watched life in Maldon pass him by:

> Often on a Sunday I look through the window of my little cottage to see the world go by . . . Men go out to the Bush with their guns and greyhounds . . . well dressed couples walk to churches and chapels, people play cards and dice on the Station platform . . . and Chinamen run to and fro with their baskets of fruits and vegetables . . . From my humble cottage I hear Church bells inviting sinners to attend . . . In front of my cottage there is an area of level ground over which men follow their separate pursuits of training dogs or horses . . . but most of these attend chapels or churches in the afternoon.

On the last day of 1886 he was again overcome by the dread that he would die like a pauper and have 'to be buried on the Parish.' This would have been the final indignity for a

Welshman with his background. To meet such a contingency he yet again set out specific instructions in his diary:

> 31 December 1886
>
> I am strange and friendless in this part. Should I happen to die suddenly, I wish to inform the person finding my corpse to read this postscript. My address in Wales was Trecefel, Tregaron, Cardiganshire. I have a friend and countryman David Evans, Rheola, near Inglewood. I wish the said person to telegraph him that I might be buried without trespassing on the public money.
>
> Joseph Jenkins, North Maldon, Victoria

The year 1887 found him 'sweating copiously' as he fought 'to clear the water channels in a temperature of 150°F.' He records that 'scores die of sunstroke and cattle and sheep perish for lack of grass and water.' Rabbits and hares had become such destructive pests that the Government declared a public holiday specially to kill them. Joseph describes how crowds of people, young and old, surged towards the bush armed with guns and sticks to hunt them. They were paid nine pence for each animal, the corpses were left to rot in the bush, and the ears cut off and brought back as evidence of the kill. According to Joseph, 'One party killed over 450 rabbits and hares and the Government spent £350,000 on attempting to curb or eliminate these rabbits.' It seems a supreme quirk of fate that many former convicts had been transported to Australia for poaching rabbits on the estates of oppressive landlords, whereas they were now being paid to shoot and trap them. Blazing gum trees continued to be a hazard to both man and beast. '12 February 1887, The bush fires destroy sheep, ponies, homesteads, hares, rabbits, foxes and all sorts of wild animals, even snakes go without mercy, . . . kangaroos, wallabies, koalas all perish – Men flee for their lives on horseback, as sparks fall like rain.'

On 27 February Joseph was 69 years old but, as usual, his birthday was far from being a joyful occasion. Instead, he was again overcome by a feeling of profound pessimism and despair and he rued the day he was born.

> 27 February 1887
>
> My mother would have done a good job by inventing some way to get rid of her hare lipped baby at once rather than leaving him to pine for 69 years on earth. Unlucky men are useless in this world and yet it is always the case when born late on Fridays and late in the last quarter of the moon. Such a thing causes me to believe firmly in Fate. The accident happened on the above date at Blaenplwyf, Ystrad, Cardiganshire, Wales.

In spite of these periodic bouts of self-pity, his faith in his ultimate salvation remained strong. On occasions he attended the Welsh Congregational Chapel in Maldon for spiritual comfort and noted that 'the attendance has declined because Welsh mine managers now opt to attend the English chapels – the Welsh do not keep together like the Scotch and the Irish.' Nevertheless, Joseph had many friends in the chapel; among them was an old couple, Mr and Mrs William Rees from Glamorganshire, who had been in Maldon for nearly 30 years. He was often invited to dinner on a Sunday after chapel when 'we had long chats about the old country.' Mr and Mrs Rees owned a small farm where Joseph would give a helping hand during harvest time.

On 21 April Joseph read that a general holiday was declared

throughout the colony of which he thoroughly approved. 'It is the 8 hours anniversary day with all Trades of Toiling men.' He saw many trains packed with thousands from Sandhurst, Ballarat, Geelong, Williamstown and other places, 'all in a grand procession through the main streets of Melbourne . . . about 16,000 in all . . . under different banners but all in unity.' The eight-hour day was a significant milestone in the cause of the workers.

On a Sunday he was often visited by his Welsh mining friends, John Davies and John Williams, 'who talk about nothing other than gold reefs and racing.' He found their visits boring and intrusive and grumbled that they prevented him from doing his necessary chores. Although the town of Maldon existed because of gold, there were times when Joseph was revolted by the whole ethos of avarice which seemed to dominate all else. 'I'm tired of hearing how they expect to strike it rich month after month and seek material solutions for spiritual needs. They have made greed their God! Lust for gold is the one great evil I have seen under the sun, and it is common here among men. He that loves gold shall not be satisfied by gold!'

> 24 June 1887
> Gold! Gold! Gold! – is on every tongue while the fine surface of the soil is shamefully neglected. Each man, myself excepted, appears to have come here to seek his fortune.

This entry smacks of crass hypocrisy: Joseph not only dug for gold on many occasions, but also bought shares in claims. During his moral spasms, however, he conveniently forgot such things.

On 24 May Joseph noted in his diary that it was the birthday of the Queen, but 1887 had the added significance of being the Jubilee commemorating the fiftieth year of her reign. Joseph was requested by the town council of Maldon to compose an anthem for the bands celebrating the 'great event'. He wrote six verses and dedicated them to Lady Loch, wife of the Governor of Victoria. It was an occasion he relished and he was hailed as the 'Bard of Maldon'. Although some of his verses are truly lyrical, much of his poetry tends to be sheer doggerel, and his feeling of pride was to be short-lived. Within a month, the 'Royalist Scavenger' found himself in the doghouse when some of the citizens of Maldon made an official complaint against the standard of his work. Joseph was rudely reminded of his true status in the town when the clerk of the works angrily called at his cottage. An indignant Joseph records, '23 June 1887, They moan that the channels are dirty and must be done up to suit the growlers. Ignorant people are not easily pleased. When they do growl at me, I do laugh and smile at them!'

However, beneath this defiant façade, Joseph fumed and struck back with venom:

> There is hellish filth in each one here from the poor to the highest in authority . . . and their ignorance is more obnoxious to the mind than any other thing. †

Because he considered himself one of life's unfortunates, Joseph was able to show a spirit of humanity and compassion towards others in distress. On 28 July 1887, he had a chance encounter with an Aborigine named Equinhup at the railway station near his cottage. Joseph had always been concerned about the barbarous treatment of the Aborigines by the early white settlers and he offered Equinhup hospitality at his own home:

28 July 1887

I met an Aborigine. He seemed half starved. I took him into my cottage and invited him to share a meal with me, and I shared my blankets with him during the night. He could speak fair English.

Joseph struck up an instant rapport with Equinhup. During the evening the Aborigine, who was nicknamed 'Tom Clarke' by the whites, informed Joseph that the Railway Commissioners had taken the land from his tribe and that he wished to claim compensation from them. Joseph was more than willing to take up Equinhup's case. He was aware of the Aboriginal belief that their land was sacred, and had been created by their ancestors in an era known as the Dreamtime. As an exile himself, he could empathise with the view that the land 'embodied their myth and history.' He had always felt a spiritual attachment to the verdant acres of Trecefel and had suffered the agony of turning his back on them. In his case this had been self-inflicted, but he could appreciate the pain of those who had been forcibly removed from their land. Not much is known of the Aborigines who lived around Maldon, but the early settlers feared them, amid reports of 'deadly boomerangs, flying spears and surprise attacks.' The Aborigines had been treated badly, with large areas of their land appropriated for sheep stations. In 1788 the Aboriginal population numbered 750,000; by 1888 it had been drastically reduced.

Later, there was a feeling of guilt among some and attempts were made at restitution. In 1841 the Reverend Edward Stone Parker was appointed Assistant Protector of the Aborigines, and a part of the Loddon River near Tarrangower, Maldon, was chosen as the site for an Aboriginal Station. Parker encountered many difficulties and an extract from his first periodical report reflects the tragic results of what happened in the enforced meeting between black and white:

> The Aborigine, left in their present state, to be beaten back 'by the white man's foot' – to be excluded, perforce, from lands which many unquestionably regard as their own property, and from scenes as dear to them as our own native homes to us – despoiled, denied the right of humanity – classed with and treated as wild dogs – I can entertain no other expectation but that they will be driven to more frequent depredations, and exposed to more rapid and certain destruction.

Joseph composed the following letter for Equinhup and advised him to present it to the Railway Commissioners:

> Maldon
> 28 July 1887
>
> Gentlemen and Brothers too,
> I am the last of the Aborigines tribes in these parts. I do humbly wish you to compare two lots of Title Deeds.
> I received mine from the Author of Nature, while the land occupied by all the railways is titled by the white man's lawyers.
> Always humble.
> Praying your charitable consideration.
> Equinhup. (Tom Clarke)

The Commissioners agreed to pay Equinhup £1 in silver as compensation, but with a promise of more. Whether or not this promise was kept is not known.

Joseph's sympathy for Equinhup was, no doubt, due to the fact that he often felt persecuted himself. Whilst clearing the channels at Maldon he was constantly plagued by a drunken Irish tinker. The Irishman deliberately aggravated him by singing, 'Taffy was a Welshman, Taffy was a thief.' He had unsuccessfully applied for Joseph's job as street cleaner and this was his revenge. But Joseph replied with the following withering riposte:

> Taffy was a Welshman,
> But never was a thief.
> It was the Tinker Satan
> That stole the leg of beef
> And cooked it for his dinner
> On a rusty piece of tin.
> And stole the pound of solder
> To buy a glass of gin.

Occasionally, he was buoyed up by good news from Wales:

> 18 September 1887
> I read in the *Cambrian News* that my youngest daughter had won a prize at her school in Kensington, London. Well done, Anne! ... I have just received the *Daily News*, where I see it reported that my youngest son John David has qualified as a doctor.

While his children excelled themselves, their father appeared destined to remain in exile clinging to one of the most thankless and demeaning jobs in the colony. Conscious of this, he admitted, 'I sometimes think I am the agent of my own destruction. At home I had 6 servants. Here, I exist in penury.' A graphic entry provides an impression of his *modus vivendi*:

> September 1887
>
> I have many miles of drains to look after . . . Tobin Street has the dirtiest drains because the sludge from the two butchers' shops run into them. Both men are on the council and when their colleagues complain they turn to blame me! . . . I do my best, but it is not good enough!

In September 1887 Joseph's health once again began to fail. He was afflicted by painful rheumatism in both his hands and hip. He continued to correspond regularly with people in Wales, and their letters had become an increasingly important emotional lifeline to him. In often trying circumstances he describes himself as 'up at five, having posted the letters and newspapers for Wales per the *Lusitania*, being the fastest steamer.' He still nurtured the hope of one day seeing his old friends and relatives, to relate to them the drama of his life in the Antipodes. 'It will be a strange hour . . . when I am able to reveal the tribulations that I encountered.'

In November Joseph was distressed by an account of the Melbourne Races in the *Argus* newspaper. It described an incident involving a Welshman. He regarded the event as indicative of the lowly status of the Welsh in Australia:

> 2 November 1887
>
> A trifling accident happened when two horses fell . . . and the two riders were carried on stretchers, an Englishman and a Welshman of the name of Williams. The former came to himself soon, but the poor Welsh boy was taken to a hospital to die. But the accident was only a trifle. Williams was only a Welshman and had no business to live. If one of the Governors present had met the same fate as Williams, the races would have been postponed on the spot.

On 24 November he was troubled by toothache and had been advised by one of his friends to adopt the following bizarre remedy, 'To spill a drop of good brandy down my ears, and soak a small bit of cotton wadding to put in the ear above the destroyed tooth, which gives a release generally.' Joseph concluded that, 'It would have been better for my feelings to take the brandy through my mouth and down my throat!'

One of the rare pleasures afforded to Joseph in the midst of his seemingly endless labours was a visit to McArthur's Bakery. Established in 1854, it still stands in Maldon's Main Street today. Among McArthur's wide-ranging collection of books, he could satisfy his insatiable curiosity and his constant quest for enlightenment:

> I have my lunch with me in order to spare a mile's walk back to my cottage . . . I generally take it at McArthur's Bakery at the baker's private room where nobody can interfere with me . . . I'm allowed to use his study where books of all description are at hand and welcomed. In fact it is a library of poetical and philosophical books of the best type.

The run-up to Christmas 1887 again proved to be a hectic time for Joseph. He reports, 'I was plagued by swarms of locusts and flies . . . I had to wear a veil to protect my eyes . . . and then a great havoc was caused by a heavy thunderstorm. I was knee deep in water. The footbridges were carried away and the flood entered the stores, cellars and houses.' He was called out and worked for up to eleven hours at a time to control the situation. He accused the Council of failing to foresee the problem of flooding. 'They cannot blame me for I have warned them many a time of such a catastrophe.'

Not surprisingly, by Christmas Day he was feeling the effect of the strenuous work. 'Sunday 25, December being my 69th Christmas Day . . . I do not feel well and cannot relish my breakfast. Having remained lonely in my cot all day reading, resting and washing. I had to have a fire on the hearth to warm myself. The Fire Brigade and Sports are on . . . all sorts of athletes, wrestling etc.' On Boxing Day he could hear the bands playing all afternoon and the pistol reports to start the races, but Joseph did not attend them. From his cottage he saw hundreds of people catch excursion trains 'all day to Castlemaine and Ballarat', noting cynically, 'Spendthrifts find a way to spend!' Over the following few days both his physical and mental fatigue are evident in the diary. '28 December 1887, my eyelids are so sore from sweating that I wear a veil to keep the flies from my eyes.' The prospect of reaching 70 years of age also worried him. 'I am full of fear of the age promised by my Bible – fifteen hours of toil in hot weather ought to be enough for a man on the eve of 70.' Despite this, he concludes his diary on a note of unexpected optimism:

31 December 1887
I do feel the moment I trespass upon Nature that both pain and discontentment are the fruits, and vice versa when I go as I ought in unity to the grand order of Nature. On this last day of the year when I look back on my pains and troubles and on my joy and contentment, they seem of no importance. It is the present that matters. The past and the future are out of our reach. I am loathsome to leave you my dear 1887.

But, alas, New Year's Day found him yet again verging on

despair. As he contemplated the future, the unhappy experiences of his past intruded. His thoughts flew back to Blaenplwyf and what his parents would now think of his wretched existence in Australia. He believed that they would have preferred to see him dead than suffering his present degradation:

> 1 January 1888
> If my mother and father were to see
> The way I have been troubled,
> They would have desired,
> In spite of the amount of love they had for me,
> For some disease or injury
> To put an end to life. †

Possibly he was closer to death than he imagined or would have wished, for the following entry reads, 'I find it best not to make my bed in the morning here, for at bed time, I have often found a poisonous snake in my cot and I may find a black or tiger snake coiled between the blankets.'

Joseph's life continued in the same vein – work, work and more work – like an exercise in masochism. He now faced the aftermath of the violent storms that had swept the country. 'The floods have left over twenty tons of mud and gravel to cart away from the gutters.' But he relished the challenge. 'I do it with ease. Nothing pleases me better than work when I am able to do it.' The more arduous the work, the more he seemed to welcome it, claiming that, 'It numbs the pain I feel when I remember my children, so that there is no space for private sorrow.' On Sunday he attended three church services at Maldon and listened to two sermons. But he confessed, 'It would have been better had I stayed in my cottage and re-read the Sermon on the Mount.'

On 27 February Joseph reached 70. He recalled the circumstances of his father's death at that age and the day of his funeral. Even so, he decided to celebrate his birthday with a glass of brandy while composing ten lines of poetry. On 9 March he noticed that the flags of Maldon were at half-mast and learned that, 'The Emperor of Germany and King of Prussia had died at the age of 91 . . . He was a peaceful monarch and led his army successfully against Napoleon III. I composed an *englyn* to mark the occasion.'

Ever since he had landed in Australia Joseph had secretly admired the way the Irish celebrated St Patrick's Day on 17 March, 'Fiddle playing, dancing, singing and carousing were everywhere. The Irish constitute one third of the inhabitants of Maldon, and their colourful way of life dominates the town. Anything will do for an excuse for people to celebrate in this country!' He wished that the Welsh exhibited the same national fervour as the Irish but, in sharp contrast, they celebrated St David's Day in a rather downbeat and sober way.

On Easter Monday Maldon held a large fair consisting of a wide variety of entertainments. The proceeds were donated to the hospital and Joseph again composed poetry to mark the occasion. Within a few days his joy was marred by extremely sad news. 'On 9 April I received a telegram informing me that my dear friend David Evans had died suddenly at the age of 49 years . . . I am broken in my breast; of all my friends he was the best. – Man that is born of a woman is of few days.' It was to David Evans that he had always turned during his darkest hours and it was at his home that he had spent his sunniest days. During his times of frequent sickness Evans and his wife had nursed him back to health.

On 10 April, sick at heart, he set out to travel the hundred miles to attend the funeral of a companion whose friendship he had cherished so much in Wales. On arrival he found that 'the whole Welsh community at Castlemaine had turned up in droves to pay their last respects . . . This is the largest funeral I have seen in the colony, 22 carriages plus the hearse and a score of riding horses, including pedestrians covering over a mile of road.' The Evans home had been a Mecca for Welshmen, 'where never a word of English was spoken,' and his loss was a blow to many who 'relived old times at his homestead.' After the interment, his widow, Margaret Evans, turned to Joseph and asked him to value the estate, which he willingly agreed to do.

On his return to Maldon he felt downcast. He looked out on a landscape ravaged by diggers, where heaps of dirt, old mullocks and tips sullied the land; deserted shafts scarred the hillsides, the towering Beehive chimney-stack scored the skyline, and all around was withered grass and cracked earth. All so different from his homeland. 'But,' wrote Joseph, 'this is a new land with a vital spark: there is freedom here, and many of my countrymen have had the chances they never had back home! I do believe that one day Australia will be a great country, but it must have the time to grow in its own way. I have read David Copperfield many times and am comforted by the fact that Mr Micawber prospered here, because people accepted him for what he was and not for what he had been. There is much talk of republicanism, but I consider Australia too young to risk this chance. When ready, it will come in the fullness of time.'

Although he could be critical, Joseph enjoyed many features of Maldon. Many different cultures and languages enriched the town. The Irish, Welsh, Scots, English, Germans, Swiss all contributed with their distinctive customs. In the early days hundreds of Chinese had settled at Maldon; they were segregated by law and were obliged to have a residential licence. They generally lived in camps in north Maldon which contained many Chinese shops, opium dens and joss houses. They were clever with herbal remedies and it was the Chinese who kept Maldon supplied with medicines, fresh fruit and vegetables. They were skilful diggers, but they ensured that all the holes dug were round in shape because they feared that evil spirits lurked in corners. Joseph described the social life of Maldon as 'flourishing, where people enjoy themselves as much as they can.' Public occasions were celebrated in street parades with great pomp and pageantry. 'This colony uses every occasion it can for a celebration ... The High Street and the Main Street have all that is necessary for life with many different stores and there are many well built public buildings, such as the Market Place, Court House, Post Office, Railway Station, Banks and Hospital.' He concluded, 'Maldon is a town of contrasts. It is like London in one respect: few are wealthy, but the majority are poor, and I belong to the latter!'

He also added, 'Here, in the midst of exuberant life, there is always death.' In November 1888, he noticed that the shutters of the stores were down and the blinds drawn in many houses. He learned that John Lewis, Llandeilo, the richest Welshman in Maldon, had died. As befitted a man of his standing, there followed an ostentatious funeral with a hearse drawn by six black horses to the sombre notes of the Dead March played by 'a full band preceding the cortege on foot.' Twenty carriages and hundreds of mourners on foot also followed; among them Joseph. A grand funeral was the most important and expensive of all Victorian rites of passage: it was a demonstration of one's place in society. Joseph's most enduring wish, so often reiterated, was that he would, one day, be accorded a decent burial.

After the funeral, Mrs Mary Lewis, the widow, asked Joseph to compose poetry and an encomium in prose to commemorate the life of her late husband. It was a commission that perfectly suited Joseph's temperament. He spent many long hours composing the verses and wrote 500 lines praising the virtues and charitable works of John Lewis in Maldon. But having completed the work, Joseph could scarcely conceal his disgust at Mary Lewis's subsequent treatment of him. 'I read it over to the widow who appeared to be well pleased with it. She offered me the princely payment of six pence for my trouble!! She was a true native of her county, having been born at Llangeitho.'

Christmas 1888 brought the usual flurry of activities and there were 'all manner of competitive meetings and sporting events . . . among them horse-racing, pigeon shooting, cricket, football, wrestling, concerts, dancing, billiards . . . betting and gambling.' But Joseph, the 'wowser', preferred to spend his time alone in his cottage complaining that, 'This is no way for a young country, heavily in debt, to carry on!' Possibly, he was made more irritable by painful rheumatism in his left knee. 'I am walking lame today . . . It's a sure sign of rain.' His prediction proved correct:

1 January 1889

The storm is coming right over Maldon . . . thunder can be heard . . . It is dark all around . . . Before 5 o'clock the flood was over most of the footbridges and some were swept away . . . I lost one of my shovels . . . The flood entered the Times Office and destroyed all the type and machinery . . . About 12 persons already reported to have been drowned and more may be counted . . . without mentioning the pecuniary losses.

This meant no rest for Joseph. '3 January 1889, I was up before 5 o'clock and hurried to examine the damage – I was ordered to mend the Eagle Hawk Bridge. I was there for three hours making room for the water to run away.' The following day was equally demanding:

> 4 January 1889
> I went to clear and wheel the mud and gravel from the water channel in front of the Railway Tavern, or rather Hotel, as they call every shanty here in this Colony . . . I have to work hard all day filling holes in the footpaths and clearing the mouths of culverts . . . I was in front of a house of ill fame; some fools were robbed at different times! Serve them right! The state of the weather is remarkably variable in this Colony and very trying for the constitution of the inhabitants . . . All storm or sun.

The weather, like his mood, was thoroughly unpredictable. By 9 January the heat of the sun had replaced the terror of the floods. 'I found it so hot . . . I was obliged to retreat under the shade of a tree close by. I met William Rees at noon and we had a conversation in the Welsh language.' William Rees, who was 80 years of age, was now Joseph's closest remaining friend in Maldon and the one to whom he invariably turned for news of Wales.

Despite having been haunted by the thought that he would

die at the same age as his father, Joseph was very much alive on 27 February and composed an *englyn* to celebrate his 71st birthday. He confessed, however, 'I do feel myself failing every day, especially in my walking.' Unfortunately, he again fell victim to the Maldon thieves. 'I had hung my waistcoat on a fence...when I returned...its pockets had been emptied of my spectacles and needle case.'

On St David's Day, despite the heavy contingent of Welsh in the town, Joseph again expressed his disappointment at the lack of patriotism shown by his countrymen in honouring their national saint in Maldon:

> 1 March 1889
>
> Very little sign of any Sports seen here on St David's Day ... There are great 'Turns' at Melbourne, Ballarat, Sandhurst, Geelong and all the big places through the Colony ... Each person wears an artificial leek ... singing Welsh Songs, with different sorts of sports that used to be patronised by the Ancient Britons ... Unlike the Irish the Welsh are very indifferent in Australia about keeping up their national and original language ...

News reached him from Wales about the 'Tithe Wars'. Farmers, who were largely Nonconformists, had long resented having to pay a tithe to the Anglican Church which they never attended. This eventually erupted into a protest in many parts of Wales, and led to episodes of violence, especially when the goods of those who refused to pay were seized. One of the areas involved was Cardiganshire. Although Joseph appreciated the justice of their cause, he could not support the actions of those prepared to use force. He was no law breaker:

> Sunday 12 May 1889
>
> I was sorry to read of a scuffle between the police and some Cardiganshire farmers about the payment of tithes. It is a very unjust tax, but that is not the right way to get rid of it. They have faithful MP's to plead their case in the House of Commons.

Despite holding progressive views on many social issues, he was vehemently opposed to granting women the vote. 'If women are allowed to vote they will turn the world upside down.' His icon, Queen Victoria, held the same viewpoint as Joseph; she was horrified by the thought of granting women the power to vote or any other equality with men. Nevertheless South Australia extended the franchise to women in 1894 and Victoria, after Federation, in 1901. Not until after World War I did Britain concede to the bitter struggle of the suffragettes.

There remained one woman, however, whom he constantly revered. Ever the loyal Victorian, he invariably took a holiday in honour of the Queen, although he frequently denounced the Australians for taking other holidays:

> Friday 24 May 1889
>
> I was up at 5 o'clock . . . It is the 70th anniversary for the Queen of the Saxons. I took a holiday in her name today
>
> > God bless the English Queen
> > I had a day of rest;
> > Of all the monarchs that have been
> > She is among the best.

On the 28 July he was granted another holiday. He proudly recorded, 'I have been invited to attend a special occasion . . . They are going to cut the first sod of the . . . Maldon to

Lanacoori Railway.' No doubt, the occasion triggered a flood of memories of his past involvement with the M&M Railway at Tregaron. But at Maldon he was not seated among the prominent guests.

By August, the state of his health had also declined and he paints a piteous picture of himself. 'I am lame and painful . . . the rheumatism is so severe in my left knee that I have a strong stick and the handle of the shovel to keep me up when trying to walk.' Despite such an affliction, for a man of 71 years he continued to show extraordinary tenacity. '4 August 1889, I managed to be at my work before 7 a.m. at the Hospital grounds. I was ordered to cross cut large fallen timber close to the Shire Hall . . . the trees were Tasmanian Gum planted 18 years previously and straight as any ship's mast . . . They were grubbed for fear of falling on the fine building during the storm.' Joseph was proud of Maldon Hospital and regularly contributed to the Easter collection for its upkeep. Strictly speaking, it was not within the terms of his contract to work within the hospital grounds, but he yielded to the 'order of the clerk of the works because I wish to be of use to my fellow men.'

Concern about his physical condition is now a frequent theme in his diary. 'I fear I will be unable to work for my health – it looks dark ahead – for I am among strangers from whom I cannot expect to get assistance of any kind!!' The larrikins and other vexations only served to exacerbate his situation:

15 August 1889
My cottage has a corrugated roof . . . it becomes unbearably hot in the sun's ray and small boys like casting stones on it deliberately to annoy me. Inside, the mice

disturb me as they tear at my books and papers. Tonight, I have placed strychnine in their oatmeal, perhaps that will quiet them.

A week later his cottage was again broken into and many of his possessions were damaged or stolen. It was too much for an old man to bear. '28 August 1889, I was at work at 6.30 a.m. ... when I came home for dinner I was astonished to find that some one or more had been in the house and took many valuable things away. No doubt, somebody was watching me planting the key of the front door, otherwise they could not find it. It was put back, but not in the same place.'

August had proved a trying month and in his vulnerable state he again fell victim to morbid thoughts. 'I am lame, very tired and shall have to give up and use my few extra pounds, then go out to the bush and starve there. That, I believe, will be my fate – The strife and struggle of life seems endless.'

Money was a constant source of worry, and with falling wool and wheat prices Joseph sensed that he was suffering because of the economic disaster on the horizon. 'September, I did not receive my usual monthly wage today . . . the council has an overdraft at the bank.' As he brooded in his cottage over fiscal affairs, he once again set himself up as the custodian of the moral standards of the nation. The Melbourne Cup, the most popular event, was a particular target and he was horrified to learn that £20,000,000 was spent each year on racing and horses:

November 1889
Horse-racing at Melbourne during the past six days. Last year's attendance was 130,000. Elaborate gambling takes place, and large sums of money change hands. Some one

half of the ladies attending are attired in borrowed dresses for which service they pay dearly . . . the maid-servants look as flash and dainty as do the countesses . . . This year the cup was won by a horse named 'Bravo' – he started at third favourite.

As the year wore on Joseph's mood vacillated from one extreme to another. Episodes of mania were followed by a sudden descent to despair. Although he admired and praised many aspects of his adopted country, sadly he seemed out of touch with the new ethos which prevailed in Australia. He was unable to appreciate the philosophy of the new settlers who had found freedom there. They believed that they were on this earth to enjoy themselves. In contrast, Joseph repeatedly wrote, 'I was not born to be content.' Still enmeshed in a puritan ethic that 'man is not here for pleasure,' the image of Australia as 'God's own country . . . the lucky country' was to him an alien one. The appetite for life among the new immigrants only reinforced his view that 'this country is hurtling towards doom.'

His feeling of isolation from the society around him was compounded by the steady loss of old Welsh friends. In September William Rees passed away. Joseph had drawn up his will and called for a doctor only an hour or so before he died. He quoted from the book of Job, 'He cometh forth like a flower . . . is cut down . . . he fleeth also as a shadow, and continueth not.' After attending his funeral, he wrote, 'Not to feel sorrow any more would be a relief, but times past can never be recovered nor can they be eliminated.'

Everywhere, it seemed that events were conspiring against him. On 9 November the excessive drinking in Maldon to celebrate the birthday of the Prince of Wales, whom he despised, disgusted him. 'Much toasting goes on in public houses . . . There are twenty two of them in this small place of less than 2,000 inhabitants, half of which are children . . . The iniquity of the world increases by seventy per cent!' Indeed, some of this iniquity was soon to present itself, yet again, on his own doorstep:

> 10 December 1889
>
> Returning home from work I found a glass pane had been removed from my window. My belongings inside had been rifled . . . lots of things missing . . . my diaries had been scattered outside . . . This is the sixth time I have been robbed in 4 years.

Although this would have been enough to break the stoutest of hearts, Joseph remained 'bloody but unbowed'. During the day he continued to drag himself to work, but each evening he consigned his troubled thoughts onto the pages of his diary, often proclaiming that death would be preferable to his present condition:

> 17 December 1889
>
> Filling in holes in the footpath to Tobin and other streets. They expect an old man to work in this country for his meals every day . . . Some employers say frankly that the old men ought to be hanged in order to make room for the young men. I think very often that they are right in respect of their merciful idea. It is better to hang a man once and give plenty of slack to the rope, than to 'pine' him in every shape for years . . . All must die once.

He was opposed to the death penalty, but apparently in favour of euthanasia.

In December the Council, at last, paid Joseph his wages for the month but he grumbled that it was 'scarcely enough for me to clear my Creditors.' He remained obsessed with the way public money was being misspent. 'It is a curious thing how the Council and the government of this colony saddle their posterity with debts . . . There must be a clash . . . as the cultivation of the soil . . . is completely neglected . . . Gold and silver are the cry all through Australasia.'

As ill health continued to make life difficult, he was obliged to follow a special diet. '22 December 1889. I prepare boiled eggs for my breakfast along with mixed tea and coffee with jam on my bread – damson jam which is binding and agrees with my complaint chronic dysentery.' But he held few hopes for a cure:

> 22 December 1889
>
> This dysentery will stick to me as long as my life. It is always fatal to an aged man in this colony. It is a very troublesome disease . . . Especially . . . when a man is obliged to attend to the call of nature about 9 times in the nine hours. I have to call at the hotel toilets. To buy a glass of beer for each time would swallow the day's wages when working opposite different Hotels!! Dysentery!

He spent Christmas alone with little appetite for food. On 31 December he prepared himself for the coming year. 'I bought a new and blank diary for the next year with a new Almanac, but to fill it is a mystery.' On New Year's Eve he decided, for once, to shrug off his worries. 'I went up to the Miners' Hotel to drink the health of the past year . . . should I be able to open my eyes at the dawn of next and outlive the year, I do hope that it will be to my advantage, comfort and improvement.'

The year 1889 had been one of sadness, sickness and intense irritation. Although he displayed great fortitude in the face of so much provocation, he continued to be stalked by thoughts of death, which he still looked upon as the one certain release from his trials in this world:

> I often think that he is best
> Who's early called for quiet rest.

What are we all but fellow travellers stumbling along this rough road called life towards the grave?

If ever a man had an endless capacity for unhappiness and morbidity, it was Joseph, who finally concluded that, 'Things are never so bad, that they cannot get worse.'

CHAPTER 20

I AM ROOTLESS

By 1890 Joseph Jenkins had been in Australia for 21 years and he was now 72 years of age. The remorseless work, the personal tragedies, sickness and the extremes of climate had all taken their toll. Yet, he stubbornly dragged himself to work. 'I was on my withered pins at 4.30 this morning . . . Picking and shovelling all day . . . The air was foul with the smoke of bush fires burning all around . . . I could not get the smoke out of my nostrils.' He returned home utterly exhausted and fell asleep under a nearby oak tree with dreams of sweet death. When he awoke he thought how peaceful it would be to quit this difficult world. Like Keats he was 'half in love with easeful death' and expressed his wish in these lines, inspired perhaps, by the sweet oblivion of laudanum:

6 February 1890

> Under the oak my bed I made
> Its spreading branches gave me shade,
> Beneath the fierce scorching sun
> There I slept till day was done.
> Oh, how lovely it would be
> To lie beneath the old yew tree,
> There to enjoy a blissful rest
> Safe in one's grave with those so blest. †

Still in this moribund mood he walked the two miles to Maldon cemetery on the following Sunday, where he spent between three and four hours studying the inscriptions on the graves. The diversity of names bore witness to the multinational origins of the early pioneers; he pondered on the inscriptions to the Cornish, Welsh, Scots, Irish, English and German and noted with curiosity the brick urns of the Chinese. Emotional to the core, he commented, 'their love, their hatreds, their envy are all now perished.' Many Welshmen he had counted as friends were now 'eternally laid to rest' in Australian soil. Full of fear that he would soon join them in earth so far removed from his native Cardiganshire, he movingly wrote, 'If I don't have a grave back home it will be as though I'd never walked this earth!'

At the beginning of March he was unlucky enough to spill boiling water over his left foot causing severe scalding. His foot became so blistered and swollen that, 'I cannot walk and I cannot work. It is serious.' He bathed it in linseed oil and each night he placed a poultice on it to ease the pain. He complained, *'Rwy'n glaf, rwy'n gloff, rwy'n boenus* ['I'm sick, I'm lame, I'm in pain] . . . I have no friends to console me at Maldon these dreary days . . . or to fetch my necessities of life such as water and firewood. I am marooned.'

Hopelessly dejected, his thoughts turned to the past and he yearned for the impossible, 'I wish my eldest daughter, Margaret, could be at hand . . . the one that is dead. I did assist her when she had her arm dreadfully scolded in boiled starch.' The excruciating pain in his foot continued for six months. On 12 April, unable to sleep, and steeped in gloom, he wrote yet another epitaph for himself:

I AM ROOTLESS

12 April 1890
Die we must and cast aside this mortal shell
How, or when, and in what place, we cannot tell. †

After an absence of two months he finally hobbled back to work, having made a special slipper for his left foot, which was still too sore and swollen to fit into his boot. He complained bitterly that, 'Maldon Council did not allow one penny of sick pay, nor did any representative of the Council visit me during my indisposition.' He was upset that his constant loyalty went unacknowledged. Still in great pain with his foot, he cut a pitiful figure. On 12 April he described himself as, 'limping between the arms of my wheelbarrow . . . raking the dead leaves from the channels, clearing sorrel roots and thistles.' All this time he worried about his loss of wages, his unpaid debts and how he would survive on his meagre savings.

His strength was also flagging. '17 May I felt myself shaky and giddy . . . I was unable to walk forward and I felt as if I was dead drunk . . . I fell backward like a loose gate.' Two men nearby helped him to his feet and tried to persuade him to enter Maldon Hospital, but he refused. Anxiety about money compounded his distress. 'No wages since these last nine weeks! How can I live? Starve Jo!' To add to his agony he contracted another severe bout of dysentery which plunged him into suicidal despair:

23 May 1890
I am completely miserable and would rather die than live. It appears now that my diaries will never go to Wales . . . I am low in body, spirit and mind. I have not eaten an ordinary meal for ten days. I have a gripping pain in my belly – the effects of chronic dysentery. I was praying to

my God last night to be released and go quickly to the Majority for lasting peace. What a man thinks makes him what he is, and I am wretched in the extreme!

Feeling abandoned and forgotten, he prepared himself for the worst. '25 May 1890, I crawled to bed at 6 o'clock . . . I am obliged to leave my door unbolted that somebody may come in to find my corpse after death.' The outlook seemed bleak. On 27 May, the wife of his old friend, William Rees, visited him, but she was hardly the harbinger of good news. Like Job's comforter, the only thing she had to offer him was a grave.

27 May 1890
The plain and kind old woman Catherine Rees came to see me, she had 2 miles to come in her 77th year of age – Mrs Rees wishes me to be buried inside their burying ground . . . she sees that I cannot exist long like this!

Even *in extremis* Joseph continued to rage against Betty. 'I had all sorts of bad and cruel treatment while in Wales, where I was robbed of all my comforts and property by one who swore to behave otherwise to-wards me.'

Whilst suffering from acute dysentery he became increasingly worried about the fate of his diaries. 'It is now unlikely that my diaries will ever be returned to Wales . . . or that anyone will ever know of what my life's journey has been here . . . I am unable to fetch water or cut firewood.' It was 'old Mrs Rees' who came to his rescue. She arranged for him to see a doctor who ordered his immediate admission to Maldon Hospital on 28 May. After medical care, good food and a period of rest he recovered sufficiently to leave hospital in late June. Much to his annoyance he was charged £2 a week for his stay; this he referred to as a 'crying shame'. Because he had lost so much pay due to his illness, he forced himself to return to work almost immediately, in spite of the horrendous conditions. 'The streets are very muddy after heavy rain and the pedestrians grumble that they are ankle deep in muck.'

Nevertheless, the resumption of work seemed to revive his spirits and the old fighting Joseph re-emerged. He was again trenchant in his criticism of the economic unrest that now swept the country and manifested itself in the great maritime strike. He had long predicted a crash in the economy and he now felt that he had been vindicated. 'This colony is lurching towards perdition because of the great boom and reckless borrowing of the 1880's which is ending in collapse! The ports are paralysed because of the mass desertion of sailors.'

20 August 1890
The strike increases through all the Colonies, 23 big ships remain at Melbourne alone. They cannot go to sea for want of hands. Every commodity is rising in price rapidly, even bread, when plenty of wheat and flour can be had inland.

The situation deteriorated daily. 'On 23 August even the Marine Officers Association joined the strike against the ship owners which is getting more serious every hour and all commodities continue to rise . . . Everything for a man's provision is dearer, even the fruits and cabbages, carrots and potatoes.' Joseph had always been a strident critic of what he saw as the profligacy of the Australian colonial governments in borrowing and spending too much. He claimed that, 'This has led to the present rather serious and troublesome situation in the colonies . . . Even the ships' officers have joined the Union and the stock of coal is out.

There is no coal to burn for gas to light the cities and towns... I fear that the thieves and burglars will take advantage of the dark season.' Alarmed lest there should be a total breakdown of law and order he noted that, 'a thousand extra Constables were sworn in at the city of Melbourne alone. The shipowners bitterly oppose the strike and are backed from England with £80 millions sterling according to the Telegrams, in order to bring the officers and men to a condition of starvation.' But there was some good news. Joseph had, mercifully, found a remedy for his illness. 'I bought two dozen eggs and boiled them hard. They keep in good condition for weeks and they keep away my threatening dysentery. Thank God!'

On 10 September 1890 Joseph received more news from Wales that took his mind back 35 years to the heady days of the construction of the M&M Railway:

> 10 September 1890
>
> David Davies, the great contractor and coal proprietor has died. He was only a poor top sawyer when 25 years old, and 71 when he died. He would have been a millionaire... The wheel of fortune did much in his favour but was stopped at last!

Both David Davies and Joseph had been born in similar circumstances, but whilst Davies had risen to become one of the most prosperous and powerful men in Wales, Joseph's many talents had remained largely unfulfilled. With a touch of self-satisfaction he observed, 'Not a day of extra time can be bought by any man, not even the exceedingly wealthy David Davies. Empty handed we come in, and empty handed we go out of this world.'

Meanwhile Joseph noted that the great strike in the colony was having tragic repercussions even in Maldon. 'While busy cleaning the Main Street on 4 October, I heard a report from inside the London and Charter Bank and did not think much of it. I then found out that the manager, aged 36, had shot himself in an act of wilful suicide. He was buried like a pauper the next day, unmourned. The reason for the suicide seems to have been a combination of financial and marital problems.'

A fortnight later, Joseph recorded yet another unexpected death in Maldon. While walking to work on 15 October 1890, he passed a crowd of people who had dragged a drowned man out of the big dam. He turned out to be a colourful local character known as the Silver King, who had once struck it rich, 'since which time he had never been sober,' and ended up penniless. Joseph was horrified to learn that local predators had stripped his dead body of his gold watch and chain and waistcoat. 'There is,' he wrote, 'no respect for the dead here.'

During this time of instability and unrest, alcoholism was rife in Maldon but Joseph attended the meetings held at Maldon Temperance Hall and contributed generously to the cause. On 6 September he again signed the pledge, witnessed by the prominent businessman Mr R. Dabb, promising 'to abstain from all Intoxicating Drinks.'

For some years there had been a crusade against alcohol led by the Protestants and strongly supported by women. More than 45,000 Victorian women signed a temperance petition describing strong drink as 'the source of broken hearts, ruined homes and blighted lives.' Joseph knew full well the truth of these sentiments, and felt proud at his long abstinence for so many years. But in a time of joy, pain can strike at any moment.

In late September he received a letter from his daughter Nel at Tyndomen informing him of the death of her seven-year-old son, Ieuan, and how he had been bled while suffering from scarlet fever. She wrote that even at his tender age he had faced death bravely, telling his parents not to grieve for him. Joseph now found himself weeping for a grandson he had never seen. 'My first born son, my first born daughter and now my first born grandchild – dead! Who can hope to understand the order of things?' But Nel's letter also contained the disturbing news that Joseph's younger brother, Benjamin, 'had been ill in bed for two months with consumption.'

Joseph's worst fears were to be confirmed when on 2 December he received copies of *The Welshman* and the *Cambrian News* informing him that Benjamin had died on 15 October, and that as a mark of respect for him 111 carriages had followed his coffin to the cemetery. These sad letters from home left Joseph 'drained by sorrow'. Turning to his Bible for consolation he quoted once again from Ecclesiastes, which he had often heard his father read aloud to the family, *'Y mae amser i bob peth ... Amser i wylo ... amser i alaru.'* ['To everything there is a season ... a time to weep ... a time to mourn.'] He read his Bible because of the magnificence of its prose and confessed, 'I am even thankful to my old teacher, Jac Llwyd, for thrashing me into learning to read it. But my soul is sore vexed and I am weary with groaning ... 2 Rhagfyr [December] 1890 *Er pelled wyf, collais beth dagrau. Yr oeddwn mor hoff o'm brawd Benjamin.* [Although I am far away I have lost a few tears, I was so fond of my brother Benjamin.]' Benjamin had been the youngest brother and a favourite with the whole family.

Meanwhile, at Maldon, a fierce thunderstorm rent the sky.

Joseph describes how bolts of lightning zigzagged wildly and from his cottage he saw a cow and a goat struck dead. Later, great clouds of locusts blackened the sky and 'covered the rail track making it so greasy that the wheels of the engine failed to grip and the train came to a halt ... These pests,' wrote Joseph, 'devour all sorts of green as they travel onward; vegetables, wines, corn, grass etc.'

Since the death of David Evans, Rheola, he had become increasingly worried about the eleven diaries which he had left with his friend. He was terrified that his lifelong work should be carelessly cast into oblivion with the impending sale of the farm. Joseph still entertained the hope of returning home one day but, ever conscious of his own mortality, he wrote, 'If I do not reach Wales, my intention is to send my diaries there, so that somebody may have the chance to know how I fared as their antipode. I want the immortality of remembrance.' After spending Christmas alone, Joseph set out for Rheola on 31 December to collect his diaries. While he was there Margaret, David Evans's widow, asked him to draw up her will and to attend to the sale of the farm. Within a month Margaret Evans also died. Joseph returned to Rheola in mid-February 1891 to witness the dismantling of the farm which had been his refuge in times of crisis. Everything was sold cheaply; there were no bids for 14 barrels of wine and the auctioneer snapped up a bargain at two shillings a gallon. The horses went well below market value, but the cattle sold well. The proceeds of the sale realised £500 and Evan Evans of New South Wales bought the vineyard, the land and the house for £775. The late David Evans and his wife of Bryn Madog, Tal-sarn, Wales, had worked hard and achieved much, but were cut down in life before they could enjoy the fruits of their labour. 'Such is the way of the world,' sighed Joseph, 'what a man will build up, time will pull down.' At 4 a.m. the following morning Joseph 'rose quietly and walked to the cemetery to visit the grave of his friends.' He stood there awhile meditating on the fact that had he not left Bryn Madog he would have been buried in Tal-sarn cemetery, but now he would forever lie at Inglewood. Joseph shivered involuntarily and then took his final leave of Rheola and returned to Maldon.

In March he attended the official opening of the Maldon to Lanacoori Railway Line. He was allowed to ride on the engine *Eastern Ho*, but he noticed that the driver 'was the worse for drink!' At the end of the month Maldon was again deluged with heavy rainstorms causing serious flooding. Because the Easter Day celebrations were threatened, Joseph, once more, was urgently called upon 'to unblock the footbridges and clear the channels' of all manner of detritus so that the water could flow freely. He grumbled that, 'It was heavy work to move by barrow the mud, sand and clay, especially for a man of 73 years of age.' Following the flood came fire, when 'a drapery shop, a shoe shop, a grocery shop and a book shop were mysteriously engulfed in flames.'

Despite his own precarious state of health, many of Joseph's compatriots had predeceased him in Maldon. In August 1891 Rees Jones, formerly of Ponterwyd, died of T.B. He had worked in the Cwmystwyth lead mines alongside his father from the age of 13. His quest for a better life in Australia had been extremely successful, but ironically he succumbed to a disease that was endemic among the lead miners of Cardiganshire. At the time of his death he was the manager of the Beehive Golden Claim, the most prosperous and largest of the 22 claims in Maldon. He and his wife had often invited Joseph to supper at their magnificent residence in Church Street. 'Rees Jones left a widow, and nine children.' According to Joseph, 'He had paid a premium of £20 to cover an insurance policy of £500 and had been ailing for some time.' He lamented the death of a fellow Welshman who had come from a part of Cardiganshire he knew so well, but he found some consolation in the fact that, 'Rees Jones had a swell funeral . . . Twenty five carriages followed a beautiful hearse drawn by two black horses. The coffin was covered with wreaths . . . withered flowers over a withered body.' It is unlikely that he would have had such an ostentatious send-off in the wilds of Ponterwyd.

At the end of November, now that her husband William Rees was dead, Mrs Catherine Rees asked Joseph to help her gather in the hay. Joseph went willingly. Because it was a blisteringly hot day and sunstroke was a very real threat, he fortified himself for the task. 'I soaked a big piece of calico in water and wrapped it around my head and I placed a green cabbage leaf inside my hat as a precaution against sun stroke and a visor to protect my eyes against the dust and flies.' It was often during such dog hot days that he longed for the cooler climes of Wales, especially after receiving a poem from his favourite nephew Aeronian, son of his brother John, which urged him to return home and assured him of a warm welcome.

Joseph was moved by Aeronian's plea for he had long suffered frequent bouts of homesickness, often confessing, 'Here, I am rootless.' In September 1892 it all became too much for him; his intense longing for home spilled over into a poem and six of his stanzas were published in the *Tarrangower Times*.

THE OLD HOME

'Tis many a year from home I've been, but I'd like to try somehow
To see the old folk once again; but they won't know me now.
But still the thought of dear old home does oft a pleasure bring,
But I have changed and they have changed, and changed has everything.

I'd like to see the old play-ground, and the green lanes where I've strolled,
I think I'd know my way around, though now I'm getting old,
And the grist mill with the water-wheel, the turnstile and the brook,
And the angler sitting by the stream, with his bait upon the hook.

With the blackberries upon the hedge, and the little birds at play,
And the willows and the meadows, do they look as green today?
And the song-birds on the branches, would their music sound as sweet?
And the glow-worms in the bushes, where the lovers used to meet.

And the old churchyard with tombstones thick, some crumbling in decay,
I think I could the old spot find, where they laid a friend away.
And the old school I remember yet, with ink-stained desk of yore,
With the scolds and birching then I got, but the master's now no more.

And by the pathway, near the church, two old graves together;
And the tombstones sinking in the earth, leant one against the other.
Beneath were friends in life, now in their graves long undisturbed they lie,
It seemed in death a touching thing, for tombstones thus to tie.

What matters it when death does come, and in the grave you're lain?
The friends you knew are very few who'd wish you back again;
And p'haps it's well, for when you're old, you're often in the way,
So it's natural-like such things should be, as age to youth gives way.

When Joseph wrote this nostalgic poem speaking of 'home and death' he could have had no idea that the very next letter would bring news of the death, not 'of old people', but of his beloved nephew, Aeronian, who had so recently pleaded with him to return home. The order of things was once again all wrong and he could not come to terms with it. In his notebook he wrote, 'Now my brother's first born son is dead! Is there no end to it?' The circumstances of Aeronian's death were particularly poignant; first, his wife, Elizabeth, died on the birth of their eleventh child on 27 April 1890 at the age of 39; on 27 May the following year his eldest daughter, Margaret, died of T.B. at the age of 23; then Aeronian himself succumbed at the age of 46 on 17 October 1892, and was buried in Nantcwnlle cemetery leaving ten orphaned children. A distraught Joseph wrote, 'I do hope I will be able to see them before I join their parents.' He also added, 'People will learn from my life how cruel the human condition can be – how much suffering there is, and so often, and how little we can do about it.'

Family tragedies were not the only matters of concern for Joseph. He felt that a national tragedy was unfolding in the affairs of Victoria itself. At the beginning of 1893 he once again became obsessed with the state of the economy. Without mincing his words he makes grim predictions, '3 January 1893, This Colony is going headlong into disaster . . . It is heavily in debt to the tune of £50 million while it craves for still more loans . . . Up to twelve banks have failed . . . The London Chartered Bank has closed its doors. It is short of half a million pounds. People are clamouring to get their money out, but the banks have shut their doors. This country is divided against itself. The politicians deceive us, they overpay themselves and they think the voters are dullards. No-one is to be trusted! Politics is all about power and money. Very few men have true principles! . . . Probity is lacking here as it was in Wales . . . Most men are gripped by greed.'

During the boom time of the 1880s over 200 million pounds had been borrowed and there had been heavy investment in buildings, public works, roads and the construction of the railways to provide employment. The Stock Exchange had a volume of business exceeding six million pounds a week but to the canny farmer from Cardiganshire, things had gone too far! Even seven years previously he had expressed serious misgivings about the economy:

> 21 December 1885
> All mortgages bear interest rates of between 7% and 12%. For how long can things go on in this way? Only time will tell, but the day of reckoning cannot be far off . . . When I arrived in the Colony in 1869, my share of the public debt was £4-13-4, but it is now £32!

For Joseph the only answer lay in the land. '1 January 1893, No nation can survive unless it improves the surface of its soil through proper cultivation, employing labour at fair wages.'

Farming methods had vastly improved over the years, but Joseph remained critical. 'Although the land is rich, the land is Nature, and Nature is honest. You may only take from it what you give to it. Properly managed, this country could feed the whole of Europe. But now they can scarcely feed themselves. Nature has so much to teach us, but we do not listen!'

The collapse of the economy had profound consequences: wages plummeted and there was mass unemployment with labourers going hungry. Even Joseph could now consider himself well off with his three shillings and four pence per day. His two Welsh mining friends, John Davies and John Williams, 'worked for half a crown a day . . . going down 1,000 feet before finding any gold. 26 July 1893, Unemployment is rife . . . many families are starving. I left a new bucket outside my door under the veranda and it was stolen. Every schoolboy here is a downright thief.'

Joseph's humble cottage had again become the target for vandals and thieves, and the larrikins continued to cause him acute distress. In November 1893, after a visit to the butcher's shop, he 'returned within 20 minutes to find my two windows broken ... they were riddled with stones thrown by schoolboys.'

Although the larrikins made his life a misery, thoughts of home caused him even more pain. The first page of his 1894 diary reveals a man still fixated by his wife:

> If I ever I return to Wales,
> I'll ask of Betty
> What evil I did commit, what was my failing –
> That I deserved to be trampled upon? †

So much of his diary is a running tide of his own private hell. He was not a saint, but he often considered himself a martyr. He never wept for Betty: his tears flowed only for himself. And underlying everything lay the conviction that the fates conspired against him even before he was born:

> POOR OLD JO
> My fate was to suffer injustice
> Long before I left my mother's womb,
> All the time my miserable fate was to be
> Like a scapegoat in the world. †

He signs this verse, 'Hare-lipped fellow, Hen pecked Husband, Scapegoat, and one who suffers for another's faults.' Joseph also listed what he considered to be the eight universal sins in the world:

1 Whoredom	5 Pride
2 Greed for money	6 Partiality
3 Ambition	7 Bigotry
4 Selfishness	8 Countercreed denomination

The Victorians loved moralizing, and no man indulged in it more than Joseph. The whole page makes grim reading but, as usual, in one leap of his wildly gyrating mind he suddenly takes us from darkness to light, casting aside his cloak of despair to show a man content with his world:

> Diary for the year 1894
> Monday, the first day of the year . . . I was up this bright, warm and dry morning. I do think to take it as a holiday like the rest, so I did; and had my little Cot to myself all day. It is remarkably busy at the Railway Station. The trains are back and fore every two hours, full of holiday passengers for different parts of the colony.

Yet on that same day, his mood plummets once again as he worried about the fate of his diaries:

> This is my 53rd diary filled by me and 25 of them filled in Australia. I would be glad to see them together before I am to die, but most likely that will not have my desired object fulfilled and very likely that some of them are devoured and burnt by my traitors in Cardiganshire but I can't help that revengeful crime.

Ironically, his concern was not without foundation. For the next three weeks he followed his strict regime of cleaning the streets, rising at 4.30, taking his lunch break at the bakehouse of his friend Alexander McArthur, and browsing through his excellent collection of books. Quoting from the Bible he wrote, 'Of the making of books there is no end.' There also seemed to be no end to Joseph's sustained ill treatment. On 29 January, instead of eating his lunch at the bakery, Joseph decided to return to his cottage for a break. There, he found 'the larrikins' again doing mischief to his property. Unable to endure any further provocation, he resorted to drastic action. 'I did load my gun in their sight, and that made them measure a safe distance, very quick! . . . They are the reckless governors of the place . . . parents have no control over them . . . they will steal and break anything they see and molest undefended people.' The threat of Joseph's gun had, temporarily, kept the 'pests' at bay. But the harassment continued.

In March he complained to Mr Smith, the headmaster of Maldon School, that the children mocked and hindered him while he tried to do his work. Mr Smith refused to intervene and merely referred him to the police, stating that he was not responsible for the children outside school hours. Joseph was greatly displeased with this response. He had expected the children to be severely disciplined. 'Their language is foul, and forty per cent of them do not know which end of a cabbage plant to put into the earth in their parents' rich gardens which are overrun with weeds and brambles.' Had the headmaster realised Joseph's poor state of health he might have been more sympathetic. Chronic dysentery now so weakened him that he was obliged to take fifty drops of laudanum 'to ease the pain and to enable me to go to work.'

'Another year, and other deadly blows.' However, the next 'ghastly blow' came, not from Australia, but from Wales.

6 May 1894

I had a letter yesterday from a friend to say that my brother John [Cerngoch] died suddenly when waiting outside the house without anybody with him on 24 March 1894. This gave me a shock, as I was very fond of him always, as we were of the same opinion on every subject.

The loss of John left him pole-axed and he scarcely knew how to express the inexpressible. He wrote, 'I feel now that I have nothing left to fear – How fragile and finite we all are. Today would be a good day for my own dissolution.' Only through poetry, which they had so often shared, could he hope to communicate his feelings:

> This brother was fervent and lovable
> The one I loved best. †

With his bardic soul mate dead, he had never felt so isolated since his arrival in Australia. In his lonely cottage he read and re-read the account of his brother's funeral when 'a large concourse of people had followed the body from Penybryn to Rhydygwin Chapel.' His mind flew back over 60 years to the death of his eight-year-old sister, Esther, in 1832. With exquisite pathos he wrote, 'I wish I could join her in the cemetery to escape the pain of living.' At this point in the diary his writing becomes scarcely legible as if, submerged in a world of grief, he was unable to cope with the trauma. His brother's death was the catalyst which finally persuaded him to return to Wales before it was too late. He gave Maldon Council one month's notice of his intention to quit his job.

In July he began to wind up his affairs, such as they were, but encountered many difficulties. Over the years he had lent money to many so-called friends and compatriots, but not one, so far, had repaid him. The time had now come to demand his payments. One day after another he tramped round his debtors, pleading for his cash, but to no avail. Even John Davies, his mining friend, who often called to see him on Sundays, would not, or could not, repay the many sums he had borrowed. In despair Joseph confessed, 'I did not get one farthing back of all the money I lent... the money amounted to over £200.' Once again, it seemed that he was destined to be one of life's losers. Worse still, he was unable to sell his cottage or belongings, owing to the depressed state of the economy.

As if all this were not enough, the local thieves and hooligans, sensing their opportunity, again swooped on his cottage like vultures for the seventh time and wrought the worst destruction yet:

28 July 1894

When I arrived at my Cot before 9 p.m. I found that burglars had been there. The front window had been broken with the frame and part of the brick wall taken down... they put my house on fire... it was a damnable and cruel attempt... my life is in danger... I was afraid to go out... I could not venture to look for the police ... I found 7 of my big diaries outside spread about.

The following day he faced the heart-rending task of attempting to make his cottage once again fit for habitation. 'I tried to block up my windows with boards and rags to keep out the cold.' He could not afford to replace the glass, and conditions were such that he found it difficult to read or write. In a scarcely legible scrawl, he describes how utterly wretched he felt:

30 July 1894

Poor Jo. Start for Wales as soon as you can or somewhere else. The grave would be safe from burglars and swindlers.

> My brother John is lucky. Nobody will disturb him in his resting place at Rhydygwin burial ground. Nobody will be able to torment me therein, death would be a boon for me ... I have suffered cruelty towards me in all shapes without the least cause or provocation – The history of my life has been wounds in this dreary world.

There seemed to be only one thing left to live for. '31 July 1894 I should like to see my grandchildren before my dissolution.' With a tormented mind in an exhausted body, he set out his pitiful predicament in poetry:

> Deep in thought the evening long
> I sit before the fire.
> If I should now compose a song
> There's no one here to listen. †

But still there was no peace from his tormentors:

> 19 August 1894
> A further £5 has been stolen from my Cot ... somebody must have a key to open my door ... I never read of so bad a thieving place as this Township ... This fine country is glorious, but her inhabitants could not be worse!

Unfortunately the actions of a mischievous few had clouded Joseph's good opinion of the town and its people. Over the years, many of Maldon's inhabitants had admired and respected him; they appreciated his erudition, his readiness to help others, and his commitment to his work.

As Joseph attempted to arrange the return voyage to Wales, he found the days endless. He confesses, 'I wish I hadn't given in my notice so early.' Without a structured day packed with hard work, time hung heavy on his hands and left him at the mercy of his confused emotions. Despite his dysentery and his rheumatism, it had been far easier to drag himself to work at dawn than to sit at home brooding. Work had been his refuge; now self-pity and despair filled the void. '27 August 1894, Poor Jo . . . No pay, no job. Cheer up. You wont be a stumbling block long to anybody in this friendless world.'

Apart from his low esteem and a sense of hopelessness, he fretted constantly about his ability to face the long voyage home. '28 August . . . It will be an odd thing if the Brokers will accept me as a passenger on the Mail Boat . . . But I will try . . . They take more crippled old men than me on board when properly paid.'

The state of Victoria remained a target for his wrath. '30 August 1894 . . . This Colony is going headlong to destruction for the mismanagement of her Legislators. Each member receives his £300 a year for blundering . . . and going millions into debt . . . we have scheming politicians mistrusted by all!' Joseph also felt that he had been unfairly treated by the Town Council and continued to allege that monies were owed to him, but Maldon Council were having none of it and threatened him with prison if he persisted with his complaints:

2 September 1894
After working hard and honestly all my life . . . according to the cruel law of Victoria they must put me in prison for a month, afterwards out to the Bush to starve! . . . Democratic Australia treats honest people worse than ordinary thieves...
This government cares not a fig for charity.

He admits that at his advanced age:

I brood continuously over diverse subjects and am reminded

of the words by the poet Clough, who was considered to be an infidel –

> And almost every man when age,
> Disease, and sorrow, strike him
> Inclines to think there is a God,
> Or something very like Him.

Unlike Clough, Joseph's belief in God remained strong throughout his life. He prayed for strength each morning and read his Bible each day. Outside, the weather matched his mood, and added to his sense of foreboding. 'There is a heavy and rattling thunderstorm over my head at this moment . . . It is dangerous . . . The thunderclaps are deafening overhead with big hail stones covering the surface two inches thick.'

As the days dragged on, Joseph complained increasingly of 'feeling far from well . . . and very cold.' He cut some firewood for the grocer for which he received 'no money, but a plug of tobacco now and then which was just as well for me. I can't live comfortable without a smoke, sometimes a chew.' He also began to worry about his appearance should he eventually reach Wales:

> 11 September 1894
> I went to the Post Office Savings Bank to order £10 in cash . . . having lodged £5-0-0 for a new suit of the best colonial tweed . . . I must try and prepare something for my intended long voyage – If I will be alive and well enough to embark on the Mail Boat . . . I am afraid of the sea voyage in my old age. I have cut and trimmed my grey beard.

After such a long exile, the prospect of returning home troubled him. But by 17 September his mood had lightened and he confessed to 'feeling much better'. He was out at 6 a.m. on a 'new and beautiful morning' and hoped that he 'would have sunny days to air and dust my manuscripts and clothes . . . many are eaten by moths etc . . . The mice did have their share of mischief.' He even began to take a renewed interest in the politics of Victoria but, as usual, his comment is scathing:

19 September 1894

It will be a busy day at Maldon tomorrow, being a General Election through the Colony. There are three sorts of Candidates. The Squatters and the Landgrabbers, the working class and Tradesmen, and the Farmers and Labourers. All of them are quite useless when they are in opposition to each other. This colony is going headlong to destruction for bad constitution . . . The Paterson Government has resigned giving way to G. Turner, St Kilda, and his Liberal Ministry.

He wrote many letters to his family in Wales informing them that he hoped to see them before Christmas 1894. His intention was to sail on the *SS Austral* on 10 November, and arrive 'before the hiring fairs of menservants and maidservants for the coming year.' But there were still many hurdles to overcome; apart from his health, shortage of money was proving a major problem. Maldon Town Council still owed him £90 in backpay and he feared, 'I will lose my wages through the stratagem of the Clerk of the Works.' His anxiety was well founded; he never did receive this money and recorded wistfully, 'I must look out, otherwise I will be unable to embark homeward.'

By mid October the suspense of trying to book a voyage home was again taking its toll on his health. He complains, 'I feel myself getting weaker everyday.' He again slipped into his old trough of despondency believing that he was at death's door. 'I have been a scapegoat long enough in this life . . . the world can go on without me, as well as the Emperor of all the Russians and even the Pope of the Vatican! But I should like to see my grandchildren before I die.' Feeling bloated and off colour, he overdosed himself on senna pods, with the result that he became 'loose and gripey'. He suffered from frequent bouts of torrential diarrhoea and wryly confessed, 'If this should happen on board among hundreds of passengers, they would fling me overboard without consultation!'

At the beginning of November he made one last ditch attempt to recover the money he had lent 'in good faith . . . to various persons . . . I took a long walk about the township to-day as a debt collector . . . but my creditors are downright swindlers and complete rogues . . . this fine country is glorious, but her inhabitants could not be worse and are ready to rob each other every way . . . many have been cruel and abusive to me and Australia has more vagabonds than saints. Nothing will satisfy this ache in my soul other than to go home.' Despite desperate attempts to sell his cottage and the small parcel of land, there were no buyers. In fact, he could not even give it away. 'I must leave all the heavy things behind; no body will give me a farthing for anything. I have no friend that deserves anything as a gift, neither money nor principles.' It was a sad admission considering all the years he had spent in Australia. On 5 November Joseph found that, after all, he was unable to travel on the *SS Austral* on 10 November, but instead obtained a passage on the *SS Ophir* due to sail on 24 November. He now began in earnest to pack his most valuable possessions and the fruits of a lifetime's labour:

14 November 1894

Busy all day mending my portmanteau in order to pack my Diaries and manuscripts for Wales. Should I happen to die on the ocean, they will dispatch me cheap and easy. I hope that my Diaries will reach their destination at Llanio Station in the care of . . . Elinor Evans. I will not live long to bother them . . . I was over 50 years when I was transported to this part of the Globe. My conscience is clear.

His constant insistence that 'my conscience is clear' suggests that he had never really addressed the question of his own guilt. Instead he seems to have attempted to expiate it by endless work, and when he could find no other reason for his lack of success he conveniently attributed everything to being 'a play thing of fate'.

Finally, the long wait was nearing its end. With his diaries safely dispatched and his meagre possessions packed, he surveyed the remnants of his life in Maldon. All that remained of his Spartan existence were a few cooking utensils and some sticks of furniture, one chair, one table, one bed, many books and a lamp. Despite the gratuitous abuse and despite his harsh words about Maldon and Australia, Joseph clearly had feelings of regret at leaving a place which had afforded him a sanctuary over the years. '22 November . . . I do consider I am to leave a home where I spent nearly ten years comfortably in spite of my defaults.' The complexity of the man meant that there was, possibly, no place on God's earth which could have provided him with a true refuge from his inner self. As far as possible for a man of his volatile nature, he had achieved some measure of contentment during the decade spent at Maldon; indeed, he would later come to realise that his years spent in Australia were happier than he'd thought.

He conceded that since coming to Australia he had 'never gone hungry', although he had been very close to it during his early years. He was, nevertheless, a survivor. 'Whenever I was out of work ... I would find a place to put down my swag for the night ... and in the morning I would walk into pastures new ... perhaps 100 miles in search of work to keep body and soul together.' He remained convinced that Australia, 'In spite of its many failings ... can offer young men the best of opportunities to succeed in this life.' His tragedy was that he was not a young man when he set out on his eventful journey. 'If only I had been twenty years younger, I could have gained land cheaply and prospered here – but fate decreed otherwise.'

Eccentric, dogmatic and opinionated are adjectives that might well describe him, but he was also cultured, knowledgeable and, above all, industrious. His diaries put a human face to those hundreds of thousands of anonymous swagmen who made their own unique contribution to the development of Australia in the nineteenth century. Ever proud to count himself among them, he used his pen to seek to improve their lot. Even so, he had never been able to sever the umbilical cord that bound him to Wales. Death itself he could take, for he had courted it many times when he had been at his lowest ebb, but his recurring nightmare was the 'fear of being buried in alien soil.' While most Welsh immigrants had eagerly adopted the Australian way of life, Joseph continued to refer to himself as 'rootless – locked in my own loneliness.'

On the evening before his departure for Wales, he was understandably tense. Uptight and restless, he wrote, 'I was in bed early . . . but could not remain in bed for two hours and was quite sleepless.' At daybreak, on the morning of 23 November 1894, he left North Gate Railway Lodge for the last time, when 'two neighbours helped me carry my box and portmanteau to catch the 6.15 a.m. Castlemaine-Melbourne train.' Almost 25 years previously he had written in the margin of his 1869 diary, 'Home is where the soul is.' If truth be told, despite the long exile, his soul had never really left Wales. As a stranger he had arrived and as a stranger he departed.

CHAPTER 21

I TRUST ALL OF US WILL BE RECONCILED

Three hours after leaving Maldon, Joseph reached Melbourne, where he proceeded immediately to the Orient Line Shipping Office and paid £26 15s 6d for a single cabin on the *SS Ophir*, bound for Tilbury Docks. He probably heaved a sigh of relief that the whole procedure had gone so smoothly. For the previous three months he had been frantic with worry that he might be refused a passage on account of his age and poor state of health.

The following day, 24 November 1894, he boarded the *SS Ophir*, which was due to sail at 6.30 p.m. When he first saw the vessel, it appeared so huge that he wrote, 'it is a wonder to me that it would move!' The *SS Ophir*, built in Glasgow in 1891, was 6,814 tons 'with four decks and steam driven by 10,000 horse power.' Joseph's neighbour from Llanddewibrefi, Jonathan Ceredig Davies, a noted traveller and author, also sailed on the *SS Ophir* in 1898. He described the vessel as 'one of the finest steamers of the Orient Line . . . a Monarch of the Ocean and a favourite boat of their majesties; the present King and Queen travelled by it to Australia and other parts of the world.' As an implacable royalist, Joseph would, no doubt, have been proud to learn that Lloyd's Register of Shipping described the *SS Ophir* as 'the Royal Yacht which conveyed the Duke and Duchess of York to Australia in 1901 to open the Federal Parliament.'

But all that lay in the future. The Australia that Joseph was now leaving was a very different country from the one he had entered 25 years previously. When he had stepped ashore in 1869, Australia still retained several features of the old convict colony from which it sprang. But Joseph had witnessed a sea change, for by the 1890s Australia was beginning to find its own identity. The population was now made up, in the main, of descendants of early immigrants and many did not feel the same sense of loyalty towards the 'old world' with its hereditary privileges and class distinctions. It was now a developing country with a new confidence in its future, where a spirit of egalitarianism prevailed. The poet Henry Lawson's line reflects this mounting sense of nationhood, 'We are lords of ourselves, our land is our own.' Joseph would most certainly have taken an interest in these developments, but now his only concern was that the *SS Ophir* should weigh anchor and head for Britain as soon as possible.

Sea travel had advanced significantly during the past quarter of a century. As Joseph stood on the deck watching Port Melbourne recede, he marvelled at the fact that the ship was infinitely more luxurious than the 1,163-ton schooner *Eurynome* that had brought him to Australia. As the *SS Ophir* steamed majestically out of Melbourne, 'past the Heads where many good ships were wrecked,' Joseph could hardly believe that at last he was going home after so many years of self-imposed exile. Inevitably, his feelings were mixed, for in spite of his tirades and frequent criticisms, he had become accustomed to the freedom that Australia offered. Now an old man, he would have to adjust to a world that he had forsaken all those years ago. However, his main concern was for a safe voyage back to Wales and that he 'would not be plunged into a watery grave.'

He travelled as a second-class passenger, but conditions had vastly improved since his outward-bound journey, for he now had the luxury of a cabin. On his first day aboard he records, 'up early, ship steaming well all night on a smooth and pleasant sea.' This contrasted starkly to his previous turbulent voyage, when he was thrown from his bunk four times in one night off the coast of Anglesey. On deck he recorded that 'there is nothing but order and civility to be seen among sailors and passengers.' This time, no farm animals fouled the deck; the invention of refrigeration meant that there was a plenteous supply of meat for all. After leaving Melbourne the ship dropped anchor three miles from Adelaide 'because it was too large to enter closer.' With everything under way, on the evening of 28 November, the officers and sailors had a concert on deck to mark the commencement of the long voyage to Tilbury Docks, London.

After three days at sea Joseph decided to place his worldly wealth in the ship's safe: it amounted to a Postal Order for £32 and three sovereigns. It did not seem much after a quarter of a century of hard work; the failure to retrieve the £200 owed to him by many 'friends' in Australia still rankled. He confesses that, 'I was a fool to trust people and have been sorely cheated . . . I was obliged to leave without my due payment of hundreds of pounds.' Recalling the warmth and concern of old Mrs Catherine Rees towards him, he wrote a letter to thank her 'for being like a mother to me when I was unable to take care of myself.' He also recalled her generous but chilling suggestion that he 'be buried with her husband in the family vault.' He firmly reiterated in his diary, 'my wish is to be buried in Welsh soil! My heart is too deeply rooted in the land of my birth.'

From the very start, Joseph seemed set fair to enjoy his return voyage. Ever curious, he set out to inspect the ship and described it as having 'three big anchors in the forecastle between one and four tons and two main anchors on deck each weighing seven tons . . . the crew consisted of 160 officers and the passengers numbered around 300.' He does not seem to have been tormented by the gibes and goading of fellow passengers, as had happened on the *Eurynome*. Perhaps he himself had mellowed with age and could observe life around him with a more benign attitude. Certainly his first Sunday on board was tranquil. '2 December 1894, It is a cool and lovely Sunday. We are going over the Indian Ocean towards Colombo in Ceylon. We are not far from the Equator. I cannot tell how many parsons or preachers or priests we have, but I know that we have two of the latter and they are very busy. Although I had no sermon, only Iolo's psalms. There was no-body on board that could neither read or understand them.'

Joseph's pleasure, for once, seemed unalloyed. '4 December, I am able to relish my meals and enjoy my sleep. The jolly sailors have put up the frame of the shade to prepare for the heat under the Line . . . Anchored at Albany at 4.30 taking on mail, wool etc.'

The *SS Ophir* offered far more in the way of amusements and activities to occupy the passengers than the *Eurynome*. Joseph paints a lively, busy scene on deck, 'a big sports day and all sorts of racing was held . . . two good runners ran 10 times around the ship without stopping. Even women and children ran short stages for money ... scores of small children from one to eight years of age are on board – they have their passage free – and it is a wonder to see how straight the two and three year olds can run along joyfully even when the ship is rolling sideways. A mighty tug of war contest was arranged, on which there was a great deal of betting. All sorts of sales and raffles were held on deck consisting mostly of watches, pocket knives, valuable pipes, rings and jewels.'

After a fascinating day of observing all these events, he retired to bed at 9 o'clock and 'left them paying the winners, most of whom drank away the money they had won.'

Powered by double screw propellers and twin keels to keep her steady, the *SS Ophir* entered the beautiful harbour of Colombo, Ceylon, on 12 December 1894. Here, the sight of dozens of half-naked native vendors clambering aboard 'with scores of different things to sell' intrigued him. Believing that he was getting a bargain, he bought a large box of 120 cigars for half a crown. Later in the day, he was incensed to discover that 'some had bought the same quantity for 1/6.' Despising himself for his rash haste to buy, he wrote, 'Poor Jo! Always in too much of a hurry!'

The scene in Colombo harbour kept him enthralled. He watched twenty barges 'with 2,000 tons of Welsh coal ... by far the best in the World for steam ships ... loaded into the hold.' The engines consumed huge amounts of coal, not only for driving the ship, but also for powering the cooling engine to preserve meat, vegetables and butter. He also noticed that hundreds of boxes of Ceylon tea had been loaded on to the ship for transportation to London. While the loading was in progress, he became apprehensive on hearing some of the sailors remarking casually that, 'the cargo is so heavy she may stick in the mud of the Suez Canal!'

As the ship steamed across the Indian Ocean to the Red Sea, Joseph found the whole experience sheer bliss. 'What a delightful scene all round, the ship goes well and steady. Last night one third of the passengers were sleeping on the decks. Most of them took their bedding with them.'

As was his usual practice, Joseph arose each morning between 5 and 6 a.m. but he strongly disapproved of the 'many passengers' who slept on the open deck. He referred to them as 'sleeping bundles' and considered them a nuisance because they impeded his morning progress round the deck.

For the first time in 25 years, since the far-off days when he was wined and dined at the Talbot Hotel by Colonel Powell, Nanteos, we find Joseph living a life of luxury. Not even the Queen herself seemed better placed than he:

> I went on deck and had a smoke ... read for two hours in the forecastle of the ship ... Nothing can hinder my pleasure ... I can see more than I wish to possess. I really think that I have seen as much as her Majesty the Queen Victoria ... This is as well, if not better, than to possess it and be growled at when any part of the estate goes wrong through war or famine.

He enjoyed the ship's facilities to the full, 'barbers and hair cutters are plentiful and are ready to attend for sixpence ... The ship has plenty of bars with an endless supply of Bass beer and all sorts of spirits at reasonable prices.'

What gave him the most pleasure, however, was the incessant throb of the engines taking the ship day and night closer to Wales. 'I live in hope,' he wrote, 'to see Welsh soil early next year.' Even so, he still had a few qualms, for he was far from being a well man:

> 19 December 1894
>
> Approaching the Red Sea . . . Yr wyf yn hiraethu am weld Cymru er fy mod yn ddigartref yno [I long to see Wales although I have no home there] . . . I wish I was in Wales to see my children and grand children . . . I am doubtful whether I will be able to succeed . . . I am shaking all over from head to toe, and painful to myself in many movements . . . Even dressing and undressing myself twice a day. I feel nearly unable to put my stockings off and on . . . I am longing to see Wales once more before going to my last rest.

The excitement of approaching the Suez Canal momentarily banished all self-pity. He describes the Red Sea as 'not a wide one, but rather long from Aden to the Suez Canal.' As he peered over the side, he was struck by the fact that the Red Sea was, in fact, a deep blue colour, and nobody was able to explain to him why it was called 'Red'. On 22 December he recorded, 'I can see the land of Egypt and a fine lighthouse on two rocks.' To him, this was a profound spiritual experience. As the ship approached the Suez Canal, his diary is filled with relevant Old Testament references to Joseph and Moses.

On 23 December 1894, Joseph's long awaited expectation was realised when at 9 a.m. the *SS Ophir* entered the Suez Canal. He had a grand view of the entrance, which 'had fine buildings of brick walls with roofs with ornamental trees.'

Extreme caution was required in navigating the ship through this man-made wonder, which Joseph described as a 'great and miraculous achievement'. He had read that the Egyptians had 'worked 18 hours a day digging and scooping the sand with their bare hands into baskets so that it was 70' wide and 70' deep.'

> 24 December 1894
> The Suez canal is 85 miles long . . . sandy and level as far as the naked eye could see . . . not straight but it zigzags like an ordinary river . . . There are many beds and narrow places . . . the ship is obliged to be steered by a pilot with caution . . . not over five miles an hour otherwise it would disturb the water and swell it to break down the brittle and sandy sides.

Dykes and waterways had always fascinated Joseph. He had once fancied himself as an engineer with his projects on the river Teifi; now to witness and pass through this colossal feat conceived by Ferdinand de Lesseps was one of the great thrills of his life. The completion of the Suez Canal shortened the distance from Australia to Britain by 8,000 kilometres. It was officially opened in 1869 and Joseph's old acquaintance, David Davies, Llandinam, had attended the opening ceremony as an official guest because he was one of the chief exporters of Welsh steam coal. Uncertain about its future, Davies wrote, 'I fear the sand . . . will fall in and soon fill it up – There are thousands of men, camels and asses employed.' But, for once, he was wrong.

On 24 December Joseph confirmed that 'the ship has arrived at Port Said . . . the end of the big canal . . . It was anchored here for coaling. They are going to put 2,000 tons of Welsh coal in, enough to reach London . . . They began to coal early in the morning . . . about 15 coal barges were full of Welsh coal on both sides.' Joseph was astonished to see how quickly the Italian and Sicilian labourers carried the coal on deck. 'They were working like slaves . . . running back and fore with wicker bags containing from 56 to 60 lbs of coal, two abreast along a broad plank . . . about a hundred of them on both sides of the ship.'

As they left Port Said, he noticed that, 'the water was muddy for miles, and drives the sand as far as the canal which cause much expensive dredging.' Christmas Day dawned wet and windy, the air became chilly and the sea rough. Joseph recorded, 'it began to blow hard. We are in a storm, not a tea cup storm as Shakespeare termed it . . . The ship began to dance a little . . . the sea depositing its breakers on our high decks . . . pitching from bow to stern . . . but very little rolling.' Despite the stormy weather, the passengers 'enjoyed a good Christmas dinner.' As on the previous voyage, there were no roasted geese, 'but plenty of plum puddings' and all sorts of other festive foods.

Soon the stormy conditions caused the ship to pitch and roll, and Joseph was obliged to spend all day below on his bed listening to the loud clatter and banging. He compared the noise to 'the loose tins and other things being thrown in all directions, as if scores of Tinkers plied their trade throughout the ship.' With dry humour he adds, 'It was a storm at sea, but I have seen many worse in my lifetime!' – a fact that could scarcely be denied. Such was the severity of the storm that he wrote, 'one of the big funnels was damaged, but I pray a prayer that the propellers will hold, and the Welsh coal will drive the vessel on.' One of his constant concerns was the lack of a quiet place to continue his Journal. All around him, the experiences of a lifetime were taking place and with so much to observe and record, he longed for peace to write it all down. As a second-class passenger he envied the infinitely better facilities of the luxurious reading and writing rooms available to the first-class travellers, which he could only observe from a distance. He deplored class differences and drew comfort from the thought that death would be the great leveller:

> 26 December 1894
>
> One of my main discomforts on board is I that have no convenient place to write or any sort of reading . . . It is too crowded . . . and my cabin is too dark. There is plenty of light and air, day and night in the grand saloon with libraries, writing desks etc etc . . . We dare not enter their premises and walk on their fine decks . . . There are all sorts of swells, M.P.'s, lawyers, preachers, priests etc etc. How long will the world continue to support two sorts of inhabitants – one sort to scorn and tramp on the other? . . . Death will relieve both, and that will be all in all.

On 27 December the ship approached Italy and he was intrigued to see 'Mount Etna glowing with the mountains covered in snow.' As the ship neared Naples, he saw 'steamers of all sizes . . . and Mount Vesuvius pouring out its smoke and glowing fire at the top.' Such was his excitement that he wrote two letters, one to his brother Jenkin at Blaenplwyf and the other to his daughter Nel at Tyndomen, describing the sights of the voyage. He only just caught the post, 'these letters went by the mail bags taken from the ship at 4 a.m. this morning; there are many scores of bags to be distributed throughout Europe.'

At 5 a.m. the following morning the *SS Ophir* left Naples

'steering fast and easy of movement towards Gibraltar.' He sat on deck, relaxing, and watching 'the majority of passengers busily engaged in all sorts of sports, principally rope coits.' Although 'troubled by a severe cough,' he still found the voyage 'very pleasant with something new to meet my eyes all along. Besides the lively sea, many big steamers and sailing ships appear now and then ... But this ship goes faster than them all.' 28 December proved less enjoyable when 'a sudden storm blew up'; but worse still, 'I lost my manuscript of the voyage from my pocket – I'm afraid that my life will go next!' To cap it all, the practice fire alarm went off with a deafening clanging noise. Joseph praised the whole procedure, 'each man was stationed in his proper places ... hoses and buckets ready in hand ... should a fire break out.'

On the last day of 1894 Joseph arose early to catch the imposing sight of 'the rock and strong forts of Gibraltar ... our ship did steer round the steep high rock.' Gibraltar was an important harbour and he marvelled at the many warships anchored there:

31 December 1894

Our ship did cast her anchor close to some of the strongest ships of war that England possesses, called the Mediterranean Fleet, including torpedo boats and other ships of war. I did count over a hundred and so many others cruising about ... There was a fine Township on the N. West Side of the Straits ... It was a grand view to me, a full regiment of soldiers are stationed there always with 7 years of provision for them and the artillery men ready for action, should it be required.

The power of Britannia's naval and military might greatly impressed him and he was proud of the fact that, 'it had the largest fleet in the world and a vast Empire under a most wonderful queen.'

Rough weather at Gibraltar caused problems and provisions were taken on board only with difficulty, 'scores of small boats were approaching our ship with all sorts of vegetables, tobacco, shirts etc etc ... But because of the roughness of the sea ... there was very little trading they were able to do. One of them fell overboard ... but was soon picked up ... The anchor was hauled up and the *Ophir* began to steer westward against a strong head wind. Her middle decks and forecastle were visited by heavy breakers drenching some of us often.' After the excitement of Gibraltar, Joseph's mood of elation suddenly switched to one of despair. The thought of a new year and the future frightened him and he was again haunted by the spectre of death, especially being buried at sea.

Although he was unsure as to whether he would ever reach 'terra firma', he wrote, 'I have a covenant in my heart to return to the earth which nurtured me, and to be laid to rest in the valley of my birth.'

New Year's Day found the *Ophir* steaming swiftly towards the Bay of Biscay which, as Joseph knew from past experience, was capable of 'throwing up the most terrifying storms.' His opening entry of 1895 confirmed his worst fears:

SS Ophir
Tuesday, 1 January 1895
On board the ship *SS Ophir* ... Rough and stormy ...
Very cold and uncomfortable on deck ... she steers against

the head in a complete gale ... The breakers are thrown heavily over the decks and even as high as the Bridge.

Joseph described the storm that raged around the ship in detail. It could also be said that, with each mile that took him nearer home, the storm within the man himself was gathering force. His diary reflects his feeling of insecurity. 'Will I', he asked anxiously, 'have a home back in Wales? Will they welcome an old man?' His emotions were as churned up as the seas that battered the ship. Crippling rheumatism made his life more difficult. 'I grip my pen with a cramped hand, and write only with difficulty.' His writing, at this point, is barely legible, but he still struggled to register his tortured thoughts.

When Joseph had informed his family of his intention to return home, the news had evoked mixed feelings. For Betty, the return of her husband after an absence of 25 years would inevitably prove to be an ordeal. As she did not keep a diary we are not privy to her thoughts at this time. It is fortunate, however, that Joseph's youngest daughter, Anne, had emulated her father and kept a daily journal of events. It is through her that we are able to view the situation at Trecefel. Joseph was now within one week of reaching Tilbury. By allowing the diaries of father and daughter to intersect, we catch a glimpse of two contrasting worlds; one the storm-tossed Bay of Biscay, and the other an ice-bound Trecefel. Anne sets the scene at home:

Trecefel

1 January 1895

Hard frost with snow on the ground. Children came for their new year's gifts ... which has been the custom for more than half a century here. Daniel Pugh, servant, had to take the horses to put some sharp nails in their shoes, the road being too slippery for them to walk. Tom went to Tregaron to arrange about meeting father in London. Uncle Jenkin [Blaenplwyf] kindly wrote to inform us that the *SS Ophir* is due at Tilbury Docks, Friday next.

Joseph's long-felt desire to reach Wales was nearing its fulfilment, but the storm in the Bay of Biscay, rather ominously, kept up its momentum. The weather, both at sea and in Wales, seemed to reflect the general mood of apprehension that gripped all concerned:

Bay of Biscay

2 January 1895

Wednesday. It looks boisterous. We may have a dance by the ship. We can see Portugal on our right, it gets more boisterous and the sea showing more sprays on its surface, sign of storm ahead!

Joseph tried to stay on deck but was ordered to go below by the sailors for his own safety.

While Joseph was fighting to maintain his balance in a 'pitching and rolling ship', the conditions in Tregaron were also perilous and slippery. Preparations were now being made to greet a father whom Anne and her brother Tom could scarcely remember. When Joseph had left Tregaron in 1868 Tom was six, Anne was four, and John David the youngest was eighteen months. With all the other daughters now married, the responsibility for welcoming him fell to Tom and Anne, as their mother Betty was still in a state of confusion and shock. For the past 25 years she had struggled to be both mother and father to the children. She had ensured that they all received a good education and she had been successful in retaining the farm despite the increases in rent and all the other difficulties which had confronted her. Clearly, the prospect of receiving Joseph back did not fill her with elation. Anne duly records in her diary the latest information concerning her father:

> Trecefel
> 2 January 1895
> Roads very slippery ... letters from Uncle Jenkin [Blaenplwyf] and another from brother John [in London] both containing information about my father. He has fortunately been in very good health during the voyage, therefore able to enjoy and appreciate the grand sights.

On the Atlantic, Joseph was experiencing one of the worst nights of the voyage, describing himself as 'being upside down in my cabin':

> Bay of Biscay
> 3 January
> The storms were increasing before I got asleep and the ship was both side rolling and pitching. We are enclosed down in our cabins ... The swells were coming down to our cabins. The storm increases. It is furious now. We dare not go out for the strength of the wind.

Outside Trecefel farmhouse the weather was also treacherous, and inside the tension was mounting:

> Trecefel
> 3 January 1895
> Snow falling during the night ... when Mother and I seated ourselves by the breakfast table Tom came in wrapped in

his overcoat, he had been with Uncle Jenkin... Tom told us they had arranged to meet Father at Tilbury Docks, London. Daniel Pugh, the servant, drove him to meet Uncle and make for Lampeter where they intend to catch the train for Carmarthen or Aberystwyth en route for London by night mail.

During the night of 3 January, Joseph described conditions on board as being so bad that, 'I could not keep my feet... and had to fight for my life.' The following day brought only a slight improvement:

SS Ophir
4 January 1895
This morning I went on Deck and found that the wet and windy storm is still raging... The ship had her anchor cast last night about 8 o'clock; after stopping about 4 hours she resumed her voyage for London... not quite as rough... but still a complete storm.

Meanwhile, at Tregaron station, Tom and Jenkin, Joseph's brother, caught the London mail train to reach Tilbury Docks in time to meet Joseph. Anne and Betty remained at Trecefel, anxiously preparing for his imminent return. That morning a neighbour, unable to contain her curiosity, called at Trecefel to see what was happening:

Trecefel
4 January 1895
Thawing and slippery... Miss Owens Penrallt called to see and sympathise with us in our loneliness during Tom's absence.

Joseph's final entry in the Australian diaries, which is little short of an illegible scrawl, records his last day at sea and his arrival at Tilbury:

London

5 January 1895

Before I went to bed last night I went on deck. It was rough and stormy . . . the breakers were coming over the deck and up to the forecastle to the annoyance of the big folks . . . I heard the Anchor dropped on the mouth of the Thames at 4.30 a.m., but went back again for an hour till 5.30. I went on deck and found it wet and windy . . . not so boisterous as it was last night – we are on a smooth sea. Mouth of the Thames. The ships will not be taken to the Dock for hours yet.

At Trecefel the weather took a turn for the worse and the waiting was taking its toll on the two women:

Trecefel

5 January 1895

Cold and snowing . . . Late getting up having spent a restless night . . . The latest intelligence we have received was a letter from brother John to say the ship *SS Ophir* was not expected until some time today, and that he had met Tom and Uncle Jenkin at Paddington Station.

By now, many other relatives were getting anxious about Joseph's imminent arrival:

Trecefel

6 January 1895

Uncle Tynant, John Maestir and Mary Fro drove up to get news about father, we were very sorry we could not acquaint them with much.

Late in the afternoon of Saturday, 5 January, a party of five stood anxiously at Tilbury Docks awaiting the arrival of the *SS Ophir*, which had been delayed by the storms. They included his sons Tom and John, who had now qualified as a doctor and was employed at Bethnal Green Hospital, two cousins and Joseph's brother, Jenkin. All were tense and uneasy. When the passengers finally disembarked, no one recognised Joseph at first.

The wasted, arthritic man they saw shuffling down the ship's gangway was a figure so broken by time, toil and the trials of life that Jenkin actually had to approach the stranger and tentatively ask, *'Ai ti yn wir yw Joseph?'* ['Are you indeed Joseph?'] His brother was shocked at Joseph's appearance. The man who had left Trecefel in 1868 had been well over six feet tall, erect, and powerfully built; the figure they now greeted was a mere husk of the man he once was. Because of his fragile condition, it was decided that he should stay two nights in London to allow him time to recover from his voyage. On the Monday morning they caught the first train from Paddington for Wales.

When, ten hours later, the train pulled into Tregaron, a servant was waiting with a wagonette to drive the party the last mile through the freezing air, past fields blanketed with snow, to Trecefel. We can only imagine what thoughts went through Joseph's mind as the wagonette crossed the Teifi Bridge and approached the farm.

His daughter Anne described his arrival in her diary. Her style is less flamboyant than her father's, and she records the event in a matter-of-fact way. Even so, she manages to convey the understandable apprehension felt by the family at the return of this stranger to their midst:

Trecefel

7 January 1895

Hard frost . . . The wagonette arrived containing Father, Uncle Jenkin, cousin J. Lloyd, brother Tom and Evan Jonathon. I went out to welcome them. Mother could not, she felt it very much. Wil Lloyd, Llanfairfach, Hugh Williams, Derigaron and Gwilym Evans called later to see Father. It seems he has altered very much and his memory is defective. I trust Mother and all of us will be reconciled after his coming and that we will all feel comfortable.

After the long years of separation and the inevitable tension brought about by his return, Anne had expressed a sincere hope that a spirit of forgiveness and friendship should now prevail at Trecefel. Only time would reveal whether her wish could be fulfilled, and whether Joseph and Betty could rebuild a relationship so cruelly shattered a quarter of a century earlier.

CHAPTER 22
GRIEF SUBSIDES – LOVE ABIDES

The escape to Australia in 1868 had been a liberating experience, but the past has a habit of catching up. Day dawned on 8 January 1895 to reveal a landscape sealed by snow and ice; it was Joseph's first day home. So often under the blistering Australian sun he had longed to walk his fields in the cool of daybreak; above all he had yearned to see his children. But he had been chasing shadows, for they were no longer the young innocents he had left in 1868. They were now strangers: adults he scarcely knew. Anne, the little girl of four, was thirty, Tom, the young boy of six, was thirty-two, and John David, the eight-month baby, was twenty-six. But most painful must have been the realisation that Joseph himself was, in fact, the real stranger. He had turned his back on their childhood, which was irretrievably gone, and he was paying the price for his action.

Betty had been civil on his return, but it was obvious that she tolerated his arrival as a dutiful wife rather than relished it, for the sake of the children. She had been too overwrought to go out to the farmyard to greet him and one can sympathise with her emotional predicament. Understandably, her feelings were in turmoil, for during his time in Australia her husband had continued to harbour a deep resentment against her and she had been well aware of it. Even as Joseph stepped down from the wagonette he must have feared that his dream of Trecefel as a final haven might turn out to be a bitter illusion. Would it be a case of, 'It is better to travel hopefully than to arrive'? Perhaps he should, after all, have accepted old Catherine Rees's offer of a free burial plot in Maldon cemetery; at least it would have spared him the pain of awakening to the reality that he was barely welcome in his own home.

Throughout his life Joseph had considered himself something of a philosopher. In nearly every diary he commented on the meaning and significance of time. Not until now was he to feel the full impact of those words written by him in Australia, 'But I have changed and they have changed and changed has everything.' These were not the people he had left in 1868 and he was certainly not the man who was once master of Trecefel. His long years of absence had caused a huge divide, which was not to be easily bridged. In many ways he no longer belonged here. 'Time,' he wrote, 'is a one way road. I can't stop and I can't turn back... Is my journey worth the pain? Soon my life will flicker out like a common rush light – and my diary will reflect the human condition – a mixture of joy and pain, but more of the latter.' As the chill of the Cardiganshire winter penetrated the marrow of his bones, he realised that one factor alone had not changed, and that was the weather. Beyond his window the rushes along the Teifi banks stood stiff and bleached with hoar frost, just as they had always done in midwinter.

To the local people of Tregaron, the return of Joseph to Trecefel after all those years in Australia was a matter of considerable interest. Although thousands had emigrated from the county, only a very few returned, and it was extremely unusual to see an emigrant re-emerge after a quarter of a century. The circumstances of Joseph's departure had also created something of a scandal – country folk have long memories – and there was much curiosity concerning the welcome he would now receive from his wife and family.

On his first day home, Anne's diary records that a stream of visitors came to Trecefel, but Joseph, still in his disorientated condition, scarcely recognised them. Most seemed to pass before him like a dim succession of phantoms from a distant past. Of the many relatives and friends who called on that first day, according to Anne, 'His sister Jane was the only one he recognised since his arrival in this country, and he seemed exceedingly pleased to see her. They had a long chat by the parlour fire.'

On his second day home an unwelcome caller hammered late at night on the Trecefel door. It was William Rees, a neighbour and former drinking companion of Joseph's. Reluctantly, Betty and Anne were obliged to admit him into the farmhouse. Anne recorded in her diary, '9 January 1895, Wil Rees, Waunfawr, who was under the influence of drink called late in the evening and insisted on seeing Father.' It was an ominous visit.

The intrusion of the inebriated Wil Rees was anathema to both mother and daughter, but also alarming in that it stirred up fears of the 'old demon', which they both dreaded. After Joseph had abandoned them, Betty had brought up her children to despise and fear alcohol. Anne, in particular, was vehemently opposed to all forms of drink and became an active member of the British Women's Temperance Association. She was also elected to the executive of the Tregaron Temperance

Association. Both women considered alcohol to have been the curse of Trecefel and the cause of all the ensuing pain and trauma. No alcohol was allowed in the Trecefel farmhouse except for medicinal purposes. We do not know what happened after Wil Rees was admitted that night, but almost certainly there would have been none of the warm hospitality usually afforded to visitors at the farm.

The following day, 10 January, Joseph, still exhausted by the return journey and weakened by the number of callers, contracted a severe cold that confined him to bed. He needed time to adjust psychologically and physically; six weeks previously he had been at risk from sunstroke in the Antipodes, now he had to contend with the biting sub-zero temperature of a Welsh winter.

For the past 17 years Tom had managed Trecefel farm for his mother. When his elder brother Lewis had died suddenly at the age of twenty in 1869, ten months after Joseph left for Australia, Tom had been seven years old. In subsequent years Betty's strength of character and tenacity had been severely tested, but assisted by servants and helped by her elder daughters, she had survived the difficult early years, successfully running the farm until Tom had come of age to take charge. With the reappearance of the long lost father, who had returned only when it suited him, Tom now felt a measure of resentment and feared a threat to his authority. The clash of temperament is evidenced in Anne's diary. 'Tom was peeved . . . suspicious, and in a bad mood.' In Australia, it had been easier for Joseph to exorcise his anger, frustrations and self-doubts; here, there was the resentment of age over youth. Ironically, Tom resembled his father in one respect. In spite of his mother's dire warnings, he had acquired a predilection for alcohol. This upset Betty and Anne and posed a constant challenge to their fierce teetotal stance. Despairingly Anne wrote, 'Tom is the worse for alcohol.' Sadly, as the years progressed, Tom would develop a craving for alcohol just as Joseph had done, and Anne's diaries testify to her heroic but unsuccessful efforts to curb his addiction.

During the early days after Joseph's return, many people continued to call at Trecefel, some out of curiosity, others in friendship to greet the 'exile'. While most visitors were welcomed, many of Joseph's former drinking companions who called were more coolly received. Other callers came to request information about their relatives in Australia. On 19 January Anne records that 'Mr Jones Penwern came to see Father to get an account of his brother Walter, who had been in Australia for 26 years.' Joseph was able to give Mr Jones a full account of Walter's activities, since they had often dug together for gold at Forest Creek; he had also lent Walter Jones money which was never repaid. In September a young man from Bryn Madog, Tal-sarn, came 'seeking information on the disposal of David Evans, Rheola's property in Australia.' This caller stirred many memories for Joseph, who was able to give precise information on the sale of the contents and the price paid for the farm.

After his return to Wales Joseph continued to keep his diary, but regrettably the last four diaries recording his life were destroyed and with them went his secret thoughts. It is therefore fortunate that his daughter Anne followed in the best tradition of her father and began to keep a diary in 1886 at 21. Like her father, she diligently wrote in her diary every day until her death in 1948, thus completing 61 diaries. Between them, father and daughter covered a period of 120 years.

Anne's diary informs us than on 21 January 1895, just over a fortnight after her father's return, he had felt sufficiently fit to venture out on his first visit to Tregaron. Accompanied by an old friend, Thomas Jones the Mason, 'he walked the mile or so into Tregaron without difficulty.' It was an emotional occasion. Ever since learning of the death of his favourite daughter Margaret in 1883, he had longed to grieve over her grave. Guided by Thomas Jones, he now visited the new cemetery adjacent to the National School, built on land given by Colonel Powell of Nanteos. This new cemetery had been consecrated shortly before Margaret's death in May 1883, and her grave lay alongside the boundary fence with her name only engraved on the headstone. Joseph remained there for some time. Reflecting on the past, he felt many mixed emotions as he knelt at the grave of his eldest daughter and murmured, *'Pylodd y galar, ond erys y cariad.'* ['The grief has subsided, but the love abides.']

Finally, he got up and, helped by his friends, returned to Tregaron Square to inspect the imposing new statue erected to Henry Richard M.P. (1812-1888). Joseph had known him when he was an aspiring politician. The statue was built in recognition of his efforts to promote international peace and for his contribution to developing secondary and higher education in Wales. Henry Richard had realised his political ambition and been elected M.P. for Merthyr Tydfil, but Joseph's life had been a mixture of achievement and disaster. Many times he had declared, 'My Journal shall be my monument.' As he admired the grand memorial to Henry Richard, he could not have dreamt that almost a hundred years later, a fountain dedicated to his own memory would be placed in Maldon. This was unveiled on 27 November 1994 in recognition of 'his monumental contribution to the life of a rural worker in Victoria as recorded in his diaries.'

Slowly, Joseph began to settle in again to life in Wales. On 18 February he returned to his old home of Blaenplwyf where his brother Jenkin, now a prominent member of Cardiganshire County Council, lived alone, apart from one manservant who slept in *y dowlad*, the loft above the cowshed adjoining the farmhouse. Memories came flooding back, for according to Anne, 'He was much affected by the visit and recalled the days of his youth when his mother, father and all the many children were still alive.' In old age Joseph's mind teemed with Biblical phrases and in his notebook at Blaenplwyf, he wrote:

> The child I once was is now an old man. The only things which linger here now are in my memory. I hear my father's white mare galloping on to the farmyard and through the window I see my mother stir the cauldron of cawl. These are but shadows of times that have been, they have no consciousness except in my heart. Those with me see and feel nothing: 'Un genhedlaeth a â ymaith, a chenhedlaeth arall a ddaw.' ['One generation passeth away, and another generation cometh.'] But every stone in this old house holds a memory for me.

The atmosphere of neglect and decay around the farm depressed him as he viewed the abandoned farm implements, rusting ploughshares and the pond choked by invading reeds. He strolled across to Cefnbysbach which now lay crumbling in a tangle of thicket. He remembered it as a 'mud cottage with only a hole for a window, stuffed with rags at night to keep out the cold and the family living on sucan and cawl.' Recalling the lives of the former sons of the humble dwelling, he commented ruefully, 'Daniel and David Davies in their bungalows at Ballarat now have a life as different from night as day!' On 18 February 1895 his thoughts turned once again to Australia as he contemplated its future. 'No doubt, they will one day want to go their own way, but the destinies of both us and them will remain for ever entwined as long as our glorious Queen prevails… There are no ghosts from the past out there, as there are here. It's a free place. I was out of harness there. Unbound!' Clearly, Joseph had forgotten his hardships as a swagman and remembered only the sunnier times. Rather woefully, he added, 'If only I could remould my life and find an easier path in the sun's reflection . . . Money can be remade, ground can be reclaimed, but time – NEVER!' Always intrigued by the question of time, it now played havoc with him. After all the angst of longing to return home he now confessed to feeling like a displaced person where the past clashed with the present, where he saw youth superseding old age. Turning to his old favourite, the Preacher in Ecclesiastes, he summed up his feelings in a single line, 'Y mae amser i bob peth.' ['To everything there is a season.']

Regrettably, Anne's diary also reveals a more disturbing aspect of his homecoming. Within a mere six weeks of his return, he had abandoned all those earnestly sworn pledges to abstain from alcohol and began to drink regularly in the taverns of Tregaron. After 25 years of virtual sobriety in Australia, the old temptations again ensnared him. Ironically, Anne's opening entry for her 1895 diary had been, 'How little we know of the future and what 1895 will bring us . . . It is well that the veil cannot be lifted.'

It was indeed 'well' that they could not have foreseen what

lay on the horizon, for his behaviour soon became a source of acute embarrassment to the family, particularly to Betty and Anne. The entries in Anne's diary reveal almost an exact replay of the discord which had so plagued the family 25 years previously. '15 February 1895, Father went into town which put Mother in a very bad humour . . . 19 March 1895, Father went into town. Thomas George, Shoemaker, brought him home . . . 3 July 1895, Father went to town early and came home in a very bad humour and much the worse for drink.' The family seemed fated to relive all the torments of the past.

As the old tensions surfaced, the long conflict between Joseph and Betty, where nothing was forgotten or forgiven, especially on his part, was now renewed. For Betty, it must have been the realisation of her worst nightmare. Her father's drinking also compromised Anne's position as a leading member of the National Temperance Association. She had long been committed to the fight against alcohol and in August 1895 she had proudly recorded in her diary that, 'In Tregaron forty new people have signed the pledge.' Alcoholism still posed a very real problem in the town as in the country in general. In an attempt to curb these excesses a Welsh Sunday Closing Act was introduced in 1881 – which forced all public houses to close on the Sabbath. Despite Anne's prominent role in the Temperance Movement, her father rode roughshod over her feelings and once again turned his steps towards the pubs of Tregaron. '4 July 1895, Father and Joseph [his friend] on the spree all day . . . 15 July 1895, Father in town and returned home late, very much the worse for drink. David Lewis brought him home.'

To compound her suffering, Betty suffered a serious accident. Anne describes what happened, 'The mare Star, while drawing the gambo trod on Mother's foot causing her to fall ... The wheel went over her at waist level and she sustained fractures of both collar bones and ribs.' It was as if Joseph's homecoming had upset the equilibrium at Trecefel.

Her nephew, Dr Evan Evans, Greengrove, attended to her injuries. He also diagnosed cardiac disease and strongly advised Betty to rest. This left Anne with the heavy responsibility of caring for both her mother and her father as well as assisting Tom in the running of Trecefel. In some ways little had changed since the time when Joseph was master of Trecefel. Anne clung to the old ways and records that she and her servant still 'made 500 candles a week' and sold large quantities of butter and cheese at the Tregaron market. She even continued to carry water from the spring using a wooden yoke across her shoulders, on which was suspended two full buckets of water. However, prices had risen: in 1896 Anne 'hired a new servant Eliza for £14 10s per annum.' Instead of granting a strip of land for planting potatoes, as in the old days, the contract included 'an allowance for the cost of a new dress.' Inflation had risen in Wales as well as in Australia. 'Paid the mole catcher 5/- for 3 dozen tails.' Like her father, Anne was an avid reader and spent every spare moment reading the classics. She read George Eliot, Dickens and Trollope among many other famous authors and poets. It is obvious from her diary that she also had a deep Christian faith which sustained her during her many crises. 'May God be with us,' she prayed in 1895, 'for we are but few now.'

Trecefel was a busy farm and, as he regained his strength, Joseph began once again to do odd jobs on the land which, 50 years previously, he had worked so hard to establish. Anne records, '26 March 1895, Tom and father mending gaps in Caesharno hedge . . . 3 April 1895, all hands carrying corn to stack – father included.' He also trimmed the hay stacks, looked after the sheep and carried out less strenuous chores such as weeding the garden. On 19 July he enjoyed the challenge of 'being out with his gun to keep the crows from spoiling Caepant field.' The last time he had held a gun was a year previously in Maldon when he had scared the 'larrikins' away from his cottage. Joseph had always been considered 'an excellent shot', and it restored some of his self-esteem to handle a gun again, even if only to scare away the feathered predators.

Sometimes, in late summer afternoons, he took a walk to look out over Cors Caron to watch the land and sky dissolving into an orange sunset. His love of nature and memories of Australia never deserted him:

> Out there, I'll always remember the huge canopy of sky lit by the brightest stars I ever beheld ... The birds were of bright colours too, and I'll never forget the sound of the kookaburra laughing like old Jac Llwyd my teacher ... But the bush fires frightened me with the tall columns of flames shooting up, and the loud bangs and cracking sounds as the oil from the gum trees fuelled the blaze.

Although there had been some modern advancement, many of the old methods of farming still prevailed at Trecefel. In 1897 Anne's diary informs us that:

> many hands were engaged in the laborious task of lifting stones from the face of the field – which is hard because of bending and straightening the back which induces much pain and discomfort.

But there was some financial inducement attached to this arduous task and Anne paints a vivid scene describing the activity at the entrance to Trecefel lane:

> The loaded cart of stones was led to the main road and tipped on the verge, where the elderly stone-breaker would sit on his tripod stool and break up the stone with his long handled hammer. Later, the surveyor would measure the heap and pay him for each cubic yard of broken stone. Eventually, we received payment for transportation, horse and cart, and labour for stones supplied for macadamising.

Because of Joseph's renewed drinking, husband and wife, to all intents and purposes, led independent lives. Joseph often visited his sister Jane, but he spent most of his time with his daughter Nel at Tyndomen. They had corresponded regularly while he was in Australia, and after Margaret's death Nel seems to have taken her place in his affections. It was his custom to walk across the fields to Tyndomen smoking his pipe. On one occasion he was distressed to lose his tobacco pouch and 'spent days searching for it in the meadows.' He ultimately found his pouch but he does not appear to have found that recollection in tranquillity which he had hoped for in his declining years.

The entries in Anne's diary suggest that the atmosphere within Trecefel was often charged with tension; she refers to her father's 'bad humour', 'foul moods' and 'melancholic days'; a quotation copied from Sophocles illustrates his perverse zest for the dismal, 'Man's happiest lot is not to be!'

Joseph's condition gradually deteriorated, and prescient of his declining health he noted the following moving lines, 'I've sometimes seen little reason to life except that to live it has not been easy. Yet, I trust eternity awaits me.'

In June 1898 he had a premonition of death and called for Anne. Her diary tells us that, 'Father informed me that he was going to die tonight and proceeded to give me some wise counselling.' Joseph always prided himself on his ability to give advice to others, but what this was, we shall never know, as Anne did not reveal it. The following morning he was very much alive, but he evidently felt a sense of unease about his condition, for he confessed, 'like every other human being, I am a fallible, stumbling fellow, for whom the grave now beckons.'

In the late summer of 1898, three years after his return, Joseph became so frail that he was no longer able to walk across the fields to Cors Caron or through the meadows to Tyndomen. For 40 years he had flirted with the idea of death, fearing that he would 'die like an old crow, unburied, in the bush.' But towards the end of August it seemed that, finally, the 'grim reaper' was within striking distance. Anne writes, '28 August 1898, Father created a disturbance during the night and prevented Mother and I from having our usual sleep.' By the following month his condition had become serious. '3 September 1898, Father did not leave his bed all day.' One of his last undated comments was, 'Keeping my diary has given me the greatest pleasure and enriched my life; it is, above all else, a narrative of human nature.'

Over the next few weeks Joseph lay dying. Despite all the acrimony which had prevailed at Trecefel since his return, he was given the best of care and attention. Almost daily, Dr Evan Evans called at the farm to attend to his needs. Brief references in Anne's diary give us a glimpse of his last days. '19 September,

Father very peevish . . . Father worse . . . he floats in and out of consciousness.'

By 25 September his condition had become so critical that his brother Jenkin rode at a gallop from Blaenplwyf to Trecefel and his sister Jane also rushed to his side. Anne tells us that, 'He was conscious of their presence but could not speak to them.' A few months previously he had written in his Black Book, 'The day will come when I shall not recover . . . nor will I write another word in my book. But my diaries will breathe after me unless my family destroy them!'

That 'day' was nigh. On 26 September, when Anne went to his room she found that, 'Father was fast sinking.' She quickly sent for her sister Nel from Tyndomen, 'who watched over him with me until the end came about 1 p.m.' His life had come full circle and he quietly ended his earthly pilgrimage among his family in his own home as he had devoutly hoped he would. He had written, 'In Wales was my beginning, and in Wales I wish to have my end.' Significantly, Anne makes no mention of her mother being at his side in these last hours. Possibly, once again, Betty felt the strain of it too much. After he had breathed his last, the two sisters 'sent for Mrs Jones, Tanrhiw, to come and assist to do the last services for him, after which his body was laid in the spare bedroom.' So often in the past Joseph had graphically recounted his illnesses and his close to death encounters; this was the one experience he was never to describe.

Tom went immediately to Tregaron 'to make arrangements for the hearse and wagonette.' Although Anne specifically states in her diary that there were to be 'no mourning cards', a mourning card does exist which was paid for by his youngest son John David out of respect for his father. However, no obituary or account of his funeral appeared in the local newspapers: the only official reference to his death is a brief entry, which appeared in the Unitarian magazine, *Yr Ymofynydd*, in December 1898. His brothers Benjamin and John and other members of the Blaenplwyf family had all been accorded lengthy, eulogistic obituaries in the local papers, and Joseph, doubtless, would have welcomed a similar encomium, but it was not to be.

Possibly Joseph Jenkins had been away too long and his many contributions in the early years to the life of the community had now been largely forgotten. Had the details of his dramatic life in Australia been generally known, he might well have been accorded the fulsome tributes he deserved. It is evident, however, that the Trecefel family were minded to make Joseph's funeral a low-key affair.

The funeral took place on 30 September with interment at the Unitarian Chapel of Capel y Groes, Llanwnnen. Anne wrote, 'The day was wet and stormy.' As was customary, a service was first held in the house 'when Uncle John preached at 10.30 on the very appropriate words from 2 Kings, *'Trefna dy dŷ, canys farw fyddi, ac ni byddi byw.'* ['Set thine house in order; for thou shalt die and live not.'] Scores of people had turned up to pay their last respects; 80 vehicles made up the funeral cortege which followed the hearse on the winding road to the cemetery where the Reverend Enoch Jenkins officiated at the graveside.

But on that miserable windswept day there was another bizarre twist to this story. Following the burial, the family filed into the chapel to hear the reading of Joseph's last will and testament: they were stunned by its contents. Even from beyond the grave Joseph managed one final act of revenge, causing Betty profound anguish. Anne's diary relates the incident:

> 30 September 1898
> After all was over, my Father's will was read by Uncle John, Tancoed at the chapel; – it was given him by sister Nel, to whom Father had bequeathed all his property both personal and real. It was a shock to us all that they could have behaved so cruelly to-wards us all.

The atmosphere within the chapel was sepulchral. No one had envisaged this. Joseph's will now placed his wife Betty, his son Tom and daughter Anne in severely straitened circumstances, since they depended on the farm for their livelihood. This inequitable disposal of the estate to which he had contributed nothing for the past 25 years left Betty crushed, and she asked poignantly, *'Ody hwn yn golygu sdim hawl da fi fynd adre i Drecefel heno?'* ['Does this mean I can't go home to Trecefel to-night?'] Sadly, Joseph had let the sun set upon his wrath.

Fortunately, the will did not cause a legacy of lasting bitterness. John David, the youngest son, acted as a conciliator between Nel, the sole beneficiary, and his mother and the whole affair was satisfactorily resolved. Betty could remain in Trecefel after all. A happy entry in Anne's diary refers to this:

> 5 October 1898
> Brother John went to Tyndomen and brought sister Nel up [to Trecefel] to settle affairs regarding Father's will, which was done amicably to our pleasure.

For Joseph, after the anguish of his experiences in Australia and his irrepressible fear of being buried there, his great wish was at last realised. At the age of 80, he was laid to rest in Welsh soil alongside his two sons in the family vault at Capel y Groes cemetery. His great odyssey in this life was finally done.

Whatever his faults – and there were many – he was an original spirit who, through his diaries, bequeathed to us a vivid account of his life and times. He had chosen Australia as the anvil to hammer out his own tortured personality and had worked like a man possessed, believing that toil and hardship could redeem all things. But only rarely did he manage to still his heart's passions: he remained a prisoner to his past and allowed old hatreds and recriminations to intrude upon the present, casting a malign shadow over his life.

Betty did not keep diaries so we never really get to know her innermost thoughts. Unlike Joseph, she never gave direct voice to her fears and pain, nor did she have the time to indulge in self-pity. Occasionally, we get glimpses of her suffering in the diaries of her daughter Anne, but compared to Joseph, she remains a shadowy figure. We are left in no doubt, however, as to her strength of character. Following her husband's departure she shouldered the responsibility of raising her family and running the farm successfully. That she was prepared to give Joseph a home on his return also reveals a breadth of compassion and tolerance.

She was greatly loved by her children, and on reaching her ninetieth birthday her youngest son John, now a Medical Officer of Health, spoke on their behalf:

October 20, 1917

My Dear Mother,

I remember whilst a child hearing you express the wish

that you might live until your youngest child reached the age of 14 – and this by now was almost 50 years ago. I am thankful that there are so many reasons for saying that the duration of your life has been such a blessing in many ways to every one of us to-day, and I fear greatly, as do the rest of your children, the day when nature will take its course, for this old world will appear emptier and less delightful ...

With feelings of love and tenderness,

Your son, John

Surrounded by her six sorrowing children, Betty died on 24 February 1919, having lived to the grand old age of 91, surviving Joseph by 21 years. She was buried on Joseph's birthday, 27 February, and was laid beside him in the family vault at Capel y Groes.

With all emotion spent – after an extraordinary life – husband and wife lie side by side in the tranquillity of this country cemetery. Alongside the grave is a lump of brain coral from the Great Barrier Reef, placed there by their grandson Tom Jo Davies as a reminder of Joseph's time in Australia. As in life, so in death, the 'Swagman' has the last word. Inscribed on his tombstone is the epitaph which he wrote for himself during one sleepless night in Maldon:

> Die we must, and cast aside this mortal shell
> How, or when, and in what place we cannot tell.
> If we assign to life a gift so rare,
> Then death itself claims equal share.
> Whate'er our fate, it is quite clear,
> We'll get fair play from Earth's Creator. †

Appendix 1

CHAPTER 3
pp. 32-33

CERNGOCH (John)

Dydd a i chwi gyfeillion,
Anfoniaid ydym ni;
Down tros ein mistir ffyddlon
Ar neges atoch chwi.

AMNON II (Joseph)

Pa beth yw'r holl ymgrwydro
Sydd arnoch o bob man?
A ddaliwyd rhyw hen gadno,
A'i hudo tua'r llan?

CERNGOCH

Peth gwael yw hir ymddiddan,
Mae'r amser bron myn'd allan;
Mae Lloyd, y Bettws, wrth y llan
Yn disgwyl rhan o'i harian.

CERNGOCH

Pa'm rhwystrwch ni ar ein siwrnai,
Os felly ceir meddianau?
Mae gyda Deio dros dri chant
I roi i'r plant a hithau.

AMNON II

O dewch i mewn, gyfeillion,
Mae'r drws ar 'gored ddigon;
Cewch fwyd a diod yn ddilai,
Mae arian yn rhai purion.

p. 39
Mae'n haws byw, mi wn, os bydd
Dwy galon gyda'i gilydd,
Cael ti Betty mewn llety llon
Ydyw golud fy nghalon.

p. 40
I'W GARIAD
Dynes fach net, net yw Betty – ei gwedd
A'i gwaddol wy'n hoffi ...
Ei chusan sy'n achosi – i'r galon
O'i gwaelod orferwi.
Mewn serch myna'i pharchu
O! gad fam, daw gyda fi.

CHAPTER 4
pp. 62-63
26 Mawrth 1854
Fy Annwyl Rieni,
Yr wyf gwedi mynd i'r fath amgylchiadau fel nas gallaf yn bosibl ei gwrthsefyll, gan fy mod braidd yn sicr, pe bawn yn ei chymryd, priodi, na byddwn byw nemawr o amser achos fy iechyd. Mae hyn a llawer o bethau eraill yn fy nhemtio i gynorthwyo natur i'm symud o'r byd helbulus hwn, gan fawr hyderu y bydd i'r Hollalluog Dad faddau i mi'r fath erchyll waith.

Fy rhieni annwyl, a'm perthnasau serchog a hoff, na wylwch ar fy ôl, ond yn hytrach byddwch byw yn ddichlynedd yn y byd hwn; fel nas bo euogrwydd cydwybod nac un temtasiwn arall

APPENDIX 1

ddyfod i'ch cyfarfod yn nhaith yr anial. Er fy mod yn ddyrmygus wrth wneud y fath weithred, gwnewch gymaint a hyn o'm dymuniad eto, sef fy hebrwng i Fynwent Capel y Groes a'r testun a bregethir arno fydd hwn – Gwyliwch a gweddiwch – fel nad eloch i brofedigaeth – canys yr ysbryd yn ddiau sydd barod, ond y cnawd sydd wan. Gadewch i'm chwaer Margaret a Jenkin fod yma ar fy ôl, oherwydd mae llawer diferyn o'm chwys yma ymhob man, er nad oes nemawr i weld eto ...

Ffarwel, ffarwel bob un tan nawdd ein tirion Dad. Wele y tro olaf y caf ysgrifennu gair byth i chwi fy Rhieni anwyl.

D.S. Rhoddwch yn hael at yr achos, dros yr hwn y croeshoeliwyd. Y mae hiraeth neillduol arnaf wrth feddwl ymadael a'r cyfryw ...

Even from a dead man to his friends and relations in this uncertain world.

p. 63
O'w diwael oedd, a diwyd, yn ei oes
    Un isel o ysbryd.
  Bu'n glaf dan bwn o glefyd
  A thrwy y baich, aeth o'r byd.

CHAPTER 5

p. 66
Dysg ddarllen a 'sgrifennu,
Dysg rifo a sillebu,
Dysg roi dy feddwl yn ddifai
Ar bapur a'i fynegi.

p. 68
Oes gwaeledd ein hysgolion, heibio aeth
   A'i bythod oer lwydion:

CHAPTER 7

p. 104
Dechrau wnaeth y flwyddyn hon
A'i holl beryglon ganddi.

p. 105
Gwelir blodyn y bedd
Yn gorwedd ar ei wedd.

p. 109
Bu'n ufudd, er byw'n afiach – bu'n eirwir
   Bu'n arwain cyfeillach.
 Bu'n bwyllog, diboen bellach,
   I well oes cwyd yn holliach.

CHAPTER 8

p. 121
Yfed gwydriad ar ryw bryd
Yw holl bechodau hyn o fyd,
A phe bai'r cwrw'n mynd ar goll
Doi dynol ryw'n angylion oll.

APPENDIX 1

CHAPTER 9
p. 138
Fan hyn y gorwedd Jo mab Syncyn
Yn gorph ac enaid yn y priddyn,
A phan bo'r byd yn ei gollfarnu
Tan fantell mam mewn hedd mae'n llechu.

CHAPTER 12
p. 208
Fel crwydryn rwyf yn cerdded
Yn wag fy mol a'm poced.

CHAPTER 14
p. 235
Hedd i'w enaid ddihuno
A dywyll fedd diwall fo.
Mae'n ddiwedd ar bob stormydd
Pob tristwch a llawenydd

p. 235
Ond Lewis aeth mor bell nas ceir
Mwy glywed gair oddiwrtho.

p. 237
Wrth gloddio, rhawio pob rhych,
O na chawn beth rwy'n chwennych.
Chwilio'r aur a chwalu rwyf,
Hedeg i ddyled ydwyf.

p. 240
Hardd yw gweled Meibion Gwalia
Heddy'n tario yn Victoria,
Gan gasglu nghyd i noddi'u hiaith
Ar diroedd maith Awstralia.

pp. 241-242
Fy Unig Briod
Yr wyf yn hela atoch, efallai i godi mwy o gasineb attaf, ond os felly y bydd, nid oes dim i wneud, waeth yr wyf yn darllen rhai o'ch llythyron chwi at y plant a fy nghefnder pa rai sydd yn dangos i mi mai fi a Lewis oedd yr achos o'ch ymadawiad, os felly yr oedd, chwi sydd yn gwybod, ond yr wyf i yn siwr nad oedd neb yn dymuno mwy o ddaioni i chwi na'r plant a finnau. Ond nid oes gyda nhw na finnau dim help i wneud, ond mi allwn ni hela rhai dillad atoch chwi a'r llyfrau. Y mae yr awrlais i'w chael hefyd ond mi leiciwn ei chadw, ond os ydych yn meddwl hela eich oes yn Australia, efallai y bydd i'r plant i'w danfon i chwi. Y mae arian yn brin, ac nid oes gobaith y daw'n well, gan nad oes gennym neb i hela gwaith yn mlaen. Dim ond Daniel Lloyd ag un crwt bach, yr hwn nas gall ddala yr arad, ond yr ydym wedi cael y cynhaeaf yn dda, ond mae yn rhaid trio cael rhyw fachgen, ond nid wyf yn gwybod pa le i'w gael. Yr ydym yn meddwl hau gwenith yn cae cnwcsarn os nad aiff yn rhy ddiweddar. Yr ydym heb dynnu tato. Nid oes gennyf un newydd i'w hela attoch gan fod eich brodyr a'ch brodyr yng nghyfraith a'r plant yn hela pob newydd a popeth yn mynd yn y blaen. Yr oeddech yn gofyn pa faint o ddyled yr

ydym wedi talu, nid wyf yn gwybod pa faint dalodd Lewis, canys yr oedd yn dyweud y gwnai ei orau i'w dalu i gyd a magu y rhai bach – Ond och yn awr nid oes gennyf neb i ofalu amdanynt mwy, ond mi wnaf fy ngorau. Mae Jane Lloyd, eich chwaer heb fod yn iach ers pum wythnos. Ei phen y mae yn achwyn.

Mae Marged a Mary heb fod yn iach – dolur gwddwg sydd ar Mary, y mae wedi torri dair gwaith – a mae Mary wedi derbyn llythyr oddi wrthych yr hwn sydd yn cynnwys llawer o bethau siarad – Ond y mae yn ddrwg gennyf glywed eich bod heb fod yn iach, ond efallai ei bod yn well na phe byddech yma gyda ni – canys yr ydych yn dangos fi yw mam y drwg, a thrwy hynny, mae yn well cadw draw – Ond cofiwch mae bara a chaws i'w cael a lle i gysgu.

Ni fuodd gwraig David eich brawd a finnau yn auction Sunny Hill – fe barodd bedwar diwrnod. Mae y plant a finnau yn cofio attoch, gan obeithio eich bod wedi gwella, a cawn eich gweld etto os byw fyddwn,

Hyn yn anhrefnus oddiwrth
Elizabeth Jenkins

CHAPTER 15
pp. 250-251
HIRAETH AM EI BLANT
Rwy'n edrych tua'r dalar draw
Gan ddisgwyl gweled Tom ac Anne
Yno'n chwareu'n llaw yn llaw,
Och! cofio'r pellder yn y fan,

Yn y nos wrth hanner huno
Gyda'r plantos iengaf wyf,
Am wladyddiaeth yn ymgomio
Ond wedi deffro, dyna'r clwyf!'

p. 251
Mi gofiaf am y wlad
A pryd gadewais Cymru,
Blin cofio y sarhad
A gefais gan fy nheulu.

p. 252
Rhag treulio oriau segur
Dysg gadw dydd gofiadur;
Caiff rhywrai addysg yn ddi-os,
Wrth edrych ar dy lafur.
Y penaf peth it wneuthur,
Cydnabod Awdur Natur;
Ble byna' byddot ar dy daith,
Mae Ef a'i waith yn eglur.

CHAPTER 17
p. 282
Cwrdd i arddel iaith ein teidiau,
A'i harferion gyda chlod,
Cwrdd i wella ein bucheddau
Gwir frawdgarwch fyddo'n nod.

CHAPTER 18

p. 301

Tri Chardi'n chwilio aur,
Ym mysg y pridd a'r cerrig,
Y cyfan yno geir
Yw lliw neu rhywbeth tebyg.

pp. 308-309

Dymunwn gael ei gweled
Cyn iddi fynd i'w bedd;
Ond dyna fel bu'r dynged,
Does dim ond cofio'i gwedd
Roedd hon yn annwyl gennyf ...

CHAPTER 19

p. 323

Mae budredd uffernol ym mhob un o'r tlawd i'r uchaf ei awdurdod . . . a mae eu hanwybodaeth yn fwy drewllyd i'r meddwl na dim arall.

p. 330

Pe gwelsai mam a thad
Y dull y cawn fy mhoeni,
Dymuno wnaethent hwy
Cans faint eu serch tuag ataf,
Am i ryw haint neu glwy
Roi diwedd arall arnaf.

CHAPTER 20

p. 344

Tan bren derwen mi orweddais
Un tewfrig a changhennog iawn
Tan ei chysgod yno cysgais
Heibio hanner y prynhawn,
Fel pe buaswn yn y gladdfa
Tan bren ywen wyrdd ei wedd
O! mor hyfryd yw gorphwysfa
Y mwyafrif yn y bedd.

p. 346

Marw sydd rhaid, nis gwyddom pryd,
Pa fodd, pa fan, yn hyn o fyd.

p. 358

Os byth dof nol i Gymru
Gofyn wnaf i Betty
Pwy ddrwg a wnês, a phle bu'm ffael,
Fel haeddwn gael fy sarnu?

p. 358

Fy nhynged fu goddef cam
Ym mhell cyn gadael groth fy mam!
'Run fath bu'm tynged dost o hyd
Fel plocyn taro yn y byd.

APPENDIX 1

p. 361
Brwd a hoff oedd y brawd hwn
Y goreu un a garwn.

p. 363
Rwy'n eistedd wrth y tân
Heb neb yn agos ataf,
Pe bawn i'n llunio cân
Does neb i wrando arnaf.

CHAPTER 22

p. 407
Marw sydd raid, nis gwyddom pryd
Pa fodd, pa fan yn hyn o fyd.
Ac os yw bywyd i ni'n rhodd,
Mae marw hefyd yr un modd.
Can's beth fo'n rhan, mae'n eithaf eglur,
Cawn chwareu teg gan Awdur Natur.

Appendix 2

This is a copy of the will of Joseph Jenkins which he made before embarking on the *SS Eurynome* in Liverpool at the beginning of his voyage to Australia.
Will of Joseph Jenkins dated 10 December 1868
Deed of Gift
To all to Whom present shall come; I Joseph Jenkins parish of Caron Isclawdd, county of Cardigan. Know ye that I the said Joseph Jenkins for and in consideration of the love and affection which I have and do bear towards my loving wife and children, Elizabeth, Lewis, Margaret, Elinor, Mary, Jane, Tom Jo., Ann and John David Jenkins all in the same parish and county, have given and granted and by these presnts [sic] do freely give and grant unto the said my wife and children their heirs, executors and ofspring [sic.], all my property consisting all the live and dead stock now remain on my farm according to schedule. I do hereby attached and signed, being now my property and the same to be equally divided between my said wife and children according to the value of the attached inventory signed by my own hand and bearing even date. To have and to hold all the goods chattels, Money and security for Money now belonging to me, their heirs, executors, administrators or assigns from this date, also I appoint my father in law Jenkin Evans of Caemawr Dihewid,

APPENDIX 2

Cardiganshire, and the Rev. Latimer Maurice Jones the Vicarage Carmarthen to be the Trustees in order to carry out my intention in these presents of equally dividing my said property according to whats [sic] inserted in the schedule and inventory hereinafter described and signed. Also I do wish to have an additional stamp of 1 12 0 to this deed in due time and let authority know that I could not procure it at the time of my writings and signature hereof. I witness whereof I have hereunto set my hand and seal this day of December 1868.

JOSEPH JENKINS

Witnesses   Francis Mc Namee   9 Islington Liverpool
P.W. Mc Namee, 38 Manchester St. L'Pool

Inventory of Property

Corn at the barn and so on	40	0	0
6 stacks of Corn at the haggard	120	0	0
2 ricks of hay at	75	0	0
Thatch and straw	12	0	0
Wheat in the ground at	20	0	0
8 horses at	110	0	0
32 head of horned cattle	160	0	0
53 sheep at	38	0	0
37 lambs at	14	0	0
15 pigs at	12	0	0
Fowl at	1	0	0
2 pairs of harness	10	0	0
1 Thrashing Machine at	28	0	0
1 Winnowing Machine	4	0	0
4 Wheelbarrows at	2	0	0

1 Spring Cart	10	0	0
3 ploughs and 8 harnesses	15	0	0
1-4 horse gwebber [sic]	4	0	0
1 scuffler at	1	10	0
1 potato digger at	4	10	0
1 chaffing machine at	5	10	0
Farming tools, carpentry and so on at	10	0	0
Timber in lower shed	7	10	0
Ladders and so on	1	0	0
Timber outside doors	3	0	0
Timber at storehouse	5	6	0
Do. at Kiln house	3	0	0
Potatoes in greves and so on	45	0	0
Turnips at	5	0	0
Manure in ground for next crop	60	0	0
20 Gates and posts	8	0	0
Iron and steel wire	4	0	0
Household furniture	65	0	0
1 Roller – 2 cars at	1	10	0
Turff	6	0	0
Aeron Vale share	100	0	0
Llanddewi cots.	130	0	0
Sister Anne's share	15	0	0
Club Money Beehive			
per bond of Miss Jones Executors –			
Bond at Mr Jones of Llandysul	1800	0	0
Interest for 3 years	45	0	0
Sundry debts due on Diary	50	0	0

Re Witness my hand this 10th day of December 1868 Joseph Jenkins

APPENDIX 2

Debts again.
To Father in law	70	10	0
Lampeter Bank Deed at	51	10	0
Sundry debts to Mr Morgan David Rowlands			
Smiths Shoemakers Servants etc.	30	0	0
	152	0	0

Source: NLW G.E. Owen Collection 12816

APPENDIX 3

SS EURYNOME AND SS OPHIR

The following information was received by the Guildhall Library (Lloyd's Marine Collection) London.

Joseph travelled to Australia on *SS Eurynome* in 1868.

SS Eurynome

An iron schooner with two bulkheads built on the Clyde at Glasgow in 1862. It was 210 feet in length, 35 feet wide, 22.9 feet deep and the gross tonnage was 1163. The vessel was owned by J. Heap and registered at Liverpool port. The master during Joseph Jenkins' voyage in 1868 was Walter Watson, born in Devonshire in 1828. The ship was built as a cargo vessel but also carried a limited number of passengers. In 1881 the *Eurynome* disappeared without trace on a voyage to Australia.

Joseph travelled from Australia on *SS Ophir* in 1894.

SS Ophir

Steel Twin Screw Steamer.

Built at Glasgow October 1891, by R. Napier and Sons.

Gross tonnage 6910. Length 465 feet.

Owned by Orient Steam Navigation Co. Ltd.

Class + 100 Al.

The *Ophir* was designed for passenger and mail service with little carrying space for cargo and was the first twinscrew ship on the Australian run. Her luxury made her popular with passengers and she was generally considered the 'Queen' of the Indian Ocean. In 1901 she was chosen as the Royal Yacht for the Duke and Duchess of Kent, later King George V and Queen Mary, when they toured Australia. During the First World War she became *SS Ophir*, an armed merchant cruiser and later a hospital vessel. The Ministry of Shipping Service List (World War One) adds the information that she was an armed merchant cruiser from 26 January 1915 to 29 July 1919. She was purchased by the Admiralty in 1918 and converted into a hospital ship. In February 1919 she was laid up in the River Clyde with other surplus ships and finally broken up in Troon, Scotland in 1922.

BIBLIOGRAPHY

Primary Sources (Unpublished Material)

Diaries of Joseph Jenkins:
    Trecefel Diaries, 1839-1869, National Library of Wales, Aberystwyth.
    Australian Diaries, 1870-1894, State Library of Victoria, Melbourne.
    Shipboard Diary of Voyage Liverpool to Melbourne Dec. 1868-March 1869, National Library of Wales.
Diaries of Anne Jenkins, National Library of Wales.
Letters of Dr John Jenkins, in the possession of Mair Owen, Bronant.
Blaenplwyf Account Book, in the possession of Gareth and Beti Davies, Sychbant.
'Reminiscences of the Jenkins Family', compiled by Beti Evans and Mair Owen.
Will of Joseph Jenkins, NLW, G.E. Owen Collection, 12816.
Letter of Lewis Jenkins, State Library of Victoria, Melbourne.
Shipboard Diary of voyage from Melbourne to Tilbury 1894-1895, State Library of Victoria.
Miscellaneous papers, letters, notebooks and literary fragments in the possession of Frances Evans, Tyndomen.

Secondary Sources

ap Huw, *Gwlad yr Aur neu Cydymaith yr Ymfudwyr Cymreig i Awstralia*, 1852
Beaglehole, C.J., *Captain James Cook*, London 1974
Beatty, Bill, *Tales of Old Australia*, London 1966
Blackman, Grant & Larkin, John, *Australia's First Notable Town*, Maldon 1978
Blainey, Geoffrey, *The Rush That Never Ended*, Melbourne 1963
    The Tyranny of Distance, Melbourne 1966
    Our Side of the Country. The Story of Victoria, National Library of Australia 1984
Borrow, George, *Wild Wales*, London 1906
Bradfield, Raymond, *Castlemaine*, London 1972
Brown, Max, *Ned Kelly: Australian Son*, Angus Robertson 1941
Burt, Jocelyn, *A Land Down Under*, Melbourne 1984
Carey, Peter, *True History of the Kelly Gang*, Faber 2001
Carless, Ronald Leslie, *History of Rheola*, Dominion Press 1985
Clark, Mary Ryllis, *Discover Historic Australia*, Viking 1996
Clark, Manning, *A Short History of Australia*, Melbourne 1981
Davies, John, *History of Wales*, Penguin 1994
Davies, Jonathon Ceredig, *Life, Travels and Reminiscences*, Llanddewi 1927
Dickens, Charles, *David Copperfield*, 1890
Eames, Aled, *Y Fordaith Bell*, Caernarfon 1993
Evans, William, *Diary of a Welsh Swagman*, Melbourne 1975
Hughes, Robert, *The Fatal Shore*, Pan Books 1988
Keneally, Thomas, *Outback*, 1983
    Australia. Beyond the Dream Time. Facts on File, New York 1887

Kilvert, Francis (ed. William Plomer), *Kilvert's Diary*, London 1938

Lacour-Gayet, Robert, *A Concise History of Australia*, Penguin 1976

Macintyre, Stuart, *A Concise History of Australia*, Oxford 1999

Pilger, John, *A Secret Country*, London 1989

Rees, Siân, *The Floating Brothel*, Headline 2001

Reynolds, Henry, *The Other Side of the Frontier*, Maryborough 1982

Roberts, Gwyneth Tyson, *The Language of the Blue Books*, 1988

Rowley, C.D., *The Destruction of Aboriginal Society*, Penguin 1978

Serle, Geoffrey, *The Golden Age: A History of the Colony of Victoria 1851-1861*, Melbourne 1968

Shaw, A.G.L., *The Story of Australia*, Faber 1960

Thomas, Ivor, *Top Sawyer: History of David Davies, Llandinam*, Carmarthen 1988

Ward, Russel, *Australia Since the Coming of Man*, MacMillan 1987

White, Charles, *History of Australian Bushranging*, Sydney 1976

NEWSPAPERS

British Newspapers 1855-69

Aberystwyth Observer
Cambrian, The
Cambrian News
Chester Chronicle
Daily News
Weekly Dispatch, The
Welsh Gazette, The
Welshman, The

Australian Newspapers 1869-94

Age, The
Australian, The
(Melbourne) Argus
Geelong Times
Leader, The
Maldon Times
Tarrangower Times

Articles

Beddoe, Deirdre, 'Eleanor James, Cardiganshire's only female transportee to Australia', *Ceredigion,* 1978

Jones, Bill, 'Welsh Identities in Ballarat, Australia, During the Late Nineteenth Century', *The Welsh History Review – Cylchgrawn Hanes Cymru,* Vol. 20, Dec. 2000

Jones, Ieuan Gwynedd, 'The Elections of 1865 and 1868', *Transactions of the Honourable Society of Cymmrodorion,* 1964

Reference

Seventh Report of the Medical Officer of the Privy Council: 1864

Ned Kelly in Pictures: The man who became an Australian legend Produced by the National Trust, Old Melbourne Gaol, Melbourne

Crockford's Clerical Dictionary, 1870

INDEX

Aberaeron
    fair 37
    Quarter Sessions 53-4
Abercerdin tavern (Fish and
    Anchor) 43
Allt-ddu farm 5
Arch, Tom, gamekeeper 56

Ballarat 217, 219, 236-9, 244,
    256-7
    eisteddfod 238-9, 280-2,
    304
Banc, cottage 21
Bateman, farmer 230
Beeston, Frederick, contractor
    70, 74, 77-9
Benbow, James, engine driver 4,
    77-8, 127
Bendigo 209, 219
Blaencwm, cottage 21
Blaenplwyf farm 7-26
Bronbyrfe farm 25-6
Bryngolau, Daniel 15
Butler, Joseph, gamekeeper 159
Byrne, Joe 291

Caemawr farm 40
Capel y Groes, Llanwnnen 42,
    43, 62, 63, 108, 403-6
Cardiganshire Yeomanry 81
Carn, Jac 15
Castlemaine 209, 214-5, 218-21

Cefnbysbach, cottage 14, 21
Chewton 215
Cilpill, sale 59
Clarke, Mrs 264, 274
Clarke, Tom (Equinhup) 323-4
Clarke, William, Mount
    Cameron Farm 263-4, 273-4
Clunes 257
customs, Cardiganshire
    bidding 33-5, 46
    candle making 97-8, 398
    fairs 31, 36-8
    funerals 9, 15, 17-8
    lime collecting 13, 24-5
    New Year 11, 13, 58
    peat cutting 5, 27, 162
    shearing day 25
    weddings 30-6
Cwm Bettws family 18

Dabb, R. 349
Dafis, Dafydd, Castell Hywel 8
Davies, Daniel, Cefnbysbach 14,
    217, 237-8, 396
Davies, David, Cefnbysbach 14,
    42, 217, 237, 396
Davies, David, Cefnbysbach and
    Australia 237-8
Davies, David, Llandinam 70-2,
    74-5, 77-81, 90-6, 160, 348
Davies, Reverend David,
    Bethania 158
Davies, David, Tymawr 158

Davies, Evan 124
Davies, John 108
Davies, John, miner 356, 361
Davies, John, Allt-ddu 137
Davies, John, Lodge, Derry Ormond 111
Davies, John, Tynrhos 35
Davies, Jonathan Ceredig 370
Davies, Mary, Cefnbysbach 14
Davies, Reverend Rees, Cribyn 10, 43
Davies, Dr S., 42
Davies, Tim 54
Davies, Tom Jo 406
Davies, Walter, Tregaron and Forest Creek 216
drovers 57

Edward, porter 4, 142
elections
    1849 50
    1859 84-9, 96
    1865 89-96
Eliza, servant 398
Equinhup *see* Clarke, Tom (Equinhup)
Evans, Dr, Lloydjack farm 41, 42
Evans, Mrs, Bank 15
Evans, Reverend David 108
Evans, David, Rheola and Tal-sarn 265-7, 270, 272, 279, 286, 290, 300, 302, 306, 319, 330-1, 351, 393
Evans, Elinor 367
Evans, Elizabeth, Blaencwm 32
Evans, Evan, New South Wales 351
Evans, Dr Evan, Greengrove 398, 401
Evans, Reverend Evan 25
Evans, Gwilym 388
Evans, Jenkin, Tynant 39-40, 61, 272, 275, 277

Evans, John, Gogoyan 58
Evans, Joseph, Tyndomen 81
Evans, Lewis, Tynant (brother of Elizabeth (Betty) Jenkins) 50, 61-3, 108
Evans, Margaret 265, 267, 331, 351
Evans, Morgan 129
Evans, Thomas, servant 17
Evans, Thomas, Tynant 101, 107

Forest Creek 215-9, 221, 223
Francis, Mr 56
Froncaemawr farm 21

Galaway, Mr 247
George, Thomas, shoemaker 397
Gilfach Frân, Elinor, 62
Glanbrenig 74
Glendenning, Mr, Summerset Farm, Kingston 301
Gors y Gelad 61
Gwargors, cottage 21
Gwlad yr Aur (ap Huw) 216

Harford, Sir John, Falcondale 120
Harries, Thomas, Llechryd 158
Hart, Steve 291, 294
Hawkins, John, Coghill's Creek 259
Hepburn, George, Smeaton 228-31, 233
Howel, Howel, Ynys, Tal-sarn, bidder 34
Howells, Thomas, carpenter 43
Hughes, Mr 54
Hughes, David, Banc, carpenter 32
Hughes, Reverend John, Tregaron 53, 56, 67, 68, 86, 145, 153, 160

INDEX

Ibbotson, C. 268, 271

Jane, maid 97, 143-4
Jenkins, Anne (daughter of Joseph Jenkins) 137, 147, 202, 249, 389
  her education 325
  her relationship with her father 134, 135
  notes from her diary 81, 382-8, 391-405
Jenkins, Anne (sister of Joseph Jenkins) 18, 46
Jenkins, Benjamin (brother of Joseph Jenkins) 25, 27, 110
  his death 350, 403
  solicitor at Lampeter 46
Jenkins, David 54
Jenkins, David (brother of Joseph Jenkins) 38, 45, 164
Jenkins, Elinor (Nel) (daughter of Joseph Jenkins) 101-3, 110, 133-4, 143, 147-8, 245, 300, 350, 379, 400, 402, 404
Jenkins, Elinor (mother of Joseph Jenkins) 8, 16, 17-18, 22, 26, 41
Jenkins, Elizabeth (Betty née Evans, wife of Joseph Jenkins)
  birth of Jenkin 44, 50
  birth of John David 145
  birth of Lewis 50-1
  death of Jenkin 104-11
  her attack on Joseph 148-51
  her death 406
  her letter to Joseph in Australia 240-1
  her marriage 2, 40
  leaves for Tynant 109, 133
  returns to Trecefel 135-6
Jenkins, Elizabeth (wife of Jenkin Aeronian Jenkins) 355
Jenkins, Elizabeth (daughter of Elinor (Nel) Jenkins) 301
Jenkins, Elizabeth, Tyndomen 110
Jenkins, Reverend Enoch 403
Jenkins, Esther (sister of Joseph Jenkins) 18, 360
Jenkins, Evan, carpenter 107
Jenkins, Griffith (brother of Joseph Jenkins) 107
Jenkins, Ieuan (son of Elinor (Nel) Jenkins) 351
Jenkins, Jane (daughter of Joseph Jenkins) 99
Jenkins, Jane (sister of Joseph Jenkins) 129, 241, 391, 400, 402
Jenkins, Jenkin (brother of Joseph Jenkins) 25, 35, 202, 207, 379-80, 383-8, 395, 402
Jenkins, Jenkin (father of Joseph Jenkins) 8, 9, 21, 23, 108
  his death 40-5
Jenkins, Jenkin (son of Joseph Jenkins) 44, 46, 47, 100-1, 102, 103
  sickness and death 104-8
Jenkins, Jenkin Aeronian 35, 353-5
Jenkins, John (Cerngoch, brother of Joseph Jenkins) 8, 15, 18, 20, 21, 24, 27, 87, 107, 135, 151, 153, 384
  his death 359, 403
  his poetry 30-3
  his wedding 34-6
Jenkins, John David (son of Joseph Jenkins) 145, 325, 383, 386, 389, 403-4
Jenkins, Joseph (Amnon II) (1818-98) 31
  agent and agricultural adviser at Nanteos 59
  and Ants Mole Cottage 304

and astrology 50-1
and elections 83-96
and Fenianism 138-9
and fishing 56
and gold digging 216-23, 233, 300-1, 321
and hunting 56-7, 60, 131-2, 150
and North Railway Gate Lodge 315-69
and snakes 211, 246, 258-9, 270, 275, 320, 329
and stag hunting 132
and the fountain to his memory at Maldon 394-5
and the Good Templars 260
and the railway 3, 70-82
and the Unitarian credo 39-40, 47-8
and Tregaron Literary Society 69
and Tregaron school 68-9
as a diarist 10-13, 44-5
as a road cleaner at Maldon 316-60
as Church Warden 53, 130, 138
as Parish Constable 51, 52
at Ballarat Eisteddfod 280-1, 304
attacked by his family 148-51
'Bard of Maldon' 322
farming at Trecefel 49-50, 52-5
his alcoholism 37, 38-9, 56, 113, 114, 115, 117-18, 119, 120, 121, 122-3, 125-6, 128, 131, 132-3, 135, 141-4, 397
his Black Book 149-50, 310, 402
his death and funeral 402-3
his departure from Tregaron 1-6, 162

his education 8-10, 66
his epitaph 138, 406
his interest in cricket 260
his letter 'Pity the Swagman' 235
his letter 'State of the Working Man' 299
his opinion of Aborigines, 264-7, 322-3
his opinion of Catholicism 113, 117, 127, 129, 139-40, 170, 226
his opinion of Methodism 39, 75, 120-1, 276
his opinion on emigration to Patagonia 116
his opinion on the Tithe Wars 335-6
his poem 'Cors Caron' 78
his poem 'From the Scavenger's Diary' 315
his poem 'Gold, Its Power and Influence' 222
his poem 'Home' 124
his poem 'Ploughboy weeping over Smeaton' 261-2
his poem 'Poor Old Jo' 357
his poem 'The Old Home' 354
his poem 'To a friend in the old country' 256
his poem to his son Jenkin 109, 110
his poem to his son Tom 66, 251
his poem 'To my Love' 40
his poem 'Yearning for his children' 249-50
his reading habits 117
his verses defending the rights of Swagmen 253-4
his visit to Borth 110-11
his visit to Llanwrtyd Wells 100, 101-3

INDEX

his visit to London 63-5
his visit to *The Great Eastern*, Milford Haven 115
his visit to the Great Exhibition at Melbourne 301
his voyage on the *Eurynome* 164-99
his voyage on the *SS Ophir* 366, 370-87
his wills 162, 404, 420-23
in Ballarat District hospital 284-5
in Castlemaine hospital 286-9
in court 160-1
in Inglewood hospital 266-7
in Maldon hospital 346
in Maryborough hospital 266
member of the Board of Guardians 53
Jenkins, Lewis (son of Joseph Jenkins) 74, 109, 110, 122, 126, 127, 143-5, 147-8, 151, 392
his birth 50-1
his death 234, 240-2
his education 129, 134, 136
his illness 137
his letter to his father in Australia 231-3
Jenkins, Margaret (daughter of John Jenkins)
her death 87
Jenkins, Margaret (daughter of Joseph Jenkins) 110, 116, 147-8, 177, 202, 241, 256, 258, 270
her death 306-8, 344, 355, 394
Jenkins, Margaret, née Evans, Tynygwndwn 34-5
Jenkins, Mary (daughter of Joseph Jenkins) 101, 241
Jenkins, Thomas 143, 147

Jenkins, Thomas, excise officer, Tregaron 52
Jenkins, Timothy (brother of Joseph Jenkins) 25, 27, 45
Jenkins, Tom Jo (son of Joseph Jenkins) 66, 103, 109, 134, 135, 137, 147, 202, 249-51, 398, 402-4
and alcoholism 392-3
arranges to meet his father on his return from Australia 383, 384, 385, 386, 387, 388, 389
John, Edwin 314
Johnes, John, Judge, Dolaucothi 275-6
Jonathon, Evan 388
Jones, Mr, Penwern 393
Jones, Mrs, Tanrhiw 402
Jones, David 119
Jones, David, Brynchwyth 158
Jones, David, Llanbadarn Trefeglwys 158
Jones, David, Rhiwonen 217, 300
Jones, David, Tregaron 54
Jones, Evan, headmaster, Tregaron 68-9
Jones, John, Camer 86
Jones, John, Gwent and Smeaton 227
Jones, John, Llwynbrain 22-4
Jones, John Inglis, Derry Ormond 59, 72, 155
Jones, Reverend Latimer, vicar of St Peter's Church, Carmarthen 48, 74, 84, 114-15, 127, 146, 242, 277
Jones, Mary 54
Jones, Mary, Llanfihangel-y-Pennant 192
Jones, Rees, Ponterwyd and Maldon 352-3
Jones, Richard, Cricieth 202
Jones, Stephen John, Cilpill 152

Jones, Thomas, mason 394
Jones, Walter, Pen-y-wern Ystrad and Australia 218, 393
Jones, William 54
Joseph, Griffith, Glamorgan and Australia 221

Kelly Gang 290-7
Kelly, Dan 291, 294
Kelly, Ned 291-7
Kinnersley, Mr, Spring Vale Farm 248, 255-6

Lady Elizabeth, train engine 78
Lamb, Wil 101, 103
Lampeter
    Black Lion 121
    Bush Inn 144
    Hiring Fair 126
    Ivy Bush 113
    Pig's Fair 141
    Royal Oak 141
    show 55
Lane, Morgan, Smeaton 225, 226-7
Lewis, David 397
Lewis, David, Silian, carrier 24
Lewis, Mr and Mrs Edward, Golden Age Hotel 272
Lewis, Evan 216, 286, 288, 302
Lewis, John (Ioan Mynyw) 68
Lewis, John, Llandeilo and Maldon 312, 313, 332-3
Lewis, John, Llan-non and Forest Creek 215-6, 219-21, 223, 233, 252, 279, 285-6, 288-9, 290, 302, 314
Lewis, Mary, Glyn Uchaf and Maldon 312, 333
Llangeitho fair 137
Llan-non cemetery 29
Llewelyn, Dr, Dean of St David's College, Lampeter 231

Lloyd, Bettws, vicar 33
Lloyd, Daniel 63, 143, 147, 241
Lloyd, David 63
Lloyd, David, servant 76
Lloyd, J. 388
Lloyd, Sir Thomas Davies, Bronwydd 75, 89, 91-5
Lloyd, Wil, Llanfairfach 388
Llwyd, Jac, schoolmaster 8-9, 350, 399

McArthur's Bakery 327, 358
McCrea, Dr 286
McKay, Mr, Lake Learmouth 260
Martin, C. N. 165, 169, 179, 186
Mason, Jenkin 43
Mechosk, John G. 311
Melbourne 219
    races 210
Minster, Herr, Cumberland Hotel 228
Morgan, Mrs, Lletem-ddu, healer 99
Morgan, Thomas, Tynffordd, Llanfihangel-y-Creuddyn 158

Nantserni 66, 123
Nash, William, Lorrumberry 253-4

Owen, Dr, Denbigh and Ballarat 284-5
Owens, Miss, Penrallt 385

Pantyblawd 76
Parker, Reverend Edward Stone 323
Penbrynmawr farm 35-6
Penrallt 48, 74

INDEX

Penrhiw, cottage 21
Philips, Mr, agent of Colonel Powell 150
Powell, Edwyna, Nanteos 99
Powell, Colonel William, Nanteos, 56, 59, 60, 69, 84-9, 90-1, 112, 115, 119, 132, 144, 151, 154, 158, 283
Pryse, John Pugh, Gogerddan 50, 56, 90, 92
Pugh, Daniel, servant 382, 385

Raw, Charles, landlord, Talbot Hotel 245
Rebecca riots 13-14
Rees, Catherine 320, 346, 353, 372-3, 390
Rees, William 320, 334-5, 339
Rees, William, Waunfawr 391
Rhydygwin chapel 87
Richard, Henry M.P. 90-1, 394
Richards, Evan Matthew 150-8
Richards, George, Waunfawr 54-5
Richards, William, Cefncoch 159
Roberts, Mr, photographer 256
Roberts, Alexander, Carmarthen and Australia 213
Rogers, Dr J., Tal-sarn 29
Rogers, J. E., Abermeurig 25, 160
Rowe, Mr, butcher 308-9
Rowlands, Dr, Strata Florida 131, 143
Rowlands, Dr John, Garth 137, 143, 232

Saunders-Davies, A. H., Pentre 84, 88
Silver King 349
Smith, Miss, schoolmistress 66
Smith, Mr, headmaster of Maldon school 359

Smith, William, child of 17
Spite family 18
SS Austral 365-6
Szlumper, James Weekes 73, 79, 81-2, 160

Tait, John 175, 181
Tal-sarn Fair 36, 38
Taradale 215
Teifi, train engine 78
Thomas, Mrs Ann 282
Thomas, Daniel, Hafod 72
Thomas, Ellis, Melbourne 204, 207
Thomas, T. O., Aberystwyth 92
Thomas, Reverend Thomas 63
Thomas, Thomas, undertaker 43-4
Thomas, Reverend William, Llandysul 203
Trecefel 47, 49, 50, 52-3, 55-65, 97
Trefynor family 18
Tregaron
  Beehive Society 117, 141
  Bwlchgwynt chapel 121
  Day School 67
  Ffair Garon 36-7, 125, 137, 144
  Ffair Iwan 106
  Fountain Inn 142
  Hiring Fair 48
  Pig's Fair 125
  Red Lion 118, 130
  St Silyn Fair 141
  school 68-9
  Talbot Hotel 52, 60, 69, 72, 84, 85, 86, 87, 112, 117, 119, 150, 154-5
Tregaron Literary Society 69
Tregaron Temperance Association 391-2
Tremble, Henry 275-6
Tyndomen 48, 66, 74

Vaughan, Mr, Trawsgoed 59
Vaughan, Edmund Mallet,
    Trawsgoed 150-9
Vaughan, John, Brynog 16

Watson, Captain W., 163, 170-98
weather
    1845 14-15, 26-7
    1846 28-9
    1857 84-5
    1859 98-9
    1863 111
    1864 118-19
    1867 129-30, 131
    1868 155
wells
    Ffynnon Elwad 100
    Ffynnon Garon 99-100
    near Pont Einon 100
Westcott, William, Morabool
    Creek 274-6
Whelan, John, Irishman 268
Williams, Mr, Sunnyhill 86
Williams, Eleanor 101
Williams, Evan, Abergwesyn
    102, 103
Williams, Hugh, Derigaron 388
Williams, John, miner 321, 356
Wilson, Mr, Spring Gardens
    237-8

Yolland, Colonel, Board of
    Trade 79
Ystrad Benefit Society 16

Also from Y Lolfa:

£14.95

Bilingual volume. Collection of photographs of ordinary working people by John Thomas, forming an important record of rural life in Wales during the Victorian period.

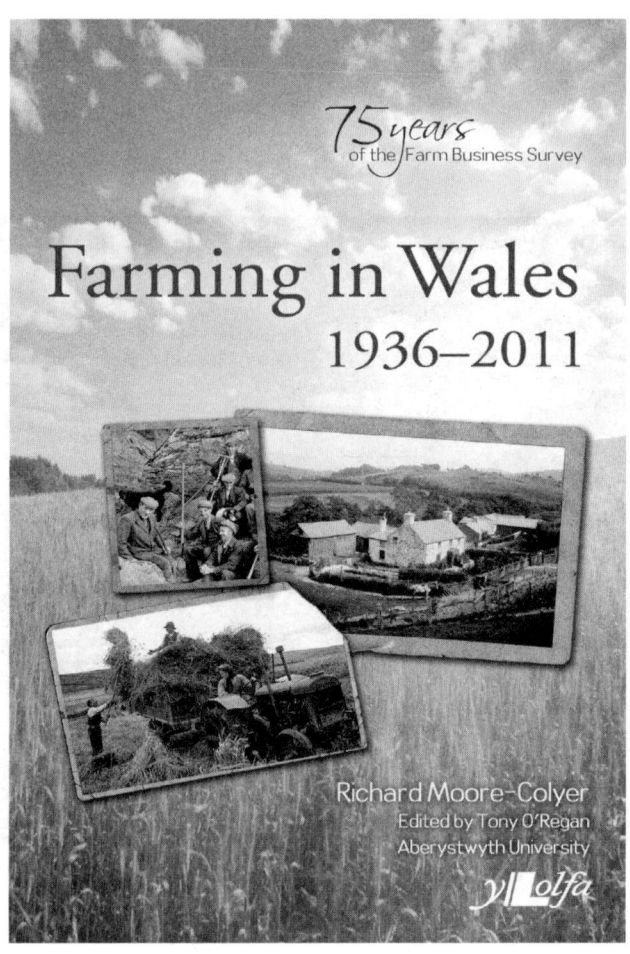

£9.95

Book tracing the development of Welsh agriculture in the context of the Farm Business Survey, and the story of one of the nation's biggest assets: farmed land and those who nurture it.

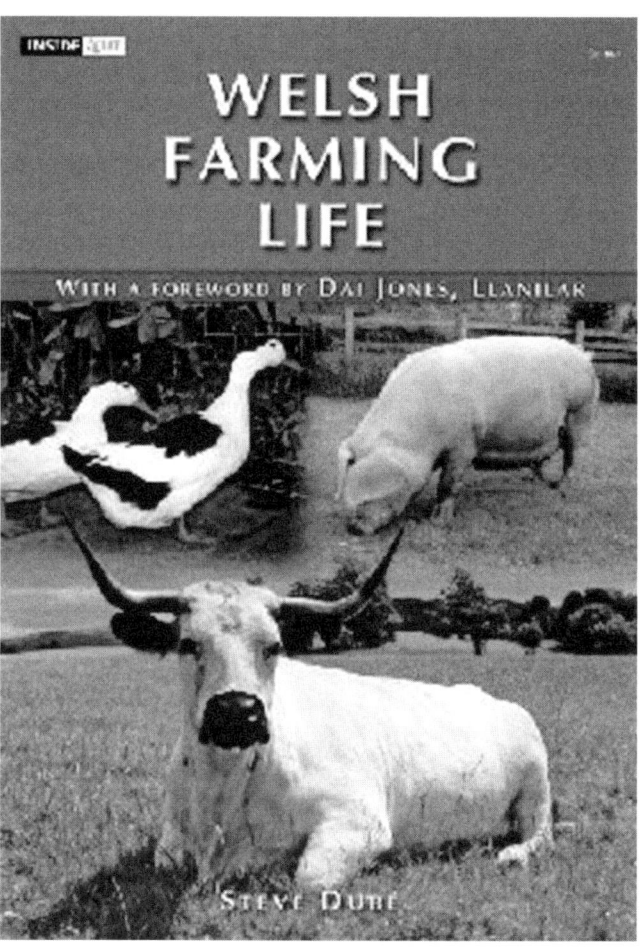

£4.99

An informed and entertaining glance at
Welsh breeds and Welsh farming traditions.